THE MESSAGE:
THE OLD TESTAMENT
HISTORY BOOKS
IN CONTEMPORARY LANGUAGE

൧

*The Message is a contemporary rendering
of the Bible from the original languages,
crafted to present its tone, rhythm, events,
and ideas in everyday language.*

൧

The New Testament with Psalms and Proverbs

The Old Testament Wisdom Books
Job, Psalms, Proverbs, Ecclesiastes, Song of Songs

The Old Testament Prophets
Isaiah, Jeremiah, Lamentations, Ezekiel, Daniel, Hosea, Joel, Amos,
Obadiah, Jonah, Micah, Nahum, Habakkuk, Zephaniah, Haggai,
Zechariah, Malachi

The Old Testament Books of Moses
Genesis, Exodus, Leviticus, Numbers, Deuteronomy

The Old Testament History Books
Joshua, Judges, Ruth, 1 Samuel, 2 Samuel, 1 Kings, 2 Kings,
1 Chronicles, 2 Chronicles, Ezra, Nehemiah, Esther

The Message Bible Available July 2002
Old and New Testaments combined into one volume

For a free Message/NavPress catalog or to inquire about large quantity purchases for your business, ministry, church, or organization, please call 1-800-366-7788; send an e-mail to themessage@navpress.com; or write to The Message, P.O. Box 35001, Colorado Springs, CO 80935.
www.messagebible.com

The MESSAGE

THE HISTORY BOOKS

EUGENE H. PETERSON

NAVPRESS

Bringing Truth to Life

P.O. Box 35001, Colorado Springs, Colorado 80935

The Old Testament History Books Exegetical Consultants:

Dr. Robert L Hubbard Jr.
North Park Theological Seminary
CHAIRMAN

Dr. Bryan E. Beyer
Columbia Biblical University
Ezra, Nehemiah

Dr. Paul R. House
Trinity Episcopal School for Ministry
1 & 2 Kings

Dr. V. Philips Long
Regent College
Joshua, Judges, Ruth, Esther

Dr. Richard L. Pratt Jr.
Reformed Theological Seminary
1 & 2 Chronicles

Dr. John H. Walton
Wheaton College
1 & 2 Samuel

THE MESSAGE: *The Old Testament History Books in Contemporary Language*
Copyright © 2002 by Eugene H. Peterson. All rights reserved.

Library of Congress Catalog Card Number: 2002016699
ISBN 1-57683-194-9

Bible, O.T. Historical books. English. Peterson. 2002.
    The message : the Old Testament history books in contemporary language / Eugene H. Peterson.
        p. cm.
    ISBN 1-57683-194-9
        I. Peterson, Eugene H., 1932- II. Title.

    BS1203 .P48 2002
    222'.05209—dc21

                                                                        2002016699

Published in association with the literary agency of Alive Communications, Inc., 7680 Goddard St., Suite 200, Colorado Springs, CO 80920.

Printed in the United States of America
1 2 3 4 5 6 7 8 9 10 11 12 13 14 15 16 17 / 10 09 08 07 06 05 04 03 02 01

CONTENTS

INTRODUCTION TO THE HISTORY BOOKS

The twelve biblical books stretching from Joshua to Esther are conventionally designated "the history books." But the word "history" doesn't tell the whole story, for this is history attentive to the conditions in which people encounter and experience God. The Hebrew people were intent on observing and participating in what happened in and around them because they believed that God was personally alive and active in the world, in their community, and in them. Life could not be accounted for by something less than the life of God, no matter how impressive and mysterious their experience was, whether an eclipse of the sun, spots on the liver of a goat, or the hiss of steam from a fissure in the earth. God could not be reduced to astronomical, physiological, geological, or psychological phenomena; God was alive, always and everywhere working his will, challenging people with his call, evoking faith and obedience, shaping a worshiping community, showing his love and compassion, and working out judgments on sin. And none of this "in general" or "at large," but at particular times, in specific places, with named persons: history.

For biblical people, God is not an idea for philosophers to discuss or a force for priests to manipulate. God is not a part of creation that can be studied and observed and managed. God is person—a person to be worshiped or defied, believed or rejected, loved or hated, in time and place. That is why these books immerse us in dates and events, in persons and circumstances—in history. God meets us in the ordinary and extraordinary occurrences that make up the stuff of our daily lives. It never seemed to have occurred to our biblical ancestors that they could deal better with God by escaping from history, "getting away from it all" as we say. History is the medium in which God works salvation, just as paint and canvas is the medium in which Rembrandt made created works of art. We cannot get closer to God by distancing ourselves from the mess of history.

This deeply pervasive sense of history—the dignity of their place in history, the presence of God in history—accounts for the way in which the Hebrew people talked and wrote. They did not, as was the fashion in the ancient world, make up and embellish fanciful stories. Their writings did not entertain or explain; they revealed the ways of God with men and women and the world. They gave narrative shape to actual people and circumstances in their dealings with God, and in God's dealings with them.

But for the Hebrews there simply was no secular history. None. Everything that happened, happened in a world penetrated by God. Since they do not talk a lot about God in their storytelling, it is easy to forget that God is always the invisible and mostly silent presence in everything that is taking place. But if we forget for very long, we will understand neither what is written nor the way it is written. God is never absent from these narratives and never peripheral to them. As far as these writers were concerned, the only reason for paying attention to people and events was to stay alert to God.

This is a difficult mindset for us to acquire, for we are used to getting our history from so-called historians, scholars, and journalists for whom God is not involved or present in what they study and write. We are thoroughly trained by our schools, daily newspapers, and telecasts to read history solely in terms of politics and economics, human interest and environmental conditions. If we have a mind for it, we can go ahead and fit God in somewhere or other. These historical books—Joshua through Esther—are radically and refreshingly different. They pull us into a way of reading history that involves us and everyone around us in all the operations of God.

JOSHUA

L and. Land flowing with milk and honey. Promised land. Holy land. Canaan land. The land. Joshua, Moses' successor as leader of Israel, was poised at the River Jordan to enter and take possession of Canaan, an unremarkable stretch of territory sandwiched between massive and already ancient civilizations. It would have been unimaginable to anyone at the time that anything of significance could take place on that land. This narrow patch had never been significant economically or culturally, but only as a land bridge between the two great cultures and economies of Egypt and Mesopotamia. But it was about to become important in the religious consciousness of humankind. In significant ways, this land would come to dwarf everything that had gone on before and around it.

The People of Israel had been landless for nearly five hundred years. The "fathers"—Abraham, Isaac, Jacob and his twelve sons—had been nomads in the land of Canaan. That was followed by a long period of slavery in Egypt (over 400 years!), a miraculous deliverance into freedom led by Moses, and then forty years of testing and training for living as a free people under God's guidance and blessing.

The company camped at the Jordan on the day that opens the Book of Joshua had nearly half a millennium of slavery behind them. They were a dispossessed, ragtag crew—and only very recently set free. The transition from being landless slaves to landholding free men and women was huge. Joshua leads the transition, first in taking the land (chapters 1 through 12), then in distributing it among the twelve tribes (chapters 13 through 22), and concluding with a solemn covenant-witness (chapters 23 through 24) that bound the people to the gift of land and the worship of the God from whom they received it.

For most modern readers of Joshua, the toughest barrier to embracing this story as sacred is the military strategy of "holy war," what I have translated as the "holy curse"—killing everyone in the conquered cities and totally destroying all the plunder, both animals and goods. Massacre and destruction. "No survivors" is the recurrent refrain. We look back from our time in history and think, "How horrible." But if we were able to put ourselves back in the thirteenth century B.C., we might see it differently, for that Canaanite culture was a snake pit of child sacrifice and sacred prostitution, practices ruthlessly devoted to using the most innocent and vulnerable members of the community (babies and virgins) to manipulate God or gods for gain.

As the Book of Joshua takes the story of salvation forward from the leadership and teaching of Moses, it continues to keep us grounded in places and connected to persons: place names, personal names—hundreds of them. What we often consider to be the subjects of religion—ideas, truths, prayers, promises, beliefs—are never permitted to have a life of their own apart from particular persons and actual places. Biblical religion has a low tolerance for "great ideas" or "sublime truths" or "inspirational thoughts" apart from the people and places in which they occur. God's great love and purposes for us are worked out in the messes, storms and sins, blue skies, daily work, and dreams of our common lives, working with us as we are and not as we should be.

People who want God as an escape from reality, from the often hard conditions of this life, don't find this much to their liking. But to the man or woman wanting more reality, not less—this continuation of the salvation story—Joshua's fierce and devout determination to win land for his people and his extraordinary attention to getting all the tribes and their families name by name assigned to their own place, is good news indeed. Joshua lays a firm foundation for a life that is grounded.

JOSHUA

1 After the death of Moses the servant of GOD, GOD spoke to Joshua, Moses' assistant:

"Moses my servant is dead. Get going. Cross this Jordan River, you and all the people. Cross to the country I'm giving to the People of Israel. I'm giving you every square inch of the land you set your foot on—just as I promised Moses. From the wilderness and this Lebanon east to the Great River, the Euphrates River—all the Hittite country—and then west to the Great Sea. It's all yours. All your life, no one will be able to hold out against you. In the same way I was with Moses, I'll be with you. I won't give up on you; I won't leave you. Strength! Courage! You are going to lead this people to inherit the land that I promised to give their ancestors. Give it everything you have, heart and soul. Make sure you carry out The Revelation that Moses commanded you, every bit of it. Don't get off track, either left or right, so as to make sure you get to where you're going. And don't for a minute let this Book of The Revelation be out of mind. Ponder and meditate on it day and night, making sure you practice everything written in it. Then you'll get where you're going; then you'll succeed. Haven't I commanded you? Strength! Courage! Don't be timid; don't get discouraged. GOD, your God, is with you every step you take."

THE TAKING OF THE LAND

Then Joshua gave orders to the people's leaders: "Go through the camp and give this order to the people: 'Pack your bags. In three days you will cross this Jordan River to enter and take the land GOD, your God, is giving you to possess.'"

Then Joshua addressed the Reubenites, the Gadites, and the half-tribe of Manasseh. He said, "Remember what Moses the servant of GOD commanded you: GOD, your God, gives you rest and he gives you this land. Your wives, your children, and your livestock can stay here east of the Jordan, the country Moses gave you; but you, tough soldiers all, must cross the River in battle formation, leading your brothers, helping them until GOD, your God, gives your brothers a place of rest just as he has done for you. They also will take possession of the land that GOD, your God, is giving them. Then you will be free to return to your possession, given to you by Moses the servant of GOD, across the Jordan to the east."

They answered Joshua: "Everything you commanded us, we'll do. Wherever you send us, we'll go. We obeyed Moses to the letter; we'll also obey you—we just pray that GOD, your God, will be with you as he was with Moses. Anyone who questions what you say and refuses to obey whatever you command him will be put to death. Strength! Courage!"

RAHAB

2 Joshua son of Nun secretly sent out from Shittim two men as spies: "Go. Look over the land. Check out Jericho." They left and arrived at the house of a harlot named Rahab and stayed there.

The king of Jericho was told, "We've just learned that men arrived tonight to spy out the land. They're from the People of Israel."

The king of Jericho sent word to Rahab: "Bring out the men who came to you to stay the night in your house. They're spies; they've come to spy out the whole country."

The woman had taken the two men and hidden them. She said, "Yes, two men did come to me, but I didn't know where they'd come from. At dark, when the gate was about to be shut, the men left. But I have no idea where they went. Hurry up! Chase them—you can still catch them!" (She had actually taken them up on the roof and hidden them under the stalks of flax that were spread out for her on the roof.) So the men set chase down the Jordan road toward the fords. As soon as they were gone, the gate was shut.

Before the spies were down for the night, the woman came up to them on the roof and said, "I know that GOD has given you the land. We're all afraid. Everyone in the country feels hopeless. We heard how GOD dried up the waters of the Red Sea before you when you left Egypt, and what he did to the two Amorite kings east of the Jordan, Sihon and Og, whom you put under a holy curse and destroyed. We heard it and our hearts sank. We all had the wind knocked out of us. And all because of you, you and GOD, your God, God of the heavens above and God of the earth below.

"Now promise me by GOD. I showed you mercy; now show my family mercy. And give me some tangible proof, a guarantee of life for my father and mother, my brothers and sisters—everyone connected with my family. Save our souls from death!"

"Our lives for yours!" said the men. "But don't tell anyone our business. When GOD turns this land over to us, we'll do right by you in loyal mercy."

She lowered them down out a window with a rope because her house was on the city wall to the outside. She told them, "Run for the hills so your pursuers won't find you. Hide out for three days and give your pursuers time to return. Then get on your way."

The men told her, "In order to keep this oath you made us swear, here is what you must do: Hang this red rope out the window through which you let us down and gather your entire family with you in your house—father, mother, brothers, and sisters. Anyone who goes out the doors of your house into the street and is killed, it's his own fault— we aren't responsible. But for everyone within the house we take full responsibility. If anyone lays a hand on one of them, it's our fault. But if you tell anyone of our business here, the oath you made us swear is canceled—we're no longer responsible."

She said, "If that's what you say, that's the way it is," and sent them off. They left and she hung the red rope out the window.

They headed for the hills and stayed there for three days until the pursuers had returned. The pursuers had looked high and low but found nothing.

The men headed back. They came down out of the hills, crossed the river, and returned to Joshua son of Nun and reported all their experiences. They told Joshua, "Yes! GOD has given the whole country to us. Everybody there is in a state of panic because of us."

THE JORDAN

3 Joshua was up early and on his way from Shittim with all the People of Israel with him. He arrived at the Jordan and camped before crossing over. After three days, leaders went through the camp and gave out orders to the people: "When you see the Covenant-Chest of GOD, your God, carried by the Levitical priests, start moving. Follow it. Make sure you keep a proper distance between you and it, about half a mile—be sure now to keep your distance! —and you'll see clearly the route to take. You've never been on this road before."

Then Joshua addressed the people: "Sanctify yourselves. Tomorrow GOD will work miracle-wonders among you."

Joshua instructed the priests, "Take up the Chest of the Covenant and step out before the people." So they took it up and processed before the people.

GOD said to Joshua, "This very day I will begin to make you great in the eyes of all Israel. They'll see for themselves that I'm with you in the same way that I was with Moses. You will command the priests who are carrying the Chest of the Covenant: 'When you come to the edge of the Jordan's waters, stand there on the river bank.'"

Then Joshua addressed the People of Israel: "Attention! Listen to what GOD, your God, has to say. This is how you'll know that God is alive among you—he will completely dispossess before you the Canaanites, Hittites, Hivites, Perizzites, Girgashites, Amorites, and Jebusites. Look at what's before you: the Chest of the Covenant. Think of it—the Master of the entire earth is crossing the Jordan as you watch. Now take twelve men from the tribes of Israel, one man from each tribe. When the soles of the feet of the priests carrying the Chest of GOD, Master of all the earth, touch the Jordan's water, the flow of water will be stopped—the water coming from upstream will pile up in a heap."

And that's what happened. The people left their tents to cross the Jordan, led by the priests carrying the Chest of the Covenant. When the priests got to the Jordan and their feet touched the water at the edge (the Jordan overflows its banks throughout the harvest), the flow of water stopped. It piled up in a heap—a long way off—at Adam, which is near Zarethan. The river went dry all the way down to the Arabah Sea (the Salt Sea). And the people crossed, facing Jericho.

And there they stood; those priests carrying the Chest of the Covenant stood firmly planted on dry ground in the middle of the Jordan while all Israel crossed on dry ground. Finally the whole nation was across the Jordan, and not one wet foot.

4 When the whole nation was finally across, GOD spoke to Joshua: "Select twelve men from the people, a man from each tribe, and tell them, 'From right here, the middle of the Jordan where the feet of the priests are standing firm, take twelve stones. Carry them across with you and set them down in the place where you camp tonight.'"

Joshua called out the twelve men whom he selected from the People of Israel, one man from each tribe. Joshua directed them, "Cross to the middle of the Jordan and take your place in front of the Chest of GOD, your God. Each of you heft a stone to your shoulder, a stone for each of the tribes of the People of Israel, so you'll have something later to mark the occasion. When your children ask you, 'What are these stones to you?' you'll say, 'The flow of the Jordan was stopped in front of the Chest of the Covenant of GOD as it crossed the Jordan—stopped in its tracks. These stones are a permanent memorial for the People of Israel.'"

The People of Israel did exactly as Joshua commanded: They took twelve stones from the middle of the Jordan—a stone for each of the twelve tribes, just as GOD had instructed Joshua—carried them across with them to the camp, and set them down there. Joshua set up the twelve stones taken from the middle of the Jordan that had marked the place where the priests who carried the Chest of the Covenant had stood. They are still there today.

The priests carrying the Chest continued standing in the middle of the Jordan until everything GOD had instructed Joshua to tell the people to do was done (confirming what Moses had instructed Joshua). The people crossed; no one dawdled. When the crossing of all the people was complete, they watched as the Chest of the Covenant and the priests crossed over.

The Reubenites, Gadites, and the half-tribe of Manasseh had crossed over in battle formation in front of the People of Israel, obedient to Moses' instructions. All told, about 40,000 armed soldiers crossed over before GOD to the plains of Jericho, ready for battle.

GOD made Joshua great that day in the sight of all Israel. They were in awe of him just as they had been in awe of Moses all his life.

✝

GOD told Joshua, "Command the priests carrying the Chest of the Testimony to come up from the Jordan."

Joshua commanded the priests, "Come up out of the Jordan."

They did it. The priests carrying GOD's Chest of the Covenant came up from the middle of the Jordan. As soon as the soles of the priests' feet touched dry land, the Jordan's waters resumed their flow within the banks, just as before.

The people came up out of the Jordan on the tenth day of the first month. They set up camp at The Gilgal (The Circle) to the east of Jericho. Joshua erected a monument at The Gilgal, using the twelve stones that they had taken from the Jordan. And then he told the People of Israel, "In the days to come, when your children ask their fathers, 'What are these stones doing here?' tell your children this: 'Israel crossed over this Jordan on dry ground.'

"Yes, GOD, your God, dried up the Jordan's waters for you until you had crossed, just as GOD, your God, did at the Red Sea, which had dried up before us until we had crossed. This was so that everybody on earth would recognize how strong GOD's rescuing hand is and so that you would hold GOD in solemn reverence always."

✝

5 When all the Amorite kings west of the Jordan and the Canaanite kings along the seacoast heard how GOD had stopped the Jordan River before the People of Israel until they had crossed over, their hearts sank; the courage drained out of them just thinking about the People of Israel.

At that time GOD said to Joshua, "Make stone knives and circumcise the People of Israel a second time." So Joshua made stone knives and circumcised the People of Israel at Foreskins Hill.

This is why Joshua conducted the circumcision. All the males who had left Egypt, the soldiers, had died in the wilderness on the journey out of Egypt. All the people who had come out of Egypt, of course, had been circumcised, but all those born in the wilderness along the way since leaving Egypt had not been. The fact is that the People of Israel had walked through that wilderness for forty years until the entire nation died out, all the men of military age who had come out of Egypt but had disobeyed the call of GOD. GOD vowed that these would never lay eyes on the land GOD had solemnly promised their ancestors to give us, a land flowing with milk and honey. But their children had replaced them. These are the ones Joshua circumcised. They had never been circumcised; no one had circumcised them along the way.

When they had completed the circumcising of the whole nation, they stayed where they were in camp until they were healed.

GOD said to Joshua, "Today I have rolled away the reproach of Egypt." That's why the place is called The Gilgal. It's still called that.

✝

The People of Israel continued to camp at The Gilgal. They celebrated the Passover on the evening of the fourteenth day of the month on the plains of Jericho.

Right away, the day after the Passover, they started eating the produce of that country, unraised bread and roasted grain. And then no more manna; the manna stopped. As soon as they started eating food grown in the land, there was no more manna for the People of Israel. That year they ate from the crops of Canaan.

✝

And then this, while Joshua was there near Jericho: He looked up and saw right in front of him a man standing, holding his drawn sword. Joshua stepped up to him and said, "Whose side are you on—ours or our enemies'?"

He said, "Neither. I'm commander of GOD's army. I've just arrived." Joshua fell, face to the ground, and worshiped. He asked, "What orders does my Master have for his servant?"

GOD's army commander ordered Joshua, "Take your sandals off your feet. The place you are standing is holy."

Joshua did it.

JERICHO

6 Jericho was shut up tight as a drum because of the People of Israel: no one going in, no one coming out.

GOD spoke to Joshua, "Look sharp now. I've already given Jericho to you, along with its king and its crack troops. Here's what you are to do: March around the city, all your soldiers. Circle the city once. Repeat this for six days. Have seven priests carry seven ram's horn trumpets in front of the Chest. On the seventh day march around the city seven times, the priests blowing away on the trumpets. And then, a long blast on the ram's horn—when you hear that, all the people are to shout at the top of their lungs. The city wall will collapse at once. All the people are to enter, every man straight on in."

So Joshua son of Nun called the priests and told them, "Take up the Chest of the Covenant. Seven priests are to carry seven ram's horn trumpets leading GOD's Chest."

Then he told the people, "Set out! March around the city. Have the armed guard march before the Chest of GOD."

And it happened. Joshua spoke, the people moved: Seven priests with their seven ram's horn trumpets set out before GOD. They blew the trumpets, leading GOD's Chest of the Covenant. The armed guard marched ahead of the trumpet-blowing priests; the rear guard was marching after the Chest, marching and blowing their trumpets.

Joshua had given orders to the people, "Don't shout. In fact, don't even speak—not so much as a whisper until you hear me say, 'Shout!'—then shout away!"

He sent the Chest of GOD on its way around the city. It circled once, came back to camp, and stayed for the night. Joshua was up early the next morning and the priests took up the Chest of GOD. The seven priests carrying the seven ram's horn trumpets marched before the Chest of GOD, marching and blowing the trumpets, with the armed guard marching before and the rear guard marching after. Marching and blowing of trumpets!

On the second day they again circled the city once and returned to camp. They did this six days.

When the seventh day came, they got up early and marched around the city this same way but seven times—yes, this day they circled the city seven times. On the seventh time around the priests blew the trumpets and Joshua signaled the people, "Shout!—GOD has given you the city! The city and everything in it is under a holy curse and offered up to GOD.

"Except for Rahab the harlot—she is to live, she and everyone in her house with her, because she hid the agents we sent.

"As for you, watch yourselves in the city under holy curse. Be careful that you don't covet anything in it and take something that's cursed, endangering the camp of Israel with the curse and making trouble for everyone. All silver and gold, all vessels of bronze and iron are holy to GOD. Put them in GOD's treasury."

The priests blew the trumpets.

When the people heard the blast of the trumpets, they gave a thunderclap shout. The wall fell at once. The people rushed straight into the city and took it.

They put everything in the city under the holy curse, killing man and woman, young and old, ox and sheep and donkey.

Joshua ordered the two men who had spied out the land, "Enter the house of the harlot and rescue the woman and everyone connected with her, just as you promised her." So the young spies went in and brought out Rahab, her father, mother, and brothers—everyone connected with her. They got the whole family out and gave them a place outside the camp of Israel. But they burned down the city and everything in it, except for the gold and silver and the bronze and iron vessels—all that they put in the treasury of GOD's house.

But Joshua let Rahab the harlot live—Rahab and her father's household and everyone connected to her. She is still alive and well in Israel because she hid the agents whom Joshua sent to spy out Jericho.

Joshua swore a solemn oath at that time:

Cursed before GOD is the man
    who sets out to rebuild this city Jericho.
He'll pay for the foundation with his firstborn son,
    he'll pay for the gates with his youngest son.

GOD was with Joshua. He became famous all over the land.

ACHAN

7 Then the People of Israel violated the holy curse. Achan son of Carmi, the son of Zabdi, the son of Zerah of the tribe of Judah, took some of the cursed things. GOD became angry with the People of Israel.

Joshua sent men from Jericho to Ai (The Ruin), which is near Beth Aven just east of Bethel. He instructed them, "Go up and spy out the land." The men went up and spied out Ai.

They returned to Joshua and reported, "Don't bother sending a lot of people—two or three thousand men are enough to defeat Ai. Don't wear out the whole army; there aren't that many people there."

So three thousand men went up—and then fled in defeat before the men of Ai! The men of Ai killed thirty-six—chased them from the city gate as far as The Quarries, killing them at the descent. The heart of the people sank, all spirit knocked out of them.

Joshua ripped his clothes and fell on his face to the ground before the Chest of GOD, he and the leaders throwing dirt on their heads, prostrate until evening.

Joshua said, "Oh, oh, oh . . . Master, GOD. Why did you insist on bringing this people across the Jordan? To make us victims of the Amorites? To wipe us out? Why didn't we just settle down on the east side of the Jordan? Oh, Master, what can I say after this, after Israel has been run off by its enemies? When the Canaanites and all the others living here get wind of this, they'll gang up on us and make short work of us—and then how will you keep up *your* reputation?"

GOD said to Joshua, "Get up. Why are you groveling? Israel has sinned: They've broken the covenant I commanded them; they've taken forbidden plunder—stolen and then covered up the theft, squirreling it away with their own stuff. The People of Israel can no longer look their enemies in the eye—they themselves are plunder. I can't continue with you if you don't rid yourselves of the cursed things.

"So get started. Purify the people. Tell them: Get ready for tomorrow by purifying yourselves. For this is what GOD, the God of Israel, says: There are cursed things in the camp. You won't be able to face your enemies until you have gotten rid of these cursed things.

"First thing in the morning you will be called up by tribes. The tribe GOD names will come up clan by clan; the clan GOD names will come up family by family; and the family GOD names will come up man by man. The person found with the cursed things will be burned, he and everything he has, because he broke GOD's covenant and did this despicable thing in Israel."

Joshua was up at the crack of dawn and called Israel up tribe by tribe. The tribe of Judah was singled out. Then he called up the clans and singled out the Zerahites. He called up the Zerahite families and singled out the Zabdi family. He called up the family members one by one and singled out Achan son of Carmi, the son of Zabdi, the son of Zerah of the tribe of Judah.

Joshua spoke to Achan, "My son, give glory to GOD, the God of Israel. Make your confession to him. Tell me what you did. Don't keep back anything from me."

Achan answered Joshua, "It's true. I sinned against GOD, the God of Israel. This is how I did it. In the plunder I spotted a beautiful Shinar robe, two hundred shekels of silver, and a fifty-shekel bar of gold, and I coveted and took them. They are buried in my tent with the silver at the bottom."

Joshua sent off messengers. They ran to the tent. And there it was, buried in the tent with the silver at the bottom. They took the stuff from the tent and brought it to Joshua and to all the People of Israel and spread it out before GOD.

Joshua took Achan son of Zerah, took the silver, the robe, the gold bar, his sons and daughters, his ox, donkey, sheep, and tent—everything connected with him. All Israel was there. They led them off to the Valley of Achor (Trouble Valley).

Joshua said, "Why have you troubled us? GOD will now trouble you. Today!" And all Israel stoned him—burned him with fire and stoned him with stones. They piled a huge pile of stones over him. It's still there. Only then did GOD turn from his hot anger. That's how the place came to be called Trouble Valley right up to the present time.

AI

8 GOD said to Joshua, "Don't be timid and don't so much as hesitate. Take all your soldiers with you and go back to Ai. I have turned the king of Ai over to you—his people, his city, and his land.

"Do to Ai and its king what you did to Jericho and its king. Only this time you may plunder its stuff and cattle to your heart's content. Set an ambush behind the city."

Joshua and all his soldiers got ready to march on Ai. Joshua chose thirty thousand men, tough, seasoned fighters, and sent them off at night with these orders: "Look sharp now. Lie in ambush behind the city. Get as close as you can. Stay alert. I and the troops with me will approach the city head-on. When they come out to meet us just as before, we'll turn and run. They'll come after us, leaving the city. As we are off and running, they'll say, 'They're running away just like the first time.' That's your signal to spring from your ambush and take the city. GOD, your God, will hand it to you on a platter. Once you have the city, burn it down. GOD says it, you do it. Go to it. I've given you your orders."

Joshua sent them off. They set their ambush and waited between Bethel and Ai, just west of Ai. Joshua spent the night with the people.

Joshua was up early in the morning and mustered his army. He and the leaders of Israel led the troops to Ai. The whole army, fighting men all, marched right up within sight of the city and set camp on the north side of Ai. There was a valley between them and Ai. He had taken about five thousand men and put them in ambush between Bethel and Ai, west of the city. They were all deployed, the main army to the north of the city and the ambush to the west. Joshua spent the night in the valley.

So it happened that when the king of Ai saw all this, the men of the city lost no time; they were out of there at the crack of dawn to join Israel in battle, the king and his troops, at a field en route to the Arabah. The king didn't know of the ambush set against him behind the city.

Joshua and all Israel let themselves be chased; they ran toward the wilderness. Everybody in the city was called to the chase. They pursued Joshua and were led away from the city. There wasn't a soul left in Ai or Bethel who wasn't out there chasing after Israel. The city was left empty and undefended as they were chasing Israel down.

Then GOD spoke to Joshua: "Stretch out the javelin in your hand toward Ai—I'm giving it to you." Joshua stretched out the javelin in his hand toward Ai. At the signal the men in ambush sprang to their feet, ran to the city, took it, and quickly had it up in flames.

The men of Ai looked back and, oh! saw the city going up in smoke. They found themselves trapped with nowhere to run. The army on the run toward the wilderness did an about-face—Joshua and all Israel, seeing that the ambush had taken the city, saw it going up in smoke, turned and attacked the men of Ai.

Then the men in the ambush poured out of the city. The men of Ai were caught in the middle with Israelites on both sides—a real massacre. And not a single survivor. Except for the king of Ai; they took him alive and brought him to Joshua.

When it was all over, Israel had killed everyone in Ai, whether in the fields or in the wilderness where they had chased them. When the killing was complete, the Israelites returned to Ai and completed the devastation. The death toll that day came to 12,000 men and women—everyone in Ai.

Joshua didn't lower his outstretched javelin until the sacred destruction of Ai and all its people was completed. Israel did get to take the livestock and loot left in the city; GOD's instructions to Joshua allowed for that.

Joshua burned Ai to the ground. A "heap" of nothing forever, a "no-place"—go see for yourself. He hanged the king of Ai from a tree. At evening, with the sun going down, Joshua ordered the corpse cut down. They dumped it at the entrance to the city and piled it high with stones—you can go see that also.

✢

Then Joshua built an altar to the GOD of Israel on Mount Ebal. He built it following the instructions of Moses the servant of GOD to the People of Israel and written in the Book of The Revelation of Moses, an altar of whole stones that hadn't been chiseled or shaped by an iron tool. On it they offered to GOD Whole-Burnt-Offerings and sacrificed Peace-Offerings. He also wrote out a copy of The Revelation of Moses on the stones. He wrote it with the People of Israel looking on.

All Israel was there, foreigners and citizens alike, with their elders, officers, and judges, standing on opposite sides of the Chest, facing the Levitical priests who carry GOD's Covenant Chest. Half of the people stood with their backs to Mount Gerizim and half with their backs to Mount Ebal to bless the People of Israel, just as Moses the servant of GOD had instructed earlier.

After that, he read out everything written in The Revelation, the Blessing and the Curse, everything in the Book of The Revelation. There wasn't a word of all that Moses commanded that Joshua didn't read to the entire congregation—men, women, children, and foreigners who had been with them on the journey.

GIBEON

9 All the kings west of the Jordan in the hills and foothills and along the Mediterranean seacoast north toward Lebanon—the Hittites, Amorites, Canaanites, Perizzites, Hivites, Girgashites, and Jebusites—got the news. They came together in a coalition to fight against Joshua and Israel under a single command.

The people of Gibeon heard what Joshua had done to Jericho and Ai and cooked up a ruse. They posed as travelers: their donkeys loaded with patched sacks and mended wineskins, threadbare sandals on their feet, tattered clothes on their bodies, nothing but dry crusts and crumbs for food. They came to Joshua at Gilgal and spoke to the men of Israel, "We've come from a far-off country; make a covenant with us."

The men of Israel said to these Hivites, "How do we know you aren't local people? How could we then make a covenant with you?"

They said to Joshua, "We'll be your servants."

Joshua said, "Who are you now? Where did you come from?"

They said, "From a far-off country, very far away. Your servants came because we'd heard such great things about GOD, your God—all those things he did in Egypt! And the two Amorite kings across the Jordan, King Sihon of Heshbon and King Og of Bashan, who ruled in Ashtaroth! Our leaders and everybody else in our country told us, 'Pack up some food for the road and go meet them. Tell them, We're your servants; make a covenant with us.'

"This bread was warm from the oven when we packed it and left to come and see you. Now look at it—crusts and crumbs. And our cracked and mended wineskins, good as new when we filled them. And our clothes and sandals, in tatters from the long, hard traveling."

The men of Israel looked them over and accepted the evidence. But they didn't ask GOD about it.

So Joshua made peace with them and formalized it with a covenant to guarantee their lives. The leaders of the congregation swore to it.

And then, three days after making this covenant, they learned that they were next-door neighbors who had been living there all along! The

People of Israel broke camp and set out; three days later they reached their towns—Gibeon, Kephirah, Beeroth, and Kiriath Jearim. But the People of Israel didn't attack them; the leaders of the congregation had given their word before the GOD of Israel. But the congregation was up in arms over their leaders.

The leaders were united in their response to the congregation: "We promised them in the presence of the GOD of Israel. We can't lay a hand on them now. But we can do this: We will let them live so we don't get blamed for breaking our promise." Then the leaders continued, "We'll let them live, but they will be woodcutters and water carriers for the entire congregation."

And that's what happened; the leaders' promise was kept.

But Joshua called the Gibeonites together and said, "Why did you lie to us, telling us, 'We live far, far away from you,' when you're our next-door neighbors? For that you are cursed. From now on it's menial labor for you—woodcutters and water carriers for the house of my God."

They answered Joshua, "We got the message loud and clear that GOD, your God, commanded through his servant Moses: to give you the whole country and destroy everyone living in it. We were terrified because of you; that's why we did this. That's it. We're at your mercy. Whatever you decide is right for us, do it."

And that's what they did. Joshua delivered them from the power of the People of Israel so they didn't kill them. But he made them wood-cutters and water carriers for the congregation and for the Altar of GOD at the place GOD chooses. They still are.

THE FIVE KINGS

10 It wasn't long before My-Master-Zedek king of Jerusalem heard that Joshua had taken Ai and destroyed it and its king under a holy curse, just as he had done to Jericho and its king. He also learned that the people of Gibeon had come to terms with Israel and were living as neighbors. He and his people were alarmed: Gibeon was a big city—as big as any with a king and bigger than Ai—and all its men were seasoned fighters.

Adoni-Zedek king of Jerusalem sent word to Hoham king of Hebron, Piram king of Jarmuth, Japhia king of Lachish, and Debir king of Eglon: "Come and help me. Let's attack Gibeon; they've joined up with Joshua and the People of Israel."

So the five Amorite (Western) kings—the king of Jerusalem, the king of Hebron, the king of Jarmuth, the king of Lachish, and the king of Eglon—combined their armies and set out to attack Gibeon.

The men of Gibeon sent word to Joshua camped at Gilgal, "Don't let us down now! Come up here quickly! Save us! Help us! All the Amorite kings who live up in the hills have ganged up on us."

So Joshua set out from Gilgal, his whole army with him—all those tough soldiers! GOD told him, "Don't give them a second thought. I've put them under your thumb—not one of them will stand up to you."

Joshua marched all night from Gilgal and took them by total surprise. GOD threw them into total confusion before Israel, a major victory at Gibeon. Israel chased them along the ridge to Beth Horon and fought them all the way down to Azekah and Makkedah. As they ran from the People of Israel, down from the Beth Horon ridge and all the way to Azekah, GOD pitched huge stones on them out of the sky and many died. More died from the hailstones than the People of Israel killed with the sword.

The day GOD gave the Amorites up to Israel, Joshua spoke to GOD, with all Israel listening:

"Stop, Sun, over Gibeon;
Halt, Moon, over Aijalon Valley."
And Sun stopped,
Moon stood stock still
Until he defeated his enemies.

(You can find this written in the Book of Jashar.) The sun stopped in its tracks in mid sky; just sat there all day. There's never been a day like that before or since—GOD took orders from a human voice! Truly, GOD fought for Israel.

Then Joshua returned, all Israel with him, to the camp at Gilgal.

Meanwhile the five kings had hidden in the cave at Makkedah. Joshua was told, "The five kings have been found, hidden in the cave at Makkedah."

Joshua said, "Roll big stones against the mouth of the cave and post guards to keep watch. But don't you hang around—go after your enemies. Cut off their retreat. Don't let them back into their cities. GOD has given them to you."

Joshua and the People of Israel then finished them off, total devastation. Only a few got away to the fortified towns. The whole army then returned intact to the camp and to Joshua at Makkedah. There was no criticism that day from the People of Israel!

Then Joshua said, "Open the mouth of the cave and bring me those five kings."

They did it. They brought him the five kings from the cave: the king of Jerusalem, the king of Hebron, the king of Jarmuth, the king of Lachish, and the king of Eglon.

When they had them all there in front of Joshua, he called up the army and told the field commanders who had been with him, "Come here. Put your feet on the necks of these kings."

They stepped up and put their feet on their necks.

Joshua told them, "Don't hold back. Don't be timid. Be strong! Be confident! This is what GOD will do to all your enemies when you fight them."

Then Joshua struck and killed the kings. He hung them on five trees where they remained until evening. At sunset Joshua gave the command. They took them down from the trees and threw them into the cave where they had hidden. They put large stones at the mouth of the cave. The kings are still in there.

No Survivors

That same day Joshua captured Makkedah, a massacre that included the king. He carried out the holy curse. No survivors. Makkedah's king got the same treatment as Jericho's king.

Joshua, all Israel with him, moved on from Makkedah to Libnah and fought against Libnah. GOD gave Libnah to Israel. They captured city and king and massacred the lot. No survivors. Libnah's king got the same treatment as Jericho's king.

Joshua, all Israel with him, moved on from Libnah to Lachish. He set up camp nearby and attacked. GOD gave Lachish to Israel. Israel took it in two days and killed everyone. He carried out the holy curse, the same as with Libnah.

Horam, king of Gezer, arrived to help Lachish. Joshua attacked him and his army until there was nothing left of them. No survivors.

Joshua, all Israel with him, moved on from Lachish to Eglon. They set up camp and attacked. They captured it and killed everyone, carrying out the holy curse, the same as they had done with Lachish.

Joshua, all Israel with him, went up from Eglon to Hebron. He attacked and captured it. They killed everyone, including its king, its villages, and their people. No survivors, the same as with Eglon. They carried out the holy curse on city and people.

Then Joshua, all Israel with him, turned toward Debir and attacked it. He captured it, its king, and its villages. They killed everyone. They put everyone and everything under the holy curse. No survivors. Debir and its king got the same treatment as Hebron and its king, and Libnah and its king.

⊹

Joshua took the whole country: hills, desert, foothills, and mountain slopes, including all kings. He left no survivors. He carried out the holy curse on everything that breathed, just as GOD, the God of Israel, had commanded. Joshua's conquest stretched from Kadesh Barnea to Gaza and from the entire region of Goshen to Gibeon. Joshua took all these kings and their lands in a single campaign because GOD, the God of Israel, fought for Israel.

Then Joshua, all Israel with him, went back to the camp at Gilgal.

⊹

11 When Jabin king of Hazor heard of all this, he sent word to Jobab king of Madon; to the king of Shimron; to the king of Acshaph; to all the kings in the northern mountains; to the kings in the valley south of Kinnereth; to the kings in the western foothills and Naphoth Dor; to the Canaanites both east and west; to the Amorites, Hittites, Perizzites, and Jebusites in the hill country; and to the Hivites below Hermon in the region of Mizpah.

They came out in full force, all their troops massed together—a huge army, in number like sand on an ocean beach—to say nothing of all the horses and chariots. All these kings met and set up camp together at the Waters of Merom, ready to fight against Israel.

GOD said to Joshua: "Don't worry about them. This time tomorrow I'll hand them over to Israel, all dead. You'll hamstring their horses. You'll set fire to their chariots."

Joshua, his entire army with him, took them by surprise, falling on them at the Waters of Merom. GOD gave them to Israel, who struck and chased them all the way to Greater Sidon, to Misrephoth Maim, and then to the Valley of Mizpah on the east. No survivors. Joshua treated them following GOD's instructions: he hamstrung their horses; he burned up their chariots.

Then Joshua came back and took Hazor, killing its king. Early on Hazor had been head of all these kingdoms. They killed every person there, carrying out the holy curse—not a breath of life left anywhere. Then he burned down Hazor.

Joshua captured and massacred all the royal towns with their kings, the holy curse commanded by Moses the servant of GOD. But Israel didn't burn the cities that were built on mounds, except for Hazor—Joshua did burn down Hazor. The People of Israel plundered all the loot, including the cattle, from these towns for themselves. But they killed the people—total destruction. They left nothing human that breathed.

Just as GOD commanded his servant Moses, so Moses commanded Joshua, and Joshua did it. He didn't leave incomplete one thing that GOD had commanded Moses.

✛

Joshua took the whole country: the mountains, the southern desert, all of Goshen, the foothills, the valley (the Arabah), and the Israel mountains with their foothills, from Mount Halak, which towers over the region of Seir, all the way to Baal Gad in the Valley of Lebanon in the shadows of Mount Hermon. He captured their kings and then killed them. Joshua fought against these kings for a long time. Not one town made peace with the People of Israel, with the one exception of the Hivites who lived in Gibeon. Israel fought and took all the rest. It was GOD's idea that they all would stubbornly fight the Israelites so he could put them under the holy curse without mercy. That way he could destroy them just as GOD had commanded Moses.

✛

Joshua came out at that time also to root out the Anakim from the hills, from Hebron, from Debir, from Anab, from the mountains of Judah, from the mountains of Israel. Joshua carried out the holy curse on them and their cities. No Anakim were left in the land of the People of Israel, except in Gaza, Gath, and Ashdod—there were a few left there.

Joshua took the whole region. He did everything that GOD had told Moses. Then he parceled it out as an inheritance to Israel according to their tribes.

And Israel had rest from war.

THE DEFEATED KINGS

12 These are the kings that the People of Israel defeated and whose land they took on the east of the Jordan, from the Arnon Gorge to Mount Hermon, with the whole eastern side of the Arabah Valley.

Sihon king of the Amorites, who reigned from Heshbon: His rule extended from Aroer, which sits at the edge of the Arnon Gorge, from the middle of the gorge and over half of Gilead to the Gorge of the Jabbok River, which is the border of the Ammonites. His rule included the eastern Arabah Valley from the Sea of Kinnereth to the Arabah Sea (the Salt Sea), eastward toward Beth Jeshimoth and southward to the slopes of Pisgah.

And Og king of Bashan, one of the last of the Rephaim who reigned from Ashtaroth and Edrei: His rule extended from Mount Hermon and Salecah over the whole of Bashan to the border of the Geshurites and the Maacathites (the other half of Gilead) to the border of Sihon king of Heshbon.

Moses the servant of GOD and the People of Israel defeated them. And Moses the servant of GOD gave this land as an inheritance to the Reubenites, the Gadites, and half of the tribe of Manasseh.

✝

And these are the kings of the land that Joshua and the People of Israel defeated in the country west of the Jordan, from Baal Gad in the Valley of Lebanon south to Mount Halak, which towers over Seir. Joshua gave this land to the tribes of Israel as a possession, according to their divisions: lands in the mountains, the western foothills, and the Arabah Valley, on the slopes, and in the wilderness and the Negev desert (lands on which Hittites, Amorites and Canaanites, Perizzites, Hivites, and Jebusites had lived). The kings were:

The king of Jericho	one
The king of Ai (near Bethel)	one
The king of Jerusalem	one
The king of Hebron	one
The king of Jarmuth	one
The king of Lachish	one
The king of Eglon	one
The king of Gezer	one
The king of Debir	one

The king of Geder	one
The king of Hormah	one
The king of Arad	one
The king of Libnah	one
The king of Adullam	one
The king of Makkedah	one
The king of Bethel	one
The king of Tappuah	one
The king of Hepher	one
The king of Aphek	one
The king of Lasharon	one
The king of Madon	one
The king of Hazor	one
The king of Shimron Meron	one
The king of Acshaph	one
The king of Taanach	one
The king of Megiddo	one
The king of Kedesh	one
The king of Jokneam in Carmel	one
The king of Dor (Naphoth Dor)	one
The king of Goyim in Gilgal	one
The king of Tirzah	one

A total of thirty-one kings.

THE RECEIVING OF THE LAND

13 When Joshua had reached a venerable age, GOD said to him, "You've had a good, long life, but there is a lot of land still to be taken. This is the land that remains:

all the districts of the Philistines and Geshurites;
the land from the Shihor River east of Egypt to the border of
    Ekron up north, Canaanite country (there were five
    Philistine tyrants—in Gaza, in Ashdod, in Ashkelon, in
    Gath, in Ekron); also the Avvim from the south;
all the Canaanite land from Arah (belonging to the Sidonians) to
    Aphek at the Amorite border;
the country of the Gebalites;

all Lebanon eastward from Baal Gad in the shadow of Mount
 Hermon to the Entrance of Hamath;
all who live in the mountains, from Lebanon to Misrephoth
 Maim;
all the Sidonians.

"I myself will drive them out before the People of Israel. All you
have to do is allot this land to Israel as an inheritance, as I have
instructed you. Do it now: Allot this land as an inheritance to the nine
tribes and the half-tribe of Manasseh."

LAND EAST OF THE JORDAN

The other half-tribe of Manasseh, with the Reubenites and Gadites, had
been given their inheritance by Moses on the other side of the Jordan
eastward. Moses the servant of GOD gave it to them.

This land extended from Aroer at the edge of the Arnon Gorge and
the city in the middle of the valley, taking in the entire tableland of
Medeba as far as Dibon, and all the towns of Sihon king of the Amorites,
who ruled from Heshbon, and out to the border of the Ammonites. It
also included Gilead, the country of the people of Geshur and Maacah,
all of Mount Hermon, and all Bashan as far as Salecah—the whole kingdom of Og in Bashan, who reigned in Ashtaroth and Edrei. He was one
of the last survivors of the Rephaim. Moses had defeated them and
taken their land. The People of Israel never did drive out the Geshurites
and the Maacathites—they're still there, living in Israel.

Levi was the only tribe that did not receive an inheritance. The
Fire-Gift offerings to GOD, the God of Israel, are their inheritance, just
as he told them.

REUBEN

To the tribe of Reuben, clan by clan, Moses gave:
the land from Aroer at the edge of the Arnon Gorge and the town
 in the middle of the valley, including the tableland around
 Medeba;
Heshbon on the tableland with all its towns (Dibon, Bamoth Baal, Beth
 Baal Meon, Jahaz, Kedemoth, Mephaath, Kiriathaim, Sibmah,
 Zereth Shahar on Valley Mountain, Beth Peor, the slopes of Pisgah,
 Beth Jeshimoth);
and all the cities of the tableland, the whole kingdom of Sihon

king of the Amorites, who ruled at Heshbon, whom Moses put to death along with the princes of Midian: Evi, Rekem, Zur, Hur, and Reba, who lived in that country, all puppets of Sihon. (In addition to those killed in battle, Balaam son of Beor, the soothsayer, was put to death by the People of Israel.)

The boundary for the Reubenites was the bank of the Jordan River. This was the inheritance of the Reubenites, their villages and cities, according to their clans.

GAD

To the tribe of Gad, clan by clan, Moses gave:
the territory of Jazer and all the towns of Gilead and half the
Ammonite country as far as Aroer near Rabbah;
the land from Heshbon to Ramath Mizpah and Betonim, and from
Mahanaim to the region of Debir;
in the valley: Beth Haram, Beth Nimrah, Succoth, and Zaphon,
with the rest of the kingdom of Sihon king of Heshbon (the
east side of the Jordan, north to the end of the Sea of
Kinnereth).

This was the inheritance of the Gadites, their cities and villages, clan by clan.

HALF-TRIBE OF MANASSEH

To the half-tribe of Manasseh, clan by clan, Moses gave:
the land stretching out from Mahanaim;
all of Bashan, which is the entire kingdom of Og king of Bashan,
and all the settlements of Jair in Bashan—sixty towns in all.
Half of Gilead with Ashtaroth and Edrei, the royal cities of Og in
Bashan, belong to the descendants of Makir, a son of Manasseh
(in other words, the half-tribe of the children of Makir) for
their clans.

This is the inheritance that Moses gave out when he was on the plains of Moab across the Jordan east of Jericho. But Moses gave no inheritance to the tribe of Levi. GOD, the God of Israel, is their inheritance, just as he told them.

LAND WEST OF THE JORDAN

14 Here are the inheritance allotments that the People of Israel received in the land of Canaan. Eleazar the priest, Joshua son of Nun, and the heads of the family clans made the allotments. Each inheritance was assigned by lot to the nine and a half tribes, just as GOD had commanded Moses.

Moses had given the two and a half tribes their inheritance east of the Jordan, but hadn't given an inheritance to the Levites, as he had to the others. Because the sons of Joseph had become two tribes, Manasseh and Ephraim, they gave no allotment to the Levites; but they did give them cities to live in with pasture rights for their flocks and herds.

The People of Israel followed through exactly as GOD had commanded Moses. They apportioned the land.

CALEB

The people of Judah came to Joshua at Gilgal. Caleb son of Jephunneh the Kenizzite spoke: "You'll remember what GOD said to Moses the man of God concerning you and me back at Kadesh Barnea. I was forty years old when Moses the servant of GOD sent me from Kadesh Barnea to spy out the land. And I brought back an honest and accurate report. My companions who went with me discouraged the people, but I stuck to my guns, totally with GOD, my God. That was the day that Moses solemnly promised, 'The land on which your feet have walked will be your inheritance, you and your children's, forever. Yes, you have lived totally for GOD.' Now look at me: GOD has kept me alive, as he promised. It is now forty-five years since GOD spoke this word to Moses, years in which Israel wandered in the wilderness. And here I am today, eighty-five years old! I'm as strong as I was the day Moses sent me out. I'm as strong as ever in battle, whether coming or going. So give me this hill country that GOD promised me. You yourself heard the report, that the Anakim were there with their great fortress cities. If GOD goes with me, I will drive them out, just as GOD said."

Joshua blessed him. He gave Hebron to Caleb son of Jephunneh as an inheritance. Hebron belongs to Caleb son of Jephunneh the Kenizzite still today, because he gave himself totally to GOD, the God of Israel.

The name of Hebron used to be Kiriath Arba, named after Arba, the greatest man among the Anakim.

And the land had rest from war.

JUDAH

15 The lot for the people of Judah, their clans, extended south to the border of Edom, to the wilderness of Zin in the extreme south.

The southern border ran from the tip of the Salt Sea south of The Tongue; it ran southward from Scorpions Pass, went around Zin and just south of Kadesh Barnea; then it ran past Hezron, ascended to Addar, and curved around to Karka; from there it passed along to Azmon, came out at the Brook of Egypt, ending at the Sea. This is the southern boundary.

The eastern boundary: the Salt Sea up to the mouth of the Jordan.

The northern boundary started at the shallows of the Sea at the mouth of the Jordan, went up to Beth Hoglah and around to the north of Beth Arabah and to the Stone of Bohan son of Reuben. The border then ascended to Debir from Trouble Valley and turned north toward Gilgal, which lies opposite Red Pass, just south of the gorge. The border then followed the Waters of En Shemesh and ended at En Rogel. The border followed the Valley of Ben Hinnom along the southern slope of the Jebusite ridge (that is, Jerusalem). It ascended to the top of the mountain opposite Hinnom Valley on the west, at the northern end of Rephaim Valley; the border then took a turn at the top of the mountain to the spring, the Waters of Nephtoah, and followed the valley out to Mount Ephron, turned toward Baalah (that is, Kiriath Jearim), took another turn west of Baalah to Mount Seir, curved around to the northern shoulder of Mount Jearim (that is, Kesalon), descended to Beth Shemesh, and crossed to Timnah. The border then went north to the ridge of Ekron, turned toward Shikkeron, passed along to Mount Baalah, and came out at Jabneel. The border ended at the Sea.

The western border: the coastline of the Great Sea.

This is the boundary around the people of Judah for their clans.

Joshua gave Caleb son of Jephunneh a section among the people of Judah, according to GOD's command. He gave him Kiriath Arba, that is, Hebron. Arba was the ancestor of Anak.

Caleb drove out three Anakim from Hebron: Sheshai, Ahiman, and Talmai, all descendants of Anak. He marched up from there against the people of Debir. Debir used to be called Kiriath Sepher.

Caleb said, "Whoever attacks Kiriath Sepher and takes it, I'll give my daughter Acsah to him as his wife." Othniel son of Kenaz, Caleb's brother, took it; so Caleb gave him his daughter Acsah as his wife.

When she arrived she got him
    to ask for farm land from her father.
As she dismounted from her donkey
    Caleb asked her, "What would you like?"
She said, "Give me a marriage gift.
    You've given me desert land;
Now give me pools of water!"
    And he gave her the upper and the lower pools.

✝

This is the inheritance of the tribe of the people of Judah, clan by clan.

The southern towns of the tribe of Judah in the Negev were near the boundary of Edom:

Kabzeel, Eder, Jagur,
Kinah, Dimonah, Adadah,
Kedesh, Hazor, Ithnan,
Ziph, Telem, Bealoth,
Hazor Hadattah, Kerioth Hezron (that is, Hazor),
Amam, Shema, Moladah,
Hazar Gaddah, Heshmon, Beth Pelet,
Hazar Shual, Beersheba, Biziothiah,
Baalah, Iim, Ezem,
Eltolad, Kesil, Hormah,
Ziklag, Madmannah, Sansannah,
Lebaoth, Shilhim, Ain, and Rimmon—
    a total of twenty-nine towns and their villages.

In the Shephelah (the western foothills) there were:
Eshtaol, Zorah, Ashnah,
Zanoah, En Gannim, Tappuah, Enam,
Jarmuth, Adullam, Socoh, Azekah,
Shaaraim, Adithaim, and Gederah (or Gederothaim)—
    fourteen towns and their villages.
Zenan, Hadashah, Migdal Gad,
Dilean, Mizpah, Joktheel,
Lachish, Bozkath, Eglon,
Cabbon, Lahmas, Kitlish,
Gederoth, Beth Dagon, Naamah, and Makkedah—
    sixteen towns and their villages.

Libnah, Ether, Ashan,
Iphtah, Ashnah, Nezib,
Keilah, Aczib, and Mareshah—
    nine towns and their villages.
Ekron with its towns and villages;
From Ekron, west to the sea, all that bordered Ashdod with its
    villages;
Ashdod with its towns and villages;
Gaza with its towns and villages all the way to the Brook of Egypt.
The Great Sea is the western border.

In the hill country:
Shamir, Jattir, Socoh,
Dannah, Kiriath Sannah (that is, Debir),
Anab, Eshtemoh, Anim,
Goshen, Holon, and Giloh—
    eleven towns and their villages.
Arab, Dumah, Eshan,
Janim, Beth Tappuah, Aphekah,
Humtah, Kiriath Arba (that is, Hebron), and Zior—
    nine towns and their villages.
Maon, Carmel, Ziph, Juttah,
Jezreel, Jokdeam, Zanoah,
Kain, Gibeah, and Timnah—
    ten towns and their villages.
Halhul, Beth Zur, Gedor,
Maarath, Beth Anoth, and Eltekon—
    six towns and their villages.
Kiriath Baal (that is, Kiriath Jearim) and Rabbah—
    two towns and their villages.

In the wilderness:
Beth Arabah, Middin, Secacah,
Nibshan, the City of Salt, and En Gedi—
    six towns and their villages.

The people of Judah couldn't get rid of the Jebusites who lived in
Jerusalem. The Jebusites stayed put, living alongside the people of
Judah. They are still living there in Jerusalem.

JOSEPH

16 The lot for the people of Joseph went from the Jordan near Jericho, east of the spring of Jericho, north through the desert mountains to Bethel. It went on from Bethel (that is, Luz) to the territory of the Arkites in Ataroth. It then descended westward to the territory of the Japhletites to the region of Lower Beth Horon and on to Gezer, ending at the Sea.

This is the region from which the people of Joseph—Manasseh and Ephraim—got their inheritance.

✢

Ephraim's territory by clans:

The boundary of their inheritance went from Ataroth Addar in the east to Upper Beth Horon and then west to the Sea. From Micmethath on the north it turned eastward to Taanath Shiloh and passed along, still eastward, to Janoah. The border then descended from Janoah to Ataroth and Naarah; it touched Jericho and came out at the Jordan. From Tappuah the border went westward to the Brook Kanah and ended at the Sea. This was the inheritance of the tribe of Ephraim by clans, including the cities set aside for Ephraim within the inheritance of Manasseh—all those towns and their villages.

But they didn't get rid of the Canaanites who were living in Gezer. Canaanites are still living among the people of Ephraim, but they are made to do forced labor.

✢

17 This is the lot that fell to the people of Manasseh, Joseph's first-born. (Gilead and Bashan had already been given to Makir, Manasseh's firstborn and father of Gilead, because he was an outstanding fighter.) So the lot that follows went to the rest of the people of Manasseh and their clans, the clans of Abiezer, Helek, Asriel, Shechem, Hepher, and Shemida. These are the male descendants of Manasseh son of Joseph by their clans.

Zelophehad son of Hepher, the son of Gilead, the son of Makir, the son of Manasseh, had no sons, only daughters. Their names were Mahlah, Noah, Hoglah, Milcah, and Tirzah. They went to Eleazar the priest, Joshua son of Nun, and the leaders and said, "GOD commanded Moses to give us an inheritance among our kinsmen." And Joshua did it; he gave them, as GOD commanded, an inheritance amid their father's brothers.

Manasseh's lot came to ten portions, in addition to the land of Gilead and Bashan on the other side of the Jordan, because Manasseh's daughters got an inheritance along with his sons. The land of Gilead belonged to the rest of the people of Manasseh.

The boundary of Manasseh went from Asher all the way to Micmethath, just opposite Shechem, then ran southward to the people living at En Tappuah. (The land of Tappuah belonged to Manasseh, but Tappuah itself on the border of Manasseh belonged to the Ephraimites.) The boundary continued south to the Brook Kanah. (The cities there belonged to Ephraim although they lay among the cities of Manasseh.) The boundary of Manasseh ran north of the brook and ended at the Sea. The land to the south belonged to Ephraim; the land to the north to Manasseh, with the Sea as their western border; they meet Asher on the north and Issachar on the east.

Within Issachar and Asher, Manasseh also held Beth Shan, Ibleam, and the people of Dor, Endor, Taanach, and Megiddo, together with their villages, and the third in the list is Naphoth.

The people of Manasseh never were able to take over these towns — the Canaanites wouldn't budge. But later, when the Israelites got stronger, they put the Canaanites to forced labor. But they never did get rid of them.

⊹

The people of Joseph spoke to Joshua: "Why did you give us just one allotment, one solitary share? There are a lot of us, and growing — GOD has extravagantly blessed us."

Joshua responded, "Since there are so many of you, and you find the hill country of Ephraim too confining, climb into the forest and clear ground there for yourselves in the land of the Perizzites and the Rephaim."

But the people of Joseph said, "There's not enough hill country for us; and the Canaanites who live down in the plain, both those in Beth Shan and its villages and in the Valley of Jezreel, have iron chariots."

Joshua said to the family of Joseph (to Ephraim and Manasseh): "Yes, there are a lot of you, and you are very strong. One lot is not enough for you. You also get the hill country. It's nothing but trees now, but you will clear the land and make it your own from one end to the other. The powerful Canaanites, even with their iron chariots, won't stand a chance against you."

THE SHILOH SURVEY

18 Then the entire congregation of the People of Israel got together at Shiloh. They put up the Tent of Meeting.

The land was under their control but there were still seven Israelite tribes who had yet to receive their inheritance.

Joshua addressed the People of Israel: "How long are you going to sit around on your hands, putting off taking possession of the land that GOD, the God of your ancestors, has given you? Pick three men from each tribe so I can commission them. They will survey and map the land, showing the inheritance due each tribe, and report back to me. They will divide it into seven parts. Judah will stay in its territory in the south and the people of Joseph will keep to their place in the north.

"You are responsible for preparing a survey map showing seven portions. Then bring it to me so that I can cast lots for you here in the presence of our GOD.

"Only the Levites get no portion among you because the priesthood of GOD is their inheritance. And Gad, Reuben, and the half-tribe of Manasseh already have their inheritance on the east side of the Jordan, given to them by Moses the servant of GOD."

So the men set out. As they went out to survey the land, Joshua charged them: "Go. Survey the land and map it. Then come back to me and I will cast lots for you here at Shiloh in the presence of GOD."

So off the men went. They covered the ground and mapped the country by towns in a scroll. Then they reported back to Joshua at the camp at Shiloh.

Joshua cast the lots for them at Shiloh in the presence of GOD. That's where Joshua divided up the land to the People of Israel, according to their tribal divisions.

BENJAMIN

The first lot turned up for the tribe of Benjamin with its clans. The border of the allotment went between the peoples of Judah and Joseph.

The northern border began at the Jordan, then went up to the ridge north of Jericho, ascending west into the hill country into the wilderness of Beth Aven. From there the border went around to Luz, to its southern ridge (that is, Bethel), and then down from Ataroth Addar to the mountain to the south of Lower Beth Horon.

There the border took a turn on the west side and swung south from the mountain to the south of Beth Horon and ended at Kiriath

Baal (that is, Kiriath Jearim), a town of the people of Judah. This was the west side.

The southern border began at the edge of Kiriath Jearim on the west, then ran west until it reached the spring, the Waters of Nephtoah. It then descended to the foot of the mountain opposite the Valley of Ben Hinnom (which flanks the Valley of Rephaim to the north), descended to the Hinnom Valley, just south of the Jebusite ridge, and went on to En Rogel. From there it curved north to En Shemesh and Geliloth, opposite the Red Pass (Adummim), down to the Stone of Bohan the son of Reuben, continued toward the north flank of Beth Arabah, then plunged to the Arabah. It then followed the slope of Beth Hoglah north and came out at the northern bay of the Salt Sea—the south end of the Jordan. This was the southern border.

The east border was formed by the Jordan.

This was the inheritance of the people of Benjamin for their clans, marked by these borders on all sides.

The cities of the tribe of Benjamin, clan by clan, were:

Jericho, Beth Hoglah, Emek Keziz,
Beth Arabah, Zemaraim, Bethel,
Avvim, Parah, Ophrah,
Kephar Ammoni, Ophni, and Geba—
    twelve towns with their villages.
Gibeon, Ramah, Beeroth,
Mizpah, Kephirah, Mozah,
Rekem, Irpeel, Taralah,
Zelah, Haeleph, the Jebusite city (that is, Jerusalem), Gibeah,
and Kiriath Jearim—
    fourteen cities with their villages.

This was the inheritance for Benjamin, according to its clans.

SIMEON

19 The second lot went to Simeon for its clans. Their inheritance was within the territory of Judah. In their inheritance they had:

Beersheba (or Sheba), Moladah,
Hazar Shual, Balah, Ezem,
Eltolad, Bethul, Hormah,

Ziklag, Beth Marcaboth, Hazar Susah,
Beth Lebaoth, and Sharuhen—
thirteen towns and their villages.
Ain, Rimmon, Ether, and Ashan—
four towns and their villages—plus all the villages around
these towns as far as Baalath Beer, the Ramah of the Negev.

This is the inheritance of the tribe of Simeon according to its clans. The inheritance of Simeon came out of the share of Judah, because Judah's portion turned out to be more than they needed. That's how the people of Simeon came to get their lot from within Judah's portion.

ZEBULUN

The third lot went to Zebulun, clan by clan:
The border of their inheritance went all the way to Sarid. It ran west to Maralah, met Dabbesheth, and then went to the brook opposite Jokneam. In the other direction from Sarid, the border ran east; it followed the sunrise to the border of Kisloth Tabor, on to Daberath and up to Japhia. It continued east to Gath Hepher and Eth Kazin, came out at Rimmon, and turned toward Neah. There the border went around on the north to Hannathon and ran out into the Valley of Iphtah El. It included Kattath, Nahalal, Shimron, Idalah, and Bethlehem—twelve cities with their villages.

This is the inheritance of the people of Zebulun for their clans— these towns and their villages.

ISSACHAR

The fourth lot went to Issachar, clan by clan. Their territory included:

Jezreel, Kesulloth, Shunem,
Hapharaim, Shion, Anaharath,
Rabbith, Kishion, Ebez,
Remeth, En Gannim, En Haddah, and Beth Pazzez.

The boundary touched Tabor, Shahazumah, and Beth Shemesh and ended at the Jordan—sixteen towns and their villages.
These towns with their villages were the inheritance of the tribe of Issachar, clan by clan.

ASHER

The fifth lot went to the tribe of Asher, clan by clan:

Their territory included Helkath, Hali, Beten, Acshaph, Allammelech, Amad, and Mishal. The western border touched Carmel and Shihor Libnath, then turned east toward Beth Dagon, touched Zebulun and the Valley of Iphtah El, and went north to Beth Emek and Neiel, skirting Cabul on the left. It went on to Abdon, Rehob, Hammon, and Kanah, all the way to Greater Sidon. The border circled back toward Ramah, extended to the fort city of Tyre, turned toward Hosah, and came out at the Sea in the region of Aczib, Ummah, Aphek, and Rehob—twenty-two towns and their villages.

These towns and villages were the inheritance of the tribe of Asher, clan by clan.

NAPHTALI

The sixth lot came to Naphtali and its clans.

Their border ran from Heleph, from the oak at Zaanannim, passing Adami Nekeb and Jabneel to Lakkum and ending at the Jordan.

The border returned on the west at Aznoth Tabor and came out at Hukkok, meeting Zebulun on the south, Asher on the west, and the Jordan on the east.

The fort cities were:

Ziddim, Zer, Hammath, Rakkath, Kinnereth,
Adamah, Ramah, Hazor,
Kedesh, Edrei, En Hazor,
Iron, Migdal El, Horem, Beth Anath, and Beth Shemesh—
    nineteen towns and their villages.

This is the inheritance of the tribe of Naphtali, the cities and their villages, clan by clan.

DAN

The seventh lot fell to Dan. The territory of their inheritance included:

Zorah, Eshtaol, Ir Shemesh,
Shaalabbin, Aijalon, Ithlah,

Elon, Timnah, Ekron,
Eltekeh, Gibbethon, Baalath,
Jehud, Bene Berak, Gath Rimmon,
Me Jarkon, and Rakkon, with the region facing Joppa.

But the people of Dan failed to get rid of the Westerners (Amorites), who pushed them back into the hills. The Westerners kept them out of the plain and they didn't have enough room. So the people of Dan marched up and attacked Leshem. They took it, killed the inhabitants, and settled in. They renamed it Leshem Dan after the name of Dan their ancestor.

This is the inheritance of the tribe of Dan, according to its clans, these towns with their villages.

✛

They completed the dividing of the land as inheritance and the setting of its boundaries. The People of Israel then gave an inheritance among them to Joshua son of Nun. In obedience to GOD's word, they gave him the city which he had requested, Timnath Serah in the hill country of Ephraim. He rebuilt the city and settled there.

These are the inheritances which Eleazar the priest and Joshua son of Nun and the ancestral leaders assigned by lot to the tribes of Israel at Shiloh in the presence of GOD at the entrance of the Tent of Meeting. They completed the dividing of the land.

ASYLUM-CITIES

20 Then GOD spoke to Joshua: "Tell the People of Israel: Designate the asylum-cities, as I instructed you through Moses, so that anyone who kills a person accidentally—that is, unintentionally—may flee there as a safe place of asylum from the avenger of blood.

"A person shall escape for refuge to one of these cities, stand at the entrance to the city gate, and lay out his case before the city's leaders. The leaders must then take him into the city among them and give him a place to live with them.

"If the avenger of blood chases after him, they must not give him up—he didn't intend to kill the person; there was no history of ill-feeling. He may stay in that city until he has stood trial before the congregation and until the death of the current high priest. Then he may go back to his own home in his hometown from which he fled."

They set apart Kedesh in Galilee in the hills of Naphtali, Shechem in the hills of Ephraim, and Kiriath Arba (that is, Hebron) in the hills of Judah.

On the other side of the Jordan, east of Jericho, they designated Bezer on the desert plateau from the tribe of Reuben, Ramoth in Gilead from the tribe of Gad, and Golan in Bashan from the tribe of Manasseh. These were the designated cities for the People of Israel and any resident foreigner living among them, so that anyone who killed someone unintentionally could flee there and not die by the hand of the avenger of blood without a fair trial before the congregation.

CITIES FOR THE LEVITES

21 The ancestral heads of the Levites came to Eleazar the priest and Joshua son of Nun and to the heads of the other tribes of the People of Israel. This took place at Shiloh in the land of Canaan. They said, "GOD commanded through Moses that you give us cities to live in with access to pastures for our cattle."

So the People of Israel, out of their own inheritance, gave the Levites, just as GOD commanded, the following cities and pastures:

The lot came out for the families of the Kohathites this way: Levites descended from Aaron the priest received by lot thirteen cities out of the tribes of Judah, Simeon, and Benjamin. The rest of the Kohathites received by lot ten cities from the families of the tribes of Ephraim, Dan, and the half-tribe of Manasseh.

The Gershonites received by lot thirteen cities from the families of the tribes of Issachar, Asher, Naphtali, and the half-tribe of Manasseh in Bashan.

The families of the Merarites received twelve towns from the tribes of Reuben, Gad, and Zebulun.

So the People of Israel gave these cities with their pastures to the Levites just as GOD had ordered through Moses, that is, by lot.

CITIES FOR THE DESCENDANTS OF AARON

They assigned from the tribes of Judah, Simeon, and Benjamin the following towns, here named individually (these were for the descendants of Aaron who were from the families of the Kohathite branch of Levi because the first lot fell to them):

Kiriath Arba (Arba was the ancestor of Anak), that is, Hebron, in the hills of Judah, with access to the pastures around it. The fields of the city and its open lands they had already given to Caleb son of Jephunneh as his possession.

To the descendants of Aaron the priest they gave Hebron (the asylum-city for the unconvicted killers), Libnah, Jattir, Eshtemoa, Holon, Debir, Ain, Juttah, and Beth Shemesh, all with their accompanying pastures—nine towns from these two tribes.

And from the tribe of Benjamin: Gibeon, Geba, Anathoth, and Almon, together with their pastures—four towns.

The total for the cities and pastures for the priests descended from Aaron came to thirteen.

The rest of the Kohathite families from the tribe of Levi were assigned their cities by lot from the tribe of Ephraim: Shechem (the asylum-city for the unconvicted killer) in the hills of Ephraim, Gezer, Kibzaim, and Beth Horon, with their pastures—four towns.

From the tribe of Dan they received Eltekeh, Gibbethon, Aijalon, and Gath Rimmon, all with their pastures—four towns.

And from the half-tribe of Manasseh they received Taanach and Gath Rimmon with their pastures—two towns.

All told, ten cities with their pastures went to the remaining Kohathite families.

The Gershonite families of the tribe of Levi were given from the half-tribe of Manasseh: Golan in Bashan (an asylum-city for the unconvicted killer), and Be Eshtarah, with their pastures—two cities.

And from the tribe of Issachar: Kishion, Daberath, Jarmuth, and En Gannim, with their pastures—four towns.

From the tribe of Asher: Mishal, Abdon, Helkath, and Rehob, with their pastures—four towns.

From the tribe of Naphtali: Kedesh in Galilee (an asylum-city for the unconvicted killer), Hammoth Dor, and Kartan, with their pastures—three towns.

For the Gershonites and their families: thirteen towns with their pastures.

The Merari families, the remaining Levites, were given from the tribe of Zebulun: Jokneam, Kartah, Dimnah, and Nahalal, with their pastures—four cities.

From the tribe of Reuben: Bezer, Jahaz, Kedemoth, and Mephaath, with their pastures—four towns.

From the tribe of Gad: Ramoth in Gilead (an asylum-city for the unconvicted killer), Mahanaim, Heshbon, and Jazer, with their pastures—a total of four towns.

All these towns were assigned by lot to the Merarites, the remaining Levites—twelve towns.

The Levites held forty-eight towns with their accompanying pastures within the territory of the People of Israel. Each of these towns had pastures surrounding it—this was the case for all these towns.

☩

And so GOD gave Israel the entire land that he had solemnly vowed to give to their ancestors. They took possession of it and made themselves at home in it. And GOD gave them rest on all sides, as he had also solemnly vowed to their ancestors. Not a single one of their enemies was able to stand up to them—GOD handed over all their enemies to them.

Not one word failed from all the good words GOD spoke to the house of Israel. Everything came out right.

☩

22 Then Joshua called together the Reubenites, Gadites, and the half-tribe of Manasseh. He said: "You have carried out everything Moses the servant of GOD commanded you, and you have obediently done everything I have commanded you. All this time and right down to this very day you have not abandoned your brothers; you've shouldered the task laid on you by GOD, your God. And now GOD, your God, has given rest to your brothers just as he promised them. You're now free to go back to your homes, the country of your inheritance that Moses the servant of GOD gave you on the other side of the Jordan. Only this: Be vigilant in keeping the Commandment and The Revelation that Moses the servant of GOD laid on you: Love GOD, your God, walk in all his ways, do what he's commanded, embrace him, serve him with everything you are and have."

Then Joshua blessed them and sent them on their way. They went home. (To the half-tribe of Manasseh, Moses had assigned a share in Bashan. To the other half, Joshua assigned land with their brothers west of the Jordan.)

When Joshua sent them off to their homes, he blessed them. He said: "Go home. You're going home rich—great herds of cattle, silver and gold, bronze and iron, huge piles of clothing. Share the wealth with your friends and families—all this plunder from your enemies!"

✝

The Reubenites, Gadites, and the half-tribe of Manasseh left the People of Israel at Shiloh in the land of Canaan to return to Gilead, the land of their possession, which they had taken under the command of Moses as ordered by GOD.

They arrived at Geliloth on the Jordan (touching on Canaanite land). There the Reubenites, Gadites, and the half-tribe of Manasseh built an altar on the banks of the Jordan—a huge altar!

The People of Israel heard of it: "What's this? The Reubenites, Gadites, and the half-tribe of Manasseh have built an altar facing the land of Canaan at Geliloth on the Jordan, across from the People of Israel!"

When the People of Israel heard this, the entire congregation mustered at Shiloh to go to war against them. They sent Phinehas son of Eleazar the priest to the Reubenites, Gadites, and the half-tribe of Manasseh (that is, to the land of Gilead). Accompanying him were ten chiefs, one chief for each of the ten tribes, each the head of his ancestral family. They represented the military divisions of Israel.

They went to the Reubenites, Gadites, and the half-tribe of Manasseh and spoke to them: "The entire congregation of GOD wants to know: What is this violation against the God of Israel that you have committed, turning your back on GOD and building your own altar— a blatant act of rebellion against GOD? Wasn't the crime of Peor enough for us? Why, to this day we aren't rid of it, still living with the fallout of the plague on the congregation of GOD! Look at you—turning your back on GOD! If you rebel against GOD today, tomorrow he'll vent his anger on all of us, the entire congregation of Israel.

"If you think the land of your possession isn't holy enough but somehow contaminated, come back over to GOD's possession, where GOD's Dwelling is set up, and take your land there, but don't rebel against GOD. And don't rebel against us by building your own altar apart from the Altar of our GOD. When Achan son of Zerah violated the holy curse, didn't anger fall on the whole congregation of Israel? He wasn't the only one to die for his sin."

The Reubenites, Gadites, and the half-tribe of Manasseh replied to the heads of the tribes of Israel:

The God of Gods is GOD,
The God of Gods is GOD!

"He knows and he'll let Israel know if this is a rebellious betrayal of GOD. And if it is, don't bother saving us. If we built ourselves an altar in rebellion against GOD, if we did it to present on it Whole-Burnt-Offerings or Grain-Offerings or to enact there sacrificial Peace-Offerings, let GOD decide.

"But that's not it. We did it because we cared. We were anxious lest someday your children should say to our children, 'You're not connected with GOD, the God of Israel! GOD made the Jordan a boundary between us and you. You Reubenites and Gadites have no part in GOD.' And then your children might cause our children to quit worshiping GOD.

"So we said to ourselves, 'Let's do something. Let's build an altar—but not for Whole-Burnt-Offerings, not for sacrifices.'

"We built this altar as a witness between us and you and our children coming after us, a witness to the Altar where we worship GOD in his Sacred Dwelling with our Whole-Burnt-Offerings and our sacrifices and our Peace-Offerings.

"This way, your children won't be able to say to our children in the future, 'You have no part in GOD.'

"We said to ourselves, 'If anyone speaks disparagingly to us or to our children in the future, we'll say: Look at this model of GOD's Altar which our ancestors made. It's not for Whole-Burnt-Offerings, not for sacrifices. It's a witness connecting us with you.'

"Rebelling against or turning our backs on GOD is the last thing on our minds right now. We never dreamed of building an altar for Whole-Burnt-Offerings or Grain-Offerings to rival the Altar of our GOD in front of his Sacred Dwelling."

Phinehas the priest, all the heads of the congregation, and the heads of the military divisions of Israel who were also with him heard what the Reubenites, Gadites, and the half-tribe of Manasseh had to say. They were satisfied.

Priest Phinehas son of Eleazar said to Reuben, Gad, and Manasseh, "Now we're convinced that GOD is present with us since you haven't been disloyal to GOD in this matter. You saved the People of Israel from GOD's discipline."

Then Priest Phinehas son of Eleazar left the Reubenites, Gadites, and the half-tribe of Manasseh (from Gilead) and, with the chiefs, returned to the land of Canaan to the People of Israel and gave a full report. They were pleased with the report. The People of Israel blessed God—there was no more talk of attacking and destroying the land in which the Reubenites and Gadites were living.

Reuben and Gad named the altar:

A Witness Between Us.
GOD Alone Is God.

JOSHUA'S CHARGE

23 A long time later, after GOD had given Israel rest from all their surrounding enemies, and Joshua was a venerable old man, Joshua called all Israel together—elders, chiefs, judges, and officers. Then he spoke to them:

"I'm an old man. I've lived a long time. You have seen everything that GOD has done to these nations because of you. He did it because he's GOD, your God. He fought for you.

"Stay alert: I have assigned to you by lot these nations that remain as an inheritance to your tribes—these in addition to the nations I have already cut down—from the Jordan to the Great Sea in the west. GOD, your God, will drive them out of your path until there's nothing left of them and you'll take over their land just as GOD, your God, promised you.

"Now, stay strong and steady. Obediently do everything written in the Book of The Revelation of Moses—don't miss a detail. Don't get mixed up with the nations that are still around. Don't so much as speak the names of their gods or swear by them. And by all means don't worship or pray to them. Hold tight to GOD, your God, just as you've done up to now.

"GOD has driven out superpower nations before you. And up to now, no one has been able to stand up to you. Think of it—one of you, single-handedly, putting a thousand on the run! Because GOD is GOD, your God. Because he fights for you, just as he promised you.

"Now, vigilantly guard your souls: Love GOD, your God. Because if you wander off and start taking up with these remaining nations still among you (intermarry, say, and have other dealings with them), know for certain that GOD, your God, will not get rid of these nations for you. They'll be nothing but trouble to you—horsewhips on your backs and sand in your eyes—until you're the ones who will be driven out of this good land that GOD, your God, has given you.

"As you can see, I'm about to go the way we all end up going. Know this with all your heart, with everything in you, that not one detail has failed of all the good things GOD, your God, promised you. It has all happened. Nothing's left undone—not so much as a word.

"But just as sure as everything good that GOD, your God, has promised has come true, so also GOD will bring to pass every bad thing until there's nothing left of you in this good land that GOD has given you. If you leave the path of the Covenant of GOD, your God, that he commanded you, go off and serve and worship other gods, GOD's anger will blaze out against you. In no time at all there'll be nothing left of you, no sign that you've ever been in this good land he gave you."

THE COVENANT AT SHECHEM

24 Joshua called together all the tribes of Israel at Shechem. He called in the elders, chiefs, judges, and officers. They presented themselves before God. Then Joshua addressed all the people:

"This is what GOD, the God of Israel, says: A long time ago your ancestors, Terah and his sons Abraham and Nahor, lived to the east of the River Euphrates. They worshiped other gods. I took your ancestor Abraham from the far side of The River. I led him all over the land of Canaan and multiplied his descendants. I gave him Isaac. Then I gave Isaac Jacob and Esau. I let Esau have the mountains of Seir as home, but Jacob and his sons ended up in Egypt. I sent Moses and Aaron. I hit Egypt hard with plagues and then led you out of there. I brought your ancestors out of Egypt. You came to the sea, the Egyptians in hot pursuit with chariots and cavalry, to the very edge of the Red Sea!

"Then they cried out for help to GOD. He put a cloud between you and the Egyptians and then let the sea loose on them. It drowned them.

"You watched the whole thing with your own eyes, what I did to Egypt. And then you lived in the wilderness for a long time. I brought you to the country of the Amorites, who lived east of the Jordan, and they fought you. But I fought for you and you took their land. I destroyed them for you. Then Balak son of Zippor made his appearance. He was the king of Moab. He got ready to fight Israel by sending for Balaam son of Beor to come and curse you. But I wouldn't listen to Balaam—he ended up blessing you over and over! I saved you from him.

"You then crossed the Jordan and came to Jericho. The Jericho leaders ganged up on you as well as the Amorites, Perizzites, Canaanites, Hittites, Girgashites, Hivites, and Jebusites, but I turned them over to you.

"I sent the Hornet ahead of you. It drove out the two Amorite kings—did your work for you. You didn't have to do a thing, not so much as raise a finger.

"I handed you a land for which you did not work, towns you did not build. And here you are now living in them and eating from vineyards and olive groves you did not plant.

"So now: Fear GOD. Worship him in total commitment. Get rid of the gods your ancestors worshiped on the far side of The River (the Euphrates) and in Egypt. You, worship GOD.

"If you decide that it's a bad thing to worship GOD, then choose a god you'd rather serve—and do it today. Choose one of the gods your ancestors worshiped from the country beyond The River, or one of the gods of the Amorites, on whose land you're now living. As for me and my family, we'll worship GOD."

The people answered, "We'd never forsake GOD! Never! We'd never leave GOD to worship other gods.

"GOD is our God! He brought up our ancestors from Egypt and from slave conditions. He did all those great signs while we watched. He has kept his eye on us all along the roads we've traveled and among the nations we've passed through. Just for us he drove out all the nations, Amorites and all, who lived in the land.

"Count us in: We too are going to worship GOD. He's our God."

Then Joshua told the people: "You can't do it; you're not able to worship GOD. He is a holy God. He is a jealous God. He won't put up with your fooling around and sinning. When you leave GOD and take up the worship of foreign gods, he'll turn right around and come down on you hard. He'll put an end to you—and after all the good he has done for you!"

But the people told Joshua: "No! No! We worship GOD!"

And so Joshua addressed the people: "You are witnesses against yourselves that you have chosen GOD for yourselves—to worship him."

And they said, "We are witnesses."

Joshua said, "Now get rid of all the foreign gods you have with you. Say an unqualified Yes to GOD, the God of Israel."

The people answered Joshua, "We will worship GOD. What he says, we'll do."

Joshua completed a Covenant for the people that day there at Shechem. He made it official, spelling it out in detail. Joshua wrote out all the directions and regulations into the Book of The Revelation of God. Then he took a large stone and set it up under the oak that was in the holy place of GOD.

Joshua spoke to all the people: "This stone is a witness against us. It has heard every word that GOD has said to us. It is a standing witness against you lest you cheat on your God."

Then Joshua dismissed the people, each to his own place of inheritance.

✝

After all this, Joshua son of Nun, the servant of GOD, died. He was 110 years old. They buried him in the land of his inheritance at Timnath Serah in the mountains of Ephraim, north of Mount Gaash.

Israel served GOD through the lifetime of Joshua and of the elders who outlived him, who had themselves experienced all that GOD had done for Israel.

Joseph's bones, which the People of Israel had brought from Egypt, they buried in Shechem in the plot of ground that Jacob had purchased from the sons of Hamor (who was the father of Shechem). He paid a hundred silver coins for it. It belongs to the inheritance of the family of Joseph.

Eleazar son of Aaron died. They buried him at Gibeah, which had been allotted to his son Phinehas in the mountains of Ephraim.

JUDGES

S ex and violence, rape and massacre, brutality and deceit do not seem to be congenial materials for use in developing a story of salvation. Given the Bible's subject matter—God and salvation, living well and loving deeply—we quite naturally expect to find in its pages leaders for us who are good, noble, honorable men and women showing us the way. So it is always something of a shock to enter the pages of the Book of Judges and find ourselves immersed in nearly unrelieved mayhem.

It might not gravel our sensibilities so much if these flawed and reprobate leaders were held up as negative moral examples, with lurid, hellfire descriptions of the punishing consequences of living such bad lives. But the story is not told quite that way. There is a kind of matter-of-fact indifference in the tone of the narration, almost as if God is saying, "Well, if this is all you're going to give me to work with, I'll use *these* men and women, just as they are, and get on with working out the story of salvation." These people are even given a measure of dignity as they find their place in the story; they are most certainly not employed for the sake of vilification or lampoon.

God, it turns out, does not require good people in order to do good work. He can and does work with us in whatever moral and spiritual condition he finds us. God, we are learning, does some of his best work using the most unlikely people. If God found a way to significantly include these leaders ("judges") in what we know is on its way to becoming a glorious conclusion, he can certainly use us along with our sometimes impossible friends and neighbors.

Twice in Judges (17:6 and 21:25) there is the telling refrain: "At that time there was no king in Israel. People did whatever they felt like doing." But we readers know that there *was* a king in Israel: *God* was king. And so, while the lack of an earthly king accounts for the moral and political anarchy, the presence of the sovereign God, however obscurely realized, means that the reality of the kingdom is never in doubt.

JUDGES

1 A time came after the death of Joshua when the People of Israel asked GOD, "Who will take the lead in going up against the Canaanites to fight them?"

And GOD said, "Judah will go. I've given the land to him."

The men of Judah said to those of their brother Simeon, "Go up with us to our territory and we'll fight the Canaanites. Then we'll go with you to your territory." And Simeon went with them.

So Judah went up. GOD gave them the Canaanites and the Perizzites. They defeated them at Bezek — ten military units!

They caught up with My-Master-Bezek there and fought him. They smashed the Canaanites and the Perizzites. My-Master-Bezek ran, but they gave chase and caught him. They cut off his thumbs and big toes. My-Master-Bezek said, "Seventy kings with their thumbs and big toes cut off used to crawl under my table, scavenging. Now God has done to me what I did to them."

They brought him to Jerusalem and he died there.

✜

The people of Judah attacked and captured Jerusalem, subduing the city by sword and then sending it up in flames. After that they had gone down to fight the Canaanites who were living in the hill country, the Negev, and the foothills. Judah had gone on to the Canaanites who lived in Hebron (Hebron used to be called Kiriath Arba) and brought Sheshai, Ahiman, and Talmai to their knees.

From there they had marched against the population of Debir (Debir used to be called Kiriath Sepher). Caleb had said, "Whoever attacks Kiriath Sepher and takes it, I'll give my daughter Acsah to him as his wife."

Othniel son of Kenaz, Caleb's brother, took it, so Caleb gave him his daughter Acsah as his wife.

When she arrived she got him
    to ask for farm land from her father.
As she dismounted from her donkey
    Caleb asked her, "What would you like?"
She said, "Give me a marriage gift.
    You've given me desert land;

Now give me pools of water!"
And he gave her the upper and the lower pools.

⊹

The people of Hobab the Kenite, Moses' relative, went up with the people of Judah from the City of Palms to the wilderness of Judah at the descent of Arad. They settled down there with the Amalekites.

The people of Judah went with their kin the Simeonites and struck the Canaanites who lived in Zephath. They carried out the holy curse and named the city Curse-town.

But Judah didn't manage to capture Gaza, Ashkelon, and Ekron with their territories. GOD was certainly with Judah in that they took over the hill country. But they couldn't oust the people on the plain because they had iron chariots.

They gave Hebron to Caleb, as Moses had directed. Caleb drove out the three sons of Anak.

But the people of Benjamin couldn't get rid of the Jebusites living in Jerusalem. Benjaminites and Jebusites live side by side in Jerusalem to this day.

⊹

The house of Joseph went up to attack Bethel. GOD was with them. Joseph sent out spies to look the place over. Bethel used to be known as Luz. The spies saw a man leaving the city and said to him, "Show us a way into the city and we'll treat you well." The man showed them a way in. They killed everyone in the city but the man and his family. The man went to Hittite country and built a city. He named it Luz; that's its name to this day.

But Manasseh never managed to drive out Beth Shan, Taanach, Dor, Ibleam, and Megiddo with their territories. The Canaanites dug in their heels and wouldn't budge. When Israel became stronger they put the Canaanites to forced labor, but they never got rid of them.

Neither did Ephraim drive out the Canaanites who lived in Gezer. The Canaanites stuck it out and lived there with them.

Nor did Zebulun drive out the Canaanites in Kitron or Nahalol. They kept living there, but they were put to forced labor.

Nor did Asher drive out the people of Acco, Sidon, Ahlab, Aczib, Helbah, Aphek, and Rehob. Asher went ahead and settled down with the Canaanites since they could not get rid of them.

Naphtali fared no better. They couldn't drive out the people of Beth Shemesh or Beth Anath so they just moved in and lived with them. They did, though, put them to forced labor.

The Amorites pushed the people of Dan up into the hills and wouldn't let them down on the plains. The Amorites stubbornly continued to live in Mount Heres, Aijalon, and Shaalbim. But when the house of Joseph got the upper hand, they were put to forced labor.

The Amorite border extended from Scorpions' Pass and Sela upward.

✛

2 GOD's angel went up from Gilgal to Bokim and said, "I brought you out of Egypt; I led you to the land that I promised to your fathers; and I said, I'll never break my covenant with you—never! And you're never to make a covenant with the people who live in this land. Tear down their altars! But you haven't obeyed me! What's this that you're doing?

"So now I'm telling you that I won't drive them out before you. They'll trip you up and their gods will become a trap."

When GOD's angel had spoken these words to all the People of Israel, they cried out—oh! how they wept! They named the place Bokim (Weepers). And there they sacrificed to GOD.

✛

After Joshua had dismissed them, the People of Israel went off to claim their allotted territories and take possession of the land. The people worshiped GOD throughout the lifetime of Joshua and the time of the leaders who survived him, leaders who had been in on all of GOD's great work that he had done for Israel. Then Joshua son of Nun, the servant of GOD, died. He was 110 years old. They buried him in his allotted inheritance at Timnath Heres in the hills of Ephraim north of Mount Gaash.

Eventually that entire generation died and was buried. Then another generation grew up that didn't know anything of GOD or the work he had done for Israel.

✛

The People of Israel did evil in GOD's sight: they served Baal-gods; they deserted GOD, the God of their parents who had led them out of Egypt;

they took up with other gods, gods of the peoples around them. They actually worshiped them! And oh, how they angered GOD as they worshiped god Baal and goddess Astarte! GOD's anger was hot against Israel: He handed them off to plunderers who stripped them; he sold them cheap to enemies on all sides. They were helpless before their enemies. Every time they walked out the door GOD was with them—but for evil, just as GOD had said, just as he had sworn he would do. They were in a bad way.

But then GOD raised up judges who saved them from their plunderers. But they wouldn't listen to their judges; they prostituted themselves to other gods—worshiped them! They lost no time leaving the road walked by their parents, the road of obedience to GOD's commands. They refused to have anything to do with it.

When GOD was setting up judges for them, he would be right there with the judge: He would save them from their enemies' oppression as long as the judge was alive, for GOD was moved to compassion when he heard their groaning because of those who afflicted and beat them. But when the judge died, the people went right back to their old ways—but even worse than their parents!—running after other gods, serving and worshiping them. Stubborn as mules, they didn't drop a single evil practice.

And GOD's anger blazed against Israel. He said, "Because these people have thrown out my covenant that I commanded their parents and haven't listened to me, I'm not driving out one more person from the nations that Joshua left behind when he died. I'll use them to test Israel and see whether they stay on GOD's road and walk down it as their parents did."

That's why GOD let those nations remain. He didn't drive them out or let Joshua get rid of them.

3 These are the nations that GOD left there, using them to test the Israelites who had no experience in the Canaanite wars. He did it to train the descendants of Israel, the ones who had no battle experience, in the art of war. He left the five Philistine tyrants, all the Canaanites, the Sidonians, and the Hivites living on Mount Lebanon from Mount Baal Hermon to Hamath's Pass. They were there to test Israel and see whether they would obey GOD's commands that were given to their parents through Moses.

But the People of Israel made themselves at home among the Canaanites, Hittites, Amorites, Perizzites, Hivites, and Jebusites. They married their daughters and gave their own daughters to their sons in marriage. And they worshiped their gods.

OTHNIEL

The People of Israel did evil in GOD's sight. They forgot their GOD and worshiped the Baal gods and Asherah goddesses. GOD's hot anger blazed against Israel. He sold them off to Cushan-Rishathaim king of Aram Naharaim. The People of Israel were in servitude to Cushan-Rishathaim for eight years.

The People of Israel cried out to GOD and GOD raised up a savior who rescued them: Caleb's nephew Othniel, son of his younger brother Kenaz. The Spirit of GOD came on him and he rallied Israel. He went out to war and GOD gave him Cushan-Rishathaim king of Aram Naharaim. Othniel made short work of him.

The land was quiet for forty years. Then Othniel son of Kenaz died.

EHUD

But the People of Israel went back to doing evil in GOD's sight. So GOD made Eglon king of Moab a power against Israel because they did evil in GOD's sight. He recruited the Ammonites and Amalekites and went out and struck Israel. They took the City of Palms. The People of Israel were in servitude to Eglon fourteen years.

The People of Israel cried out to GOD and GOD raised up for them a savior, Ehud son of Gera, a Benjaminite. He was left-handed. The People of Israel sent tribute by him to Eglon king of Moab. Ehud made himself a short two-edged sword and strapped it on his right thigh under his clothes. He presented the tribute to Eglon king of Moab. Eglon was grossly fat. After Ehud finished presenting the tribute, he went a little way with the men who had carried it. But when he got as far as the stone images near Gilgal, he went back and said, "I have a private message for you, O king."

The king told his servants, "Leave." They all left.

Ehud approached him—the king was now quite alone in his cool rooftop room—and said, "I have a word of God for you." Eglon stood up from his throne. Ehud reached with his left hand and took his sword from his right thigh and plunged it into the king's big belly. Not only the blade but the hilt went in. The fat closed in over it so he couldn't pull it out. Ehud slipped out by way of the porch and shut and locked the doors of the rooftop room behind him. Then he was gone.

When the servants came, they saw with surprise that the doors to the rooftop room were locked. They said, "He's probably relieving himself in the restroom."

They waited. And then they worried—no one was coming out of those locked doors. Finally, they got a key and unlocked them. There was their master, fallen on the floor, dead!

While they were standing around wondering what to do, Ehud was long gone. He got past the stone images and escaped to Seirah. When he got there, he sounded the trumpet on Mount Ephraim. The People of Israel came down from the hills and joined him. He took his place at their head.

He said, "Follow me, for GOD has given your enemies—yes, Moab!—to you." They went down after him and secured the fords of the Jordan against the Moabites. They let no one cross over.

At that time, they struck down about ten companies of Moabites, all of them well-fed and robust. Not one escaped. That day Moab was subdued under the hand of Israel.

The land was quiet for eighty years.

SHAMGAR

Shamgar son of Anath came after Ehud. Using a cattle prod, he killed six hundred Philistines single-handed. He too saved Israel.

DEBORAH

4 The People of Israel kept right on doing evil in GOD's sight. With Ehud dead, GOD sold them off to Jabin king of Canaan who ruled from Hazor. Sisera, who lived in Harosheth Haggoyim, was the commander of his army. The People of Israel cried out to GOD because he had cruelly oppressed them with his nine hundred iron chariots for twenty years.

Deborah was a prophet, the wife of Lappidoth. She was judge over Israel at that time. She held court under Deborah's Palm between Ramah and Bethel in the hills of Ephraim. The People of Israel went to her in matters of justice.

She sent for Barak son of Abinoam from Kedesh in Naphtali and said to him, "It has become clear that GOD, the God of Israel, commands you: Go to Mount Tabor and prepare for battle. Take ten companies of soldiers from Naphtali and Zebulun. I'll take care of getting Sisera, the leader of Jabin's army, to the Kishon River with all his chariots and troops. And I'll make sure you win the battle."

Barak said, "If you go with me, I'll go. But if you don't go with me, I won't go."

She said, "Of course I'll go with you. But understand that with an attitude like that, there'll be no glory in it for you. GOD will use a woman's hand to take care of Sisera."

Deborah got ready and went with Barak to Kedesh. Barak called Zebulun and Naphtali together at Kedesh. Ten companies of men followed him. And Deborah was with him.

It happened that Heber the Kenite had parted company with the other Kenites, the descendants of Hobab, Moses' in-law. He was now living at Zaanannim Oak near Kedesh. They told Sisera that Barak son of Abinoam had gone up to Mount Tabor. Sisera immediately called up all his chariots to the Kishon River—nine hundred iron chariots!—along with all his troops who were with him at Harosheth Haggoyim.

Deborah said to Barak, "Charge! This very day GOD has given you victory over Sisera. Isn't GOD marching before you?"

Barak charged down the slopes of Mount Tabor, his ten companies following him.

GOD routed Sisera—all those chariots, all those troops!—before Barak. Sisera jumped out of his chariot and ran. Barak chased the chariots and troops all the way to Harosheth Haggoyim. Sisera's entire fighting force was killed—not one man left.

Meanwhile Sisera, running for his life, headed for the tent of Jael, wife of Heber the Kenite. Jabin king of Hazor and Heber the Kenite were on good terms with one another. Jael stepped out to meet Sisera and said, "Come in, sir. Stay here with me. Don't be afraid."

So he went with her into her tent. She covered him with a blanket. He said to her, "Please, a little water. I'm thirsty."

She opened a bottle of milk, gave him a drink, and then covered him up again.

He then said, "Stand at the tent flap. If anyone comes by and asks you, 'Is there anyone here?' tell him, 'No, not a soul.'"

Then while he was fast asleep from exhaustion, Jael wife of Heber took a tent peg and hammer, tiptoed toward him, and drove the tent peg through his temple and all the way into the ground. He convulsed and died.

Barak arrived in pursuit of Sisera. Jael went out to greet him. She said, "Come, I'll show you the man you're looking for." He went with her and there he was — Sisera, stretched out, dead, with a tent peg through his neck.

On that day God subdued Jabin king of Canaan before the People of Israel. The People of Israel pressed harder and harder on Jabin king of Canaan until there was nothing left of him.

✝

5 That day Deborah and Barak son of Abinoam sang this song:

> When they let down their hair in Israel,
>> they let it blow wild in the wind.
> The people volunteered with abandon,
>> bless GOD!

> Hear O kings! Listen O princes!
>> To GOD, yes to GOD, I'll sing,
> Make music to GOD,
>> to the God of Israel.

> GOD, when you left Seir,
>> marched across the fields of Edom,
> Earth quaked, yes, the skies poured rain,
>> oh, the clouds made rivers.
> Mountains leapt before GOD, the Sinai God,
>> before GOD, the God of Israel.

> In the time of Shamgar son of Anath,
>> and in the time of Jael,
> Public roads were abandoned,
>> travelers went by backroads.
> Warriors became fat and sloppy,
>> no fight left in them.
> Then you, Deborah, rose up;
>> you got up, a mother in Israel.
> God chose new leaders,
>> who then fought at the gates.
> And not a shield or spear to be seen
>> among the forty companies of Israel.

Lift your hearts high, O Israel,
    with abandon, volunteering yourselves with the people—
bless GOD!

✠

You who ride on prize donkeys
    comfortably mounted on blankets
And you who walk down the roads,
    ponder, attend!
Gather at the town well
    and listen to them sing,
Chanting the tale of GOD's victories,
    his victories accomplished in Israel.

Then the people of GOD
    went down to the city gates.

Wake up, wake up, Deborah!
    Wake up, wake up, sing a song!
On your feet, Barak!
    Take your prisoners, son of Abinoam!

✠

Then the remnant went down to greet the brave ones.
    The people of GOD joined the mighty ones.
The captains from Ephraim came to the valley,
    behind you, Benjamin, with your troops.
Captains marched down from Makir,
    from Zebulun high-ranking leaders came down.
Issachar's princes rallied to Deborah,
    Issachar stood fast with Barak,
    backing him up on the field of battle.
But in Reuben's divisions there was much second-guessing.
    Why all those campfire discussions?
Diverted and distracted,
    Reuben's divisions couldn't make up their minds.
Gilead played it safe across the Jordan,
    and Dan, why did he go off sailing?

Asher kept his distance on the seacoast,
  safe and secure in his harbors.
But Zebulun risked life and limb, defied death,
  as did Naphtali on the battle heights.

The kings came, they fought,
  the kings of Canaan fought.
At Taanach they fought, at Megiddo's brook,
  but they took no silver, no plunder.
The stars in the sky joined the fight,
  from their courses they fought against Sisera.
The torrent Kishon swept them away,
  the torrent attacked them, the torrent Kishon.
  Oh, you'll stomp on the necks of the strong!
Then the hoofs of the horses pounded,
  charging, stampeding stallions.
"Curse Meroz," says GOD's angel.
  "Curse, double curse, its people,
Because they didn't come when GOD needed them,
  didn't rally to GOD's side with valiant fighters."

Most blessed of all women is Jael,
  wife of Heber the Kenite,
  most blessed of homemaking women.
He asked for water,
  she brought milk;
In a handsome bowl,
  she offered cream.
She grabbed a tent peg in her left hand,
  with her right hand she seized a hammer.
She hammered Sisera, she smashed his head,
  she drove a hole through his head.
He slumped at her feet. He fell. He sprawled.
  He slumped at her feet. He fell.
  Slumped. Fallen. Dead.

✝

Sisera's mother waited at the window,
  a weary, anxious watch.
"What's keeping his chariot?
  What delays his chariot's rumble?"
The wisest of her ladies-in-waiting answers
  with calm, reassuring words,
"Don't you think they're busy at plunder,
  dividing up the loot?
A girl, maybe two girls,
  for each man,
And for Sisera a bright silk shirt,
  a prize, fancy silk shirt!
And a colorful scarf—make it two scarves—
  to grace the neck of the plunderer."

☩

Thus may all GOD's enemies perish,
  while his lovers be like the unclouded sun.

The land was quiet for forty years.

GIDEON

6 Yet again the People of Israel went back to doing evil in GOD's sight. GOD put them under the domination of Midian for seven years. Midian overpowered Israel. Because of Midian, the People of Israel made for themselves hideouts in the mountains—caves and forts. When Israel planted its crops, Midian and Amalek, the easterners, would invade them, camp in their fields, and destroy their crops all the way down to Gaza. They left nothing for them to live on, neither sheep nor ox nor donkey. Bringing their cattle and tents, they came in and took over, like an invasion of locusts. And their camels—past counting! They marched in and devastated the country. The People of Israel, reduced to grinding poverty by Midian, cried out to GOD for help.

One time when the People of Israel had cried out to GOD because of Midian, GOD sent them a prophet with this message: "GOD, the God of Israel, says,

I delivered you from Egypt,
  I freed you from a life of slavery;

64

I rescued you from Egypt's brutality
    and then from every oppressor;
I pushed them out of your way
    and gave you their land.

"And I said to you, 'I am GOD, your God. Don't for a minute be afraid of the gods of the Amorites in whose land you are living.' But you didn't listen to me."

One day the angel of GOD came and sat down under the oak in Ophrah that belonged to Joash the Abiezrite, whose son Gideon was threshing wheat in the winepress, out of sight of the Midianites. The angel of GOD appeared to him and said,

"GOD is with you,
O mighty warrior!"

Gideon replied, "With *me*, my master? If GOD is with us, why has all this happened to us? Where are all the miracle-wonders our parents and grandparents told us about, telling us, 'Didn't GOD deliver us from Egypt?' The fact is, GOD has nothing to do with us—he has turned us over to Midian."

But GOD faced him directly: "Go in this strength that is yours. Save Israel from Midian. Haven't I just sent you?"

Gideon said to him, "*Me*, my master? How and with what could I ever save Israel? Look at me. My clan's the weakest in Manasseh and I'm the runt of the litter."

GOD said to him, "I'll be with you. Believe me, you'll defeat Midian as one man."

Gideon said, "If you're serious about this, do me a favor: Give me a sign to back up what you're telling me. Don't leave until I come back and bring you my gift."

He said, "I'll wait till you get back."

Gideon went and prepared a young goat and a huge amount of unraised bread (he used over half a bushel of flour!). He put the meat in a basket and the broth in a pot and took them back under the shade of the oak tree for a sacred meal.

The angel of God said to him, "Take the meat and unraised bread, place them on that rock, and pour the broth on them." Gideon did it.

The angel of GOD stretched out the tip of the stick he was holding and touched the meat and the bread. Fire broke out of the rock and burned up the meat and bread while the angel of God slipped away out of sight. And Gideon knew it was the angel of God!

Gideon said, "Oh no! Master, GOD! I have seen the angel of God face to face!"

But GOD reassured him, "Easy now. Don't panic. You won't die."

Then Gideon built an altar there to GOD and named it "GOD's Peace." It's still called that at Ophrah of Abiezer.

That night this happened. GOD said to him, "Take your father's best seven-year-old bull, the prime one. Tear down your father's Baal altar and chop down the Asherah fertility pole beside it. Then build an altar to GOD, your God, on the top of this hill. Take the prime bull and present it as a Whole-Burnt-Offering, using firewood from the Asherah pole that you cut down."

Gideon selected ten men from his servants and did exactly what GOD had told him. But because of his family and the people in the neighborhood, he was afraid to do it openly, so he did it that night.

Early in the morning, the people in town were shocked to find Baal's altar torn down, the Asherah pole beside it chopped down, and the prime bull burning away on the altar that had been built.

They kept asking, "Who did this?"

Questions and more questions, and then the answer: "Gideon son of Joash did it."

The men of the town demanded of Joash: "Bring out your son! He must die! Why, he tore down the Baal altar and chopped down the Asherah tree!"

But Joash stood up to the crowd pressing in on him, "Are you going to fight Baal's battles for him? Are you going to save him? Anyone who takes Baal's side will be dead by morning. If Baal is a god in fact, let him fight his own battles and defend his own altar."

They nicknamed Gideon that day Jerub-Baal because after he had torn down the Baal altar, he had said, "Let Baal fight his own battles."

⁜

All the Midianites and Amalekites (the easterners) got together, crossed the river, and made camp in the Valley of Jezreel. GOD's Spirit came over Gideon. He blew his ram's horn trumpet and the Abiezrites came out, ready to follow him. He dispatched messengers all through Manasseh, calling them to the battle; also to Asher, Zebulun, and Naphtali. They all came.

Gideon said to God, "If this is right, if you are using me to save Israel as you've said, then look: I'm placing a fleece of wool on the threshing floor. If dew is on the fleece only, but the floor is dry, then I know that you will use me to save Israel, as you said."

That's what happened. When he got up early the next morning, he wrung out the fleece—enough dew to fill a bowl with water!

Then Gideon said to God, "Don't be impatient with me, but let me say one more thing. I want to try another time with the fleece. But this time let the fleece stay dry, while the dew drenches the ground."

God made it happen that very night. Only the fleece was dry while the ground was wet with dew.

☩

7 Jerub-Baal (Gideon) got up early the next morning, all his troops right there with him. They set up camp at Harod's Spring. The camp of Midian was in the plain, north of them near the Hill of Moreh.

GOD said to Gideon, "You have too large an army with you. I can't turn Midian over to them like this—they'll take all the credit, saying, 'I did it all myself,' and forget about me. Make a public announcement: 'Anyone afraid, anyone who has any qualms at all, may leave Mount Gilead now and go home.'" Twenty-two companies headed for home. Ten companies were left.

GOD said to Gideon: "There are still too many. Take them down to the stream and I'll make a final cut. When I say, 'This one goes with you,' he'll go. When I say, 'This one doesn't go,' he won't go." So Gideon took the troops down to the stream.

GOD said to Gideon: "Everyone who laps with his tongue, the way a dog laps, set on one side. And everyone who kneels to drink, drinking with his face to the water, set to the other side." Three hundred lapped with their tongues from their cupped hands. All the rest knelt to drink.

GOD said to Gideon: "I'll use the three hundred men who lapped at the stream to save you and give Midian into your hands. All the rest may go home."

After Gideon took all their provisions and trumpets, he sent all the Israelites home. He took up his position with the three hundred. The camp of Midian stretched out below him in the valley.

That night, GOD told Gideon: "Get up and go down to the camp. I've given it to you. If you have any doubts about going down, go down with Purah your armor bearer; when you hear what they're saying, you'll be bold and confident." He and his armor bearer Purah went down near the place where sentries were posted. Midian and Amalek, all the easterners, were spread out on the plain like a swarm of locusts. And their camels! Past counting, like grains of sand on the seashore!

Gideon arrived just in time to hear a man tell his friend a dream. He said, "I had this dream: A loaf of barley bread tumbled into the Midianite camp. It came to the tent and hit it so hard it collapsed. The tent fell!"

His friend said, "This has to be the sword of Gideon son of Joash, the Israelite! God has turned Midian—the whole camp!—over to him."

When Gideon heard the telling of the dream and its interpretation, he went to his knees before God in prayer. Then he went back to the Israelite camp and said, "Get up and get going! GOD has just given us the Midianite army!"

He divided the three hundred men into three companies. He gave each man a trumpet and an empty jar, with a torch in the jar. He said, "Watch me and do what I do. When I get to the edge of the camp, do exactly what I do. When I and those with me blow the trumpets, you also, all around the camp, blow your trumpets and shout, 'For GOD and for Gideon!'"

Gideon and his hundred men got to the edge of the camp at the beginning of the middle watch, just after the sentries had been posted. They blew the trumpets, at the same time smashing the jars they carried. All three companies blew the trumpets and broke the jars. They held the torches in their left hands and the trumpets in their right hands, ready to blow, and shouted, "A sword for GOD and for Gideon!" They were stationed all around the camp, each man at his post. The whole Midianite camp jumped to its feet. They yelled and fled. When the three hundred blew the trumpets, GOD aimed each Midianite's sword against his companion, all over the camp. They ran for their lives—to Beth Shittah, toward Zererah, to the border of Abel Meholah near Tabbath.

Israelites rallied from Naphtali, from Asher, and from all over Manasseh. They had Midian on the run.

Gideon then sent messengers through all the hill country of Ephraim, urging them, "Come down against Midian! Capture the fords of the Jordan at Beth Barah."

So all the men of Ephraim rallied and captured the fords of the Jordan at Beth Barah. They also captured the two Midianite commanders

Oreb (Raven) and Zeeb (Wolf). They killed Oreb at Raven Rock; Zeeb they killed at Wolf Winepress. And they pressed the pursuit of Midian. They brought the heads of Oreb and Zeeb to Gideon across the Jordan.

8 Then the Ephraimites said to Gideon, "Why did you leave us out of this, not calling us when you went to fight Midian?" They were indignant and let him know it.

But Gideon replied, "What have I done compared to you? Why, even the gleanings of Ephraim are superior to the vintage of Abiezer. God gave you Midian's commanders, Oreb and Zeeb. What have I done compared with you?"

When they heard this, they calmed down and cooled off.

✝

Gideon and his three hundred arrived at the Jordan and crossed over. They were bone-tired but still pressing the pursuit. He asked the men of Succoth, "Please, give me some loaves of bread for my troops I have with me. They're worn out, and I'm hot on the trail of Zebah and Zalmunna, the Midianite kings."

But the leaders in Succoth said, "You're on a wild goose chase; why should we help you on a fool's errand?"

Gideon said, "If you say so. But when GOD gives me Zebah and Zalmunna, I'll give you a thrashing, whip your bare flesh with desert thorns and thistles!"

He went from there to Peniel and made the same request. The men of Peniel, like the men of Succoth, also refused. Gideon told them, "When I return safe and sound, I'll demolish this tower."

Zebah and Zalmunna were in Karkor with an army of about fifteen companies, all that was left of the fighting force of the easterners—they had lost 120 companies of soldiers.

Gideon went up the caravan trail east of Nobah and Jogbehah, found and attacked the undefended camp. Zebah and Zalmunna fled, but he chased and captured the two kings of Midian. The whole camp had panicked.

Gideon son of Joash returned from the battle by way of the Heres Pass. He captured a young man from Succoth and asked some questions. The young man wrote down the names of the officials and leaders of

Succoth, seventy-seven men. Then Gideon went to the men of Succoth and said, "Here are the wild geese, Zebah and Zalmunna, you said I'd never catch. You wouldn't give so much as a scrap of bread to my worn-out men; you taunted us, saying that we were on a fool's errand."

Then he took the seventy-seven leaders of Succoth and thrashed them with desert thorns and thistles. And he demolished the tower of Peniel and killed the men of the city.

He then addressed Zebah and Zalmunna: "Tell me about the men you killed at Tabor."

"They were men much like you," they said, "each one like a king's son."

Gideon said, "They were my brothers, my mother's sons. As GOD lives, if you had let them live, I would let you live."

Then he spoke to Jether, his firstborn: "Get up and kill them." But he couldn't do it, couldn't draw his sword. He was afraid—he was still just a boy.

Zebah and Zalmunna said, "Do it yourself—if you're man enough!" And Gideon did it. He stepped up and killed Zebah and Zalmunna. Then he took the crescents that hung on the necks of their camels.

✢

The Israelites said, "Rule over us, you and your son and your grand-son. You have saved us from Midian's tyranny."

Gideon said, "I most certainly will not rule over you, nor will my son. GOD will reign over you."

Then Gideon said, "But I do have one request. Give me, each of you, an earring that you took as plunder." Ishmaelites wore gold ear-rings, and the men all had their pockets full of them.

They said, "Of course. They're yours!"

They spread out a blanket and each man threw his plundered ear-rings on it. The gold earrings that Gideon had asked for weighed about forty-three pounds—and that didn't include the crescents and pen-dants, the purple robes worn by the Midianite kings, and the orna-ments hung around the necks of their camels.

Gideon made the gold into a sacred ephod and put it on display in his hometown, Ophrah. All Israel prostituted itself there. Gideon and his family, too, were seduced by it.

Midian's tyranny was broken by the Israelites; nothing more was heard from them. The land was quiet for forty years in Gideon's time.

✣

Jerub-Baal son of Joash went home and lived in his house. Gideon had seventy sons. He fathered them all—he had a lot of wives! His concubine, the one at Shechem, also bore him a son. He named him Abimelech.

Gideon son of Joash died at a good old age. He was buried in the tomb of his father Joash at Ophrah of the Abiezrites.

ABIMELECH

Gideon was hardly cool in the tomb when the People of Israel had gotten off track and were prostituting themselves to Baal—they made Baal-of-the-Covenant their god. The People of Israel forgot all about GOD, their God, who had saved them from all their enemies who had hemmed them in. And they didn't keep faith with the family of Jerub-Baal (Gideon), honoring all the good he had done for Israel.

✣

9 Abimelech son of Jerub-Baal went to Shechem to his uncles and all his mother's relatives and said to them, "Ask all the leading men of Shechem, 'What do you think is best, that seventy men rule you—all those sons of Jerub-Baal—or that one man rule? You'll remember that I am your own flesh and blood.'"

His mother's relatives reported the proposal to the leaders of Shechem. They were inclined to take Abimelech. "Because," they said, "he is, after all, one of us."

They gave him seventy silver pieces from the shrine of Baal-of-the-Covenant. With the money he hired some reckless riff-raff soldiers and they followed along after him. He went to his father's house in Ophrah and killed his half brothers, the sons of Jerub-Baal—seventy men! And on one stone! The youngest, Jotham son of Jerub-Baal, managed to hide, the only survivor.

Then all the leaders of Shechem and Beth Millo gathered at the Oak by the Standing Stone at Shechem and crowned Abimelech king.

When this was all told to Jotham, he climbed to the top of Mount Gerizim, raised his voice, and shouted:

Listen to me, leaders of Shechem.
And let God listen to you!

71

The trees set out one day
    to anoint a king for themselves.
They said to Olive Tree,
    "Rule over us."
But Olive Tree told them,
    "Am I no longer good for making oil
That gives glory to gods and men,
    and to be demoted to waving over trees?"

The trees then said to Fig Tree,
    "You come and rule over us."
But Fig Tree said to them,
    "Am I no longer good for making sweets,
My mouthwatering sweet fruits,
    and to be demoted to waving over trees?"

The trees then said to Vine,
    "You come and rule over us."
But Vine said to them,
    "Am I no longer good for making wine,
Wine that cheers gods and men,
    and to be demoted to waving over trees?"

All the trees then said to Tumbleweed,
    "You come and reign over us."
But Tumbleweed said to the trees:
    "If you're serious about making me your king,
Come and find shelter in my shade.
    But if not, let fire shoot from Tumbleweed
    and burn down the cedars of Lebanon!"

"Now listen: Do you think you did a right and honorable thing when you made Abimelech king? Do you think you treated Jerub-Baal and his family well, did for him what he deserved? My father fought for you, risked his own life, and rescued you from Midian's tyranny, and you have, just now, betrayed him. You massacred his sons—seventy men on a single stone! You made Abimelech, the son by his maidservant, king over Shechem's leaders because he's your relative. If you think that this is an honest day's work, this way you have treated Jerub-

Baal today, then enjoy Abimelech and let him enjoy you. But if not, let
fire break from Abimelech and burn up the leaders of Shechem and
Beth Millo. And let fire break from the leaders of Shechem and Beth
Millo and burn up Abimelech."

And Jotham fled. He ran for his life. He went to Beer and settled
down there, because he was afraid of his brother Abimelech.

✢

Abimelech ruled over Israel for three years. Then God brought bad
blood between Abimelech and Shechem's leaders, who now worked
treacherously behind his back. Violence boomeranged: The murderous
violence that killed the seventy brothers, the sons of Jerub-Baal, was
now loose among Abimelech and Shechem's leaders, who had supported the violence.

To undermine Abimelech, Shechem's leaders put men in ambush
on the mountain passes who robbed travelers on those roads. And
Abimelech was told.

At that time Gaal son of Ebed arrived with his relatives and moved
into Shechem. The leaders of Shechem trusted him. One day they went
out into the fields, gathered grapes in the vineyards, and trod them in
the winepress. Then they held a celebration in their god's temple, a
feast, eating and drinking. And then they started putting down
Abimelech.

Gaal son of Ebed said, "Who is this Abimelech? And who are we
Shechemites to take orders from him? Isn't he the son of Jerub-Baal,
and isn't this his henchman Zebul? We belong to the race of Hamor
and bear the noble name of Shechem. Why should we be toadies of
Abimelech? If I were in charge of this people, the first thing I'd do is
get rid of Abimelech! I'd say, 'Show me your stuff, Abimelech — let's
see who's boss here!'"

Zebul, governor of the city, heard what Gaal son of Ebed was saying and got angry. Secretly he sent messengers to Abimelech with the
message, "Gaal son of Ebed and his relatives have come to Shechem and
are stirring up trouble against you. Here's what you do: Tonight bring
your troops and wait in ambush in the field. In the morning, as soon
as the sun breaks, get moving and charge the city. Gaal and his troops
will come out to you, and you'll know what to do next."

Abimelech and his troops, four companies of them, went up that
night and waited in ambush approaching Shechem. Gaal son of Ebed

had gotten up and was standing in the city gate. Abimelech and his troops left their cover. When Gaal saw them he said to Zebul, "Look at that, people coming down from the tops of the mountains!"

Zebul said, "That's nothing but mountain shadows; they just look like men." Gaal kept chattering away.

Then he said again, "Look at the troops coming down off Tabbur-erez (the Navel of the World)—and one company coming straight from the Oracle Oak."

Zebul said, "Where is that big mouth of yours now? You who said, 'And who is Abimelech that we should take orders from him?' Well, there he is with the troops you ridiculed. Here's your chance. Fight away!"

Gaal went out, backed by the leaders of Shechem, and did battle with Abimelech. Abimelech chased him, and Gaal turned tail and ran. Many fell wounded, right up to the city gate.

Abimelech set up his field headquarters at Arumah while Zebul kept Gaal and his relatives out of Shechem.

⊹

The next day the people went out to the fields. This was reported to Abimelech. He took his troops, divided them into three companies, and placed them in ambush in the fields. When he saw that the people were well out in the open, he sprang up and attacked them. Abimelech and the company with him charged ahead and took control of the entrance to the city gate; the other two companies chased down those who were in the open fields and killed them. Abimelech fought at the city all that day. He captured the city and massacred everyone in it. He leveled the city to the ground, then sowed it with salt.

When the leaders connected with Shechem's Tower heard this, they went into the fortified God-of-the-Covenant temple. This was reported to Abimelech that the Shechem's Tower bunch were gathered together. He and his troops climbed Mount Zalmon (Dark Mountain). Abimelech took his ax and chopped a bundle of firewood, picked it up, and put it on his shoulder. He said to his troops, "Do what you've seen me do, and quickly." So each of his men cut his own bundle. They followed Abimelech, piled their bundles against the Tower fortifications, and set the whole structure on fire. Everyone in Shechem's Tower died, about a thousand men and women.

Abimelech went on to Thebez. He camped at Thebez and captured it. The Tower-of-Strength stood in the middle of the city; all the men and women of the city along with the city's leaders had fled there and locked themselves in. They were up on the tower roof. Abimelech got as far as the tower and assaulted it. He came up to the tower door to set it on fire. Just then some woman dropped an upper millstone on his head and crushed his skull. He called urgently to his young armor-bearer and said, "Draw your sword and kill me so they can't say of me, 'A woman killed him.'" His armor bearer drove in his sword, and Abimelech died.

When the Israelites saw that Abimelech was dead, they went home.

✝

God avenged the evil Abimelech had done to his father, murdering his seventy brothers. And God brought down on the heads of the men of Shechem all the evil that they had done, the curse of Jotham son of Jerub-Baal.

TOLA

10Tola son of Puah, the son of Dodo, was next after Abimelech. He rose to the occasion to save Israel. He was a man of Issachar. He lived in Shamir in the hill country of Ephraim. He judged Israel for twenty-three years and then died and was buried at Shamir.

JAIR

After him, Jair the Gileadite stepped into leadership. He judged Israel for twenty-two years. He had thirty sons who rode on thirty donkeys and had thirty towns in Gilead. The towns are still called Jair's Villages. Jair died and was buried in Kamon.

✝

And then the People of Israel went back to doing evil in GOD's sight. They worshiped the Baal gods and Ashtoreth goddesses: gods of Aram, Sidon, and Moab; gods of the Ammonites and the Philistines. They just walked off and left GOD, quit worshiping him. And GOD exploded in hot anger at Israel and sold them off to the Philistines and Ammonites, who, beginning that year, bullied and battered the People of Israel mercilessly. For eighteen years they had them under their thumb, all the People of Israel who lived east of the Jordan in the Amorite country of Gilead.

Then the Ammonites crossed the Jordan to go to war also against Judah, Benjamin, and Ephraim. Israel was in a bad way!

The People of Israel cried out to GOD for help: "We've sinned against you! We left our God and worshiped the Baal gods!"

GOD answered the People of Israel: "When the Egyptians, Amorites, Ammonites, Philistines, Sidonians—even Amalek and Midian!—oppressed you and you cried out to me for help, I saved you from them. And now you've gone off and betrayed me, worshiping other gods. I'm not saving you anymore. Go ahead! Cry out for help to the gods you've chosen—let them get you out of the mess you're in!"

The People of Israel said to GOD: "We've sinned. Do to us whatever you think best, but please, get us out of this!"

Then they cleaned house of the foreign gods and worshiped only GOD. And GOD took Israel's troubles to heart.

JEPHTHAH

The Ammonites prepared for war, setting camp in Gilead. The People of Israel set their rival camp in Mizpah. The leaders in Gilead said, "Who will stand up for us against the Ammonites? We'll make him head over everyone in Gilead!"

11 Jephthah the Gileadite was one tough warrior. He was the son of a whore, but Gilead was his father. Meanwhile Gilead's legal wife had given him other sons, and when they grew up, his wife's sons threw Jephthah out. They told him: "You're not getting any of our family inheritance—you're the son of another woman." So Jephthah fled from his brothers and went to live in the land of Tob. Some riff-raff joined him and went around with him.

Some time passed. And then the Ammonites started fighting Israel. With the Ammonites at war with them, the elders of Gilead went to get Jephthah from the land of Tob. They said to Jephthah: "Come. Be our general and we'll fight the Ammonites."

But Jephthah said to the elders of Gilead: "But you hate me. You kicked me out of my family home. So why are you coming to me now? Because you are in trouble. Right?"

The elders of Gilead replied, "That's it exactly. We've come to you to get you to go with us and fight the Ammonites. You'll be the head of all of us, all the Gileadites."

Jephthah addressed the elders of Gilead, "So if you bring me back home to fight the Ammonites and GOD gives them to me, I'll be your head—is that right?"

They said, "GOD is witness between us; whatever you say, we'll do." Jephthah went along with the elders of Gilead. The people made him their top man and general. And Jephthah repeated what he had said before GOD at Mizpah.

Then Jephthah sent messengers to the king of the Ammonites with a message: "What's going on here that you have come into my country picking a fight?"

The king of the Ammonites told Jephthah's messengers: "Because Israel took my land when they came up out of Egypt—from the Arnon all the way to the Jabbok and to the Jordan. Give it back peaceably and I'll go."

Jephthah again sent messengers to the king of the Ammonites with the message: "Jephthah's word: Israel took no Moabite land and no Ammonite land. When they came up from Egypt, Israel went through the desert as far as the Red Sea, arriving at Kadesh. There Israel sent messengers to the king of Edom saying, 'Let us pass through your land, please.' But the king of Edom wouldn't let them. Israel also requested permission from the king of Moab, but he wouldn't let them cross either. They were stopped in their tracks at Kadesh. So they traveled across the desert and circled around the lands of Edom and Moab. They came out east of the land of Moab and set camp on the other side of the Arnon—they didn't set foot in Moabite territory, for Arnon was the Moabite border. Israel then sent messengers to Sihon king of the Amorites at Heshbon the capital. Israel asked, 'Let us pass, please, through your land on the way to our country.' But Sihon didn't trust Israel to cut across his land; he got his entire army together, set up camp at Jahaz, and fought Israel. But GOD, the God of Israel, gave Sihon and all his troops to Israel. Israel defeated them. Israel took all the Amorite land, all Amorite land from Arnon to the Jabbok and from the desert to the Jordan. It was GOD, the God of Israel, who pushed out the Amorites in favor of Israel; so who do you think you are to try to take it over? Why don't you just be satisfied with what your god Chemosh gives you and we'll settle for what GOD, our God, gives us? Do you think you're going to come off better than Balak son of Zippor, the king of Moab? Did he get anywhere in opposing Israel? Did he risk war? All this time—it's been three hundred years now!—that Israel has lived in Heshbon and its villages, in Aroer and its villages, and in all the towns along the Arnon, why didn't you try to snatch them away then? No, I haven't wronged you. But this is an evil thing that you are doing to me by starting a fight. Today GOD the Judge will decide between the People of Israel and the people of Ammon."

But the king of the Ammonites refused to listen to a word that Jephthah had sent him.

GOD's Spirit came upon Jephthah. He went across Gilead and Manasseh, went through Mizpah of Gilead, and from there approached the Ammonites. Jephthah made a vow before GOD: "If you give me a clear victory over the Ammonites, then I'll give to GOD whatever comes out of the door of my house to meet me when I return in one piece from among the Ammonites—I'll offer it up in a sacrificial burnt offering."

Then Jephthah was off to fight the Ammonites. And GOD gave them to him. He beat them soundly, all the way from Aroer to the area around Minnith as far as Abel Keramim—twenty cities! A massacre! Ammonites brought to their knees by the People of Israel.

Jephthah came home to Mizpah. His daughter ran from the house to welcome him home—dancing to tambourines! She was his only child. He had no son or daughter except her. When he realized who it was, he ripped his clothes, saying, "Ah, dearest daughter—I'm dirt. I'm despicable. My heart is torn to shreds. I made a vow to GOD and I can't take it back!"

She said, "Dear father, if you made a vow to GOD, do to me what you vowed; GOD did his part and saved you from your Ammonite enemies."

And then she said to her father, "But let this one thing be done for me. Give me two months to wander through the hills and lament my virginity since I will never marry, I and my dear friends."

"Oh yes, go," he said. He sent her off for two months. She and her dear girlfriends went among the hills, lamenting that she would never marry. At the end of the two months, she came back to her father. He fulfilled the vow with her that he had made. She had never slept with a man.

It became a custom in Israel that for four days every year the young women of Israel went out to mourn for the daughter of Jephthah the Gileadite.

✠

12 The men of Ephraim mustered their troops, crossed to Zaphon, and said to Jephthah, "Why did you go out to fight the Ammonites without letting us go with you? We're going to burn your house down on you!"

Jephthah said, "I and my people had our hands full negotiating with the Ammonites. And I did call to you for help but you ignored me. When I saw that you weren't coming, I took my life in my hands and confronted the Ammonites myself. And GOD gave them to me! So why did you show up here today? Are you spoiling for a fight with me?"

So Jephthah got his Gilead troops together and fought Ephraim. And the men of Gilead hit them hard because they were saying, "Gileadites are nothing but half-breeds and rejects from Ephraim and Manasseh."

Gilead captured the fords of the Jordan at the crossing to Ephraim. If an Ephraimite fugitive said, "Let me cross," the men of Gilead would ask, "Are you an Ephraimite?" and he would say, "No." And they would say, "Say, 'Shibboleth.'" But he would always say, "Sibboleth"— he couldn't say it right. Then they would grab him and kill him there at the fords of the Jordan. Forty-two Ephraimite divisions were killed on that occasion.

Jephthah judged Israel six years. Jephthah the Gileadite died and was buried in his city, Mizpah of Gilead.

IBZAN

After him, Ibzan of Bethlehem judged Israel. He had thirty sons and thirty daughters. He gave his daughters in marriage outside his clan and brought in thirty daughters-in-law from the outside for his sons.

He judged Israel seven years. Ibzan died and was buried in Bethlehem.

ELON

After him, Elon the Zebulunite judged Israel. He judged Israel ten years. Elon the Zebulunite died and was buried at Aijalon in the land of Zebulun.

ABDON

After him, Abdon son of Hillel the Pirathonite judged Israel. He had forty sons and thirty grandsons who rode on seventy donkeys. He judged Israel eight years. Abdon son of Hillel the Pirathonite died and was buried at Pirathon in the land of Ephraim in the Amalekite hill country.

SAMSON

13 And then the People of Israel were back at it again, doing what was evil in GOD's sight. GOD put them under the domination of the Philistines for forty years.

At that time there was a man named Manoah from Zorah from the tribe of Dan. His wife was barren and childless. The angel of God appeared to her and told her, "I know that you are barren and childless, but you're going to become pregnant and bear a son. But take much care: Drink no wine or beer; eat nothing ritually unclean. You are, in fact, pregnant right now, carrying a son. No razor will touch his head—the boy will be God's Nazirite from the moment of his birth. He will launch the deliverance from Philistine oppression."

The woman went to her husband and said, "A man of God came to me. He looked like the angel of God—terror laced with glory! I didn't ask him where he was from and he didn't tell me his name, but he told me, 'You're pregnant. You're going to give birth to a son. Don't drink any wine or beer and eat nothing ritually unclean. The boy will be God's Nazirite from the moment of birth to the day of his death.'"

Manoah prayed to GOD: "Master, let the man of God you sent come to us again and teach us how to raise this boy who is to be born."

God listened to Manoah. God's angel came again to the woman. She was sitting in the field; her husband Manoah wasn't there with her. She jumped to her feet and ran and told her husband: "He's back! The man who came to me that day!"

Manoah got up and, following his wife, came to the man. He said to him, "Are you the man who spoke to my wife?"

He said, "I am."

Manoah said, "So. When what you say comes true, what do you have to tell us about this boy and his work?"

The angel of God said to Manoah, "Keep in mind everything I told the woman. Eat nothing that comes from the vine: Drink no wine or beer; eat no ritually unclean foods. She's to observe everything I commanded her."

Manoah said to the angel of God, "Please, stay with us a little longer; we'll prepare a meal for you—a young goat."

GOD's angel said to Manoah, "Even if I stay, I won't eat your food.

But if you want to prepare a Whole-Burnt-Offering for GOD, go ahead—offer it!" Manoah had no idea that he was talking to the angel of God.

Then Manoah asked the angel of God, "What's your name? When your words come true, we'd like to honor you."

The angel of GOD said, "What's this? You ask for my name? You wouldn't understand—it's sheer wonder."

So Manoah took the kid and the Grain-Offering and sacrificed them on a rock altar to GOD who works wonders. As the flames leapt up from the altar to heaven, GOD's angel also ascended in the altar flames. When Manoah and his wife saw this, they fell facedown to the ground. Manoah and his wife never saw the angel of GOD again.

Only then did Manoah realize that this was GOD's angel. He said to his wife, "We're as good as dead! We've looked on God!"

But his wife said, "If GOD were planning to kill us, he wouldn't have accepted our Whole-Burnt-Offering and Grain-Offering, or revealed all these things to us—given us this birth announcement."

The woman gave birth to a son. They named him Samson. The boy grew and GOD blessed him. The Spirit of GOD began working in him while he was staying at a Danite camp between Zorah and Eshtaol.

✠

14 Samson went down to Timnah. There in Timnah a woman caught his eye, a Philistine girl. He came back and told his father and mother, "I saw a woman in Timnah, a Philistine girl; get her for me as my wife."

His parents said to him, "Isn't there a woman among the girls in the neighborhood of our people? Do you have to go get a wife from the uncircumcised Philistines?"

But Samson said to his father, "Get her for me. She's the one I want—she's the right one."

(His father and mother had no idea that GOD was behind this, that he was arranging an opportunity against the Philistines. At the time the Philistines lorded it over Israel.)

Samson went down to Timnah with his father and mother. When he got to the vineyards of Timnah, a young lion came at him, roaring. The Spirit of GOD came on him powerfully and he ripped it open barehanded, like tearing a young goat. But he didn't tell his parents what he had done.

Then he went on down and spoke to the woman. In Samson's eyes, she was the one.

Some days later when he came back to get her, he made a little detour to look at what was left of the lion. And there a wonder: a swarm of bees in the lion's carcass—and honey! He scooped it up in his hands and kept going, eating as he went. He rejoined his father and mother and gave some to them and they ate. But he didn't tell them that he had scooped out the honey from the lion's carcass.

His father went on down to make arrangements with the woman, while Samson prepared a feast there. That's what the young men did in those days. Because the people were wary of him, they arranged for thirty friends to mingle with him.

Samson said to them: "Let me put a riddle to you. If you can figure it out during the seven days of the feast, I'll give you thirty linen garments and thirty changes of fine clothing. But if you can't figure it out then you'll give me thirty linen garments and thirty changes of fine clothing."

They said, "Put your riddle. Let's hear it." So he said,

From the eater came something to eat,
From the strong came something sweet.

They couldn't figure it out. After three days they were still stumped. On the fourth day they said to Samson's bride, "Worm the answer out of your husband or we'll burn you and your father's household. Have you invited us here to bankrupt us?"

So Samson's bride turned on the tears, saying to him, "You hate me. You don't love me. You've told a riddle to my people but you won't even tell me the answer."

He said, "I haven't told my own parents—why would I tell you?"

But she turned on the tears all the seven days of the feast. On the seventh day, worn out by her nagging, he told her. Then she went and told it to her people.

The men of the town came to him on the seventh day, just before sunset and said,

What is sweeter than honey?
What is stronger than a lion?

And Samson said,

If you hadn't plowed with my heifer,
You wouldn't have found out my riddle.

Then the Spirit of GOD came powerfully on him. He went down to Ashkelon and killed thirty of their men, stripped them, and gave their clothing to those who had solved the riddle. Stalking out, smoking with anger, he went home to his father's house. Samson's bride became the wife of the best man at his wedding.

✠

15 Later on—it was during the wheat harvest—Samson visited his bride, bringing a young goat. He said, "Let me see my wife—show me her bedroom."

But her father wouldn't let him in. He said, "I concluded that by now you hated her with a passion, so I gave her to your best man. But her little sister is even more beautiful. Why not take her instead?"

Samson said, "That does it. This time when I wreak havoc on the Philistines, I'm blameless."

Samson then went out and caught three hundred jackals. He lashed the jackals' tails together in pairs and tied a torch between each pair of tails. He then set fire to the torches and let them loose in the Philistine fields of ripe grain. Everything burned, both stacked and standing grain, vineyards and olive orchards—everything.

The Philistines said, "Who did this?"

They were told, "Samson, son-in-law of the Timnite who took his bride and gave her to his best man."

The Philistines went up and burned both her and her father to death.

Samson then said, "If this is the way you're going to act, I swear I'll get even with you. And I'm not quitting till the job's done!"

With that he tore into them, ripping them limb from limb—a huge slaughter. Then he went down and stayed in a cave at Etam Rock.

✠

The Philistines set out and made camp in Judah, preparing to attack Lehi (Jawbone). When the men of Judah asked, "Why have you come up against us?" they said, "We're out to get Samson. We're going after Samson to do to him what he did to us."

Three companies of men from Judah went down to the cave at Etam Rock and said to Samson, "Don't you realize that the Philistines already bully and lord it over us? So what's going on with you, making things even worse?"

He said, "It was tit for tat. I only did to them what they did to me."

They said, "Well, we've come down here to tie you up and turn you over to the Philistines."

Samson said, "Just promise not to hurt me."

"We promise," they said. "We will tie you up and surrender you to them but, believe us, we won't kill you." They proceeded to tie him with new ropes and led him up from the Rock.

As he approached Lehi, the Philistines came to meet him, shouting in triumph. And then the Spirit of GOD came on him with great power. The ropes on his arms fell apart like flax on fire; the thongs slipped off his hands. He spotted a fresh donkey jawbone, reached down and grabbed it, and with it killed the whole company. And Samson said,

> With a donkey's jawbone
> I made heaps of donkeys of them.
> With a donkey's jawbone
> I killed an entire company.

When he finished speaking, he threw away the jawbone. He named that place Ramath Lehi (Jawbone Hill).

Now he was suddenly very thirsty. He called out to GOD, "You have given your servant this great victory. Are you going to abandon me to die of thirst and fall into the hands of the uncircumcised?" So God split open the rock basin in Lehi; water gushed out and Samson drank. His spirit revived—he was alive again! That's why it's called En Hakkore (Caller's Spring). It's still there at Lehi today.

Samson judged Israel for twenty years in the days of the Philistines.

✝

16 Samson went to Gaza and saw a prostitute. He went to her. The news got around: "Samson's here." They gathered around in hiding, waiting all night for him at the city gate, quiet as mice, thinking, "At sunrise we'll kill him."

Samson was in bed with the woman until midnight. Then he got up, seized the doors of the city gate and the two gateposts, bolts and all, hefted them on his shoulder, and carried them to the top of the hill that faces Hebron.

✛

Some time later he fell in love with a woman in the Valley of Sorek (Grapes). Her name was Delilah. The Philistine tyrants approached her and said, "Seduce him. Discover what's behind his great strength and how we can tie him up and humble him. Each man's company will give you a hundred shekels of silver."

So Delilah said to Samson, "Tell me, dear, the secret of your great strength, and how you can be tied up and humbled."

Samson told her, "If they were to tie me up with seven bow-strings—the kind made from fresh animal tendons, not dried out—then I would become weak, just like anyone else."

The Philistine tyrants brought her seven bowstrings, not dried out, and she tied him up with them. The men were waiting in ambush in her room. Then she said, "The Philistines are on you, Samson!" He snapped the cords as though they were mere threads. The secret of his strength was still a secret.

Delilah said, "Come now, Samson—you're playing with me, making up stories. Be serious; tell me how you can be tied up."

He told her, "If you were to tie me up tight with new ropes, ropes never used for work, then I would be helpless, just like anybody else."

So Delilah got some new ropes and tied him up. She said, "The Philistines are on you, Samson!" The men were hidden in the next room. He snapped the ropes from his arms like threads.

Delilah said to Samson, "You're still playing games with me, teasing me with lies. Tell me how you can be tied up."

He said to her, "If you wove the seven braids of my hair into the fabric on the loom and drew it tight, then I would be as helpless as any other mortal."

When she had him fast asleep, Delilah took the seven braids of his hair and wove them into the fabric on the loom and drew it tight. Then she said, "The Philistines are on you, Samson!" He woke from his sleep and ripped loose from both the loom and fabric!

She said, "How can you say 'I love you' when you won't even trust me? Three times now you've toyed with me, like a cat with a mouse, refusing to tell me the secret of your great strength."

She kept at it day after day, nagging and tormenting him. Finally, he was fed up—he couldn't take another minute of it. He spilled it.

He told her, "A razor has never touched my head. I've been God's

Nazirite from conception. If I were shaved, my strength would leave me; I would be as helpless as any other mortal."

When Delilah realized that he had told her his secret, she sent for the Philistine tyrants, telling them, "Come quickly—this time he's told me the truth." They came, bringing the bribe money.

When she got him to sleep, his head on her lap, she motioned to a man to cut off the seven braids of his hair. Immediately he began to grow weak. His strength drained from him.

Then she said, "The Philistines are on you, Samson!" He woke up, thinking, "I'll go out, like always, and shake free." He didn't realize that GOD had abandoned him.

The Philistines grabbed him, gouged out his eyes, and took him down to Gaza. They shackled him in irons and put him to the work of grinding in the prison. But his hair, though cut off, began to grow again.

The Philistine tyrants got together to offer a great sacrifice to their god Dagon. They celebrated, saying,

> Our god has given us
> Samson our enemy!

And when the people saw him, they joined in, cheering their god,

> Our god has given
> Our enemy to us,
> The one who ravaged our country,
> Piling high the corpses among us.

Then this: Everyone was feeling high and someone said, "Get Samson! Let him show us his stuff!" They got Samson from the prison and he put on a show for them.

They had him standing between the pillars. Samson said to the young man who was acting as his guide, "Put me where I can touch the pillars that hold up the temple so I can rest against them." The building was packed with men and women, including all the Philistine tyrants. And there were at least 3,000 in the stands watching Samson's performance.

And Samson cried out to GOD:

> Master, GOD!
> Oh, please, look on me again,
> Oh, please, give strength yet once more.

God!
> With one avenging blow let me be avenged
> On the Philistines for my two eyes!

Then Samson reached out to the two central pillars that held up the building and pushed against them, one with his right arm, the other with his left. Saying, "Let me die with the Philistines," Samson pushed hard with all his might. The building crashed on the tyrants and all the people in it. He killed more people in his death than he had killed in his life.

☩

His brothers and all his relatives went down to get his body. They carried him back and buried him in the tomb of Manoah his father, between Zorah and Eshtaol.

He judged Israel for twenty years.

MICAH

17 There was a man from the hill country of Ephraim named Micah. He said to his mother, "Remember that 1,100 pieces of silver that were taken from you? I overheard you when you pronounced your curse. Well, I have the money; I stole it. But now I've brought it back to you."

His mother said, "GOD bless you, my son!"

As he returned the 1,100 silver pieces to his mother, she said, "I had totally consecrated this money to GOD for my son to make a statue, a cast god." Then she took 200 pieces of the silver and gave it to a sculptor and he cast them into the form of a god.

This man, Micah, had a private chapel. He had made an ephod and some teraphim-idols and had ordained one of his sons to be his priest.

In those days there was no king in Israel. People did whatever they felt like doing.

☩

Meanwhile there was a young man from Bethlehem in Judah and from a family of Judah. He was a Levite but was a stranger there. He left that town, Bethlehem in Judah, seeking his fortune. He got as far as the hill country of Ephraim and showed up at Micah's house.

Micah asked him, "So where are you from?"

He said, "I'm a Levite from Bethlehem in Judah. I'm on the road, looking for a place to settle down."

Micah said, "Stay here with me. Be my father and priest. I'll pay you ten pieces of silver a year, whatever clothes you need, and your meals."

The Levite agreed and moved in with Micah. The young man fit right in and became one of the family. Micah appointed the young Levite as his priest. This all took place in Micah's home.

Micah said, "Now I know that GOD will make things go well for me—why, I've got a Levite for a priest!"

✣

18 In those days there was no king in Israel. But also in those days, the tribe of Dan was looking for a place to settle down. They hadn't yet occupied their plot among the tribes of Israel.

The Danites sent out five robust warriors from Zorah and Eshtaol to look over the land and see what was out there suitable for their families. They said, "Go and explore the land."

They went into the hill country of Ephraim and got as far as the house of Micah. They camped there for the night. As they neared Micah's house, they recognized the voice of the young Levite. They went over and said to him, "How on earth did you get here? What's going on? What are you doing here?"

He said, "One thing led to another: Micah hired me and I'm now his priest."

They said, "Oh, good—inquire of God for us. Find out whether our mission will be a success."

The priest said, "Go assured. GOD's looking out for you all the way."

The five men left and headed north to Laish. They saw that the people there were living in safety under the umbrella of the Sidonians, quiet and unsuspecting. They had everything going for them. But the people lived a long way from the Sidonians to the west and had no treaty with the Arameans to the east.

When they got back to Zorah and Eshtaol, their brothers asked, "So, how did you find things?"

They said, "Let's go for it! Let's attack. We've seen the land and it is excellent. Are you going to just sit on your hands? Don't dawdle! Invade and conquer! When you get there, you'll find they're sitting ducks, totally unsuspecting. Wide open land—God is handing it over to you, everything you could ever ask for."

So 600 Danite men set out from Zorah and Eshtaol, armed to the teeth. Along the way they made camp at Kiriath Jearim in Judah. That is why the place is still today called Dan's Camp—it's just west of Kiriath Jearim. From there they proceeded into the hill country of Ephraim and came to Micah's house.

The five men who earlier had explored the country of Laish told their companions, "Did you know there's an ephod, teraphim-idols, and a cast god-sculpture in these buildings? What do you think? Do you want to do something about it?"

So they turned off the road there, went to the house of the young Levite at Micah's place and asked how things had been with him. The 600 Danites, all well-armed, stood guard at the entrance to the gate while the five scouts who had gone to explore the land went in and took the carved idol, the ephod, the teraphim-idols, and the god-sculpture. The priest was standing at the gate entrance with the 600 armed men. When the five went into Micah's house and took the carved idol, the ephod, the teraphim-idols, and the sculpted god, the priest said to them, "What do you think you're doing?"

They said to him, "Hush! Don't make a sound. Come with us. Be our father and priest. Which is more important, that you be a priest to one man or that you become priest to a whole tribe and clan in Israel?"

The priest jumped at the chance. He took the ephod, the teraphim-idols, and the idol and fell in with the troops.

They turned away and set out, putting the children, the cattle, and the gear in the lead. They were well on their way from Micah's house before Micah and his neighbors got organized. But they soon overtook the Danites. They shouted at them. The Danites turned around and said, "So what's all the noise about?"

Micah said, "You took my god, the one I made, and you took my priest. And you marched off! What do I have left? How can you now say, 'What's the matter?'"

But the Danites answered, "Don't yell at us; you just might provoke some fierce, hot-tempered men to attack you, and you'll end up an army of dead men."

The Danites went on their way. Micah saw that he didn't stand a chance against their arms. He turned back and went home.

So they took the things that Micah had made, along with his priest, and they arrived at Laish, that city of quiet and unsuspecting people.

They massacred the people and burned down the city.

There was no one around to help. They were a long way from Sidon and had no treaty with the Arameans. Laish was in the valley of Beth Rehob. When they rebuilt the city they renamed it Dan after their ancestor who was a son of Israel, but its original name was Laish.

The Danites set up the god-figure for themselves. Jonathan son of Gershom, the son of Moses, and his descendants were priests to the tribe of Dan down to the time of the land's captivity. All during the time that there was a sanctuary of God in Shiloh, they kept for their private use the god-figure that Micah had made.

THE LEVITE

19 It was an era when there was no king in Israel. A Levite, living as a stranger in the backwoods hill country of Ephraim, got himself a concubine, a woman from Bethlehem in Judah. But she quarreled with him and left, returning to her father's house in Bethlehem in Judah. She was there four months. Then her husband decided to go after her and try to win her back. He had a servant and a pair of donkeys with him. When he arrived at her father's house, the girl's father saw him, welcomed him, and made him feel at home. His father-in-law, the girl's father, pressed him to stay. He stayed with him three days; they feasted and drank and slept.

On the fourth day, they got up at the crack of dawn and got ready to go. But the girl's father said to his son-in-law, "Strengthen yourself with a hearty breakfast and then you can go." So they sat down and ate breakfast together.

The girl's father said to the man, "Come now, be my guest. Stay the night—make it a holiday." The man got up to go, but his father-in-law kept after him, so he ended up spending another night.

On the fifth day, he was again up early, ready to go. The girl's father said, "You need some breakfast." They went back and forth, and the day slipped on as they ate and drank together. But the man and his concubine were finally ready to go. Then his father-in-law, the girl's father, said, "Look, the day's almost gone—why not stay the night? There's very little daylight left; stay another night and enjoy yourself. Tomorrow you can get an early start and set off for your own place."

But this time the man wasn't willing to spend another night. He got things ready, left, and went as far as Jebus (Jerusalem) with his pair of saddled donkeys, his concubine, and his servant. At Jebus, though, the day was nearly gone. The servant said to his master, "It's late; let's go into this Jebusite city and spend the night."

But his master said, "We're not going into any city of foreigners. We'll go on to Gibeah." He directed his servant, "Keep going. Let's go on ahead. We'll spend the night either at Gibeah or Ramah."

So they kept going. As they pressed on, the sun finally left them in the vicinity of Gibeah, which belongs to Benjamin. They left the road there to spend the night at Gibeah.

The Levite went and sat down in the town square, but no one invited them in to spend the night. Then, late in the evening, an old man came in from his day's work in the fields. He was from the hill country of Ephraim and lived temporarily in Gibeah where all the local citizens were Benjaminites. When the old man looked up and saw the traveler in the town square, he said, "Where are you going? And where are you from?"

The Levite said, "We're just passing through. We're coming from Bethlehem on our way to a remote spot in the hills of Ephraim. I come from there. I've just made a trip to Bethlehem in Judah and I'm on my way back home, but no one has invited us in for the night. We wouldn't be any trouble: We have food and straw for the donkeys, and bread and wine for the woman, the young man, and me—we don't need anything."

The old man said, "It's going to be all right; I'll take care of you. You aren't going to spend the night in the town square." He took them home and fed the donkeys. They washed up and sat down to a good meal.

They were relaxed and enjoying themselves when the men of the city, a gang of local hell-raisers all, surrounded the house and started pounding on the door. They yelled for the owner of the house, the old man, "Bring out the man who came to your house. We want to have sex with him."

He went out and told them, "No, brothers! Don't be obscene— this man is my guest. Don't commit this outrage. Look, my virgin daughter and his concubine are here. I'll bring them out for you. Abuse them if you must, but don't do anything so senselessly vile to this man."

But the men wouldn't listen to him. Finally, the Levite pushed his concubine out the door to them. They raped her repeatedly all night long. Just before dawn they let her go. The woman came back and fell at the door of the house where her master was sleeping. When the sun rose, there she was.

It was morning. Her master got up and opened the door to continue his journey. There she was, his concubine, crumpled in a heap at the door, her hands on the threshold.

"Get up," he said. "Let's get going." There was no answer.

He lifted her onto his donkey and set out for home. When he got home he took a knife and dismembered his concubine—cut her into twelve pieces. He sent her, piece by piece, throughout the country of Israel. And he ordered the men he sent out, "Say to every man in Israel: 'Has such a thing as this ever happened from the time the Israelites came up from the land of Egypt until now? Think about it! Talk it over. Do something!'"

⁜

20 Then all the People of Israel came out. The congregation met in the presence of GOD at Mizpah. They were all there, from Dan to Beersheba, as one person! The leaders of all the people, representing all the tribes of Israel, took their places in the gathering of God's people. There were 400 divisions of sword-wielding infantry.

Meanwhile the Benjaminites got wind that the Israelites were meeting at Mizpah.

The People of Israel said, "Now tell us. How did this outrageous evil happen?"

The Levite, the husband of the murdered woman, spoke: "My concubine and I came to spend the night at Gibeah, a Benjaminite town. That night the men of Gibeah came after me. They surrounded the house, intending to kill me. They gang-raped my concubine and she died. So I took my concubine, cut up her body, and sent her piece by piece—twelve pieces!—to every part of Israel's inheritance. This vile and outrageous crime was committed *in Israel*! So, Israelites, make up your minds. Decide on some action!"

All the people were at once and as one person on their feet. "None of us will go home; not a single one of us will go to his own house. Here's our plan for dealing with Gibeah: We'll march against it by drawing lots. We'll take ten of every hundred men from all the tribes of Israel (a hundred of every thousand, and a thousand of every ten thousand) to carry food for the army. When the troops arrive at Gibeah they will settle accounts for this outrageous and vile evil that was done in Israel." So all the men in Israel were gathered against the city, totally united.

The Israelite tribes sent messengers throughout the tribe of

92

Benjamin saying, "What's the meaning of this outrage that took place among you? Surrender the men right here and now, these hell-raisers of Gibeah. We'll put them to death and burn the evil out of Israel."

But they wouldn't do it. The Benjaminites refused to listen to their brothers, the People of Israel. Instead they raised an army from all their cities and rallied at Gibeah to go to war against the People of Israel. In no time at all they had recruited from their cities twenty-six divisions of sword-wielding infantry. From Gibeah they got 700 hand-picked fighters, the best. There were another 700 super marksmen who were ambidextrous—they could sling a stone at a hair and not miss.

The men of Israel, excluding Benjamin, mobilized 400 divisions of sword-wielding fighting men.

✠

They set out and went to Bethel to inquire of God. The People of Israel said, "Who of us shall be first to go into battle with the Benjaminites?"

GOD said, "Judah goes first."

The People of Israel got up the next morning and camped before Gibeah. The army of Israel marched out against Benjamin and took up their positions, ready to attack Gibeah. But the Benjaminites poured out of Gibeah and devastated twenty-two Israelite divisions on the ground.

The Israelites went back to the sanctuary and wept before GOD until evening. They again inquired of GOD, "Shall we again go into battle against the Benjaminites, our brothers?"

GOD said, "Yes. Attack."

The army took heart. The men of Israel took up the positions they had deployed on the first day.

On the second day, the Israelites again advanced against Benjamin. This time as the Benjaminites came out of the city, on this second day, they devastated another eighteen Israelite divisions, all swordsmen.

All the People of Israel, the whole army, were back at Bethel, weeping, sitting there in the presence of GOD. That day they fasted until evening. They sacrificed Whole-Burnt-Offerings and Peace-Offerings before GOD.

And they again inquired of GOD. The Chest of God's Covenant was there at that time with Phinehas son of Eleazar, the son of Aaron, as the ministering priest. They asked, "Shall we again march into battle against the Benjaminites, our brothers? Or should we call it quits?"

And GOD said, "Attack. Tomorrow I'll give you victory."

This time Israel placed men in ambush all around Gibeah. On the third day when Israel set out, they took up the same positions before the Benjaminites as before. When the Benjaminites came out to meet the army, they moved out from the city. Benjaminites began to cut down some of the troops just as they had before. About thirty men fell in the field and on the roads to Bethel and Gibeah.

The Benjaminites started bragging, "We're dropping them like flies, just as before!"

But the Israelites strategized: "Now let's retreat and pull them out of the city onto the main roads." So every Israelite moved farther out to Baal Tamar; at the same time the Israelite ambush rushed from its place west of Gibeah.

Ten crack divisions from all over Israel now arrived at Gibeah— intense, bloody fighting! The Benjaminites had no idea that they were about to go down in defeat—GOD routed them before Israel. The Israelites decimated twenty-five divisions of Benjamin that day— 25,100 killed. They were all swordsmen. The Benjaminites saw that they were beaten.

The men of Israel acted like they were retreating before Benjamin, knowing that they could depend on the ambush they had prepared for Gibeah.

The ambush erupted and made quick work of Gibeah. The ambush spread out and massacred the city. The strategy for the main body of the ambush was that they send up a smoke signal from the city. Then the men of Israel would turn in battle. When that happened, Benjamin had killed about thirty Israelites and thought they were on their way to victory, yelling out, "They're on the run, just as in the first battle!" But then the signal went up from the city—a huge column of smoke. When the Benjaminites looked back, there it was, the whole city going up in smoke.

By the time the men of Israel had turned back on them, the men of Benjamin fell apart—they could see that they were trapped. Confronted by the Israelites, they tried to get away down the wilderness road, but by now the battle was everywhere. The men of Israel poured out of the towns, killing them right and left, hot on their trail, picking them off east of Gibeah.

✠

Eighteen divisions of Benjaminites were wiped out, all their best fighters.

Five divisions turned to escape to the wilderness, to Rimmon Rock, but the Israelites caught and slaughtered them on roads.

Keeping the pressure on, the Israelites brought down two more divisions.

The total of the Benjaminites killed that day came to twenty-five divisions of infantry, their best swordsmen.

Six hundred men got away. They made it to Rimmon Rock in the wilderness and held out there for four months.

The men of Israel came back and killed all the Benjaminites who were left, all the men and animals they found in every town, and then torched the towns, sending them up in flames.

WIVES

21 Back at Mizpah the men of Israel had taken an oath: "No man among us will give his daughter to a Benjaminite in marriage."

Now, back in Bethel, the people sat in the presence of God until evening. They cried loudly; there was widespread lamentation. They said, "Why, O GOD, God of Israel, has this happened? Why do we find ourselves today missing one whole tribe from Israel?"

Early the next morning, the people got busy and built an altar. They sacrificed Whole-Burnt-Offerings and Peace-Offerings.

Then the Israelites said, "Who from all the tribes of Israel didn't show up as we gathered in the presence of GOD?" For they had all taken a sacred oath that anyone who had not gathered in the presence of GOD at Mizpah had to be put to death.

✠

But the People of Israel were feeling sorry for Benjamin, their brothers. They said, "Today, one tribe is cut off from Israel. How can we get wives for those who are left? We have sworn by GOD not to give any of our daughters to them in marriage."

They said, "Which one of the tribes of Israel didn't gather before GOD at Mizpah?"

It turned out that no one had come to the gathering from Jabesh Gilead. When they took a roll call of the people, not a single person from Jabesh Gilead was there.

So the congregation sent twelve divisions of their top men there with the command, "Kill everyone of Jabesh Gilead, including women and children. These are your instructions: Every man and woman who has had sexual intercourse you must kill. But keep the virgins alive." And that's what they did.

And they found 400 virgins among those who lived in Jabesh Gilead; they had never had sexual intercourse with a man. And they brought them to the camp at Shiloh, which is in the land of Canaan.

Then the congregation sent word to the Benjaminites who were at the Rimmon Rock and offered them peace. And Benjamin came. They gave them the women they had let live at Jabesh Gilead. But even then, there weren't enough for all the men.

The people felt bad for Benjamin; GOD had left out Benjamin—the missing piece from the Israelite tribes.

✠

The elders of the congregation said, "How can we get wives for the rest of the men, since all the Benjaminite women have been killed? How can we keep the inheritance alive for the Benjaminite survivors? How can we prevent an entire tribe from extinction? We certainly can't give our own daughters to them as wives." (Remember, the Israelites had taken the oath: "Cursed is anyone who provides a wife to Benjamin.")

Then they said, "There is that festival of GOD held every year in Shiloh. It's north of Bethel, just east of the main road that goes up from Bethel to Shechem and a little south of Lebonah."

So they told the Benjaminites, "Go and hide in the vineyards. Stay alert—when you see the Shiloh girls come out to dance the dances, run out of the vineyards, grab one of the Shiloh girls for your wife, and then hightail it back to the country of Benjamin. When their fathers or brothers come to lay charges against us, we'll tell them, 'We did them a favor. After all we didn't go to war and kill to get wives for men. And it wasn't as if you were in on it by giving consent. But if you keep this up, you will incur blame.'"

And that's what the Benjaminites did: They carried off girls from the dance, wives enough for their number, got away, and went home to their inheritance. They rebuilt their towns and settled down.

From there the People of Israel dispersed, each man heading back to his own tribe and clan, each to his own plot of land.

At that time there was no king in Israel. People did whatever they felt like doing.

RUTH

A s we read the broad, comprehensive biblical story of God at work in the world, most of us are entirely impressed: God speaking creation into being, God laying the foundations of the life of faith through great and definitive fathers and mothers, God saving a people out of a brutal slave existence and then forming them into lives of free and obedient love, God raising up leaders who direct and guide through the tangle of difficulties always involved in living joyfully and responsively before God.

Very impressive. So impressive, in fact, that many of us, while remaining impressed, feel left out. Our unimpressive, very ordinary lives make us feel like outsiders to such a star-studded cast. We disqualify ourselves. Guilt or willfulness or accident makes a loophole and we assume that what is true for everyone else is not true for us. We conclude that we are, somehow, "just not religious" and thus unfit to participate in the big story.

And then we turn a page and come on this small story of two widows and a farmer in their out-of-the-way village.

The outsider Ruth was not born into the faith and felt no natural part of it—like many of us. But she came to find herself gathered into the story and given a quiet and obscure part that proved critical to the way everything turned out.

Scripture is a vast tapestry of God's creating, saving, and blessing ways in this world. The great names in the plot that climaxes at Sinai (Abraham, Isaac, Jacob, Joseph, Moses) and the great names in the sequel (Joshua, Samuel, David, Solomon) can be intimidating to ordinary, random individuals: "Surely there is no way that I can have any significant part on such a stage." But the story of the widowed, impoverished, alien Ruth is proof to the contrary. She is the inconsequential outsider whose life turns out to be essential for telling the complete story of God's ways among us. The unassuming ending carries the punch line: "Boaz married Ruth, she had a son Obed, Obed was the father of Jesse, and Jesse the father of David."

David! In its artful telling of this "outsider" widow, uprooted and obscure, who turns out to be the great-grandmother of David and the ancestor of Jesus, the Book of Ruth makes it possible for each of us to understand ourselves, however ordinary or "out of it," as irreplaceable in the full telling of God's story. We count—every last one of us—and what we do counts.

RUTH

1 Once upon a time—it was back in the days when judges led Israel—
there was a famine in the land. A man from Bethlehem in Judah left
home to live in the country of Moab, he and his wife and his two sons.
The man's name was Elimelech; his wife's name was Naomi; his sons
were named Mahlon and Kilion—all Ephrathites from Bethlehem in
Judah. They all went to the country of Moab and settled there.

Elimelech died and Naomi was left, she and her two sons. The sons
took Moabite wives; the name of the first was Orpah, the second Ruth.
They lived there in Moab for the next ten years. But then the two brothers, Mahlon and Kilion, died. Now the woman was left without either
her young men or her husband.

✣

One day she got herself together, she and her two daughters-in-law, to
leave the country of Moab and set out for home; she had heard that
GOD had been pleased to visit his people and give them food. And so
she started out from the place she had been living, she and her two
daughters-in-law with her, on the road back to the land of Judah.

After a short while on the road, Naomi told her two daughters-in-
law, "Go back. Go home and live with your mothers. And may GOD
treat you as graciously as you treated your deceased husbands and me.
May GOD give each of you a new home and a new husband!" She kissed
them and they cried openly.

They said, "No, we're going on with you to your people."

But Naomi was firm: "Go back, my dear daughters. Why would you
come with me? Do you suppose I still have sons in my womb who can
become your future husbands? Go back, dear daughters—on your way,
please! I'm too old to get a husband. Why, even if I said, 'There's still
hope!' and this very night got a man and had sons, can you imagine being
satisfied to wait until they were grown? Would you wait that long to get
married again? No, dear daughters; this is a bitter pill for me to swallow—
more bitter for me than for you. GOD has dealt me a hard blow."

Again they cried openly. Orpah kissed her mother-in-law good-bye;
but Ruth embraced her and held on.

Naomi said, "Look, your sister-in-law is going back home to live
with her own people and gods; go with her."

But Ruth said, "Don't force me to leave you; don't make me go home. Where you go, I go; and where you live, I'll live. Your people are my people, your God is my god; where you die, I'll die, and that's where I'll be buried, so help me God—not even death itself is going to come between us!"

When Naomi saw that Ruth had her heart set on going with her, she gave in. And so the two of them traveled on together to Bethlehem.

When they arrived in Bethlehem the whole town was soon buzzing: "Is this really our Naomi? And after all this time!"

But she said, "Don't call me Naomi; call me Bitter. The Strong One has dealt me a bitter blow. I left here full of life, and God has brought me back with nothing but the clothes on my back. Why would you call me Naomi? God certainly doesn't. The Strong One ruined me."

And so Naomi was back, and Ruth the foreigner with her, back from the country of Moab. They arrived in Bethlehem at the beginning of the barley harvest.

2 It so happened that Naomi had a relative by marriage, a man prominent and rich, connected with Elimelech's family. His name was Boaz.

One day Ruth, the Moabite foreigner, said to Naomi, "I'm going to work; I'm going out to glean among the sheaves, following after some harvester who will treat me kindly."

Naomi said, "Go ahead, dear daughter."

And so she set out. She went and started gleaning in a field, following in the wake of the harvesters. Eventually she ended up in the part of the field owned by Boaz, her father-in-law Elimelech's relative. A little later Boaz came out from Bethlehem, greeting his harvesters, "God be with you!" They replied, "And God bless you!"

Boaz asked his young servant who was foreman over the farm hands, "Who is this young woman? Where did she come from?"

The foreman said, "Why, that's the Moabite girl, the one who came with Naomi from the country of Moab. She asked permission. 'Let me glean,' she said, 'and gather among the sheaves following after your harvesters.' She's been at it steady ever since, from early morning until now, without so much as a break."

Then Boaz spoke to Ruth: "Listen, my daughter. From now on don't go to any other field to glean—stay right here in this one. And stay close to my young women. Watch where they are harvesting and follow them. And don't worry about a thing; I've given orders to my servants not to harass you. When you get thirsty, feel free to go and drink from the water buckets that the servants have filled."

She dropped to her knees, then bowed her face to the ground. "How does this happen that you should pick me out and treat me so kindly—*me*, a foreigner?"

Boaz answered her, "I've heard all about you—heard about the way you treated your mother-in-law after the death of her husband, and how you left your father and mother and the land of your birth and have come to live among a bunch of total strangers. GOD reward you well for what you've done—and with a generous bonus besides from GOD, to whom you've come seeking protection under his wings."

She said, "Oh sir, such grace, such kindness—I don't deserve it. You've touched my heart, treated me like one of your own. And I don't even belong here!"

At the lunch break, Boaz said to her, "Come over here; eat some bread. Dip it in the wine."

So she joined the harvesters. Boaz passed the roasted grain to her. She ate her fill and even had some left over.

When she got up to go back to work, Boaz ordered his servants: "Let her glean where there's still plenty of grain on the ground—make it easy for her. Better yet, pull some of the good stuff out and leave it for her to glean. Give her special treatment."

Ruth gleaned in the field until evening. When she threshed out what she had gathered, she ended up with nearly a full sack of barley! She gathered up her gleanings, went back to town, and showed her mother-in-law the results of her day's work; she also gave her the leftovers from her lunch.

Naomi asked her, "So where did you glean today? Whose field? GOD bless whoever it was who took such good care of you!"

Ruth told her mother-in-law, "The man with whom I worked today? His name is Boaz."

Naomi said to her daughter-in-law, "Why, GOD bless that man! GOD hasn't quite walked out on us after all! He still loves us, in bad times as well as good!"

Naomi went on, "That man, Ruth, is one of our circle of covenant redeemers, a close relative of ours!"

Ruth the Moabitess said, "Well, listen to this: He also told me, 'Stick with my workers until my harvesting is finished.'"

Naomi said to Ruth, "That's wonderful, dear daughter! Do that! You'll be safe in the company of his young women; no danger now of being raped in some stranger's field."

So Ruth did it—she stuck close to Boaz's young women, gleaning in the fields daily until both the barley and wheat harvesting were finished. And she continued living with her mother-in-law.

⁜

3 One day her mother-in-law Naomi said to Ruth, "My dear daughter, isn't it about time I arranged a good home for you so you can have a happy life? And isn't Boaz our close relative, the one with whose young women you've been working? Maybe it's time to make our move. Tonight is the night of Boaz's barley harvest at the threshing floor.

"Take a bath. Put on some perfume. Get all dressed up and go to the threshing floor. But don't let him know you're there until the party is well under way and he's had plenty of food and drink. When you see him slipping off to sleep, watch where he lies down and then go there. Lie at his feet to let him know that you are available to him for marriage. Then wait and see what he says. He'll tell you what to do."

Ruth said, "If you say so, I'll do it, just as you've told me."

She went down to the threshing floor and put her mother-in-law's plan into action.

Boaz had a good time, eating and drinking his fill—he felt great. Then he went off to get some sleep, lying down at the end of a stack of barley. Ruth quietly followed; she lay down to signal her availability for marriage.

In the middle of the night the man was suddenly startled and sat up. Surprise! This woman asleep at his feet!

He said, "And who are you?"

She said, "I am Ruth, your maiden; take me under your protecting wing. You're my close relative, you know, in the circle of covenant redeemers—you do have the right to marry me."

He said, "GOD bless you, my dear daughter! What a splendid expression of love! And when you could have had your pick of any of the young men around. And now, my dear daughter, don't you worry about a thing; I'll do all you could want or ask. Everybody in town knows what a courageous woman you are—a real prize! You're right, I am a close relative to you, but there is one even closer than I am. So stay the rest of the night. In the morning, if he wants to exercise his customary rights and responsibilities as the closest covenant redeemer, he'll have his chance; but if he isn't interested, as GOD lives, I'll do it. Now go back to sleep until morning."

Ruth slept at his feet until dawn, but she got up while it was still dark and wouldn't be recognized. Then Boaz said to himself, "No one must know that Ruth came to the threshing floor."

So Boaz said, "Bring the shawl you're wearing and spread it out."

She spread it out and he poured it full of barley, six measures, and put it on her shoulders. Then she went back to town.

When she came to her mother-in-law, Naomi asked, "And how did things go, my dear daughter?"

Ruth told her everything that the man had done for her, adding, "And he gave me all this barley besides—six quarts! He told me, 'You can't go back empty-handed to your mother-in-law!'"

Naomi said, "Sit back and relax, my dear daughter, until we find out how things turn out; that man isn't going to fool around. Mark my words, he's going to get everything wrapped up today."

✝

4 Boaz went straight to the public square and took his place there. Before long the "closer relative," the one mentioned earlier by Boaz, strolled by.

"Step aside, old friend," said Boaz. "Take a seat." The man sat down.

Boaz then gathered ten of the town elders together and said, "Sit down here with us; we've got some business to take care of." And they sat down.

Boaz then said to his relative, "The piece of property that belonged to our relative Elimelech is being sold by his widow Naomi, who has just returned from the country of Moab. I thought you ought to know about it. Buy it back if you want it—you can make it official in the presence of those sitting here and before the town elders. You have first redeemer rights. If you don't want it, tell me so I'll know where I stand. You're first in line to do this and I'm next after you."

He said, "I'll buy it."

Then Boaz added, "You realize, don't you, that when you buy the field from Naomi, you also get Ruth the Moabite, the widow of our dead relative, along with the redeemer responsibility to have children with her to carry on the family inheritance."

Then the relative said, "Oh, I can't do that—I'd jeopardize my own family's inheritance. You go ahead and buy it—you can have my rights—I can't do it."

✝

In the olden times in Israel, this is how they handled official business regarding matters of property and inheritance: a man would take off his shoe and give it to the other person. This was the same as an official seal or personal signature in Israel.

So when Boaz's "redeemer" relative said, "Go ahead and buy it," he signed the deal by pulling off his shoe.

Boaz then addressed the elders and all the people in the town square that day: "You are witnesses today that I have bought from Naomi everything that belonged to Elimelech and Kilion and Mahlon, including responsibility for Ruth the foreigner, the widow of Mahlon—I'll take her as my wife and keep the name of the deceased alive along with his inheritance. The memory and reputation of the deceased is not going to disappear out of this family or from his hometown. To all this you are witnesses this very day."

All the people in the town square that day, backing up the elders, said, "Yes, we are witnesses. May GOD make this woman who is coming into your household like Rachel and Leah, the two women who built the family of Israel. May GOD make you a pillar in Ephrathah and famous in Bethlehem! With the children GOD gives you from this young woman, may your family rival the family of Perez, the son Tamar bore to Judah."

✝

Boaz married Ruth. She became his wife. Boaz slept with her. By GOD's gracious gift she conceived and had a son.

The town women said to Naomi, "Blessed be GOD! He didn't leave you without family to carry on your life. May this baby grow up to be famous in Israel! He'll make you young again! He'll take care of you in old age. And this daughter-in-law who has brought him into the world and loves you so much, why, she's worth more to you than seven sons!"

Naomi took the baby and held him in her arms, cuddling him, cooing over him, waiting on him hand and foot.

The neighborhood women started calling him "Naomi's baby boy!" But his real name was Obed. Obed was the father of Jesse, and Jesse the father of David.

✠

This is the family tree of Perez:
    Perez had Hezron,
    Hezron had Ram,
    Ram had Amminadab,
    Amminadab had Nahshon,
    Nahshon had Salmon,
    Salmon had Boaz,
    Boaz had Obed,
    Obed had Jesse,
    and Jesse had David.

1-2 SAMUEL

F our lives dominate the two-volume narrative, First and Second Samuel: Hannah, Samuel, Saul, and David. Chronologically, the stories are clustered around the year 1000 B.C., the millennial midpoint between the call of Abraham, the father of Israel, nearly a thousand years earlier (about 1800 B.C.) and the birth of Jesus, the Christ, a thousand years later.

These four lives become seminal for us at the moment we realize that our ego-bound experience is too small a context in which to understand and experience what it means to believe in God and follow his ways. For these are large lives—large because they live in the largeness of God. Not one of them can be accounted for in terms of cultural conditions or psychological dynamics; God is the country in which they live.

Most of us need to be reminded that these stories are not exemplary in the sense that we stand back and admire them, like statues in a gallery, knowing all the while that we will never be able to live either that gloriously or tragically ourselves. Rather they are immersions into the actual business of living itself: this is what it means to be human. Reading and praying our way through these pages, we get it; gradually but most emphatically we recognize that what it means to be a woman, a man, mostly has to do with God. These four stories do not show us how we should live but how in fact we do live, authenticating the reality of our daily experience as the stuff that God uses to work out his purposes of salvation in us and in the world.

The stories do not do this by talking about God, for there is surprisingly little explicit God talk here—whole pages sometimes without the name of God appearing. But as the narrative develops we realize that God is the commanding and accompanying presence that provides both plot and texture to every sentence. This cluster of interlocking stories trains us in perceptions of ourselves, our sheer and irreducible humanity, that cannot be reduced to personal feelings or ideas or circumstances. If we want a life other than mere biology, we must deal with God. There is no alternate way.

One of many welcome consequences in learning to "read" our lives in the lives of Hannah, Samuel, Saul, and David is a sense of affirmation and freedom: we don't have to fit into prefabricated moral or mental or religious boxes before we are admitted into the company of God—we are taken seriously just as we are and given a place in his story, for it is, after all, his story; none of us is the leading character in the story of our life.

For the biblical way is not so much to present us with a moral code and tell us "Live up to this"; nor is it to set out a system of doctrine and say,

"Think like this and you will live well." The biblical way is to tell a story and invite us, "Live into this. This is what it looks like to be human; this is what is involved in entering and maturing as human beings." We do violence to the biblical revelation when we "use" it for what we can get out of it or what we think will provide color and spice to our otherwise bland lives. That results in a kind of "boutique spirituality" — God as decoration, God as enhancement. The Samuel narrative will not allow that. In the reading, as we submit our lives to what we read, we find that we are not being led to see God in our stories but to see our stories in God's. God is the larger context and plot in which our stories find themselves.

Such reading will necessarily be a prayerful reading — a God-listening, God-answering reading. The story, after all, is framed by prayer: Hannah's prayer at the beginning (1 Samuel 2), and David's near the end (2 Samuel 22–23).

1 SAMUEL

HANNAH POURS OUT HER HEART TO GOD

1 There once was a man who lived in Ramathaim. He was descended from the old Zuph family in the Ephraim hills. His name was Elkanah. (He was connected with the Zuphs from Ephraim through his father Jeroham, his grandfather Elihu, and his great-grandfather Tohu.) He had two wives. The first was Hannah; the second was Peninnah. Peninnah had children; Hannah did not.

Every year this man went from his hometown up to Shiloh to worship and offer a sacrifice to GOD-of-the-Angel-Armies. Eli and his two sons, Hophni and Phinehas, served as the priests of GOD there. When Elkanah sacrificed, he passed helpings from the sacrificial meal around to his wife Peninnah and all her children, but he always gave an especially generous helping to Hannah because he loved her so much, and because GOD had not given her children. But her rival wife taunted her cruelly, rubbing it in and never letting her forget that GOD had not given her children. This went on year after year. Every time she went to the sanctuary of GOD she could expect to be taunted. Hannah was reduced to tears and had no appetite.

Her husband Elkanah said, "Oh, Hannah, why are you crying? Why aren't you eating? And why are you so upset? Am I not of more worth to you than ten sons?"

So Hannah ate. Then she pulled herself together, slipped away quietly, and entered the sanctuary. The priest Eli was on duty at the entrance to GOD's Temple in the customary seat. Crushed in soul, Hannah prayed to GOD and cried and cried—inconsolably. Then she made a vow:

Oh, GOD-of-the-Angel-Armies,
If you'll take a good, hard look at my pain,
If you'll quit neglecting me and go into action for me
By giving me a son,
I'll give him completely, unreservedly to you.
I'll set him apart for a life of holy discipline.

It so happened that as she continued in prayer before GOD, Eli was watching her closely. Hannah was praying in her heart, silently. Her lips moved, but no sound was heard. Eli jumped to the conclusion that she was drunk. He approached her and said, "You're drunk! How long do you plan to keep this up? Sober up, woman!"

Hannah said, "Oh no, sir—please! I'm a woman hard used. I haven't been drinking. Not a drop of wine or beer. The only thing I've been pouring out is my heart, pouring it out to GOD. Don't for a minute think I'm a bad woman. It's because I'm so desperately unhappy and in such pain that I've stayed here so long."

Eli answered her, "Go in peace. And may the God of Israel give you what you have asked of him."

"Think well of me—and pray for me!" she said, and went her way. Then she ate heartily, her face radiant.

Up before dawn, they worshiped GOD and returned home to Ramah. Elkanah slept with Hannah his wife, and GOD began making the necessary arrangements in response to what she had asked.

DEDICATING THE CHILD TO GOD

Before the year was out, Hannah had conceived and given birth to a son. She named him Samuel, explaining, "I asked GOD for him."

When Elkanah next took his family on their annual trip to Shiloh to worship GOD, offering sacrifices and keeping his vow, Hannah didn't go. She told her husband, "After the child is weaned, I'll bring him myself and present him before GOD—and that's where he'll stay, for good."

Elkanah said to his wife, "Do what you think is best. Stay home until you have weaned him. Yes! Let GOD complete what he has begun!"

So she did. She stayed home and nursed her son until she had weaned him. Then she took him up to Shiloh, bringing also the makings of a generous sacrificial meal—a prize bull, flour, and wine. The child was so young to be sent off!

They first butchered the bull, then brought the child to Eli. Hannah said, "Excuse me, sir. Would you believe that I'm the very woman who was standing before you at this very spot, praying to GOD? I prayed for this child, and GOD gave me what I asked for. And now I have dedicated him to GOD. He's dedicated to GOD for life."

Then and there, they worshiped GOD. Hannah prayed:

2 I'm bursting with God-news!
  I'm walking on air.

I'm laughing at my rivals.
   I'm dancing my salvation.

Nothing and no one is holy like GOD,
   no rock mountain like our God.
Don't dare talk pretentiously—
   not a word of boasting, ever!
For GOD knows what's going on.
   He takes the measure of everything that happens.
The weapons of the strong are smashed to pieces,
   while the weak are infused with fresh strength.
The well-fed are out begging in the streets for crusts,
   while the hungry are getting second helpings.
The barren woman has a houseful of children,
   while the mother of many is bereft.

GOD brings death and GOD brings life,
   brings down to the grave and raises up.
GOD brings poverty and GOD brings wealth;
   he lowers, he also lifts up.
He puts poor people on their feet again;
   he rekindles burned-out lives with fresh hope,
Restoring dignity and respect to their lives—
   a place in the sun!
For the very structures of earth are GOD's;
   he has laid out his operations on a firm foundation.
He protectively cares for his faithful friends, step by step,
   but leaves the wicked to stumble in the dark.
   No one makes it in this life by sheer muscle!
GOD's enemies will be blasted out of the sky,
   crashed in a heap and burned.
GOD will set things right all over the earth,
   he'll give strength to his king,
   he'll set his anointed on top of the world!

Elkanah went home to Ramah. The boy stayed and served GOD in
the company of Eli the priest.

SAMUEL SERVES GOD

Eli's own sons were a bad lot. They didn't know GOD and could not have cared less about the customs of priests among the people. Ordinarily, when someone offered a sacrifice, the priest's servant was supposed to come up and, while the meat was boiling, stab a three-pronged fork into the cooking pot. The priest then got whatever came up on the fork. But this is how Eli's sons treated all the Israelites who came to Shiloh to offer sacrifices to GOD. Before they had even burned the fat to GOD, the priest's servant would interrupt whoever was sacrificing and say, "Hand over some of that meat for the priest to roast. He doesn't like boiled meat; he likes his rare." If the man objected, "First let the fat be burned—God's portion!—then take all you want," the servant would demand, "No, I want it now. If you won't give it, I'll take it." It was a horrible sin these young servants were committing—and right in the presence of GOD!—desecrating the holy offerings to GOD.

In the midst of all this, Samuel, a boy dressed in a priestly linen tunic, served GOD. Additionally, every year his mother would make him a little robe cut to his size and bring it to him when she and her husband came for the annual sacrifice. Eli would bless Elkanah and his wife, saying, "GOD give you children to replace this child you have dedicated to GOD." Then they would go home.

GOD was most especially kind to Hannah. She had three more sons and two daughters! The boy Samuel stayed at the sanctuary and grew up with GOD.

A HARD LIFE WITH MANY TEARS

By this time Eli was very old. He kept getting reports on how his sons were ripping off the people and sleeping with the women who helped out at the sanctuary. Eli took them to task: "What's going on here? Why are you doing these things? I hear story after story of your corrupt and evil carrying on. Oh, my sons, this is not right! These are terrible reports I'm getting, stories spreading right and left among GOD's people! If you sin against another person, there's help—God's help. But if you sin against GOD, who is around to help?"

But they were far gone in disobedience and refused to listen to a thing their father said. So GOD, who was fed up with them, decreed their death. But the boy Samuel was very much alive, growing up, blessed by GOD and popular with the people.

A holy man came to Eli and said: "This is GOD's message: I revealed myself openly to your ancestors when they were Pharaoh's slaves in Egypt. Out of all the tribes of Israel, I chose your family to be my priests: to preside at the altar, to burn incense, to wear the priestly robes in my presence. I put your ancestral family in charge of all the sacrificial offerings of Israel. So why do you now treat as mere loot these very sacrificial offerings that I commanded for my worship? Why do you treat your sons better than me, turning them loose to get fat on these offerings, and ignoring me? Therefore—this is GOD's word, the God of Israel speaking—I once said that you and your ancestral family would be my priests indefinitely, but now—GOD's word, remember!—there is no way this can continue.

I honor those who honor me;
those who scorn me I demean.

"Be well warned: It won't be long before I wipe out both your family and your future family. No one in your family will make it to old age! You'll see good things that I'm doing in Israel, but you'll see it and weep, for no one in your family will live to enjoy it. I will leave one person to serve at my altar, but it will be a hard life, with many tears. Everyone else in your family will die before their time. What happens to your two sons, Hophni and Phinehas, will be the proof: Both will die the same day. Then I'll establish for myself a true priest. He'll do what I want him to do, be what I want him to be. I'll make his position secure and he'll do his work freely in the service of my anointed one. Survivors from your family will come to him begging for handouts, saying, 'Please, give me some priest work, just enough to put some food on the table.'"

"SPEAK, GOD. I'M READY TO LISTEN"

3 The boy Samuel was serving GOD under Eli's direction. This was at a time when the revelation of GOD was rarely heard or seen. One night Eli was sound asleep (his eyesight was very bad—he could hardly see). It was well before dawn; the sanctuary lamp was still burning. Samuel was still in bed in the Temple of GOD, where the Chest of God rested.

Then GOD called out, "Samuel, Samuel!"

Samuel answered, "Yes? I'm here." Then he ran to Eli saying, "I heard you call. Here I am."

Eli said, "I didn't call you. Go back to bed." And so he did.

GOD called again, "Samuel, Samuel!"

Samuel got up and went to Eli, "I heard you call. Here I am."

Again Eli said, "Son, I didn't call you. Go back to bed." (This all happened before Samuel knew GOD for himself. It was before the revelation of GOD had been given to him personally.)

GOD called again, "Samuel!"—the third time! Yet again Samuel got up and went to Eli, "Yes? I heard you call me. Here I am."

That's when it dawned on Eli that GOD was calling the boy. So Eli directed Samuel, "Go back and lie down. If the voice calls again, say, 'Speak, GOD. I'm your servant, ready to listen.'" Samuel returned to his bed.

Then GOD came and stood before him exactly as before, calling out, "Samuel! Samuel!"

Samuel answered, "Speak. I'm your servant, ready to listen."

GOD said to Samuel, "Listen carefully. I'm getting ready to do something in Israel that is going to shake everyone up and get their attention. The time has come for me to bring down on Eli's family everything I warned him of, every last word of it. I'm letting him know that the time's up. I'm bringing judgment on his family for good. He knew what was going on, that his sons were desecrating God's name and God's place, and he did nothing to stop them. This is my sentence on the family of Eli: The evil of Eli's family can never be wiped out by sacrifice or offering."

Samuel stayed in bed until morning, then rose early and went about his duties, opening the doors of the sanctuary, but he dreaded having to tell the vision to Eli.

But then Eli summoned Samuel: "Samuel, my son!"

Samuel came running: "Yes? What can I do for you?"

"What did he say? Tell it to me, all of it. Don't suppress or soften one word, as God is your judge! I want it all, word for word as he said it to you."

So Samuel told him, word for word. He held back nothing.

Eli said, "He is GOD. Let him do whatever he thinks best."

Samuel grew up. GOD was with him, and Samuel's prophetic record was flawless. Everyone in Israel, from Dan in the north to Beersheba in the south, recognized that Samuel was the real thing—a true prophet of GOD. GOD continued to show up at Shiloh, revealed through his word to Samuel at Shiloh.

THE CHEST OF GOD IS TAKEN

4 Whatever Samuel said was broadcast all through Israel. Israel went to war against the Philistines. Israel set up camp at Ebenezer, the Philistines at Aphek. The Philistines marched out to meet Israel, the fighting spread, and Israel was badly beaten—about 4,000 soldiers left dead on the field. When the troops returned to camp, Israel's elders said, "Why has GOD given us such a beating today by the Philistines? Let's go to Shiloh and get the Chest of GOD's Covenant. It will accompany us and save us from the grip of our enemies."

So the army sent orders to Shiloh. They brought the Chest of the Covenant of GOD, the GOD-of-the-Angel-Armies, the Cherubim-Enthroned-GOD. Eli's two sons, Hophni and Phinehas, accompanied the Chest of the Covenant of God.

When the Chest of the Covenant of GOD was brought into camp, everyone gave a huge cheer. The shouts were like thunderclaps shaking the very ground. The Philistines heard the shouting and wondered what on earth was going on: "What's all this shouting among the Hebrews?"

Then they learned that the Chest of GOD had entered the Hebrew camp. The Philistines panicked: "Their gods have come to their camp! Nothing like this has ever happened before. We're done for! Who can save us from the clutches of these supergods? These are the same gods who hit the Egyptians with all kinds of plagues out in the wilderness. On your feet, Philistines! Courage! We're about to become slaves to the Hebrews, just as they have been slaves to us. Show what you're made of! Fight for your lives!"

And did they ever fight! It turned into a rout. They thrashed Israel so mercilessly that the Israelite soldiers ran for their lives, leaving behind an incredible 30,000 dead. As if that wasn't bad enough, the Chest of God was taken and the two sons of Eli—Hophni and Phinehas—were killed.

GLORY IS EXILED FROM ISRAEL

Immediately, a Benjaminite raced from the front lines back to Shiloh. Shirt torn and face smeared with dirt, he entered the town. Eli was sitting on his stool beside the road keeping vigil, for he was extremely worried about the Chest of God. When the man ran straight into town to tell the bad news, everyone wept. They were appalled. Eli heard the loud wailing and asked, "Why this uproar?" The messenger hurried over and reported. Eli was ninety-eight years old then, and blind. The man said to Eli, "I've just come from the front, barely escaping with my life."

"And so, my son," said Eli, "what happened?"

The messenger answered, "Israel scattered before the Philistines. The defeat was catastrophic, with enormous losses. Your sons Hophni and Phinehas died, and the Chest of God was taken."

At the words, "Chest of God," Eli fell backwards off his stool where he sat next to the gate. Eli was an old man, and very fat. When he fell, he broke his neck and died. He had led Israel forty years.

His daughter-in-law, the wife of Phinehas, was pregnant and ready to deliver. When she heard that the Chest of God had been taken and that both her father-in-law and her husband were dead, she went to her knees to give birth, going into hard labor. As she was about to die, her midwife said, "Don't be afraid. You've given birth to a son!" But she gave no sign that she had heard.

The Chest of God gone, father-in-law dead, husband dead, she named the boy Ichabod (Glory's-Gone), saying, "Glory is exiled from Israel since the Chest of God was taken."

THREATENED WITH MASS DEATH

5 Once the Philistines had seized the Chest of God, they took it from Ebenezer to Ashdod, brought it into the shrine of Dagon, and placed it alongside the idol of Dagon.

Next morning when the citizens of Ashdod got up, they were shocked to find Dagon toppled from his place, flat on his face before the Chest of GOD. They picked him up and put him back where he belonged. First thing the next morning they found him again, toppled and flat on his face before the Chest of GOD. Dagon's head and arms were broken off, strewn across the entrance. Only his torso was in one piece. (That's why even today, the priests of Dagon and visitors to the Dagon shrine in Ashdod avoid stepping on the threshold.)

GOD was hard on the citizens of Ashdod. He devastated them by hitting them with tumors. This happened in both the town and the surrounding neighborhoods. He let loose rats among them. Jumping from ships there, rats swarmed all over the city! And everyone was deathly afraid.

When the leaders of Ashdod saw what was going on, they decided, "The chest of the god of Israel has got to go. We can't handle this, and neither can our god Dagon." They called together all the Philistine leaders and put it to them: "How can we get rid of the chest of the god of Israel?"

The leaders agreed: "Move it to Gath." So they moved the Chest of the God of Israel to Gath.

But as soon as they moved it there, GOD came down hard on that city, too. It was mass hysteria! He hit them with tumors. Tumors broke out on everyone in town, young and old.

So they sent the Chest of God on to Ekron, but as the Chest was being brought into town, the people shouted in protest, "You'll kill us all by bringing in this Chest of the God of Israel!" They called the Philistine leaders together and demanded, "Get it out of here, this Chest of the God of Israel. Send it back where it came from. We're threatened with mass death!" For everyone was scared to death when the Chest of God showed up. God was already coming down very hard on the place. Those who didn't die were hit with tumors. All over the city cries of pain and lament filled the air.

GOLD TUMORS AND RATS

6 After the Chest of GOD had been among the Philistine people for seven months, the Philistine leaders called together their religious professionals, the priests, and experts on the supernatural for consultation: "How can we get rid of this Chest of GOD, get it off our hands without making things worse? Tell us!"

They said, "If you're going to send the Chest of the God of Israel back, don't just dump it on them. Pay compensation. Then you will be healed. After you're in the clear again, God will let up on you. Why wouldn't he?"

"And what exactly would make for adequate compensation?"

"Five gold tumors and five gold rats," they said, "to match the number of Philistine leaders. Since all of you—leaders and people—suffered the same plague, make replicas of the tumors and rats that are devastating the country and present them as an offering to the glory of the God of Israel. Then maybe he'll ease up and not be so hard on you and your gods, and on your country. Why be stubborn like the Egyptians and Pharaoh? God didn't quit pounding on them until they let the people go. Only then did he let up.

"So here's what you do: Take a brand-new oxcart and two cows that have never been in harness. Hitch the cows to the oxcart and send their calves back to the barn. Put the Chest of GOD on the cart. Secure the gold replicas of the tumors and rats that you are offering as compensation in a sack and set them next to the Chest. Then send it off. But keep your eyes on it. If it heads straight back home to where it came from, toward Beth Shemesh, it is clear that this catastrophe is a divine judgment, but if not, we'll know that God had nothing to do with it — it was just an accident."

So that's what they did: They hitched two cows to the cart, put their calves in the barn, and placed the Chest of GOD and the sack of gold rats and tumors on the cart. The cows headed straight for home, down the road to Beth Shemesh, straying neither right nor left, mooing all the way. The Philistine leaders followed them to the outskirts of Beth Shemesh.

The people of Beth Shemesh were harvesting wheat in the valley. They looked up and saw the Chest. Jubilant, they ran to meet it. The cart came into the field of Joshua, a Beth Shemeshite, and stopped there beside a huge boulder. The harvesters tore the cart to pieces, then chopped up the wood and sacrificed the cows as a burnt offering to GOD. The Levites took charge of the Chest of GOD and the sack containing the gold offerings, placing them on the boulder. Offering the sacrifices, everyone in Beth Shemesh worshiped GOD most heartily that day.

When the five Philistine leaders saw what they came to see, they returned the same day to Ekron.

The five gold replicas of the tumors were offered by the Philistines in compensation for the cities of Ashdod, Gaza, Ashkelon, Gath, and Ekron. The five gold rats matched the number of Philistine towns, both large and small, ruled by the five leaders. The big boulder on which they placed the Chest of GOD is still there in the field of Joshua of Beth Shemesh, a landmark.

IF YOU ARE SERIOUS ABOUT COMING BACK TO GOD

God struck some of the men of Beth Shemesh who, out of curiosity, irreverently peeked into the Chest of GOD. Seventy died. The whole town was in mourning, reeling under the hard blow from GOD, and questioning, "Who can stand before GOD, this holy God? And who can we get to take this Chest off our hands?"

They sent emissaries to Kiriath Jearim, saying, "The Philistines have returned the Chest of GOD. Come down and get it."

7 And they did. The men of Kiriath Jearim came and got the Chest of GOD and delivered it to the house of Abinadab on the hill. They ordained his son, Eleazar, to take responsibility for the Chest of GOD.

From the time that the Chest came to rest in Kiriath Jearim, a long time passed—twenty years it was—and throughout Israel there was a widespread, fearful movement toward GOD.

Then Samuel addressed the house of Israel: "If you are truly serious about coming back to GOD, clean house. Get rid of the foreign gods and fertility goddesses, ground yourselves firmly in GOD, worship him and him alone, and he'll save you from Philistine oppression."

They did it. They got rid of the gods and goddesses, the images of Baal and Ashtoreth, and gave their exclusive attention and service to GOD.

Next Samuel said, "Get everybody together at Mizpah and I'll pray for you."

So everyone assembled at Mizpah. They drew water from the wells and poured it out before GOD in a ritual of cleansing. They fasted all day and prayed, "We have sinned against GOD."

So Samuel prepared the Israelites for holy war there at Mizpah.

THE PLACE WHERE GOD HELPED US

When the Philistines heard that Israel was meeting at Mizpah, the Philistine leaders went on the offensive. Israel got the report and became frightened—Philistines on the move again!

They pleaded with Samuel, "Pray with all your might! And don't let up! Pray to GOD, our God, that he'll save us from the boot of the Philistines."

Samuel took a young lamb not yet weaned and offered it whole as a Whole-Burnt-Offering to GOD. He prayed fervently to GOD, interceding for Israel. And GOD answered.

While Samuel was offering the sacrifice, the Philistines came within range to fight Israel. Just then GOD thundered, a huge thunderclap exploding among the Philistines. They panicked—mass confusion!—and ran helter-skelter from Israel. Israel poured out of Mizpah and gave chase, killing Philistines right and left, to a point just beyond Beth Car. Samuel took a single rock and set it upright between Mizpah and Shen.

He named it "Ebenezer" (Rock of Help), saying, "This marks the place where GOD helped us."

The Philistines learned their lesson and stayed home—no more border crossings. GOD was hard on the Philistines all through Samuel's lifetime. All the cities from Ekron to Gath that the Philistines had taken from Israel were restored. Israel also freed the surrounding countryside from Philistine control. And there was peace between Israel and the Amorites.

Samuel gave solid leadership to Israel his entire life. Every year he went on a circuit from Bethel to Gilgal to Mizpah. He gave leadership to Israel in each of these places. But always he would return to Ramah, where he lived, and preside from there. That is where he built an altar to GOD.

REJECTING GOD AS THE KING

8 When Samuel got to be an old man, he set his sons up as judges in Israel. His firstborn son was named Joel, the name of his second, Abijah. They were assigned duty in Beersheba. But his sons didn't take after him; they were out for what they could get for themselves, taking bribes, corrupting justice.

Fed up, all the elders of Israel got together and confronted Samuel at Ramah. They presented their case: "Look, you're an old man, and your sons aren't following in your footsteps. Here's what we want you to do: Appoint a king to rule us, just like everybody else."

When Samuel heard their demand—"Give us a king to rule us!"—he was crushed. How awful! Samuel prayed to GOD.

GOD answered Samuel, "Go ahead and do what they're asking. They are not rejecting you. They've rejected me as their King. From the day I brought them out of Egypt until this very day they've been behaving like this, leaving me for other gods. And now they're doing it to you. So let them have their own way. But warn them of what they're in for. Tell them the way kings operate, just what they're likely to get from a king."

So Samuel told them, delivered GOD's warning to the people who were asking him to give them a king. He said, "This is the way the kind of king you're talking about operates. He'll take your sons and make soldiers of them—chariotry, cavalry, infantry, regimented in battalions and squadrons. He'll put some to forced labor on his farms, plowing and harvesting, and others to making either weapons of war or chariots in which he can ride in luxury. He'll put your daughters to work as beauticians and waitresses and cooks. He'll conscript your best fields, vineyards, and orchards and hand them over to his special friends. He'll tax your harvests and vintage to support his extensive bureaucracy. Your prize workers and best animals he'll take for his own use. He'll lay a tax on your flocks and you'll end up no better than slaves. The day will come when you will cry in desperation because of this king you so much want for yourselves. But don't expect GOD to answer."

But the people wouldn't listen to Samuel. "No!" they said. "We will have a king to rule us! Then we'll be just like all the other nations. Our king will rule us and lead us and fight our battles."

Samuel took in what they said and rehearsed it with GOD. GOD told Samuel, "Do what they say. Make them a king."

Then Samuel dismissed the men of Israel: "Go home, each of you to your own city."

SAUL — HEAD AND SHOULDERS ABOVE THE CROWD

9 There was a man from the tribe of Benjamin named Kish. He was the son of Abiel, grandson of Zeror, great-grandson of Becorath, great-great-grandson of Aphiah — a Benjaminite of stalwart character. He had a son, Saul, a most handsome young man. There was none finer — he literally stood head and shoulders above the crowd!

Some of Kish's donkeys got lost. Kish said to his son, "Saul, take one of the servants with you and go look for the donkeys." Saul took one of the servants and went to find the donkeys. They went into the hill country of Ephraim around Shalisha, but didn't find them. Then they went over to Shaalim — no luck. Then to Jabin, and still nothing.

When they got to Zuph, Saul said to the young man with him, "Enough of this. Let's go back. Soon my father is going to forget about the donkeys and start worrying about us."

He replied, "Not so fast. There's a holy man in this town. He carries a lot of weight around here. What he says is always right on the mark. Maybe he can tell us where to go."

Saul said, "If we go, what do we have to give him? There's no more bread in our sacks. We've nothing to bring as a gift to the holy man. Do we have anything else?"

The servant spoke up, "Look, I just happen to have this silver coin! I'll give it to the holy man and he'll tell us how to proceed!" (In former times in Israel, a person who wanted to seek God's word on a matter would say, "Let's visit the Seer," because the one we now call "the Prophet" used to be called "the Seer.")

"Good," said Saul, "let's go." And they set off for the town where the holy man lived.

As they were climbing up the hill into the town, they met some girls who were coming out to draw water. They said to them, "Is this where the Seer lives?"

They answered, "It sure is—just ahead. Hurry up. He's come today because the people have prepared a sacrifice at the shrine. As soon as you enter the town, you can catch him before he goes up to the shrine to eat. The people won't eat until he arrives, for he has to bless the sacrifice. Only then can everyone eat. So get going. You're sure to find him!"

They continued their climb and entered the city. And then there he was—Samuel!—coming straight toward them on his way to the shrine!

The very day before, GOD had confided in Samuel, "This time tomorrow, I'm sending a man from the land of Benjamin to meet you. You're to anoint him as prince over my people Israel. He will free my people from Philistine oppression. Yes, I know all about their hard circumstances. I've heard their cries for help."

The moment Samuel laid eyes on Saul, GOD said, "He's the one, the man I told you about. This is the one who will keep my people in check."

Saul came up to Samuel in the street and said, "Pardon me, but can you tell me where the Seer lives?"

"I'm the Seer," said Samuel. "Accompany me to the shrine and eat with me. In the morning I'll tell you all about what's on your mind, and send you on your way. And by the way, your lost donkeys—the ones you've been hunting for the last three days—have been found, so don't worry about them. At this moment, Israel's future is in your hands."

Saul answered, "But I'm only a Benjaminite, from the smallest of Israel's tribes, and from the most insignificant clan in the tribe at that. Why are you talking to me like this?"

Samuel took Saul and his servant and led them into the dining hall at the shrine and seated them at the head of the table. There were about thirty guests. Then Samuel directed the chef, "Bring the choice cut I pointed out to you, the one I told you to reserve."

The chef brought it and placed it before Saul with a flourish, saying, "This meal was kept aside just for you. Eat! It was especially prepared for this time and occasion with these guests."

Saul ate with Samuel—a memorable day!

Afterward they went down from the shrine into the city. A bed was prepared for Saul on the breeze-cooled roof of Samuel's house.

They woke at the break of day. Samuel called to Saul on the roof, "Get up and I'll send you off." Saul got up and the two of them went out in the street.

As they approached the outskirts of town, Samuel said to Saul, "Tell your servant to go on ahead of us. You stay with me for a bit. I have a word of God to give you."

"You'll Be a New Person"

10 Then Samuel took a flask of oil, poured it on Saul's head, and kissed him. He said, "Do you see what this means? God has anointed you prince over his people.

"This sign will confirm God's anointing of you as prince over his inheritance: After you leave me today, as you get closer to your home country of Benjamin, you'll meet two men near Rachel's Tomb. They'll say, 'The donkeys you went to look for are found. Your father has forgotten about the donkeys and is worried about you, wringing his hands—quite beside himself!'

"Leaving there, you'll arrive at the Oak of Tabor. There you'll meet three men going up to worship God at Bethel. One will be carrying three young goats, another carrying three sacks of bread, and the third a jug of wine. They'll say, 'Hello, how are you?' and offer you two loaves of bread, which you will accept.

"Next, you'll come to Gibeah of God, where there's a Philistine garrison. As you approach the town, you'll run into a bunch of prophets coming down from the shrine, playing harps and tambourines, flutes and drums. And they'll be prophesying. Before you know it, the Spirit of God will come on you and you'll be prophesying right along with them. And you'll be transformed. You'll be a new person!

"When these confirming signs are accomplished, you'll know that you're ready: Whatever job you're given to do, do it. God is with you!

"Now, go down to Gilgal and I will follow. I'll come down and join you in worship by sacrificing burnt offerings and peace offerings. Wait seven days. Then I'll come and tell you what to do next."

Saul turned and left Samuel. At that very moment God transformed him—made him a new person! And all the confirming signs took place the same day.

SAUL AMONG THE PROPHETS

When Saul and his party got to Gibeah, there were the prophets, right in front of them! Before he knew it, the Spirit of God came on Saul and he was prophesying right along with them. When those who had previously known Saul saw him prophesying with the prophets, they were totally surprised. "What's going on here? What's come over the son of Kish? How on earth did Saul get to be a prophet?" One man spoke up and said, "Who started this? Where did these people ever come from?"

That's how the saying got started, "Saul among the prophets! Who would have guessed?!"

When Saul was done prophesying, he returned home. His uncle asked him and his servant, "So where have you two been all this time?"

"Out looking for the donkeys. We looked and looked and couldn't find them. And then we found Samuel!"

"So," said Saul's uncle, "what did Samuel tell you?"

Saul said, "He told us not to worry—the donkeys had been found." But Saul didn't breathe a word to his uncle of what Samuel said about the king business.

"WE WANT A KING!"

Samuel called the people to assemble before GOD at Mizpah. He addressed the children of Israel, "This is GOD's personal message to you:

"I brought Israel up out of Egypt. I delivered you from Egyptian oppression—yes, from all the bullying governments that made your life miserable. And now you want nothing to do with your God, the very God who has a history of getting you out of troubles of all sorts.

"And now you say, 'No! We want a king; give us a king!'

"Well, if that's what you want, that's what you'll get! Present yourselves formally before GOD, ranked in tribes and families."

After Samuel got all the tribes of Israel lined up, the Benjamin tribe was picked. Then he lined up the Benjamin tribe in family groups, and the family of Matri was picked. The family of Matri took its place in the lineup, and the name Saul, son of Kish, was picked. But when they went looking for him, he was nowhere to be found.

Samuel went back to GOD: "Is he anywhere around?"

GOD said, "Yes, he's right over there—hidden in that pile of baggage."

They ran and got him. He took his place before everyone, standing tall—head and shoulders above them.

Samuel then addressed the people, "Take a good look at whom GOD has chosen: the best! No one like him in the whole country!"

Then a great shout went up from the people: "Long live the king!"

Samuel went on to instruct the people in the rules and regulations involved in a kingdom, wrote it all down in a book, and placed it before GOD. Then Samuel sent everyone home.

Saul also went home to Gibeah, and with him some true and brave men whom GOD moved to join him. But the riff-raff went off muttering, "'Deliverer'? Don't make me laugh!" They held him in contempt and refused to congratulate him. But Saul paid them no mind.

SAUL IS CROWNED KING

Nahash, king of the Ammonites, was brutalizing the tribes of Gad and Reuben, gouging out their right eyes and intimidating anyone who would come to Israel's help. There were very few Israelites living on the east side of the Jordan River who had not had their right eyes gouged out by Nahash. But seven thousand men had escaped from the Ammonites and were now living safely in Jabesh.

11 So Nahash went after them and prepared to go to war against Jabesh Gilead. The men of Jabesh petitioned Nahash: "Make a treaty with us and we'll serve you."

Nahash said, "I'll make a treaty with you on one condition: that every right eye among you be gouged out! I'll humiliate every last man and woman in Israel before I'm done!"

The town leaders of Jabesh said, "Give us time to send messengers around Israel—seven days should do it. If no one shows up to help us, we'll accept your terms."

The messengers came to Saul's place at Gibeah and told the people what was going on. As the people broke out in loud wails, Saul showed up. He was coming back from the field with his oxen.

Saul asked, "What happened? Why is everyone crying?"

And they repeated the message that had come from Jabesh.

The Spirit of God came on Saul when he heard the report and he flew into a rage. He grabbed the yoke of oxen and butchered them on the spot. He sent the messengers throughout Israel distributing the bloody pieces with this message: "Anyone who refuses to join up with Saul and Samuel, let this be the fate of his oxen!"

The terror of GOD seized the people, and they came out, one and all, not a laggard among them. Saul took command of the people at Bezek. There were 300,000 men from Israel, another 30,000 from Judah.

Saul instructed the messengers, "Tell this to the folk in Jabesh Gilead: 'Help is on the way. Expect it by noon tomorrow.'"

The messengers set straight off and delivered their message. Elated, the people of Jabesh Gilead sent word to Nahash: "Tomorrow we'll give ourselves up. You can deal with us on your terms." Long before dawn the next day, Saul had strategically placed his army in three groups. At first light they broke into the enemy camp and slaughtered Ammonites until noon. Those who were left ran for their lives, scattering every which way.

The people came to Samuel then and said, "Where are those men who said, 'Saul is not fit to rule over us'? Hand them over. We'll kill them!"

But Saul said, "Nobody is going to be executed this day. This is the day GOD saved Israel! Come, let's go to Gilgal and there reconsecrate the kingship."

They all trooped out to Gilgal. Before GOD, they crowned Saul king at Gilgal. And there they worshiped, sacrificing peace offerings. Saul and all Israel celebrated magnificently.

"DON'T CHASE AFTER GHOST-GODS"

12 Samuel addressed all Israel: "I've listened to everything you've said to me, listened carefully to every word, and I've given you a king. See for yourself: Your king among you, leading you! But now look at me: I'm old and gray, and my sons are still here. I've led you faithfully from my youth until this very day. Look at me! Do you have any complaints to bring before GOD and his anointed? Have I ever stolen so much as an ox or a donkey? Have I ever taken advantage of you or exploited you? Have I ever taken a bribe or played fast and loose with the law? Bring your complaint and I'll make it right."

"Oh no," they said, "never. You've never done any of that—never abused us, never lined your own pockets."

"That settles it then," said Samuel. "GOD is witness, and his anointed is witness that you find nothing against me—no faults, no complaints."

And the people said, "He is witness."

Samuel continued, "This is the GOD who made Moses and Aaron your leaders and brought your ancestors out of Egypt. Take your stand before him now as I review your case before God in the light of all the righteous ways in which God has worked with you and your ancestors. When Jacob's sons entered Egypt, the Egyptians made life hard for them and they cried for help to God. God sent Moses and Aaron, who led your ancestors out of Egypt and settled them here in this place.

"They soon forgot their God, so he sold them off to Sisera, commander of Hazor's army, later to a hard life under the Philistines, and still later to the king of Moab. They had to fight for their lives.

"Then they cried for help to God. They confessed, 'We've sinned! We've gone off and left God and worshiped the fertility gods and goddesses of Canaan. Oh, deliver us from the brutalities of our enemies and we'll worship you alone.'

"So God sent Jerub-Baal (Gideon), Bedan (Barak), Jephthah, and Samuel. He saved you from that hard life surrounded by enemies, and you lived in peace.

"But when you saw Nahash, king of the Ammonites, preparing to attack you, you said to me, 'No more of this. We want a king to lead us.' And God was already your king!

"So here's the king you wanted, the king you asked for. God has let you have your own way, given you a king. If you fear God, worship and obey him, and don't rebel against what he tells you. If both you and your king follow God, no problem. God will be sure to save you. But if you don't obey him and rebel against what he tells you, king or no king, you will fare no better than your fathers.

"Pay attention! Watch this wonder that God is going to perform before you now! It's summer, as you well know, and the rainy season is over. But I'm going to pray to God. He'll send thunder and rain, a sign to convince you of the great wrong you have done to God by asking for a king."

Samuel prayed to God, and God sent thunder and rain that same day. The people were greatly afraid and in awe of God and of Samuel.

Then all the people begged Samuel, "Pray to your God for us, your servants. Pray that we won't die! On top of all our other sins, we've piled on one more—asking for a king!"

Samuel said to them, "Don't be fearful. It's true that you have done something very wrong. All the same, don't turn your back on God. Worship and serve him heart and soul! Don't chase after ghost-gods. There's nothing to them. They can't help you. They're nothing but ghost-gods! God, simply because of who he is, is not going to walk off and leave his people. GOD took delight in making you into his very own people.

"And neither will I walk off and leave you. That would be a sin against GOD! I'm staying right here at my post praying for you and teaching you the good and right way to live. But I beg of you, fear GOD and worship him honestly and heartily. You've seen how greatly he has worked among you! Be warned: If you live badly, both you and your king will be thrown out."

"GOD IS OUT LOOKING FOR YOUR REPLACEMENT"

13 Saul was a young man when he began as king. He was king over Israel for many years.

Saul conscripted enough men for three companies of soldiers. He kept two companies under his command at Micmash and in the Bethel hills. The other company was under Jonathan at Gibeah in Benjamin. He sent the rest of the men home.

Jonathan attacked and killed the Philistine governor stationed at Geba (Gibeah). When the Philistines heard the news, they raised the alarm: "The Hebrews are in revolt!" Saul ordered the reveille trumpets blown throughout the land. The word went out all over Israel, "Saul has killed the Philistine governor—drawn first blood! The Philistines are stirred up and mad as hornets!" Summoned, the army came to Saul at Gilgal.

The Philistines rallied their forces to fight Israel: three companies of chariots, six companies of cavalry, and so many infantry they looked like sand on the seashore. They went up into the hills and set up camp at Micmash, east of Beth Aven.

When the Israelites saw that they were way outnumbered and in deep trouble, they ran for cover, hiding in caves and pits, ravines and brambles and cisterns—wherever. They retreated across the Jordan River, refugees fleeing to the country of Gad and Gilead. But Saul held his ground in Gilgal, his soldiers still with him but scared to death.

He waited seven days, the time set by Samuel. Samuel failed to show up at Gilgal, and the soldiers were slipping away, right and left.

So Saul took charge: "Bring me the burnt offering and the peace offerings!" He went ahead and sacrificed the burnt offering. No sooner had he done it than Samuel showed up! Saul greeted him.

Samuel said, "What on earth are you doing?"

Saul answered, "When I saw I was losing my army from under me, and that you hadn't come when you said you would, and that the Philistines were poised at Micmash, I said, 'The Philistines are about to come down on me in Gilgal, and I haven't yet come before GOD asking for his help.' So I took things into my own hands, and sacrificed the burnt offering."

"That was a fool thing to do," Samuel said to Saul. "If you had kept the appointment that your GOD commanded, by now GOD would have set a firm and lasting foundation under your kingly rule over Israel. As it is, your kingly rule is already falling to pieces. GOD is out looking for your replacement right now. This time he'll do the choosing. When he finds him, he'll appoint him leader of his people. And all because you didn't keep your appointment with GOD!"

At that, Samuel got up and left Gilgal. What army there was left followed Saul into battle. They went into the hills from Gilgal toward Gibeah in Benjamin. Saul looked over and assessed the soldiers still with him—a mere six hundred!

JONATHAN AND HIS ARMOR BEARER

Saul, his son Jonathan, and the soldiers who had remained made camp at Geba (Gibeah) of Benjamin. The Philistines were camped at Micmash. Three squads of raiding parties were regularly sent out from the Philistine camp. One squadron was assigned to the Ophrah road going toward Shual country; another was assigned to the Beth Horon road; the third took the border road that rimmed the Valley of Hyenas.

There wasn't a blacksmith to be found anywhere in Israel. The Philistines made sure of that—"Lest those Hebrews start making swords and spears." That meant that the Israelites had to go down among the Philistines to keep their farm tools—plowshares and mattocks, axes and sickles—sharp and in good repair. They charged a silver coin for the plowshares and mattocks, and half that for the rest. So when the battle of Micmash was joined, there wasn't a sword or spear to be found anywhere in Israel—except for Saul and his son Jonathan; they were both well-armed.

A patrol of Philistines took up a position at Micmash Pass.

14 Later that day, Jonathan, Saul's son, said to his armor bearer, "Come on, let's go over to the Philistine garrison patrol on the other side of the pass." But he didn't tell his father. Meanwhile, Saul was taking it easy under the pomegranate tree at the threshing floor

on the edge of town at Geba (Gibeah). There were about six hundred men with him. Ahijah, wearing the priestly Ephod, was also there. (Ahijah was the son of Ahitub, brother of Ichabod, son of Phinehas, who was the son of Eli the priest of GOD at Shiloh.) No one there knew that Jonathan had gone off.

The pass that Jonathan was planning to cross over to the Philistine garrison was flanked on either side by sharp rock outcroppings, cliffs named Bozez and Seneh. The cliff to the north faced Micmash; the cliff to the south faced Geba (Gibeah).

Jonathan said to his armor bearer, "Come on now, let's go across to these uncircumcised pagans. Maybe GOD will work for us. There's no rule that says God can only deliver by using a big army. No one can stop GOD from saving when he sets his mind to it."

His armor bearer said, "Go ahead. Do what you think best. I'm with you all the way."

Jonathan said, "Here's what we'll do. We'll cross over the pass and let the men see we're there. If they say, 'Halt! Don't move until we check you out,' we'll stay put and not go up. But if they say, 'Come on up,' we'll go right up—and we'll know GOD has given them to us. That will be our sign."

So they did it, the two of them. They stepped into the open where they could be seen by the Philistine garrison. The Philistines shouted out, "Look at that! The Hebrews are crawling out of their holes!"

Then they yelled down to Jonathan and his armor bearer, "Come on up here! We've got a thing or two to show you!"

Jonathan shouted to his armor bearer, "Up! Follow me! GOD has turned them over to Israel!" Jonathan scrambled up on all fours, his armor bearer right on his heels. When the Philistines came running up to them, he knocked them flat, his armor bearer right behind finishing them off, bashing their heads in with stones.

In this first bloody encounter, Jonathan and his armor bearer killed about twenty men. That set off a terrific upheaval in both camp and field, the soldiers in the garrison and the raiding squad badly shaken up, the ground itself shuddering—panic like you've never seen before!

STRAIGHT TO THE BATTLE

Saul's sentries posted back at Geba (Gibeah) in Benjamin saw the confusion and turmoil raging in the camp. Saul commanded, "Line up and take the roll. See who's here and who's missing." When they called the roll, Jonathan and his armor bearer turned up missing.

Saul ordered Ahijah, "Bring the priestly Ephod. Let's see what GOD has to say here." (Ahijah was responsible for the Ephod in those days.) While Saul was in conversation with the priest, the upheaval in the Philistine camp became greater and louder. Then Saul interrupted Ahijah: "Put the Ephod away."

Saul immediately called his army together and they went straight to the battle. When they got there they found total confusion—Philistines swinging their swords wildly, killing each other. Hebrews who had earlier defected to the Philistine camp came back. They now wanted to be with Israel under Saul and Jonathan. Not only that, but when all the Israelites who had been hiding out in the backwoods of Ephraim heard that the Philistines were running for their lives, they came out and joined the chase. GOD saved Israel! What a day!

The fighting moved on to Beth Aven. The whole army was behind Saul now—ten thousand strong!—with the fighting scattering into all the towns throughout the hills of Ephraim.

Saul did something really foolish that day. He addressed the army: "A curse on the man who eats anything before evening, before I've wreaked vengeance on my enemies!" None of them ate a thing all day.

There were honeycombs here and there in the fields. But no one so much as put his finger in the honey to taste it, for the soldiers to a man feared the curse. But Jonathan hadn't heard his father put the army under oath. He stuck the tip of his staff into some honey and ate it. Refreshed, his eyes lit up with renewed vigor.

A soldier spoke up, "Your father has put the army under solemn oath, saying, 'A curse on the man who eats anything before evening!' No wonder the soldiers are drooping!"

Jonathan said, "My father has imperiled the country. Just look how quickly my energy has returned since I ate a little of this honey! It would have been a lot better, believe me, if the soldiers had eaten their fill of whatever they took from the enemy. Who knows how much worse we could have whipped them!"

They killed Philistines that day all the way from Micmash to Aijalon, but the soldiers ended up totally exhausted. Then they started plundering. They grabbed anything in sight—sheep, cattle, calves—and butchered it where they found it. Then they glutted themselves—meat, blood, the works.

Saul was told, "Do something! The soldiers are sinning against

GOD. They're eating meat with the blood still in it!"

Saul said, "You're biting the hand that feeds you! Roll a big rock over here—now!" He continued, "Disperse among the troops and tell them, 'Bring your oxen and sheep to me and butcher them properly here. Then you can feast to your heart's content. Please don't sin against GOD by eating meat with the blood still in it.' "

And so they did. That night each soldier, one after another, led his animal there to be butchered.

That's the story behind Saul's building an altar to GOD. It's the first altar to GOD that he built.

FIND OUT WHAT GOD THINKS

Saul said, "Let's go after the Philistines tonight! We can spend the night looting and plundering. We won't leave a single live Philistine!"

"Sounds good to us," said the troops. "Let's do it!"

But the priest slowed them down: "Let's find out what God thinks about this."

So Saul prayed to God, "Shall I go after the Philistines? Will you put them in Israel's hand?" God didn't answer him on that occasion.

Saul then said, "All army officers, step forward. Some sin has been committed this day. We're going to find out what it is and who did it! As GOD lives, Israel's Savior God, whoever sinned will die, even if it should turn out to be Jonathan, my son!"

Nobody said a word.

Saul said to the Israelites, "You line up over on that side, and I and Jonathan my son will stand on this side."

The army agreed, "Fine. Whatever you say."

Then Saul prayed to GOD, "O God of Israel, why haven't you answered me today? Show me the truth. If the sin is in me or Jonathan, then, O GOD, give the sign Urim. But if the sin is in the army of Israel, give the sign Thummim."

The Urim sign turned up and pointed to Saul and Jonathan. That cleared the army.

Next Saul said, "Cast the lots between me and Jonathan—and death to the one GOD points to!"

The soldiers protested, "No—this is not right. Stop this!" But Saul pushed on anyway. They cast the lots, Urim and Thummim, and the lot fell to Jonathan.

Saul confronted Jonathan. "What did you do? Tell me!"

Jonathan said, "I licked a bit of honey off the tip of the staff I was carrying. That's it—and for that I'm to die?"

Saul said, "Yes. Jonathan most certainly will die. It's out of my hands—I can't go against God, can I?"

The soldiers rose up: "Jonathan—die? Never! He's just carried out this stunning salvation victory for Israel. As surely as GOD lives, not a hair on his head is going to be harmed. Why, he's been working hand-in-hand with God all day!" The soldiers rescued Jonathan and he didn't die.

Saul pulled back from chasing the Philistines, and the Philistines went home.

Saul extended his rule, capturing neighboring kingdoms. He fought enemies on every front—Moab, Ammon, Edom, the king of Zobah, the Philistines. Wherever he turned, he came up with a victory. He became invincible! He smashed Amalek, freeing Israel from the savagery and looting.

Saul's sons were Jonathan, Ishvi, and Malki-Shua. His daughters were Merab, the firstborn, and Michal, the younger. Saul's wife was Ahinoam, daughter of Ahimaaz. Abner son of Ner was commander of Saul's army (Ner was Saul's uncle). Kish, Saul's father, and Ner, Abner's father, were the sons of Abiel.

All through Saul's life there was war, bitter and relentless, with the Philistines. Saul conscripted every strong and brave man he laid eyes on.

15 Samuel said to Saul, "GOD sent me to anoint you king over his people, Israel. Now, listen again to what GOD says. This is the GOD-of-the-Angel-Armies speaking:

" 'I'm about to get even with Amalek for ambushing Israel when Israel came up out of Egypt. Here's what you are to do: Go to war against Amalek. Put everything connected with Amalek under a holy ban. And no exceptions! This is to be total destruction—men and women, children and infants, cattle and sheep, camels and donkeys—the works.' "

Saul called the army together at Telaim and prepared them to go to war—two hundred companies of infantry from Israel and another ten companies from Judah. Saul marched to Amalek City and hid in the canyon.

Then Saul got word to the Kenites: "Get out of here while you can. Evacuate the city right now or you'll get lumped in with the Amalekites. I'm warning you because you showed real kindness to the Israelites when they came up out of Egypt."

And they did. The Kenites evacuated the place.

Then Saul went after Amalek, from the canyon all the way to Shur near the Egyptian border. He captured Agag, king of Amalek, alive. Everyone else was killed under the terms of the holy ban. Saul and the army made an exception for Agag, and for the choice sheep and cattle. They didn't include them under the terms of the holy ban. But all the rest, which nobody wanted anyway, they destroyed as decreed by the holy ban.

Then GOD spoke to Samuel: "I'm sorry I ever made Saul king. He's turned his back on me. He refuses to do what I tell him."

Samuel was angry when he heard this. He prayed his anger and disappointment all through the night. He got up early in the morning to confront Saul but was told, "Saul's gone. He went to Carmel to set up a victory monument in his own honor, and then was headed for Gilgal."

By the time Samuel caught up with him, Saul had just finished an act of worship, having used Amalekite plunder for the burnt offerings sacrificed to GOD.

As Samuel came close, Saul called out, "GOD's blessings on you! I accomplished GOD's plan to the letter!"

Samuel said, "So what's this I'm hearing—this bleating of sheep, this mooing of cattle?"

"Only some Amalekite loot," said Saul. "The soldiers saved back a few of the choice cattle and sheep to offer up in sacrifice to GOD. But everything else we destroyed under the holy ban."

"Enough!" interrupted Samuel. "Let me tell you what GOD told me last night."

Saul said, "Go ahead. Tell me."

And Samuel told him. "When you started out in this, you were nothing—and you knew it. Then GOD put you at the head of Israel—made you king over Israel. Then GOD sent you off to do a job for him, ordering you, 'Go and put those sinners, the Amalekites, under a holy ban. Go to war against them until you have totally wiped them out.' So why did you not obey GOD? Why did you grab all this loot? Why, with GOD's eyes on you all the time, did you brazenly carry out this evil?"

Saul defended himself. "What are you talking about? I did obey GOD. I did the job GOD set for me. I brought in King Agag and destroyed the Amalekites under the terms of the holy ban. So the soldiers saved back a few choice sheep and cattle from the holy ban for sacrifice to GOD at Gilgal—what's wrong with that?"

Then Samuel said,

Do you think all GOD wants are sacrifices—
    empty rituals just for show?
He wants you to listen to him!
Plain listening is the thing,
    not staging a lavish religious production.
Not doing what GOD tells you
    is far worse than fooling around in the occult.
Getting self-important around GOD
    is far worse than making deals with your dead ancestors.
Because you said No to GOD's command,
    he says No to your kingship.

Saul gave in and confessed, "I've sinned. I've trampled roughshod over GOD's Word and your instructions. I cared more about pleasing the people. I let them tell me what to do. Oh, absolve me of my sin! Take my hand and lead me to the altar so I can worship GOD!"

But Samuel refused: "No, I can't come alongside you in this. You rejected GOD's command. Now GOD has rejected you as king over Israel."

As Samuel turned to leave, Saul grabbed at his priestly robe and a piece tore off. Samuel said, "GOD has just now torn the kingdom from you, and handed it over to your neighbor, a better man than you are. Israel's God-of-Glory doesn't deceive and he doesn't dither. He says what he means and means what he says."

Saul tried again, "I have sinned. But don't abandon me! Support me with your presence before the leaders and the people. Come alongside me as I go back to worship GOD."

Samuel did. He went back with him. And Saul went to his knees before GOD and worshiped.

Then Samuel said, "Present King Agag of Amalek to me." Agag came, dragging his feet, muttering that he'd be better off dead.

Samuel said, "Just as your sword made many a woman childless, so your mother will be childless among those women!" And Samuel cut Agag down in the presence of GOD right there in Gilgal.

Samuel left immediately for Ramah and Saul went home to Gibeah. Samuel never laid eyes on Saul again in this life, although he grieved long and deeply over him. But GOD was sorry he had ever made Saul king in the first place.

GOD LOOKS INTO THE HEART

16 GOD addressed Samuel: "So, how long are you going to mope over Saul? You know I've rejected him as king over Israel. Fill your flask with anointing oil and get going. I'm sending you to Jesse of Bethlehem. I've spotted the very king I want among his sons."

"I can't do that," said Samuel. "Saul will hear about it and kill me."

GOD said, "Take a heifer with you and announce, 'I've come to lead you in worship of GOD, with this heifer as a sacrifice.' Make sure Jesse gets invited. I'll let you know what to do next. I'll point out the one you are to anoint."

Samuel did what GOD told him. When he arrived at Bethlehem, the town fathers greeted him, but apprehensively. "Is there something wrong?"

"Nothing's wrong. I've come to sacrifice this heifer and lead you in the worship of GOD. Prepare yourselves, be consecrated, and join me in worship." He made sure Jesse and his sons were also consecrated and called to worship.

When they arrived, Samuel took one look at Eliab and thought, "Here he is! GOD's anointed!"

But GOD told Samuel, "Looks aren't everything. Don't be impressed with his looks and stature. I've already eliminated him. GOD judges persons differently than humans do. Men and women look at the face; GOD looks into the heart."

Jesse then called up Abinadab and presented him to Samuel. Samuel said, "This man isn't GOD's choice either."

Next Jesse presented Shammah. Samuel said, "No, this man isn't either."

Jesse presented his seven sons to Samuel. Samuel was blunt with Jesse, "GOD hasn't chosen any of these."

Then he asked Jesse, "Is this it? Are there no more sons?"

"Well, yes, there's the runt. But he's out tending the sheep."

Samuel ordered Jesse, "Go get him. We're not moving from this spot until he's here."

Jesse sent for him. He was brought in, the very picture of health—bright-eyed, good-looking.

GOD said, "Up on your feet! Anoint him! This is the one."

Samuel took his flask of oil and anointed him, with his brothers standing around watching. The Spirit of GOD entered David like a rush of wind, God vitally empowering him for the rest of his life.

Samuel left and went home to Ramah.

DAVID—AN EXCELLENT MUSICIAN

At that very moment the Spirit of GOD left Saul and in its place a black mood sent by GOD settled on him. He was terrified.

Saul's advisors said, "This awful tormenting depression from God is making your life miserable. Oh master, let us help. Let us look for someone who can play the harp. When the black mood from God moves in, he'll play his music and you'll feel better."

Saul told his servants, "Go ahead. Find me someone who can play well and bring him to me."

One of the young men spoke up, "I know someone. I've seen him myself: the son of Jesse of Bethlehem, an excellent musician. He's also courageous, of age, well-spoken, and good-looking. And GOD is with him."

So Saul sent messengers to Jesse requesting, "Send your son David to me, the one who tends the sheep."

Jesse took a donkey, loaded it with a couple of loaves of bread, a flask of wine, and a young goat, and sent his son David with it to Saul. David came to Saul and stood before him. Saul liked him immediately and made him his right-hand man.

Saul sent word back to Jesse: "Thank you. David will stay here. He's just the one I was looking for. I'm very impressed by him."

After that, whenever the bad depression from God tormented Saul, David got out his harp and played. That would calm Saul down, and he would feel better as the moodiness lifted.

GOLIATH

17 The Philistines drew up their troops for battle. They deployed them at Socoh in Judah, and set up camp between Socoh and Azekah at Ephes Dammim. Saul and the Israelites came together, camped at Oak Valley, and spread out their troops in battle readiness for the Philistines. The Philistines were on one hill, the Israelites on the opposing hill, with the valley between them.

A giant nearly ten feet tall stepped out from the Philistine line into the open, Goliath from Gath. He had a bronze helmet on his head and was dressed in armor—126 pounds of it! He wore bronze shin guards and carried a bronze sword. His spear was like a fence rail—the spear tip alone weighed over fifteen pounds. His shield bearer walked ahead of him.

Goliath stood there and called out to the Israelite troops, "Why bother using your whole army? Am I not Philistine enough for you? And you're all committed to Saul, aren't you? So pick your best fighter and pit him against me. If he gets the upper hand and kills me, the Philistines will all become your slaves. But if I get the upper hand and kill him, you'll all become our slaves and serve us. I challenge the troops of Israel this day. Give me a man. Let us fight it out together!"

When Saul and his troops heard the Philistine's challenge, they were terrified and lost all hope.

Enter David. He was the son of Jesse the Ephrathite from Bethlehem in Judah. Jesse, the father of eight sons, was himself too old to join Saul's army. Jesse's three older sons had followed Saul to war. The names of the three sons who had joined up with Saul were Eliab, the first-born; next, Abinadab; and third, Shammah. David was the youngest son. While his three oldest brothers went to war with Saul, David went back and forth from attending to Saul to tending his father's sheep in Bethlehem.

Each morning and evening for forty days, Goliath took his stand and made his speech.

One day, Jesse told David his son, "Take this sack of cracked wheat and these ten loaves of bread and run them down to your brothers in the camp. And take these ten wedges of cheese to the captain of their division. Check in on your brothers to see whether they are getting along all right, and let me know how they're doing—Saul and your brothers, and all the Israelites in their war with the Philistines in the Oak Valley."

David was up at the crack of dawn and, having arranged for some-one to tend his flock, took the food and was on his way just as Jesse had directed him. He arrived at the camp just as the army was moving into battle formation, shouting the war cry. Israel and the Philistines moved into position, facing each other, battle-ready. David left his bundles of food in the care of a sentry, ran to the troops who were deployed, and greeted his brothers. While they were talking together, the Philistine champion, Goliath of Gath, stepped out from the front lines of the Philistines, and gave his usual challenge. David heard him.

The Israelites, to a man, fell back the moment they saw the giant—totally frightened. The talk among the troops was, "Have you ever seen anything like this, this man openly and defiantly challenging Israel? The man who kills the giant will have it made. The king will give him a huge reward, offer his daughter as a bride, and give his entire family a free ride."

FIVE SMOOTH STONES

David, who was talking to the men standing around him, asked, "What's in it for the man who kills that Philistine and gets rid of this ugly blot on Israel's honor? Who does he think he is, anyway, this uncircumcised Philistine, taunting the armies of God-Alive?"

They told him what everyone was saying about what the king would do for the man who killed the Philistine.

Eliab, his older brother, heard David fraternizing with the men and lost his temper: "What are you doing here! Why aren't you minding your own business, tending that scrawny flock of sheep? I know what you're up to. You've come down here to see the sights, hoping for a ringside seat at a bloody battle!"

"What is it with you?" replied David. "All I did was ask a question." Ignoring his brother, he turned to someone else, asked the same question, and got the same answer as before.

The things David was saying were picked up and reported to Saul. Saul sent for him.

"Master," said David, "don't give up hope. I'm ready to go and fight this Philistine."

Saul answered David, "You can't go and fight this Philistine. You're too young and inexperienced—and he's been at this fighting business since before you were born."

David said, "I've been a shepherd, tending sheep for my father. Whenever a lion or bear came and took a lamb from the flock, I'd go after it, knock it down, and rescue the lamb. If it turned on me, I'd grab it by the throat, wring its neck, and kill it. Lion or bear, it made no difference—I killed it. And I'll do the same to this Philistine pig who is taunting the troops of God-Alive. GOD, who delivered me from the teeth of the lion and the claws of the bear, will deliver me from this Philistine."

Saul said, "Go. And GOD help you!"

Then Saul outfitted David as a soldier in armor. He put his bronze helmet on his head and belted his sword on him over the armor. David tried to walk but he could hardly budge.

David told Saul, "I can't even move with all this stuff on me. I'm not used to this." And he took it all off.

Then David took his shepherd's staff, selected five smooth stones from the brook, and put them in the pocket of his shepherd's pack, and with his sling in his hand approached Goliath.

As the Philistine paced back and forth, his shield bearer in front of him, he noticed David. He took one look down on him and sneered — a mere youngster, apple-cheeked and peach-fuzzed.

The Philistine ridiculed David. "Am I a dog that you come after me with a stick?" And he cursed him by his gods.

"Come on," said the Philistine. "I'll make roadkill of you for the buzzards. I'll turn you into a tasty morsel for the field mice."

David answered, "You come at me with sword and spear and battle-ax. I come at you in the name of GOD-of-the-Angel-Armies, the God of Israel's troops, whom you curse and mock. This very day GOD is handing you over to me. I'm about to kill you, cut off your head, and serve up your body and the bodies of your Philistine buddies to the crows and coyotes. The whole earth will know that there's an extraordinary God in Israel. And everyone gathered here will learn that GOD doesn't save by means of sword or spear. The battle belongs to GOD — he's handing you to us on a platter!"

That roused the Philistine, and he started toward David. David took off from the front line, running toward the Philistine. David reached into his pocket for a stone, slung it, and hit the Philistine hard in the forehead, embedding the stone deeply. The Philistine crashed, face down in the dirt.

That's how David beat the Philistine — with a sling and a stone. He hit him and killed him. No sword for David!

Then David ran up to the Philistine and stood over him, pulled the giant's sword from its sheath, and finished the job by cutting off his head. When the Philistines saw that their great champion was dead, they scattered, running for their lives.

The men of Israel and Judah were up on their feet, shouting! They chased the Philistines all the way to the outskirts of Gath and the gates of Ekron. Wounded Philistines were strewn along the Shaaraim road all the way to Gath and Ekron. After chasing the Philistines, the

Israelites came back and looted their camp. David took the Philistine's head and brought it to Jerusalem. But the giant's weapons he placed in his own tent.

✝

When Saul saw David go out to meet the Philistine, he said to Abner, commander of the army, "Tell me about this young man's family."

Abner said, "For the life of me, O King, I don't know."

The king said, "Well, find out the lineage of this raw youth."

As soon as David came back from killing the Philistine, Abner brought him, the Philistine's head still in his hand, straight to Saul.

Saul asked him, "Young man, whose son are you?"

"I'm the son of your servant Jesse," said David, "the one who lives in Bethlehem."

JONATHAN AND DAVID—SOUL FRIENDS

18 By the time David had finished reporting to Saul, Jonathan was deeply impressed with David—an immediate bond was forged between them. He became totally committed to David. From that point on he would be David's number-one advocate and friend.

Saul received David into his own household that day, no more to return to the home of his father.

Jonathan, out of his deep love for David, made a covenant with him. He formalized it with solemn gifts: his own royal robe and weapons—armor, sword, bow, and belt.

Whatever Saul gave David to do, he did it—and did it well. So well that Saul put him in charge of his military operations. Everybody, both the people in general and Saul's servants, approved of and admired David's leadership.

DAVID—THE NAME ON EVERYONE'S LIPS

As they returned home, after David had killed the Philistine, the women poured out of all the villages of Israel singing and dancing, welcoming King Saul with tambourines, festive songs, and lutes. In playful frolic the women sang,

Saul kills by the thousand,
David by the ten thousand!

This made Saul angry—very angry. He took it as a personal insult. He said, "They credit David with 'ten thousands' and me with only 'thousands.' Before you know it they'll be giving him the kingdom!" From that moment on, Saul kept his eye on David.

The next day an ugly mood was sent by God to afflict Saul, who became quite beside himself, raving. David played his harp, as he usually did at such times. Saul had a spear in his hand. Suddenly Saul threw the spear, thinking, "I'll nail David to the wall." David ducked, and the spear missed. This happened twice.

Now Saul feared David. It was clear that GOD was with David and had left Saul. So, Saul got David out of his sight by making him an officer in the army. David was in combat frequently. Everything David did turned out well. Yes, GOD was with him. As Saul saw David becoming more successful, he himself grew more fearful. He could see the handwriting on the wall. But everyone else in Israel and Judah loved David. They loved watching him in action.

One day Saul said to David, "Here is Merab, my eldest daughter. I want to give her to you as your wife. Be brave and bold for my sake. Fight GOD's battles!" But all the time Saul was thinking, "The Philistines will kill him for me. I won't have to lift a hand against him."

David, embarrassed, answered, "Do you really mean that? I'm from a family of nobodies! I can't be son-in-law to the king."

The wedding day was set, but as the time neared for Merab and David to be married, Saul reneged and married his daughter off to Adriel the Meholathite.

Meanwhile, Saul's daughter Michal was in love with David. When Saul was told of this, he rubbed his hands in anticipation. "Ah, a second chance. I'll use Michal as bait to get David out where the Philistines will make short work of him." So again he said to David, "You're going to be my son-in-law."

Saul ordered his servants, "Get David off by himself and tell him, 'The king is very taken with you, and everyone at court loves you. Go ahead, become the king's son-in-law!' "

The king's servants told all this to David, but David held back. "What are you thinking of? I can't do that. I'm a nobody; I have nothing to offer."

When the servants reported David's response to Saul, he told them to tell David this: "The king isn't expecting any money from you; only this: Go kill a hundred Philistines and bring evidence of your vengeance on the king's behalf. Avenge the king on his enemies." (Saul expected David to be killed in action.)

On receiving this message, David was pleased. There was something he could do for the king that would qualify him to be his son-in-law! He lost no time but went right out, he and his men, killed the hundred Philistines, brought their evidence back in a sack, and counted it out before the king—mission completed! Saul gave Michal his daughter to David in marriage.

As Saul more and more realized that GOD was with David, and how much his own daughter, Michal, loved him, his fear of David increased and settled into hate. Saul hated David.

Whenever the Philistine warlords came out to battle, David was there to meet them—and beat them, upstaging Saul's men. David's name was on everyone's lips.

THE BLACK MOOD OF SAUL

19 Saul called his son Jonathan together with his servants and ordered them to kill David. But because Jonathan treasured David, he went and warned him: "My father is looking for a way to kill you. Here's what you are to do. Tomorrow morning, hide and stay hidden. I'll go out with my father into the field where you are hiding. I'll talk about you with my father and we'll see what he says. Then I'll report back to you."

Jonathan brought up David with his father, speaking well of him. "Please," he said to his father, "don't attack David. He hasn't wronged you, has he? And just look at all the good he has done! He put his life on the line when he killed the Philistine. What a great victory GOD gave Israel that day! You were there. You saw it and were on your feet applauding with everyone else. So why would you even think of sinning against an innocent person, killing David for no reason whatever?"

Saul listened to Jonathan and said, "You're right. As GOD lives, David lives. He will not be killed."

Jonathan sent for David and reported to him everything that was said. Then he brought David back to Saul and everything was as it was before.

War broke out again and David went out to fight Philistines. He beat them badly, and they ran for their lives.

But then a black mood from God settled over Saul and took control of him. He was sitting at home, his spear in his hand, while David was playing music. Suddenly, Saul tried to skewer David with his spear,

141

but David ducked. The spear stuck in the wall and David got away. It was night.

Saul sent men to David's house to stake it out and then, first thing in the morning, to kill him. But Michal, David's wife, told him what was going on. "Quickly now—make your escape tonight. If not, you'll be dead by morning!" She let him out of a window, and he made his escape. Then Michal took a dummy god and put it in the bed, placed a wig of goat's hair on its head, and threw a quilt over it. When Saul's men arrived to get David, she said, "He's sick in bed."

Saul sent his men back, ordering them, "Bring him, bed and all, so I can kill him." When the men entered the room, all they found in the bed was the dummy god with its goat-hair wig!

Saul stormed at Michal: "How could you play tricks on me like this? You sided with my enemy, and now he's gotten away!"

Michal said, "He threatened me. He said, 'Help me out of here or I'll kill you.'"

David made good his escape and went to Samuel at Ramah and told him everything Saul had done to him. Then he and Samuel withdrew to the privacy of Naioth.

Saul was told, "David's at Naioth in Ramah." He immediately sent his men to capture him. They saw a band of prophets prophesying with Samuel presiding over them. Before they knew it, the Spirit of God was on them, too, and they were ranting and raving right along with the prophets!

That was reported back to Saul, and he dispatched more men. They, too, were soon prophesying. So Saul tried a third time—a third set of men—and they ended up mindlessly raving as well!

Fed up, Saul went to Ramah himself. He came to the big cistern at Secu and inquired, "Where are Samuel and David?"

A bystander said, "Over at Naioth in Ramah."

As he headed out for Naioth in Ramah, the Spirit of God was on him, too. All the way to Naioth he was caught up in a babbling trance! He ripped off his clothes and lay there rambling gibberish before Samuel for a day and a night, stretched out naked. People are still talking about it: "Saul among the prophets! Who would have guessed?"

A COVENANT FRIENDSHIP IN GOD'S NAME

20 David got out of Naioth in Ramah alive and went to Jonathan. "What do I do now? What wrong have I inflicted on your father that makes him so determined to kill me?"

"Nothing," said Jonathan. "You've done nothing wrong. And you're not going to die. Really, you're not! My father tells me everything. He does nothing, whether big or little, without confiding in me. So why would he do this behind my back? It can't be."

But David said, "Your father knows that we are the best of friends. So he says to himself, 'Jonathan must know nothing of this. If he does, he'll side with David.' But it's true—as sure as GOD lives, and as sure as you're alive before me right now—he's determined to kill me."

Jonathan said, "Tell me what you have in mind. I'll do anything for you."

David said, "Tomorrow marks the New Moon. I'm scheduled to eat dinner with the king. Instead, I'll go hide in the field until the evening of the third. If your father misses me, say, 'David asked if he could run down to Bethlehem, his hometown, for an anniversary reunion, and worship with his family.' If he says, 'Good!' then I'm safe. But if he gets angry, you'll know for sure that he's made up his mind to kill me. Oh, stick with me in this. You've entered into a covenant of GOD with me, remember! If I'm in the wrong, go ahead and kill me yourself. Why bother giving me up to your father?"

"Never!" exclaimed Jonathan. "I'd never do that! If I get the slightest hint that my father is fixated on killing you, I'll tell you."

David asked, "And whom will you get to tell me if your father comes back with a harsh answer?"

"Come outside," said Jonathan. "Let's go to the field." When the two of them were out in the field, Jonathan said, "As GOD, the God of Israel, is my witness, by this time tomorrow I'll get it out of my father how he feels about you. Then I'll let you know what I learn. May GOD do his worst to me if I let you down! If my father still intends to kill you, I'll tell you and get you out of here in one piece. And GOD be with you as he's been with my father! If I make it through this alive, continue to be my covenant friend. And if I die, keep the covenant friendship with my family—forever. And when GOD finally rids the earth of David's enemies, stay loyal to Jonathan!" Jonathan repeated his pledge of love and friendship for David. He loved David more than his own soul!

Jonathan then laid out his plan: "Tomorrow is the New Moon, and you'll be missed when you don't show up for dinner. On the third day, when they've quit expecting you, come to the place where you hid before, and wait beside that big boulder. I'll shoot three arrows in the direction of the boulder. Then I'll send off my servant, 'Go find the arrows.' If I yell after the servant, 'The arrows are on this side! Retrieve them!' that's the signal that you can return safely—as GOD lives, not a thing to fear! But if I yell, 'The arrows are farther out!' then run for it—GOD wants you out of here! Regarding all the things we've discussed, remember that GOD's in on this with us to the very end!"

David hid in the field. On the holiday of the New Moon, the king came to the table to eat. He sat where he always sat, the place against the wall, with Jonathan across the table and Abner at Saul's side. But David's seat was empty. Saul didn't mention it at the time, thinking, "Something's happened that's made him unclean. That's it—he's probably unclean for the holy meal."

But the day after the New Moon, day two of the holiday, David's seat was still empty. Saul asked Jonathan his son, "So where's that son of Jesse? He hasn't eaten with us either yesterday or today."

Jonathan said, "David asked my special permission to go to Bethlehem. He said, 'Give me leave to attend a family reunion back home. My brothers have ordered me to be there. If it seems all right to you, let me go and see my brothers.' That's why he's not here at the king's table."

Saul exploded in anger at Jonathan: "You son of a slut! Don't you think I know that you're in cahoots with the son of Jesse, disgracing both you and your mother? For as long as the son of Jesse is walking around free on this earth, your future in this kingdom is at risk. Now go get him. Bring him here. From this moment, he's as good as dead!"

Jonathan stood up to his father. "Why dead? What's he done?"

Saul threw his spear at him to kill him. That convinced Jonathan that his father was fixated on killing David.

Jonathan stormed from the table, furiously angry, and ate nothing the rest of the day, upset for David and smarting under the humiliation from his father.

In the morning, Jonathan went to the field for the appointment with David. He had his young servant with him. He told the servant, "Run and get the arrows I'm about to shoot." The boy started running and Jonathan shot an arrow way beyond him. As the boy came to the area where the arrow had been shot, Jonathan yelled out, "Isn't the arrow farther out?" He yelled again, "Hurry! Quickly! Don't just stand there!" Jonathan's servant then picked up the arrow and brought it to his master. The boy, of course, knew nothing of what was going on. Only Jonathan and David knew.

Jonathan gave his quiver and bow to the boy and sent him back to town. After the servant was gone, David got up from his hiding place beside the boulder, then fell on his face to the ground—three times prostrating himself! And then they kissed one another and wept, friend over friend, David weeping especially hard.

Jonathan said, "Go in peace! The two of us have vowed friendship in GOD's name, saying, 'GOD will be the bond between me and you, and between my children and your children forever!'"

DAVID PRETENDS TO GO CRAZY

21 David went on his way and Jonathan returned to town. David went to Nob, to Ahimelech the Priest. Ahimelech was alarmed as he went out to greet David: "What are you doing here all by yourself—and not a soul with you?"

David answered Ahimelech the Priest, "The king sent me on a mission and gave strict orders: 'This is top secret—not a word of this to a soul.' I've arranged to meet up with my men in a certain place. Now, what's there here to eat? Do you have five loaves of bread? Give me whatever you can scrounge up!"

"I don't have any regular bread on hand," said the priest. "I only have holy bread. If your men have not slept with women recently, it's yours."

David said, "None of us has touched a woman. I always do it this way when I'm on a mission: My men abstain from sex. Even when it is an ordinary mission we do that—how much more on this holy mission."

So the priest gave them the holy bread. It was the only bread he had, Bread of the Presence that had been removed from GOD's presence and replaced by fresh bread at the same time.

One of Saul's officials was present that day keeping a religious vow. His name was Doeg the Edomite. He was chief of Saul's shepherds.

David asked Ahimelech, "Do you have a spear or sword of any kind around here? I didn't have a chance to grab my weapons. The king's mission was urgent and I left in a hurry."

The priest said, "The sword of Goliath, the Philistine you killed at Oak Valley—that's here! It's behind the Ephod wrapped in a cloth. If you want it, take it. There's nothing else here."

"Oh," said David, "there's no sword like that! Give it to me!"

And at that, David shot out of there, running for his life from Saul. He went to Achish, king of Gath. When the servants of Achish saw him, they said, "Can this be David, the famous David? Is this the one they sing of at their dances?

> Saul kills by the thousand,
> David by the ten thousand!"

When David realized that he had been recognized, he panicked, fearing the worst from Achish, king of Gath. So right there, while they were looking at him, he pretended to go crazy, pounding his head on the city gate and foaming at the mouth, spit dripping from his beard. Achish took one look at him and said to his servants, "Can't you see he's crazy? Why did you let him in here? Don't you think I have enough crazy people to put up with as it is without adding another? Get him out of here!"

SAUL MURDERS THE PRIESTS OF GOD

22 So David got away and escaped to the Cave of Adullam. When his brothers and others associated with his family heard where he was, they came down and joined him. Not only that, but all who were down on their luck came around—losers and vagrants and misfits of all sorts. David became their leader. There were about four hundred in all.

Then David went to Mizpah in Moab. He petitioned the king of Moab, "Grant asylum to my father and mother until I find out what God has planned for me." David left his parents in the care of the king of Moab. They stayed there all through the time David was hiding out.

The prophet Gad told David, "Don't go back to the cave. Go to Judah." David did what he told him. He went to the forest of Hereth.

Saul got word of the whereabouts of David and his men. He was sitting under the big oak on the hill at Gibeah at the time, spear in hand, holding court surrounded by his officials. He said, "Listen here, you Benjaminites! Don't think for a minute that you have any future with the son of Jesse! Do you think he's going to hand over choice land, give you all influential jobs? Think again. Here you are, conspiring against me, whispering behind my back—not one of you is man enough to tell me that my own son is making deals with the son of Jesse, not one of you who cares enough to tell me that my son has taken the side of this, this . . . outlaw!"

Then Doeg the Edomite, who was standing with Saul's officials, spoke up: "I saw the son of Jesse meet with Ahimelech son of Ahitub, in Nob. I saw Ahimelech pray with him for GOD's guidance, give him food, and arm him with the sword of Goliath the Philistine."

Saul sent for the priest Ahimelech son of Ahitub, along with the whole family of priests at Nob. They all came to the king.

Saul said, "You listen to me, son of Ahitub!"

"Certainly, master," he said.

"Why have you ganged up against me with the son of Jesse, giving him bread and a sword, even praying with him for GOD's guidance, setting him up as an outlaw, out to get me?"

Ahimelech answered the king, "There's not an official in your administration as true to you as David, your own son-in-law and captain of your bodyguard. None more honorable either. Do you think that was the first time I prayed with him for God's guidance? Hardly! But don't accuse me of any wrongdoing, me or my family. I have no idea what you're trying to get at with this 'outlaw' talk."

The king said, "Death, Ahimelech! You're going to die—you and everyone in your family!"

The king ordered his henchmen, "Surround and kill the priests of GOD! They're hand in glove with David. They knew he was running away from me and didn't tell me." But the king's men wouldn't do it. They refused to lay a hand on the priests of GOD.

Then the king told Doeg, "You do it—massacre the priests!" Doeg the Edomite led the attack and slaughtered the priests, the eighty-five men who wore the sacred robes. He then carried the massacre into Nob, the city of priests, killing man and woman, child and baby, ox, donkey, and sheep—the works.

Only one son of Ahimelech son of Ahitub escaped: Abiathar. He got away and joined up with David. Abiathar reported to David that Saul had murdered the priests of GOD.

David said to Abiathar, "I knew it—that day I saw Doeg the Edomite there, I knew he'd tell Saul. I'm to blame for the death of everyone in your father's family. Stay here with me. Don't be afraid. The one out to kill you is out to kill me, too. Stick with me. I'll protect you."

LIVING IN DESERT HIDEOUTS

23 It was reported to David that the Philistines were raiding Keilah and looting the grain. David went in prayer to GOD: "Should I go after these Philistines and teach them a lesson?"

GOD said, "Go. Attack the Philistines and save Keilah."

But David's men said, "We live in fear of our lives right here in Judah. How can you think of going to Keilah in the thick of the Philistines?"

So David went back to GOD in prayer. GOD said, "Get going. Head for Keilah. I'm placing the Philistines in your hands."

David and his men went to Keilah and fought the Philistines. He scattered their cattle, beat them decisively, and saved the people of Keilah. After Abiathar took refuge with David, he joined David in the raid on Keilah, bringing the Ephod with him.

Saul learned that David had gone to Keilah and thought immediately, "Good! God has handed him to me on a platter! He's in a walled city with locked gates, trapped!" Saul mustered his troops for battle and set out for Keilah to lay siege to David and his men.

But David got wind of Saul's strategy to destroy him and said to Abiathar the priest, "Get the Ephod." Then David prayed to GOD: "God of Israel, I've just heard that Saul plans to come to Keilah and destroy the city because of me. Will the city fathers of Keilah turn me over to him? Will Saul come down and do what I've heard? Oh GOD, God of Israel, tell me!"

GOD replied, "He's coming down."

"And will the head men of Keilah turn me and my men over to Saul?"

And GOD said, "They'll turn you over."

So David and his men got out of there. There were about six hundred of them. They left Keilah and kept moving, going here, there, wherever—always on the move.

When Saul was told that David had escaped from Keilah, he called off the raid.

David continued to live in desert hideouts and the backcountry wilderness hills of Ziph. Saul was out looking for him day after day, but God never turned David over to him. David kept out of the way in the wilderness of Ziph, secluded at Horesh, since it was plain that Saul was determined to hunt him down.

Jonathan, Saul's son, visited David at Horesh and encouraged him in God. He said, "Don't despair. My father, Saul, can't lay a hand on you. You will be Israel's king and I'll be right at your side to help. And my father knows it." Then the two of them made a covenant before GOD. David stayed at Horesh and Jonathan went home.

Some Ziphites went to Saul at Gibeah and said, "Did you know that David is hiding out near us in the caves and canyons of Horesh? Right now he's at Hakilah Hill just south of Jeshimon. So whenever you're ready to come down, we'd count it an honor to hand him over to the king."

Saul said, "GOD bless you for thinking about me! Now go back and check everything out. Learn his routines. Observe his movements—where he goes, who he's with. He's very shrewd, you know. Scout out all his hiding places. Then meet me at Nacon and I'll go with you. If he is anywhere to be found in all the thousands of Judah, I'll track him down!"

So the Ziphites set out on their reconnaissance for Saul.

Meanwhile, David and his men were in the wilderness of Maon, in the desert south of Jeshimon. Saul and his men arrived and began their search. When David heard of it, he went south to Rock Mountain, camping out in the wilderness of Maon. Saul heard where he was and set off for the wilderness of Maon in pursuit. Saul was on one side of the mountain, David and his men on the other. David was in full retreat, running, with Saul and his men closing in, about to get him. Just then a messenger came to Saul and said, "Hurry! Come back! The Philistines have just attacked the country!"

So Saul called off his pursuit of David and went back to deal with the Philistines. That's how that place got the name Narrow Escape. David left there and camped out in the caves and canyons of En Gedi.

"I'M NO REBEL"

24 When Saul came back after dealing with the Philistines, he was told, "David is now in the wilderness of En Gedi." Saul took three companies—the best he could find in all Israel—and set out in search of David and his men in the region of Wild Goat Rocks. He came to some sheep pens along the road. There was a cave there and Saul went in to relieve himself. David and his men were huddled far back in the same cave. David's men whispered to him, "Can you believe it? This is the day GOD was talking about when he said, 'I'll put your enemy in your hands. You can do whatever you want with him.'" Quiet as a cat, David crept up and cut off a piece of Saul's royal robe.

Immediately, he felt guilty. He said to his men, "GOD forbid that I should have done this to my master, GOD's anointed, that I should so much as raise a finger against him. He's GOD's anointed!" David held his men in check with these words and wouldn't let them pounce on Saul. Saul got up, left the cave, and went on down the road.

Then David stood at the mouth of the cave and called to Saul, "My master! My king!" Saul looked back. David fell to his knees and bowed in reverence. He called out, "Why do you listen to those who say 'David is out to get you'? This very day with your very own eyes you have seen that just now in the cave GOD put you in my hands. My men wanted me to kill you, but I wouldn't do it. I told them that I won't lift a finger against my master—he's GOD's anointed. Oh, my father, look at this, look at this piece that I cut from your robe. I could have cut you—killed you!—but I didn't. Look at the evidence! I'm not against you. I'm no rebel. I haven't sinned against you, and yet you're hunting me down to kill me. Let's decide which of us is in the right. God may avenge me, but it is in his hands, not mine. An old proverb says, 'Evil deeds come from evil people.' So be assured that my hand won't touch you.

"What does the king of Israel think he's doing? Who do you think you're chasing? A dead dog? A flea? GOD is our judge. He'll decide who is right. Oh, that he would look down right now, decide right now—and set me free of you!"

When David had finished saying all this, Saul said, "Can this be the voice of my son David?" and he wept in loud sobs. "You're the one in the right, not me," he continued. "You've heaped good on me; I've dumped evil on you. And now you've done it again—treated me generously. GOD put me in your hands and you didn't kill me. Why? When a man meets his enemy, does he send him down the road with a blessing? May GOD give you a bonus of blessings for what you've done for me today! I know now beyond doubt that you will rule as king. The kingdom of Israel is already in your grasp! Now promise me under GOD that you will not kill off my family or wipe my name off the books."

David promised Saul. Then Saul went home and David and his men went up to their wilderness refuge.

TO FIGHT GOD'S BATTLES

25 Samuel died. The whole country came to his funeral. Everyone grieved over his death, and he was buried in his hometown of Ramah. Meanwhile, David moved again, this time to the wilderness of Maon.

There was a certain man in Maon who carried on his business in the region of Carmel. He was very prosperous—three thousand sheep and a thousand goats, and it was sheep-shearing time in Carmel. The man's name was Nabal (Fool), a Calebite, and his wife's name was Abigail. The woman was intelligent and good-looking, the man brutish and mean.

David, out in the backcountry, heard that Nabal was shearing his sheep and sent ten of his young men off with these instructions: "Go to Carmel and approach Nabal. Greet him in my name, 'Peace! Life and peace to you. Peace to your household, peace to everyone here! I heard that it's sheep-shearing time. Here's the point: When your shepherds were camped near us we didn't take advantage of them. They didn't lose a thing all the time they were with us in Carmel. Ask your young men—they'll tell you. What I'm asking is that you be generous with my men—share the feast! Give whatever your heart tells you to your servants and to me, David your son.'"

David's young men went and delivered his message word for word to Nabal. Nabal tore into them, "Who is this David? Who is this son of Jesse? The country is full of runaway servants these days. Do you think I'm going to take good bread and wine and meat freshly butchered for my sheepshearers and give it to men I've never laid eyes on? Who knows where they've come from?"

David's men got out of there and went back and told David what he had said. David said, "Strap on your swords!" They all strapped on their swords, David and his men, and set out, four hundred of them. Two hundred stayed behind to guard the camp.

Meanwhile, one of the young shepherds told Abigail, Nabal's wife, what had happened: "David sent messengers from the backcountry to salute our master, but he tore into them with insults. Yet these men treated us very well. They took nothing from us and didn't take advantage of us all the time we were in the fields. They formed a wall around us, protecting us day and night all the time we were out tending the sheep. Do something quickly because big trouble is ahead for our master and all of us. Nobody can talk to him. He's impossible—a real brute!"

Abigail flew into action. She took two hundred loaves of bread, two skins of wine, five sheep dressed out and ready for cooking, a bushel of roasted grain, a hundred raisin cakes, and two hundred fig cakes, and she had it all loaded on some donkeys. Then she said to her young servants, "Go ahead and pave the way for me. I'm right behind you." But she said nothing to her husband Nabal.

As she was riding her donkey, descending into a ravine, David and his men were descending from the other end, so they met there on the road. David had just said, "That sure was a waste, guarding everything this man had out in the wild so that nothing he had was lost—and now he rewards me with insults. A real slap in the face! May God do his worst to me if Nabal and every cur in his misbegotten brood isn't dead meat by morning!"

As soon as Abigail saw David, she got off her donkey and fell on her knees at his feet, her face to the ground in homage, saying, "My master, let me take the blame! Let me speak to you. Listen to what I have to say. Don't dwell on what that brute Nabal did. He acts out the meaning of his name: Nabal, Fool. Foolishness oozes from him.

"I wasn't there when the young men my master sent arrived. I didn't see them. And now, my master, as GOD lives and as you live, GOD has kept you from this avenging murder—and may your enemies, all who seek my master's harm, end up like Nabal! Now take this gift that I, your servant girl, have brought to my master, and give it to the young men who follow in the steps of my master.

"Forgive my presumption! But GOD is at work in my master, developing a rule solid and dependable. My master fights GOD's battles! As long as you live no evil will stick to you.

If anyone stands in your way,
     if anyone tries to get you out of the way,
Know this: Your God-honored life is tightly bound
     in the bundle of God-protected life;
But the lives of your enemies will be hurled aside
     as a stone is thrown from a sling.

"When GOD completes all the goodness he has promised my master and sets you up as prince over Israel, my master will not have this dead weight in his heart, the guilt of an avenging murder. And when GOD has worked things for good for my master, remember me."

And David said, "Blessed be GOD, the God of Israel. He sent you to meet me! And blessed be your good sense! Bless you for keeping me from murder and taking charge of looking out for me. A close call! As GOD lives, the God of Israel who kept me from hurting you, if you had not come as quickly as you did, stopping me in my tracks, by morning there would have been nothing left of Nabal but dead meat."

Then David accepted the gift she brought him and said, "Return home in peace. I've heard what you've said and I'll do what you've asked."

When Abigail got home she found Nabal presiding over a huge banquet. He was in high spirits—and very, very drunk. So she didn't tell him anything of what she'd done until morning. But in the morning, after Nabal had sobered up, she told him the whole story. Right then and there he had a heart attack and fell into a coma. About ten days later GOD finished him off and he died.

When David heard that Nabal was dead he said, "Blessed be GOD who has stood up for me against Nabal's insults, kept me from an evil act, and let Nabal's evil boomerang back on him."

Then David sent for Abigail to tell her that he wanted her for his wife. David's servants went to Abigail at Carmel with the message, "David sent us to bring you to marry him."

She got up, and then bowed down, face to the ground, saying, "I'm your servant, ready to do anything you want. I'll even wash the feet of my master's servants!"

Abigail didn't linger. She got on her donkey and, with her five maids in attendance, went with the messengers to David and became his wife.

David also married Ahinoam of Jezreel. Both women were his wives. Saul had married off David's wife Michal to Palti (Paltiel) son of Laish, who was from Gallim.

OBSESSED WITH A SINGLE FLEA

26 Some Ziphites came to Saul at Gibeah and said, "Did you know that David is hiding out on the Hakilah Hill just opposite Jeshimon?" Saul was on his feet in a minute and on his way to the wilderness of Ziph, taking three thousand of his best men, the pick of the crop, to hunt for David in that wild desert. He camped just off the road at the Hakilah Hill, opposite Jeshimon.

David, still out in the backcountry, knew Saul had come after him. He sent scouts to determine his precise location. Then David set out and came to the place where Saul had set up camp and saw for himself where Saul and Abner, son of Ner, his general, were staying. Saul was safely inside the camp, encircled by the army.

Taking charge, David spoke to Ahimelech the Hittite and to Abishai son of Zeruiah, Joab's brother: "Who will go down with me and enter Saul's camp?"

Abishai whispered, "I'll go with you."

So David and Abishai entered the encampment by night, and there he was—Saul, stretched out asleep at the center of the camp, his spear stuck in the ground near his head, with Abner and the troops sound asleep on all sides.

Abishai said, "This is the moment! God has put your enemy in your grasp. Let me nail him to the ground with his spear. One hit will do it, believe me; I won't need a second!"

But David said to Abishai, "Don't you dare hurt him! Who could lay a hand on GOD's anointed and even think of getting away with it?"

He went on, "As GOD lives, either GOD will strike him, or his time will come and he'll die in bed, or he'll fall in battle, but GOD forbid that I should lay a finger on GOD's anointed. Now, grab the spear at his head and the water jug and let's get out of here."

David took the spear and water jug that were right beside Saul's head, and they slipped away. Not a soul saw. Not a soul knew. No one woke up! They all slept through the whole thing. A blanket of deep sleep from GOD had fallen on them.

Then David went across to the opposite hill and stood far away on the top of the mountain. With this safe distance between them, he shouted across to the army and Abner son of Ner, "Hey Abner! How long do I have to wait for you to wake up and answer me?"

Abner said, "Who's calling?"

"Aren't you in charge there?" said David. "Why aren't you minding the store? Why weren't you standing guard over your master the king, when a soldier came to kill the king your master? Bad form! As GOD lives, your life should be forfeit, you and the entire bodyguard. Look what I have—the king's spear and water jug that were right beside his head!"

By now, Saul had recognized David's voice and said, "Is that you, my son David?"

David said, "Yes, it's me, O King, my master. Why are you after me, hunting me down? What have I done? What crime have I committed? Oh, my master, my king, listen to this from your servant: If GOD has stirred you up against me, then I gladly offer my life as a sacrifice. But if it's men who have done it, let them be banished from GOD's presence! They've expelled me from my rightful place in GOD's heritage, sneering, 'Out of here! Go get a job with some other god!' But you're not getting rid of me that easily; you'll not separate me from GOD in life or death. The absurdity! The king of Israel obsessed with a single flea! Hunting me down—a mere partridge—out in the hills!"

Saul confessed, "I've sinned! Oh, come back, my dear son David! I won't hurt you anymore. You've honored me this day, treating my life as most precious. And I've acted the fool—a moral dunce, a real clown."

David answered, "See what I have here? The king's spear. Let one of your servants come and get it. It's GOD's business to decide what to do with each of us in regard to what's right and who's loyal. GOD put your life in my hands today, but I wasn't willing to lift a finger against GOD's anointed. Just as I honored your life today, may GOD honor my life and rescue me from all trouble."

Saul said to David, "Bless you, dear son David! Yes, do what you have to do! And, yes, succeed in all you attempt!"

Then David went on his way, and Saul went home.

27 David thought to himself, "Sooner or later, Saul's going to get me. The best thing I can do is escape to Philistine country. Saul will count me a lost cause and quit hunting me down in every nook and cranny of Israel. I'll be out of his reach for good."

So David left; he and his six hundred men went to Achish son of Maoch, king of Gath. They moved in and settled down in Gath, with Achish. Each man brought his household; David brought his two wives, Ahinoam of Jezreel and Abigail, widow of Nabal of Carmel. When Saul was told that David had escaped to Gath, he called off the hunt.

Then David said to Achish, "If it's agreeable to you, assign me a place in one of the rural villages. It doesn't seem right that I, your mere servant, should be taking up space in the royal city."

So Achish assigned him Ziklag. (This is how Ziklag got to be what it is now, a city of the kings of Judah.) David lived in Philistine country a year and four months.

From time to time David and his men raided the Geshurites, the Girzites, and the Amalekites—these people were longtime inhabitants of the land stretching toward Shur and on to Egypt. When David raided an area he left no one alive, neither man nor woman, but took everything else: sheep, cattle, donkeys, camels, clothing—the works. Then he'd return to Achish.

Achish would ask, "And whom did you raid today?"

David would tell him, "Oh, the Negev of Judah," or "The Negev of Jerahmeel," or "The Negev of the Kenites." He never left a single person alive lest one show up in Gath and report what David had really been doing. This is the way David operated all the time he lived in Philistine country.

Achish came to trust David completely. He thought, "He's made himself so repugnant to his people that he'll be in my camp forever."

28 During this time the Philistines mustered their troops to make war on Israel. Achish said to David, "You can count on this: You're marching with my troops, you and your men."

And David said, "Good! Now you'll see for yourself what I can do!"

"Great!" said Achish. "I'm making you my personal bodyguard— for life!"

SAUL PRAYED, BUT GOD DIDN'T ANSWER

Samuel was now dead. All Israel had mourned his death and buried him in Ramah, his hometown. Saul had long since cleaned out all those who held seances with the dead.

The Philistines had mustered their troops and camped at Shunem. Saul had assembled all Israel and camped at Gilboa. But when Saul saw the Philistine troops, he shook in his boots, scared to death.

Saul prayed to GOD, but GOD didn't answer—neither by dream nor by sign nor by prophet.

So Saul ordered his officials, "Find me someone who can call up spirits so I may go and seek counsel from those spirits."

His servants said, "There's a witch at Endor."

Saul disguised himself by putting on different clothes. Then, taking two men with him, he went under the cover of night to the woman and said, "I want you to consult a ghost for me. Call up the person I name."

The woman said, "Just hold on now! You know what Saul did, how he swept the country clean of mediums. Why are you trying to trap me and get me killed?"

Saul swore solemnly, "As GOD lives, you won't get in any trouble for this."

The woman said, "So whom do you want me to bring up?"

"Samuel. Bring me Samuel."

When the woman saw Samuel, she cried out loudly to Saul, "Why did you lie to me? You're Saul!"

The king told her, "You have nothing to fear . . . but what do you see?"

"I see a spirit ascending from the underground."

"And what does he look like?" Saul asked.

"An old man ascending, robed like a priest."

Saul knew it was Samuel. He fell down, face to the ground, and worshiped.

Samuel said to Saul, "Why have you disturbed me by calling me up?"

"Because I'm in deep trouble," said Saul. "The Philistines are making war against me and God has deserted me—he doesn't answer me any more, either by prophet or by dream. And so I'm calling on you to tell me what to do."

"Why ask me?" said Samuel. "GOD has turned away from you and is now on the side of your neighbor. GOD has done exactly what he told you through me—ripped the kingdom right out of your hands and given it to your neighbor. It's because you did not obey GOD, refused to carry out his seething judgment on Amalek, that GOD does to you what he is doing today. Worse yet, GOD is turning Israel, along with you, over to the Philistines. Tomorrow you and your sons will be with me. And, yes, indeed, GOD is giving Israel's army up to the Philistines."

Saul dropped to the ground, felled like a tree, terrified by Samuel's words. There wasn't an ounce of strength left in him—he'd eaten nothing all day and all night. The woman, realizing that he was in deep shock, said to him, "Listen to me. I did what you asked me to do, put my life in your hands in doing it, carried out your instructions to the letter. It's your turn to do what I tell you: Let me give you some food. Eat it. It will give you strength so you can get on your way."

He refused. "I'm not eating anything."

But when his servants joined the woman in urging him, he gave in to their pleas, picked himself up off the ground, and sat on the bed. The woman moved swiftly. She butchered a grain-fed calf she had, and took some flour, kneaded it, and baked some flat bread. Then she served it all up for Saul and his servants. After dining handsomely, they got up from the table and were on their way that same night.

29 The Philistines mustered all their troops at Aphek. Meanwhile Israel had made camp at the spring at Jezreel. As the Philistine warlords marched forward by regiments and divisions, David and his men were bringing up the rear with Achish.

The Philistine officers said, "What business do these Hebrews have being here?"

Achish answered the officers, "Don't you recognize David, ex-servant of King Saul of Israel? He's been with me a long time. I've found nothing to be suspicious of, nothing to complain about, from the day he defected from Saul until now."

Angry with Achish, the Philistine officers said, "Send this man back to where he came from. Let him stick to his normal duties. He's not going into battle with us. He'd switch sides in the middle of the fight! What better chance to get back in favor with his master than by stabbing us in the back! Isn't this the same David they celebrate at their parties, singing,

Saul kills by the thousand,
David by the ten thousand!"

So Achish had to send for David and tell him, "As GOD lives, you've been a trusty ally—excellent in all the ways you have worked with me, beyond reproach in the ways you have conducted yourself. But the warlords don't see it that way. So it's best that you leave peacefully, now. It's not worth it, displeasing the Philistine warlords."

"But what have I done?" said David. "Have you had a single cause for complaint from the day I joined up with you until now? Why can't I fight against the enemies of my master the king?"

"I agree," said Achish. "You're a good man—as far as I'm concerned, God's angel! But the Philistine officers were emphatic: 'He's not to go with us into battle.' So get an early start, you and the men who came with you. As soon as you have light enough to travel, go."

David rose early, he and his men, and by daybreak they were on their way back to Philistine country. The Philistines went on to Jezreel.

DAVID'S STRENGTH WAS IN HIS GOD

30 Three days later, David and his men arrived back in Ziklag. Amalekites had raided the Negev and Ziklag. They tore Ziklag to pieces and then burned it down. They captured all the women, young and old. They didn't kill anyone, but drove them like a herd of cattle. By the time David and his men entered the village, it had been burned to the ground, and their wives, sons, and daughters all taken prisoner.

David and his men burst out in loud wails—wept and wept until they were exhausted with weeping. David's two wives, Ahinoam of Jezreel and Abigail widow of Nabal of Carmel, had been taken prisoner along with the rest. And suddenly David was in even worse trouble. There was talk among the men, bitter over the loss of their families, of stoning him.

David strengthened himself with trust in his GOD. He ordered Abiathar the priest, son of Ahimelech, "Bring me the Ephod so I can consult God." Abiathar brought it to David.

Then David prayed to GOD, "Shall I go after these raiders? Can I catch them?"

The answer came, "Go after them! Yes, you'll catch them! Yes, you'll make the rescue!"

David went, he and the six hundred men with him. They arrived at the Brook Besor, where some of them dropped out. David and four hundred men kept up the pursuit, but two hundred of them were too fatigued to cross the Brook Besor, and stayed there.

Some who went on came across an Egyptian in a field and took him to David. They gave him bread and he ate. And he drank some water. They gave him a piece of fig cake and a couple of raisin muffins. Life began to revive in him. He hadn't eaten or drunk a thing for three days and nights!

David said to him, "Who do you belong to? Where are you from?"

"I'm an Egyptian slave of an Amalekite," he said. "My master walked off and left me when I got sick—that was three days ago. We had raided the Negev of the Kerethites, of Judah, and of Caleb. Ziklag we burned."

David asked him, "Can you take us to the raiders?"

"Promise me by God," he said, "that you won't kill me or turn me over to my old master, and I'll take you straight to the raiders."

He led David to them. They were scattered all over the place, eating and drinking, gorging themselves on all the loot they had plundered from Philistia and Judah.

David pounced. He fought them from before sunrise until evening of the next day. None got away except for four hundred of the younger men who escaped by riding off on camels. David rescued everything the Amalekites had taken. And he rescued his two wives! Nothing and no one was missing—young or old, son or daughter, plunder or whatever. David recovered the whole lot. He herded the sheep and cattle before them, and they all shouted, "David's plunder!"

Then David came to the two hundred who had been too tired to continue with him and had dropped out at the Brook Besor. They came out to welcome David and his band. As he came near he called out, "Success!"

But all the mean-spirited men who had marched with David, the rabble element, objected: "They didn't help in the rescue, they don't get any of the plunder we recovered. Each man can have his wife and children, but that's it. Take them and go!"

"Families don't do this sort of thing! Oh no, my brothers!" said David as he broke up the argument. "You can't act this way with what GOD gave us! God kept us safe. He handed over the raiders who attacked us. Who would ever listen to this kind of talk? The share of the one who stays with the gear is the share of the one who fights— equal shares. Share and share alike!" From that day on, David made that the rule in Israel—and it still is.

On returning to Ziklag, David sent portions of the plunder to the elders of Judah, his neighbors, with a note saying, "A gift from the plunder of GOD's enemies!" He sent them to the elders in Bethel, Ramoth Negev, Jattir, Aroer, Siphmoth, Eshtemoa, Racal, Jerahmeelite cities, Kenite cities, Hormah, Bor Ashan, Athach, and Hebron, along with a number of other places David and his men went to from time to time.

SAUL AND JONATHAN, DEAD ON THE MOUNTAIN

31 The Philistines made war on Israel. The men of Israel were in full retreat from the Philistines, falling left and right, wounded on Mount Gilboa. The Philistines caught up with Saul and his sons. They killed Jonathan, Abinadab, and Malki-Shua, Saul's sons.

The battle was hot and heavy around Saul. The archers got his range and wounded him badly. Saul said to his weapon bearer, "Draw your sword and put me out of my misery, lest these pagan pigs come and make a game out of killing me."

But his weapon bearer wouldn't do it. He was terrified. So Saul took the sword himself and fell on it. When the weapon bearer saw that Saul was dead, he too fell on his sword and died with him. So Saul, his three sons, and his weapon bearer—the men closest to him—died together that day.

When the Israelites in the valley opposite and those on the other side of the Jordan saw that their army was in full retreat and that Saul and his sons were dead, they left their cities and ran for their lives. The Philistines moved in and occupied the sites.

The next day, when the Philistines came to rob the dead, they found Saul and his three sons dead on Mount Gilboa. They cut off Saul's head and stripped off his armor. Then they spread the good news all through Philistine country in the shrines of their idols and among the people. They displayed his armor in the shrine of the Ashtoreth. They nailed his corpse to the wall at Beth Shan.

The people of Jabesh Gilead heard what the Philistines had done to Saul. Their valiant men sprang into action. They traveled all night, took the corpses of Saul and his three sons from the wall at Beth Shan, and carried them back to Jabesh and burned off the flesh. They then buried the bones under the tamarisk tree in Jabesh and fasted in mourning for seven days.

2 SAMUEL

1 Shortly after Saul died, David returned to Ziklag from his rout of the Amalekites. Three days later a man showed up unannounced from Saul's army camp.

Disheveled and obviously in mourning, he fell to his knees in respect before David. David asked, "What brings you here?"

He answered, "I've just escaped from the camp of Israel."

"So what happened?" said David. "What's the news?"

He said, "The Israelites have fled the battlefield, leaving a lot of their dead comrades behind. And Saul and his son Jonathan are dead."

David pressed the young soldier for details: "How do you know for sure that Saul and Jonathan are dead?"

"I just happened by Mount Gilboa and came on Saul, badly wounded and leaning on his spear, with enemy chariots and horsemen bearing down hard on him. He looked behind him, saw me, and called me to him. 'Yes sir,' I said, 'at your service.' He asked me who I was, and I told him, 'I'm an Amalekite.'"

"Come here," he said, "and put me out of my misery. I'm nearly dead already, but my life hangs on."

"So I did what he asked—I killed him. I knew he wouldn't last much longer anyway. I removed his royal headband and bracelet, and have brought them to my master. Here they are."

In lament, David ripped his clothes to ribbons. All the men with him did the same. They wept and fasted the rest of the day, grieving the death of Saul and his son Jonathan, and also the army of GOD and the nation Israel, victims in a failed battle.

Then David spoke to the young soldier who had brought the report: "Who are you, anyway?"

"I'm from an immigrant family—an Amalekite."

"Do you mean to say," said David, "that you weren't afraid to up and kill GOD's anointed king?" Right then he ordered one of his soldiers, "Strike him dead!" The soldier struck him, and he died.

"You asked for it," David told him. "You sealed your death sentence when you said you killed GOD's anointed king."

Then David sang this lament over Saul and his son Jonathan, and gave orders that everyone in Judah learn it by heart. Yes, it's even inscribed in The Book of Jashar.

Oh, oh, Gazelles of Israel, struck down on your hills,
    the mighty warriors—fallen, fallen!
Don't announce it in the city of Gath,
    don't post the news in the streets of Ashkelon.
Don't give those coarse Philistine girls
    one more excuse for a drunken party!
No more dew or rain for you, hills of Gilboa,
    and not a drop from springs and wells,
For there the warriors' shields were dragged through the mud,
    Saul's shield left there to rot.

Jonathan's bow was bold—
    the bigger they were the harder they fell.
Saul's sword was fearless—
    once out of the scabbard, nothing could stop it.

Saul and Jonathan—beloved, beautiful!
    Together in life, together in death.
Swifter than plummeting eagles,
    stronger than proud lions.

Women of Israel, weep for Saul.
    He dressed you in finest cottons and silks,
    spared no expense in making you elegant.
The mighty warriors—fallen, fallen
    in the middle of the fight!
    Jonathan—struck down on your hills!

Oh my dear brother Jonathan,
    I'm crushed by your death.
Your friendship was a miracle-wonder,
    love far exceeding anything I've known—
    or ever hope to know.

The mighty warriors—fallen, fallen.
    And the arms of war broken to bits.

2 After all this, David prayed. He asked God, "Shall I move to one of the cities of Judah?"

G OD said, "Yes, move."

"And to which city?"

"To Hebron."

So David moved to Hebron, along with his two wives, Ahinoam of Jezreel and Abigail the widow of Nabal of Carmel. David's men, along with their families, also went with him and made their home in and around Hebron.

The citizens of Judah came to Hebron, and then and there made David king over the clans of Judah.

A report was brought to David that the men of Jabesh Gilead had given Saul a decent burial. David sent messengers to the men of Jabesh Gilead: "G OD bless you for this—for honoring your master, Saul, with a funeral. G OD honor you and be true to you—and I'll do the same, matching your generous act of goodness. Strengthen your resolve and do what must be done. Your master, Saul, is dead. The citizens of Judah have made me their king."

In the meantime, Abner son of Ner, commander of Saul's army, had taken Saul's son Ish-Bosheth to Mahanaim and made him king over Gilead, over Asher, over Jezreel, over Ephraim, over Benjamin—king, as it turns out, over all Israel. Ish-Bosheth, Saul's son, was forty years old when he was made king over Israel. He lasted only two years. But the people of Judah stuck with David. David ruled the people of Judah from Hebron for seven and a half years.

One day Abner son of Ner set out from Mahanaim with the soldiers of Ish-Bosheth son of Saul, headed for Gibeon. Joab son of Zeruiah, with David's soldiers, also set out. They met at the Pool of Gibeon, Abner's group on one side, Joab's on the other.

Abner challenged Joab, "Put up your best fighters. Let's see them do their stuff."

Joab said, "Good! Let them go at it!"

So they lined up for the fight, twelve Benjaminites from the side of Ish-Bosheth son of Saul, and twelve soldiers from David's side. The men from each side grabbed their opponents' heads and stabbed them with their daggers. They all fell dead—the whole bunch together. So, they called the place Slaughter Park. It's right there at Gibeon.

The fighting went from bad to worse throughout the day. Abner and the men of Israel were beaten to a pulp by David's men. The three sons of Zeruiah were present: Joab, Abishai, and Asahel. Asahel, as fast as a wild antelope on the open plain, chased Abner, staying hard on his heels.

Abner turned and said, "Is that you, Asahel?"

"It surely is," he said.

Abner said, "Let up on me. Pick on someone you have a chance of beating and be content with those spoils!" But Asahel wouldn't let up.

Abner tried again, "Turn back. Don't force me to kill you. How would I face your brother Joab?"

When he refused to quit, Abner struck him in the belly with the blunt end of his spear so hard that it came out his back. Asahel fell to the ground and died at once. Everyone who arrived at the spot where Asahel fell and died stood and gaped—Asahel dead! But Joab and Abishai kept up the chase after Abner. As the sun began to set, they came to the hill of Ammah that faced Giah on the road to the back-country of Gibeon. The Benjaminites had taken their stand with Abner there, deployed strategically on a hill.

Abner called out to Joab, "Are we going to keep killing each other till doomsday? Don't you know that nothing but bitterness will come from this? How long before you call off your men from chasing their brothers?"

"As God lives," said Joab, "if you hadn't spoken up, we'd have kept up the chase until morning!" Then he blew the ram's horn trumpet and the whole army of Judah stopped in its tracks. They quit chasing Israel and called off the fighting.

Abner and his soldiers marched all that night up the Arabah Valley. They crossed the Jordan and, after a long morning's march, arrived at Mahanaim.

After Joab returned from chasing Abner, he took a head count of the army. Nineteen of David's men (besides Asahel) were missing. David's men had cut down three hundred and sixty of Abner's men, all Benjaminites—all dead. They brought Asahel and buried him in the family tomb in Bethlehem. Joab and his men then marched all night, arriving in Hebron as the dawn broke.

3 The war between the house of Saul and the house of David dragged on and on. The longer it went on the stronger David became, with the house of Saul getting weaker.

✛

During the Hebron years, sons were born to David:
    Amnon, born of Ahinoam of Jezreel—the firstborn;
    Kileab, born of Abigail of Carmel, Nabal's widow—his second;
    Absalom, born of Maacah, daughter of Talmai, king of Geshur—
       the third;
    Adonijah, born of Haggith—the fourth;
    Shephatiah, born of Abital—the fifth;
    Ithream, born of Eglah—the sixth.
These six sons of David were born in Hebron.

✛

Abner took advantage of the continuing war between the house of Saul and the house of David to gain power for himself. Saul had had a concubine, Rizpah, the daughter of Aiah. One day Ish-Bosheth confronted Abner: "What business do you have sleeping with my father's concubine?"

Abner lost his temper with Ish-Bosheth, "Treat me like a dog, will you! Is this the thanks I get for sticking by the house of your father, Saul, and all his family and friends? I personally saved you from certain capture by David, and you make an issue out of my going to bed with a woman! What GOD promised David, I'll help accomplish—transfer the kingdom from the house of Saul and make David ruler over the whole country, both Israel and Judah, from Dan to Beersheba. If not, may God do his worst to me."

Ish-Bosheth, cowed by Abner's outburst, couldn't say another word.

Abner went ahead and sent personal messengers to David: "Make a deal with me and I'll help bring the whole country of Israel over to you."

"Great," said David. "It's a deal. But only on one condition: You're not welcome here unless you bring Michal, Saul's daughter, with you when you come to meet me."

David then sent messengers to Ish-Bosheth son of Saul: "Give me back Michal, whom I won as my wife at the cost of a hundred Philistine foreskins."

Ish-Bosheth ordered that she be taken from her husband Paltiel son of Laish. But Paltiel followed her, weeping all the way, to Bahurim. There Abner told him, "Go home." And he went home.

Abner got the elders of Israel together and said, "Only yesterday, it seems, you were looking for a way to make David your king. So do it — now! For GOD has given the go-ahead on David: 'By my servant David's hand, I'll save my people Israel from the oppression of the Philistines and all their other enemies.'"

Abner took the Benjaminites aside and spoke to them. Then he went to Hebron for a private talk with David, telling him everything that Israel in general and Benjamin in particular were planning to do.

When Abner and the twenty men who were with him met with David in Hebron, David laid out a feast for them.

Abner then said, "I'm ready. Let me go now to rally everyone in Israel for my master, the king. They'll make a treaty with you, authorizing you to rule them however you see fit." Abner was sent off with David's blessing.

Soon after that, David's men, led by Joab, came back from a field assignment. Abner was no longer in Hebron with David, having just been dismissed with David's blessing. As Joab and his raiding party arrived, they were told that Abner the son of Ner had been there with David and had been sent off with David's blessing.

Joab went straight to the king: "What's this you've done? Abner shows up, and you let him walk away scot-free? You know Abner son of Ner better than that. This was no friendly visit. He was here to spy on you, figure out your comings and goings, find out what you're up to."

Joab left David and went into action. He sent messengers after Abner; they caught up with him at the well at Sirah and brought him back. David knew nothing of all this. When Abner got back to Hebron, Joab steered him aside at the gate for a personal word with him. There he stabbed him in the belly, killed him in cold blood for the murder of his brother Asahel.

Later on, when David heard what happened, he said, "Before GOD I and my kingdom are totally innocent of this murder of Abner son of Ner. Joab and his entire family will always be under the curse of this bloodguilt. May they forever be victims of crippling diseases, violence, and famine." (Joab and his brother, Abishai, murdered Abner because he had killed their brother Asahel at the battle of Gibeon.)

David ordered Joab and all the men under him, "Rip your cloaks into rags! Wear mourning clothes! Lead Abner's funeral procession with loud lament!" King David followed the coffin. They buried Abner in Hebron. The king's voice was loud in lament as he wept at the side of Abner's grave. All the people wept, too.

Then the king sang this tribute to Abner:

Can this be? Abner dead like a nameless bum?
You were a free man, free to go and do as you wished—
Yet you fell as a victim in a street brawl.

And all the people wept—a crescendo of crying!

They all came then to David, trying to get him to eat something before dark. But David solemnly swore, "I'll not so much as taste a piece of bread, or anything else for that matter, before sunset, so help me God!" Everyone at the funeral took notice—and liked what they saw. In fact everything the king did was applauded by the people. It was clear to everyone that day, including all Israel, that the king had nothing to do with the death of Abner son of Ner.

The king spoke to his servants: "You realize, don't you, that today a prince and hero fell victim of foul play in Israel? And I, though anointed king, was helpless to do anything about it. These sons of Zeruiah are too much for me. GOD, requite the criminal for his crime!"

THE MURDER OF ISH-BOSHETH

4 Saul's son, Ish-Bosheth, heard that Abner had died in Hebron. His heart sank. The whole country was shaken.

Ish-Bosheth had two men who were captains of raiding bands— one was named Baanah, the other Recab. They were sons of Rimmon the Beerothite, a Benjaminite. (The people of Beeroth had been assigned to Benjamin ever since they escaped to Gittaim. They still live there as resident aliens.)

It so happened that Saul's son, Jonathan, had a son who was maimed in both feet. When he was five years old, the report on Saul and Jonathan came from Jezreel. His nurse picked him up and ran, but in her hurry to get away she fell, and the boy was maimed. His name was Mephibosheth.

One day Baanah and Recab, the two sons of Rimmon, headed out for the house of Ish-Bosheth. They arrived at the hottest time of the day, just as he was taking his afternoon nap. They entered the house on a ruse, pretending official business. The maid guarding the bedroom had fallen asleep, so Recab and Baanah slipped by her and entered the room where Ish-Bosheth was asleep on his bed. They killed him and then cut off his head, carrying it off as a trophy. They traveled all night long, taking the route through the Arabah Valley.

They presented the head of Ish-Bosheth to David at Hebron, telling the king, "Here's the head of Ish-Bosheth, Saul's son, your enemy. He was out to kill you, but GOD has given vengeance to my master, the king—vengeance this very day on Saul and his children!"

David answered the brothers Recab and Baanah, sons of Rimmon the Beerothite, "As surely as GOD lives—the One who got me out of every trouble I've ever been in—when the messenger told me, 'Good news! Saul is dead!' supposing I'd be delighted, I arrested him and killed him on the spot in Ziklag. That's what he got for his so-called good news! And now you show up—evil men who killed an innocent man in cold blood, a man asleep in his own house! Don't think I won't find you guilty of murder and rid the country of you!"

David then issued orders to his soldiers. They killed the two—chopped off their hands and feet, and hung the corpses at the pool in Hebron. But Ish-Bosheth's head they took and buried in Abner's tomb in Hebron.

5 Before long all the tribes of Israel approached David in Hebron and said, "Look at us—your own flesh and blood! In time past when Saul was our king, you're the one who really ran the country. Even then GOD said to you, 'You will shepherd my people Israel and you'll be the prince.'"

All the leaders of Israel met with King David at Hebron, and the king made a treaty with them in the presence of GOD. And so they anointed David king over Israel.

✝

David was thirty years old when he became king, and ruled for forty years. In Hebron he ruled Judah for seven and a half years. In Jerusalem he ruled all Israel and Judah for thirty-three years.

David and his men immediately set out for Jerusalem to take on the Jebusites, who lived in that country. But they said, "You might as well go home! Even the blind and the lame could keep you out. You can't get in here!" They had convinced themselves that David couldn't break through.

But David went right ahead and captured the fortress of Zion, known ever since as the City of David. That day David said, "To get the best of these Jebusites, one must target the water system, not to mention this so-called lame and blind bunch that David hates." (In fact, he was so sick and tired of it, people coined the expression, "No lame and blind allowed in the palace.")

David made the fortress city his home and named it "City of David." He developed the city from the outside terraces inward. David proceeded with a longer stride, a larger embrace since the GOD-of-the-Angel-Armies was with him.

It was at this time that Hiram, king of Tyre, sent messengers to David, along with timbers of cedar. He also sent carpenters and masons to build a house for David. David took this as a sign that GOD had confirmed him as king of Israel, giving his kingship world prominence for the sake of Israel, his people.

David took on more concubines and wives from Jerusalem after he left Hebron. And more sons and daughters were born to him. These are the names of those born to him in Jerusalem:

Shammua,
Shobab,
Nathan,
Solomon,
Ibhar,
Elishua,
Nepheg,
Japhia,
Elishama,
Eliada,
Eliphelet.

When the Philistines got word that David had been made king over all Israel, they came on the hunt for him. David heard of it and went down to the stronghold. When the Philistines arrived, they deployed their forces in Raphaim Valley.

Then David prayed to GOD: "Shall I go up and fight the Philistines? Will you help me beat them?"

"Go up," GOD replied. "Count on me. I'll help you beat them."

David then went straight to Baal Perazim, and smashed them to pieces. Afterwards David said, "GOD exploded on my enemies like a gush of water." That's why David named the place Baal Perazim (The-Master-Who-Explodes). The retreating Philistines dumped their idols, and David and his soldiers took them away.

Later there was a repeat performance. The Philistines came up again and deployed their troops in the Rephaim Valley. David again prayed to GOD.

This time GOD said, "Don't attack them head-on. Instead, circle around behind them and ambush them from the grove of sacred trees. When you hear the sound of shuffling in the trees, get ready to move out. It's a signal that GOD is going ahead of you to smash the Philistine camp."

David did exactly what GOD told him. He routed the Philistines all the way from Gibeon to Gezer.

6 David mustered the pick of the troops of Israel—thirty divisions of them. Together with his soldiers, David headed for Baalah to recover the Chest of God, which was called by the Name GOD-of-the-Angel-Armies, who was enthroned over the pair of angels on the Chest.

They placed the Chest of God on a brand-new oxcart and removed it from Abinadab's house on the hill. Uzzah and Ahio, Abinadab's sons, were driving the new cart loaded with the Chest of God, Ahio in the lead and Uzzah alongside the Chest. David and the whole company of Israel were in the parade, singing at the top of their lungs and playing mandolins, harps, tambourines, castanets, and cymbals. When they came to the threshing floor of Nacon, the oxen stumbled, so Uzzah reached out and grabbed the Chest of God. GOD blazed in anger against Uzzah and struck him hard because he had profaned the Chest. Uzzah died on the spot, right alongside the Chest.

Then David got angry because of GOD's deadly outburst against Uzzah. That place is still called Perez Uzzah (The-Explosion-Against-Uzzah). David became fearful of GOD that day and said, "This Chest is too hot to handle. How can I ever get it back to the City of David?" He refused to take the Chest of GOD a step farther. Instead, David removed it off the road and to the house of Obed-Edom the Gittite. The Chest of GOD stayed at the house of Obed-Edom the Gittite for three months. And GOD prospered Obed-Edom and his entire household.

It was reported to King David that GOD had prospered Obed-Edom and his entire household because of the Chest of God. So David thought, "I'll get that blessing for myself," and went and brought up the Chest of God from the house of Obed-Edom to the City of David, celebrating extravagantly all the way, with frequent sacrifices of choice bulls. David, ceremonially dressed in priest's linen, danced with great abandon before GOD. The whole country was with him as he accompanied the Chest of GOD with shouts and trumpet blasts. But as the Chest of GOD came into the City of David, Michal, Saul's daughter, happened to be looking out a window. When she saw King David leaping and dancing before GOD, her heart filled with scorn.

They brought the Chest of GOD and set it in the middle of the tent pavilion that David had pitched for it. Then and there David worshiped, offering burnt offerings and peace offerings. When David had completed the sacrifices of burnt and peace offerings, he blessed the people in the name of GOD-of-the-Angel-Armies and handed out to each person in the crowd, men and women alike, a loaf of bread, a date cake, and a raisin cake. Then everyone went home.

David returned home to bless his family. Michal, Saul's daughter, came out to greet him: "How wonderfully the king has distinguished himself today—exposing himself to the eyes of the servants' maids like some burlesque street dancer!" David replied to Michal, "In GOD's presence I'll dance all I want! He chose me over your father and the rest of our family and made me prince over GOD's people, over Israel. Oh yes, I'll dance to GOD's glory—more recklessly even than this. And as far as I'm concerned . . . I'll gladly look like a fool . . . but among these maids you're so worried about, I'll be honored no end."

Michal, Saul's daughter, was barren the rest of her life.

✣

GOD'S COVENANT WITH DAVID

7 Before long, the king made himself at home and GOD gave him peace from all his enemies. Then one day King David said to Nathan the prophet, "Look at this: Here I am, comfortable in a luxurious house of cedar, and the Chest of God sits in a plain tent."

Nathan told the king, "Whatever is on your heart, go and do it. GOD is with you."

But that night, the word of GOD came to Nathan saying, "Go and tell my servant David: This is GOD's word on the matter: You're going to build a 'house' for me to live in? Why, I haven't lived in a 'house' from the time I brought the children of Israel up from Egypt till now. All that time I've moved about with nothing but a tent. And in all my travels with Israel, did I ever say to any of the leaders I commanded to shepherd Israel, 'Why haven't you built me a house of cedar?'

"So here is what you are to tell my servant David: The GOD-of-the-Angel-Armies has this word for you: I took you from the pasture, tagging along after sheep, and made you prince over my people Israel. I was with you everywhere you went and mowed your enemies down before you. Now I'm making you famous, to be ranked with the great names on earth. And I'm going to set aside a place for my people Israel and plant them there so they'll have their own home and not be knocked around any more. Nor will evil men afflict you as they always have, even during the days I set judges over my people Israel. Finally, I'm going to give you peace from all your enemies.

"Furthermore, GOD has this message for you: GOD himself will build you a house! When your life is complete and you're buried with your ancestors, then I'll raise up your child, your own flesh and blood, to succeed you, and I'll firmly establish his rule. He will build a house to honor me, and I will guarantee his kingdom's rule permanently. I'll be a father to him, and he'll be a son to me. When he does wrong, I'll discipline him in the usual ways, the pitfalls and obstacles of this mortal life. But I'll never remove my gracious love from him, as I removed it from Saul, who preceded you and whom I most certainly did remove. Your family and your kingdom are permanently secured. I'm keeping my eye on them! And your royal throne will always be there, rock solid."

Nathan gave David a complete and accurate account of everything he heard and saw in the vision.

King David went in, took his place before GOD, and prayed: "Who am I, my Master GOD, and what is my family, that you have brought me to this place in life? But that's nothing compared to what's coming, for you've also spoken of my family far into the future, given me a glimpse into tomorrow, my Master GOD! What can I possibly say in the face of all this? You know me, Master GOD, just as I am. You've done all this not because of who I am but because of who you are—out of your very heart!—but you've let me in on it.

"This is what makes you so great, Master GOD! There is none like you, no God but you, nothing to compare with what we've heard with our own ears. And who is like your people, like Israel, a nation unique in the earth, whom God set out to redeem for himself (and became most famous for it), performing great and fearsome acts, throwing out nations and their gods left and right as you saved your people from

Egypt? You established for yourself a people—your very own Israel!—your people permanently. And you, GOD, became their God.

"So now, great GOD, this word that you have spoken to me and my family, guarantee it permanently! Do exactly what you've promised! Then your reputation will flourish always as people exclaim, 'The GOD-of-the-Angel-Armies is God over Israel!' And the house of your servant David will remain sure and solid in your watchful presence. For you, GOD-of-the-Angel-Armies, Israel's God, told me plainly, 'I will build you a house.' That's how I was able to find the courage to pray this prayer to you.

"And now, Master GOD, being the God you are, speaking sure words as you do, and having just said this wonderful thing to me, please, just one more thing: Bless my family; keep your eye on them always. You've already as much as said that you would, Master GOD! Oh, may your blessing be on my family permanently!"

8 In the days that followed, David struck hard at the Philistines—brought them to their knees and took control of the countryside.

He also fought and defeated Moab. He chose two-thirds of them randomly and executed them. The other third he spared. So the Moabites fell under David's rule and were forced to bring tribute.

On his way to restore his sovereignty at the River Euphrates, David next defeated Hadadezer son of Rehob the king of Zobah. He captured from him a thousand chariots, seven thousand cavalry, and twenty thousand infantry. He hamstrung all the chariot horses, but saved back a hundred.

When the Arameans from Damascus came to the aid of Hadadezer king of Zobah, David killed twenty-two thousand of them. David set up a puppet government in Aram-Damascus. The Arameans became subjects of David and were forced to bring tribute. GOD gave victory to David wherever he marched.

David plundered the gold shields that belonged to the servants of Hadadezer and brought them to Jerusalem. He also looted a great quantity of bronze from Tebah and Berothai, cities of Hadadezer.

Toi, king of Hamath, heard that David had struck down the entire army of Hadadezer. So he sent his son Joram to King David to greet and congratulate him for fighting and defeating them, for Toi and Hadadezer were old enemies. He brought with him gifts of silver, gold, and bronze. King David consecrated these along with the silver and gold from all the nations he had conquered—from Aram, Moab, the

Ammonites, the Philistines, and from Amalek, along with the plunder from Hadadezer son of Rehob king of Zobah.

David built a victory monument on his return from defeating the Arameans.

Abishai son of Zeruiah fought and defeated the Edomites in the Salt Valley. Eighteen thousand of them were killed. David set up a puppet government in Edom, and the Edomites became subjects under David.

GOD gave David victory wherever he marched.

Thus David ruled over all of Israel. He ruled well—fair and even-handed in all his duties and relationships.

Joab son of Zeruiah was head of the army;

Jehoshaphat son of Ahilud was clerk;

Zadok son of Ahitub and Ahimelech son of Abiathar were priests;

Seraiah was secretary;

Benaiah son of Jehoiada was over the Kerethites and Pelethites;

And David's sons were priests.

AN OPEN TABLE FOR MEPHIBOSHETH

9 One day David asked, "Is there anyone left of Saul's family? If so, I'd like to show him some kindness in honor of Jonathan."

It happened that a servant from Saul's household named Ziba was there. They called him into David's presence. The king asked him, "Are you Ziba?"

"Yes sir," he replied.

The king asked, "Is there anyone left from the family of Saul to whom I can show some godly kindness?"

Ziba told the king, "Yes, there is Jonathan's son, lame in both feet."

"Where is he?"

"He's living at the home of Makir son of Ammiel in Lo Debar."

King David didn't lose a minute. He sent and got him from the home of Makir son of Ammiel in Lo Debar.

When Mephibosheth son of Jonathan (who was the son of Saul), came before David, he bowed deeply, abasing himself, honoring David.

David spoke his name: "Mephibosheth."

"Yes sir?"

"Don't be frightened," said David. "I'd like to do something special for you in memory of your father Jonathan. To begin with, I'm returning to you all the properties of your grandfather Saul. Furthermore, from now on you'll take all your meals at my table."

Shuffling and stammering, not looking him in the eye, Mephibosheth said, "Who am I that you pay attention to a stray dog like me?"

David then called in Ziba, Saul's right-hand man, and told him, "Everything that belonged to Saul and his family, I've handed over to your master's grandson. You and your sons and your servants will work his land and bring in the produce, provisions for your master's grandson. Mephibosheth himself, your master's grandson, from now on will take all his meals at my table." Ziba had fifteen sons and twenty servants.

"All that my master the king has ordered his servant," answered Ziba, "your servant will surely do."

And Mephibosheth ate at David's table, just like one of the royal family. Mephibosheth also had a small son named Mica. All who were part of Ziba's household were now the servants of Mephibosheth.

Mephibosheth lived in Jerusalem, taking all his meals at the king's table. He was lame in both feet.

10 Sometime after this, the king of the Ammonites died and Hanun, his son, succeeded him as king. David said, "I'd like to show some kindness to Hanun, the son of Nahash—treat him as well and as kindly as his father treated me." So David sent Hanun condolences regarding his father.

But when David's servants got to the land of the Ammonites, the Ammonite leaders warned Hanun, their head delegate, "Do you for a minute suppose that David is honoring your father by sending you comforters? Don't you think it's because he wants to snoop around the city and size it up that David has sent his emissaries to you?"

So Hanun seized David's men, shaved off half their beards, cut off their robes halfway up their buttocks, and sent them packing.

When all this was reported to David, he sent someone to meet them, for they were seriously humiliated. The king told them, "Stay in Jericho until your beards grow out. Only then come back."

When it dawned on the Ammonites that as far as David was concerned they stunk to high heaven, they hired Aramean soldiers from Beth-Rehob and Zobah—twenty thousand infantry—and a thousand men from the king of Maacah, and twelve thousand men from Tob.

When David heard of this, he dispatched Joab with his strongest fighters in full force.

The Ammonites marched out and arranged themselves in battle formation at the city gate. The Arameans of Zobah and Rehob and the men of Tob and Maacah took up a position out in the open fields. When Joab saw that he had two fronts to fight, before and behind, he took his pick of the best of Israel and deployed them to confront the Arameans. The rest of the army he put under the command of Abishai, his brother, and deployed them to confront the Ammonites. Then he said, "If the Arameans are too much for me, you help me. And if the Ammonites prove too much for you, I'll come and help you. Courage! We'll fight with might and main for our people and for the cities of our God. And GOD will do whatever he sees needs doing!"

But when Joab and his soldiers moved in to fight the Arameans, they ran off in full retreat. Then the Ammonites, seeing the Arameans run for dear life, took to their heels from Abishai and went into the city.

So Joab left off fighting the Ammonites and returned to Jerusalem.

When the Arameans saw how badly they'd been beaten by Israel, they picked up the pieces and regrouped. Hadadezer sent for the Arameans who were across the River. They came to Helam. Shobach, commander of Hadadezer's army, led them. All this was reported to David.

So David mustered Israel, crossed the Jordan, and came to Helam. The Arameans went into battle formation, ready for David, and the fight was on. But the Arameans again scattered before Israel. David killed seven hundred chariot drivers and forty thousand cavalry. And he mortally wounded Shobach, the army commander, who died on the battlefield. When all the kings who were vassals of Hadadezer saw that they had been routed by Israel, they made peace and became Israel's vassals. The Arameans were afraid to help the Ammonites ever again.

DAVID'S SIN AND SORROW

11 When that time of year came around again, the anniversary of the Ammonite aggression, David dispatched Joab and his fighting men of Israel in full force to destroy the Ammonites for good. They laid siege to Rabbah, but David stayed in Jerusalem.

One late afternoon, David got up from taking his nap and was strolling on the roof of the palace. From his vantage point on the roof he saw a woman bathing. The woman was stunningly beautiful. David sent to ask about her, and was told, "Isn't this Bathsheba, daughter of Eliam and wife of Uriah the Hittite?" David sent his agents to get her. After she arrived, he went to bed with her. (This occurred during the time of "purification" following her period.) Then she returned home. Before long she realized she was pregnant.

Later she sent word to David: "I'm pregnant."

David then got in touch with Joab: "Send Uriah the Hittite to me." Joab sent him.

When he arrived, David asked him for news from the front — how things were going with Joab and the troops and with the fighting. Then he said to Uriah, "Go home. Have a refreshing bath and a good night's rest."

After Uriah left the palace, an informant of the king was sent after him. But Uriah didn't go home. He slept that night at the palace entrance, along with the king's servants.

David was told that Uriah had not gone home. He asked Uriah, "Didn't you just come off a hard trip? So why didn't you go home?"

Uriah replied to David, "The Chest is out there with the fighting men of Israel and Judah — in tents. My master Joab and his servants are roughing it out in the fields. So, how can I go home and eat and drink and enjoy my wife? On your life, I'll not do it!"

"All right," said David, "have it your way. Stay for the day and I'll send you back tomorrow." So Uriah stayed in Jerusalem the rest of the day.

The next day David invited him to eat and drink with him, and David got him drunk. But in the evening Uriah again went out and slept with his master's servants. He didn't go home.

In the morning David wrote a letter to Joab and sent it with Uriah. In the letter he wrote, "Put Uriah in the front lines where the fighting is the fiercest. Then pull back and leave him exposed so that he's sure to be killed."

So Joab, holding the city under siege, put Uriah in a place where he knew there were fierce enemy fighters. When the city's defenders came out to fight Joab, some of David's soldiers were killed, including Uriah the Hittite.

Joab sent David a full report on the battle. He instructed the messenger, "After you have given to the king a detailed report on the battle, if he flares in anger, say, 'And by the way, your servant Uriah the Hittite is dead.'"

Joab's messenger arrived in Jerusalem and gave the king a full report. He said, "The enemy was too much for us. They advanced on us in the open field, and we pushed them back to the city gate. But then arrows came hot and heavy on us from the city wall, and eighteen of the king's soldiers died."

When the messenger completed his report of the battle, David got angry at Joab. He vented it on the messenger: "Why did you get so close to the city? Didn't you know you'd be attacked from the wall? Didn't you remember how Abimelech son of Jerub-Besheth got killed? Wasn't it a woman who dropped a millstone on him from the wall and crushed him at Thebez? Why did you go close to the wall!"

"By the way," said Joab's messenger, "your servant Uriah the Hittite is dead."

Then David told the messenger, "Oh. I see. Tell Joab, 'Don't trouble yourself over this. War kills—sometimes one, sometimes another—you never know who's next. Redouble your assault on the city and destroy it.' Encourage Joab."

When Uriah's wife heard that her husband was dead, she grieved for her husband. When the time of mourning was over, David sent someone to bring her to his house. She became his wife and bore him a son.

12 But GOD was not at all pleased with what David had done, and sent Nathan to David. Nathan said to him, "There were two men in the same city—one rich, the other poor. The rich man had huge flocks of sheep, herds of cattle. The poor man had nothing but one little female lamb, which he had bought and raised. It grew up with him and his children as a member of the family. It ate off his plate and drank from his cup and slept on his bed. It was like a daughter to him.

"One day a traveler dropped in on the rich man. He was too stingy to take an animal from his own herds or flocks to make a meal for his visitor, so he took the poor man's lamb and prepared a meal to set before his guest."

David exploded in anger. "As surely as GOD lives," he said to Nathan, "the man who did this ought to be lynched! He must repay for the lamb four times over for his crime and his stinginess!"

"You're the man!" said Nathan. "And here's what GOD, the God of Israel, has to say to you: I made you king over Israel. I freed you from the fist of Saul. I gave you your master's daughter and other wives to have and to hold. I gave you both Israel and Judah. And if that hadn't been enough, I'd have gladly thrown in much more. So why have you treated the word of GOD with brazen contempt, doing this great evil? You murdered Uriah the Hittite, then took his wife as your wife. Worse, you killed him with an Ammonite sword! And now, because you treated God with such contempt and took Uriah the Hittite's wife as your wife, killing and murder will continually plague your family. This is GOD speaking, remember! I'll make trouble for you out of your own family. I'll take your wives from right out in front of you. I'll give them to some neighbor, and he'll go to bed with them openly. You did your deed in secret; I'm doing mine with the whole country watching!"

Then David confessed to Nathan, "I've sinned against GOD."

Nathan pronounced, "Yes, but that's not the last word. GOD forgives your sin. You won't die for it. But because of your blasphemous behavior, the son born to you will die."

After Nathan went home, GOD afflicted the child that Uriah's wife bore to David, and he came down sick. David prayed desperately to God for the little boy. He fasted, wouldn't go out, and slept on the floor. The elders in his family came in and tried to get him off the floor, but he wouldn't budge. Nor could they get him to eat anything. On the seventh day the child died. David's servants were afraid to tell him. They said, "What do we do now? While the child was living he wouldn't listen to a word we said. Now, with the child dead, if we speak to him there's no telling what he'll do."

David noticed that the servants were whispering behind his back, and realized that the boy must have died.

He asked the servants, "Is the boy dead?"

"Yes," they answered. "He's dead."

David got up from the floor, washed his face and combed his hair, put on a fresh change of clothes, then went into the sanctuary and worshiped. Then he came home and asked for something to eat. They set it before him and he ate.

His servants asked him, "What's going on with you? While the child was alive you fasted and wept and stayed up all night. Now that he's dead, you get up and eat."

"While the child was alive," he said, "I fasted and wept, thinking GOD might have mercy on me and the child would live. But now that he's dead, why fast? Can I bring him back now? I can go to him, but he can't come to me."

David went and comforted his wife Bathsheba. And when he slept with her, they conceived a son. When he was born they named him Solomon. GOD had a special love for him and sent word by Nathan the prophet that GOD wanted him named Jedidiah (God's Beloved).

180

✣

Joab, at war in Rabbah against the Ammonites, captured the royal city. He sent messengers to David saying, "I'm fighting at Rabbah, and I've just captured the city's water supply. Hurry and get the rest of the troops together and set up camp here at the city and complete the capture yourself. Otherwise, I'll capture it and get all the credit instead of you." So David marshaled all the troops, went to Rabbah, and fought and captured it. He took the crown from their king's head—very heavy with gold, and with a precious stone in it. It ended up on David's head. And they plundered the city, carrying off a great quantity of loot.

David emptied the city of its people and put them to slave labor using saws, picks, and axes, and making bricks. He did this to all the Ammonite cities. Then David and the whole army returned to Jerusalem.

13 Some time later, this happened: Absalom, David's son, had a sister who was very attractive. Her name was Tamar. Amnon, also David's son, was in love with her. Amnon was obsessed with his sister Tamar to the point of making himself sick over her. She was a virgin, so he couldn't see how he could get his hands on her. Amnon had a good friend, Jonadab, the son of David's brother Shimeah. Jonadab was exceptionally streetwise. He said to Amnon, "Why are you moping around like this, day after day—you, the son of the king! Tell me what's eating at you."

"In a word, Tamar," said Amnon. "My brother Absalom's sister. I'm in love with her."

"Here's what you do," said Jonadab. "Go to bed and pretend you're sick. When your father comes to visit you, say, 'Have my sister Tamar come and prepare some supper for me here where I can watch her and she can feed me.'"

So Amnon took to his bed and acted sick. When the king came to visit, Amnon said, "Would you do me a favor? Have my sister Tamar come and make some nourishing dumplings here where I can watch her and be fed by her."

David sent word to Tamar who was home at the time: "Go to the house of your brother Amnon and prepare a meal for him."

So Tamar went to her brother Amnon's house. She took dough, kneaded it, formed it into dumplings, and cooked them while he watched from his bed. But when she took the cooking pot and served him, he wouldn't eat.

Amnon said, "Clear everyone out of the house," and they all cleared out. Then he said to Tamar, "Bring the food into my bedroom, where we can eat in privacy." She took the nourishing dumplings she had prepared and brought them to her brother Amnon in his bedroom. But when she got ready to feed him, he grabbed her and said, "Come to bed with me, sister!"

"No, brother!" she said, "Don't hurt me! This kind of thing isn't done in Israel! Don't do this terrible thing! Where could I ever show my face? And you—you'll be out on the street in disgrace. Oh, please! Speak to the king—he'll let you marry me."

But he wouldn't listen. Being much stronger than she, he raped her.

No sooner had Amnon raped her than he hated her—an immense hatred. The hatred that he felt for her was greater than the love he'd had for her. "Get up," he said, "and get out!"

"Oh no, brother," she said. "Please! This is an even worse evil than what you just did to me!"

But he wouldn't listen to her. He called for his valet. "Get rid of this woman. Get her out of my sight! And lock the door after her." The valet threw her out and locked the door behind her.

She was wearing a long-sleeved gown. (That's how virgin princesses used to dress from early adolescence on.) Tamar poured ashes on her head, then she ripped the long-sleeved gown, held her head in her hands, and walked away, sobbing as she went.

Her brother Absalom said to her, "Has your brother Amnon had his way with you? Now, my dear sister, let's keep it quiet—a family matter. He is, after all, your brother. Don't take this so hard." Tamar lived in her brother Absalom's home, bitter and desolate.

King David heard the whole story and was enraged, but he didn't discipline Amnon. David doted on him because he was his firstborn. Absalom quit speaking to Amnon—not a word, whether good or bad—because he hated him for violating his sister Tamar.

Two years went by. One day Absalom threw a sheep-shearing party in Baal Hazor in the vicinity of Ephraim and invited all the king's sons. He also went to the king and invited him. "Look, I'm throwing a sheep-shearing party. Come, and bring your servants."

But the king said, "No, son—not this time, and not the whole household. We'd just be a burden to you." Absalom pushed, but David wouldn't budge. But he did give him his blessing.

Then Absalom said, "Well, if you won't come, at least let my brother Amnon come."

"And why," said the king, "should he go with you?" But Absalom was so insistent that he gave in and let Amnon and all the rest of the king's sons go.

Absalom prepared a banquet fit for a king. Then he instructed his servants, "Look sharp, now. When Amnon is well into the sauce and feeling no pain, and I give the order 'Strike Amnon,' kill him. And don't be afraid—I'm the one giving the command. Courage! You can do it!"

Absalom's servants did to Amnon exactly what their master ordered. All the king's sons got out as fast as they could, jumped on their mules, and rode off. While they were still on the road, a rumor came to the king: "Absalom just killed all the king's sons—not one is left!" The king stood up, ripped his clothes to shreds, and threw himself on the floor. All his servants who were standing around at the time did the same.

Just then, Jonadab, his brother Shimeah's son, stepped up. "My master must not think that all the young men, the king's sons, are dead. Only Amnon is dead. This happened because of Absalom's outrage since the day that Amnon violated his sister Tamar. So my master, the king, mustn't make things worse than they are, thinking that all your sons are dead. Only Amnon is dead."

Absalom fled.

Just then the sentry on duty looked up and saw a cloud of dust on the road from Horonaim alongside the mountain. He came and told the king, "I've just seen a bunch of men on the Horonaim road, coming around the mountain."

Then Jonadab exclaimed to the king, "See! It's the king's sons coming, just as I said!" He had no sooner said the words than the king's sons burst in—loud laments and weeping! The king joined in, along with all the servants—loud weeping, many tears. David mourned the death of his son a long time.

When Absalom fled, he went to Talmai son of Ammihud, king of Geshur. He was there three years. The king finally gave up trying to get back at Absalom. He had come to terms with Amnon's death.

14 Joab son of Zeruiah knew that the king, deep down, still cared for Absalom. So he sent to Tekoa for a wise woman who lived

there and instructed her, "Pretend you are in mourning. Dress in black and don't comb your hair, so you'll look like you've been grieving over a dead loved one for a long time. Then go to the king and tell him this . . ." Joab then told her exactly what to say.

The woman of Tekoa went to the king, bowed deeply before him in homage, and said, "O King, help!"

He said, "How can I help?"

"I'm a widow," she said. "My husband is dead. I had two sons. The two of them got into a fight out in the field and there was no one around to step between them. The one struck the other and killed him. Then the whole family ganged up against me and demanded, 'Hand over this murderer so we can kill him for the life of the brother he murdered!' They want to wipe out the heir and snuff out the one spark of life left to me. And then there would be nothing left of my husband—not so much as a name—on the face of the earth.

"So now I've dared come to the king, my master, about all this. They're making my life miserable, and I'm afraid. I said to myself, 'I'll go to the king. Maybe he'll do something! When the king hears what's going on, he'll step in and rescue me from the abuse of the man who would get rid of me and my son and God's inheritance—the works!' As your handmaid, I decided ahead of time, 'The word of my master, the king, will be the last word in this, for my master is like an angel of God in discerning good and evil.' GOD be with you!"

The king said, "Go home, and I'll take care of this for you."

"I'll take all responsibility for what happens," the woman of Tekoa said. "I don't want to compromise the king and his reputation."

"Bring the man who has been harassing you," the king continued. "I'll see to it that he doesn't bother you anymore."

"Let the king invoke the name of GOD," said the woman, "so this self-styled vigilante won't ruin everything, to say nothing of killing my son."

"As surely as GOD lives," he said, "not so much as a hair of your son's head will be lost."

Then she asked, "May I say one more thing to my master, the king?"

He said, "Go ahead."

"Why, then," the woman said, "have you done this very thing against God's people? In his verdict, the king convicts himself by not bringing home his exiled son. We all die sometime. Water spilled on the ground can't be gathered up again. But God does not take away life. He works out ways to get the exile back."

The king then said, "I'm going to ask you something. Answer me truthfully."

"Certainly," she said. "Let my master, the king, speak."

The king said, "Is the hand of Joab mixed up in this?"

"On your life, my master king, a body can't veer an inch right or left and get by with it in the royal presence! Yes, it was your servant Joab who put me up to this, and put these very words in my mouth. It was because he wanted to turn things around that your servant Joab did this. But my master is as wise as God's angels in knowing how to handle things on this earth."

The king spoke to Joab. "All right, I'll do it. Go and bring the young man Absalom back."

Joab bowed deeply in reverence and blessed the king. "I'm reassured to know that I'm still in your good graces and have your confidence, since the king is taking the counsel of his servant."

Joab got up, went to Geshur, and brought Absalom to Jerusalem. The king said, "He may return to his house, but he is not to see me face to face." So Absalom returned home, but was not permitted to see the king.

This Absalom! There wasn't a man in all Israel talked about so much for his handsome good looks—and not a blemish on him from head to toe! When he cut his hair—he always cut it short in the spring because it had grown so heavy—the weight of the hair from his head was over two pounds! Three sons were born to Absalom, and one daughter. Her name was Tamar—and she was a beauty.

Absalom lived in Jerusalem for two years, and not once did he see the king face to face. He sent for Joab to get him in to see the king, but Joab still wouldn't budge. He tried a second time and Joab still wouldn't. So he told his servants, "Listen. Joab's field adjoins mine, and he has a crop of barley in it. Go set fire to it." So Absalom's servants set fire to the field. That got him moving—Joab came to Absalom at home and said, "Why did your servants set my field on fire?"

Absalom answered him, "Listen, I sent for you saying, 'Come, and soon. I want to send you to the king to ask, "What's the point of my coming back from Geshur? I'd be better off still there!" Let me see the king face to face. If he finds me guilty, then he can put me to death.'"

Joab went to the king and told him what was going on. Absalom was then summoned—he came and bowed deeply in reverence before him. And the king kissed Absalom.

15 As time went on, Absalom took to riding in a horse-drawn chariot, with fifty men running in front of him. Early each morning he would take up his post beside the road at the city gate. When anyone showed up with a case to bring to the king for a decision, Absalom would call him over and say, "Where do you hail from?"

And the answer would come, "Your servant is from one of the tribes of Israel."

Then Absalom would say, "Look, you've got a strong case; but the king isn't going to listen to you." Then he'd say, "Why doesn't someone make me a judge for this country? Anybody with a case could bring it to me and I'd settle things fair and square." Whenever someone would treat him with special honor, he'd shrug it off and treat him like an equal, making him feel important. Absalom did this to everyone who came to do business with the king and stole the hearts of everyone in Israel.

After four years of this, Absalom spoke to the king, "Let me go to Hebron to pay a vow that I made to GOD. Your servant made a vow when I was living in Geshur in Aram saying, 'If GOD will bring me back to Jerusalem, I'll serve him with my life.'"

The king said, "Go with my blessing." And he got up and set off for Hebron.

Then Absalom sent undercover agents to all the tribes of Israel with the message, "When you hear the blast of the ram's horn trumpet, that's your signal: Shout, 'Absalom is king in Hebron!'" Two hundred men went with Absalom from Jerusalem. But they had been called together knowing nothing of the plot and made the trip innocently. While Absalom was offering sacrifices, he managed also to involve Ahithophel the Gilonite, David's advisor, calling him away from his home town of Giloh. The conspiracy grew powerful and Absalom's supporters multiplied.

Someone came to David with the report, "The whole country has taken up with Absalom!"

"Up and out of here!" called David to all his servants who were with him in Jerusalem. "We've got to run for our lives or none of us will escape Absalom! Hurry, he's about to pull the city down around our ears and slaughter us all!"

The king's servants said, "Whatever our master, the king, says, we'll do; we're with you all the way!"

So the king and his entire household escaped on foot. The king left ten concubines behind to tend to the palace. And so they left, step by step by step, and then paused at the last house as the whole army passed by him—all the Kerethites, all the Pelethites, and the six hundred Gittites who had marched with him from Gath, went past.

The king called out to Ittai the Gittite, "What are you doing here? Go back with King Absalom. You're a stranger here and freshly uprooted from your own country. You arrived only yesterday, and am I going to let you take your chances with us as I live on the road like a gypsy? Go back, and take your family with you. And God's grace and truth go with you!"

But Ittai answered, "As GOD lives and my master the king lives, where my master is, that's where I'll be—whether it means life or death."

"All right," said David, "go ahead." And they went on, Ittai the Gittite with all his men and all the children he had with him.

The whole country was weeping in loud lament as all the people passed by. As the king crossed the Brook Kidron, the army headed for the road to the wilderness. Zadok was also there, the Levites with him, carrying GOD's Chest of the Covenant. They set the Chest of God down, Abiathar standing by, until all the people had evacuated the city.

Then the king ordered Zadok, "Take the Chest back to the city. If I get back in GOD's good graces, he'll bring me back and show me where the Chest has been set down. But if he says, 'I'm not pleased with you'—well, he can then do with me whatever he pleases."

The king directed Zadok the priest, "Here's the plan: Return to the city peacefully, with Ahimaaz your son and Jonathan, Abiathar's son, with you. I'll wait at a spot in the wilderness across the river, until I get word from you telling us what's up." So Zadok and Abiathar took the Chest of God back to Jerusalem and placed it there, while David went up the Mount of Olives weeping, head covered but barefooted, and the whole army was with him, heads covered and weeping as they ascended.

David was told, "Ahithophel has joined the conspirators with Absalom." He prayed, "Oh, GOD—turn Ahithophel's counsel to foolishness."

As David approached the top of the hill where God was worshiped, Hushai the Arkite, clothes ripped to shreds and dirt on his head, was there waiting for him. David said, "If you come with me, you'll be just one more piece of luggage. Go back to the city and say to Absalom, 'I'm ready to be your servant, O King; I used to be your father's servant, now I'm your servant.' Do that and you'll be able to confuse Ahithophel's counsel for me. The priests Zadok and Abiathar are already there; whatever information you pick up in the palace, tell them. Their two sons—Zadok's son Ahimaaz and Abiathar's son Jonathan—are there with them—anything you pick up can be sent to me by them."

Hushai, David's friend, arrived at the same time Absalom was entering Jerusalem.

16 Shortly after David passed the crest of the hill, Mephibosheth's steward Ziba met him with a string of pack animals, saddled and loaded with a hundred loaves of bread, a hundred raisin cakes, a hundred baskets of fresh fruit, and a skin of wine.

The king said to Ziba, "What's all this?"

"The donkeys," said Ziba, "are for the king's household to ride, the bread and fruit are for the servants to eat, and the wine is for drinking, especially for those overcome by fatigue in the wilderness."

The king said, "And where is your master's grandson?"

"He stayed in Jerusalem," said Ziba. "He said, 'This is the day Israel is going to restore my grandfather's kingdom to me.'"

"Everything that belonged to Mephibosheth," said the king, "is now yours."

Ziba said, "How can I ever thank you? I'll be forever in your debt, my master and king; may you always look on me with such kindness!"

When the king got to Bahurim, a man appeared who had connections with Saul's family. His name was Shimei son of Gera. As he followed along he shouted insults and threw rocks right and left at David and his company, servants and soldiers alike. To the accompaniment of curses he shouted, "Get lost, get lost, you butcher, you hellhound! GOD has paid you back for all your dirty work in the family of Saul and for stealing his kingdom. GOD has given the kingdom to your son Absalom. Look at you now—ruined! And good riddance, you pathetic old man!"

Abishai son of Zeruiah said, "This mangy dog can't insult my master the king this way—let me go over and cut off his head!"

But the king said, "Why are you sons of Zeruiah always interfering and getting in the way? If he's cursing, it's because GOD told him, 'Curse David.' So who dares raise questions?"

"Besides," continued David to Abishai and the rest of his servants, "my own son, my flesh and bone, is right now trying to kill me; compared to that this Benjaminite is small potatoes. Don't bother with him; let him curse; he's preaching GOD's word to me. And who knows, maybe GOD will see the trouble I'm in today and exchange the curses for something good."

David and his men went on down the road, while Shimei followed along on the ridge of the hill alongside, cursing, throwing stones down on them, and kicking up dirt.

By the time they reached the Jordan River, David and all the men of the company were exhausted. There they rested and were revived.

By this time Absalom and all his men were in Jerusalem.

And Ahithophel was with them.

Soon after, Hushai the Arkite, David's friend, came and greeted Absalom, "Long live the king! Long live the king!"

Absalom said to Hushai, "Is this the way you show devotion to your good friend? Why didn't you go with your friend David?"

"Because," said Hushai, "I want to be with the person that GOD and this people and all Israel have chosen. And I want to stay with him. Besides, who is there to serve other than the son? Just as I served your father, I'm now ready to serve you."

Then Absalom spoke to Ahithophel, "Are you ready to give counsel? What do we do next?"

Ahithophel told Absalom, "Go and sleep with your father's concubines, the ones he left to tend to the palace. Everyone will hear that you have openly disgraced your father, and the morale of everyone on your side will be strengthened." So Absalom pitched a tent up on the roof in public view, and went in and slept with his father's concubines.

The counsel that Ahithophel gave in those days was treated as if God himself had spoken. That was the reputation of Ahithophel's counsel to David; it was the same with Absalom.

17 Next Ahithophel advised Absalom, "Let me handpick twelve thousand men and go after David tonight. I'll come on him when he's bone tired and take him by complete surprise. The whole army will run off and I'll kill only David. Then I'll bring the army back to you—a bride brought back to her husband! You're only after one man, after all. Then everyone will be together in peace!"

Absalom thought it was an excellent strategy, and all the elders of Israel agreed.

But then Absalom said, "Call in Hushai the Arkite—let's hear what he has to say."

So Hushai came and Absalom put it to him, "This is what Ahithophel advised. Should we do it? What do you say?"

Hushai said, "The counsel that Ahithophel has given in this instance is not good. You know your father and his men, brave and bitterly angry—like a bear robbed of her cubs. And your father is an experienced fighter; you can be sure he won't be caught napping at a time like this. Even while we're talking, he's probably holed up in some cave or other. If he jumps your men from ambush, word will soon get back, 'A slaughter of Absalom's army!' Even if your men are valiant with hearts of lions, they'll fall apart at such news, for everyone in Israel knows the kind of fighting stuff your father's made of, and also the men with him.

"Here's what I'd advise: Muster the whole country, from Dan to Beersheba, an army like the sand of the sea, and you personally lead them. We'll smoke him out wherever he is, fall on him like dew falls on the earth, and, believe me, there won't be a single survivor. If he hides out in a city, then the whole army will bring ropes to that city and pull it down and into a gully—not so much as a pebble left of it!"

Absalom and all his company agreed that the counsel of Hushai the Arkite was better than the counsel of Ahithophel. (GOD had determined to discredit the counsel of Ahithophel so as to bring ruin on Absalom.)

Then Hushai told the priests Zadok and Abiathar, "Ahithophel advised Absalom and the elders of Israel thus and thus, and I advised them thus and thus. Now send this message as quickly as possible to David: 'Don't spend the night on this side of the river; cross immediately or the king and everyone with him will be swallowed up alive.'"

Jonathan and Ahimaaz were waiting around at En Rogel. A servant girl would come and give them messages and then they would go and tell King David, for it wasn't safe to be seen coming into the city. But a soldier spotted them and told Absalom, so the two of them got out of there fast and went to a man's house in Bahurim. He had a well in his yard and they climbed into it. The wife took a rug and covered the well, then spread grain on it so no one would notice anything out of the ordinary. Shortly, Absalom's servants came to the woman's house and asked her, "Have you seen Ahimaaz and Jonathan?"

The woman said, "They were headed toward the river."

They looked but didn't find them, and then went back to Jerusalem. When the coast was clear, Ahimaaz and Jonathan climbed out of the well and went on to make their report to King David, "Get up and cross the river quickly; Ahithophel has given counsel against you!"

David and his whole army were soon up and moving and crossed the Jordan. As morning broke there was not a single person who had not made it across the Jordan.

When Ahithophel realized that his counsel was not followed, he saddled his donkey and left for his home town. After making out his will and putting his house in order, he hanged himself and died. He was buried in the family tomb.

About the time David arrived at Mahanaim, Absalom crossed the Jordan, and the whole army of Israel with him. Absalom had made Amasa head of the army, replacing Joab. (Amasa was the son of a man named Ithra, an Ishmaelite who had married Abigail, daughter of Nahash and sister of Zeruiah, the mother of Joab.) Israel and Absalom set camp in Gilead.

When David arrived at Mahanaim, Shobi son of Nahash from Ammonite Rabbah, and Makir son of Ammiel from Lo Debar, and Barzillai the Gileadite from Rogelim brought beds and blankets, bowls and jugs filled with wheat, barley, flour, roasted grain, beans and lentils, honey, and curds and cheese from the flocks and herds. They presented all this to David and his army to eat, "because," they said, "the army must be starved and exhausted and thirsty out in this wilderness."

18 David organized his forces. He appointed captains of thousands and captains of hundreds. Then David deployed his troops, a third under Joab, a third under Abishai son of Zeruiah, Joab's brother, and a third under Ittai the Gittite.

The king then announced, "I'm marching with you."

They said, "No, you mustn't march with us. If we're forced to retreat, the enemy won't give it a second thought. And if half of us die, they won't do so either. But you are worth ten thousand of us. It will be better for us if you stay in the city and help from there."

"If you say so," said the king. "I'll do what you think is best." And so he stood beside the city gate as the whole army marched out by hundreds and by thousands.

Then the king ordered Joab and Abishai and Ittai, "Deal gently for my sake with the young man Absalom." The whole army heard what the king commanded the three captains regarding Absalom.

The army took the field to meet Israel. It turned out that the battle was joined in the Forest of Ephraim. The army of Israel was beaten badly there that day by David's men, a terrific slaughter—twenty thousand men! There was fighting helter-skelter all over the place—the forest claimed more lives that day than the sword!

Absalom ran into David's men, but was out in front of them riding his mule, when the mule ran under the branches of a huge oak tree. Absalom's head was caught in the oak and he was left dangling between heaven and earth, the mule running right out from under him. A solitary soldier saw him and reported it to Joab, "I just saw Absalom hanging from an oak tree!"

Joab said to the man who told him, "If you saw him, why didn't you kill him then and there? I'd have rewarded you with ten pieces of silver and a fancy belt."

The man told Joab, "Even if I'd had a chance at a thousand pieces of silver, I wouldn't have laid a hand on the king's son. We all heard the king command you and Abishai and Ittai, 'For my sake, protect the young man Absalom.' Why, I'd be risking my life, for nothing is hidden from the king. And you would have just stood there!"

Joab said, "I can't waste my time with you." He then grabbed three knives and stabbed Absalom in the heart while he was still alive in the tree; by then Absalom was surrounded by ten of Joab's armor bearers; they hacked away at him and killed him.

Joab then blew the ram's horn trumpet, calling off the army in its pursuit of Israel. They took Absalom, dumped him into a huge pit in the forest, and piled an immense mound of rocks over him.

Meanwhile the whole army of Israel was in flight, each man making his own way home.

While alive, Absalom had erected for himself a pillar in the Valley of the King, "because," he said, "I have no son to carry on my name." He inscribed the pillar with his own name. To this day it is called "The Absalom Memorial."

Ahimaaz, Zadok's son, said, "Let me run to the king and bring him the good news that GOD has delivered him from his enemies." But Joab said, "You're not the one to deliver the good news today; some other day, maybe, but it's not 'good news' today." (This was because the king's son was dead.)

Then Joab ordered a Cushite, "You go. Tell the king what you've seen."

"Yes sir," said the Cushite, and ran off.

Ahimaaz son of Zadok kept at it, begging Joab, "What does it matter? Let me run too, following the Cushite."

Joab said, "Why all this 'Run, run'? You'll get no thanks for it, I can tell you."

"I don't care; let me run."

"Okay," said Joab, "run." So Ahimaaz ran, taking the lower valley road, and passed the Cushite.

David was sitting between the two gates. The sentry had gone up to the top of the gate on the wall and looked around. He saw a solitary runner. The sentry called down and told the king. The king said, "If he's alone, it must be good news!"

As the runner came closer, the sentry saw another runner and called down to the gate, "Another runner all by himself."

And the king said, "This also must be good news."

Then the sentry said, "I can see the first man now; he runs like Ahimaaz son of Zadok."

"He's a good man," said the king. "He's bringing good news for sure."

Then Ahimaaz called out and said to the king, "Peace!" Then he bowed deeply before the king, his face to the ground. "Blessed be your GOD; he has handed over the men who rebelled against my master the king."

The king asked, "But is the young man Absalom all right?"

Ahimaaz said, "I saw a huge ruckus just as Joab was sending me off, but I don't know what it was about."

The king said, "Step aside and stand over there." So he stepped aside.

Then the Cushite arrived and said, "Good news, my master and king! GOD has given victory today over all those who rebelled against you!"

"But," said the king, "is the young man Absalom all right?"

And the Cushite replied, "Would that all of the enemies of my master the king and all who maliciously rose against you end up like that young man."

The king was stunned. Heartbroken, he went up to the room over the gate and wept. As he wept he cried out,

O my son Absalom, my dear, dear son Absalom!
Why not me rather than you, my death and not yours,
O Absalom, my dear, dear son!

DAVID'S GRIEF FOR ABSALOM

19 Joab was told that David was weeping and lamenting over Absalom. The day's victory turned into a day of mourning as word passed through the army, "David is grieving over his son." The army straggled back to the city that day demoralized, dragging their tails. And the king held his face in his hands and lamented loudly,

> Oh my son Absalom,
> Absalom my dear, dear son!

But in private Joab rebuked the king: "Now you've done it— knocked the wind out of your loyal servants who have just saved your life, to say nothing of the lives of your sons and daughters, wives and concubines. What is this—loving those who hate you and hating those who love you? Your actions give a clear message: officers and soldiers mean nothing to you. You know that if Absalom were alive right now, we'd all be dead—would that make you happy? Get hold of yourself; get out there and put some heart into your servants! I swear to GOD that if you don't go to them they'll desert; not a soldier will be left here by nightfall. And that will be the worst thing that has happened yet."

So the king came out and took his place at the city gate. Soon everyone knew: "Oh, look! The king has come out to receive us." And his whole army came and presented itself to the king. But the Israelites had fled the field of battle and gone home.

Meanwhile, the whole populace was now complaining to its leaders, "Wasn't it the king who saved us time and again from our enemies, and rescued us from the Philistines? And now he has had to flee the country on account of Absalom. And now this Absalom whom we made king is dead in battle. So what are you waiting for? Why don't you bring the king back?"

When David heard what was being said, he sent word to Zadok and Abiathar, the priests, "Ask the elders of Judah, 'Why are you so laggard in bringing the king back home? You're my brothers! You're my own flesh and blood! So why are you the last ones to bring the king back home?' And tell Amasa, 'You, too, are my flesh and blood. As God is my witness, I'm making you the permanent commander of the army in place of Joab.'"

He captured the hearts of everyone in Judah. They were unanimous in sending for the king: "Come back, you and all your servants."

So the king returned. He arrived at the Jordan just as Judah reached Gilgal on their way to welcome the king and escort him across the Jordan. Even Shimei son of Gera, the Benjaminite from Bahurim, hurried down to join the men of Judah so he could welcome the king, a thousand Benjaminites with him. And Ziba, Saul's steward, with his fifteen sons and twenty servants, waded across the Jordan to meet the king and brought his entourage across, doing whatever they could to make the king comfortable.

Shimei son of Gera bowed deeply in homage to the king as soon as he was across the Jordan and said, "Don't think badly of me, my master! Overlook my irresponsible outburst on the day my master the king left Jerusalem—don't hold it against me! I know I sinned, but look at me now—the first of all the tribe of Joseph to come down and welcome back my master the king!"

Abishai son of Zeruiah interrupted, "Enough of this! Shouldn't we kill him outright? Why, he cursed GOD's anointed!"

But David said, "What is it with you sons of Zeruiah? Why do you insist on being so contentious? Nobody is going to be killed today. I am again king over Israel!"

Then the king turned to Shimei, "You're not going to die." And the king gave him his word.

Next Mephibosheth grandson of Saul arrived from Jerusalem to welcome the king. He hadn't combed his hair or trimmed his beard or washed his clothes from the day the king left until the day he returned safe and sound. The king said, "And why didn't you come with me, Mephibosheth?"

"My master the king," he said, "my servant betrayed me. I told him to saddle my donkey so I could ride it and go with the king, for, as you know, I am lame. And then he lied to you about me. But my master the king has been like one of God's angels: he knew what was right and did it. Wasn't everyone in my father's house doomed? But you took me in and gave me a place at your table. What more could I ever expect or ask?"

"That's enough," said the king. "Say no more. Here's my decision: You and Ziba divide the property between you."

Mephibosheth said, "Oh, let him have it all! All I care about is that my master the king is home safe and sound!"

Barzillai the Gileadite had come down from Rogelim. He crossed the Jordan with the king to give him a good send-off. Barzillai was a very old man—eighty years old! He had supplied the king's needs all the while he was in Mahanaim since he was very wealthy.

"Join me in Jerusalem," the king said to Barzillai. "Let me take care of you."

But Barzillai declined the offer, "How long do you think I'd live if I went with the king to Jerusalem? I'm eighty years old and not much good anymore to anyone. Can't taste food; can't hear music. So why add to the burdens of my master the king? I'll just go a little way across the Jordan with the king. But why would the king need to make a great thing of that? Let me go back and die in my home town and be buried with my father and mother. But my servant Kimham here; let him go with you in my place. But treat him well!"

The king said, "That's settled; Kimham goes with me. And I will treat him well! If you think of anything else, I'll do that for you, too."

The army crossed the Jordan but the king stayed. The king kissed and blessed Barzillai, who then returned home. Then the king, Kimham with him, crossed over at Gilgal.

The whole army of Judah and half the army of Israel processed with the king. The men of Israel came to the king and said, "Why have our brothers, the men of Judah, taken over as if they owned the king, escorting the king and his family and close associates across the Jordan?"

The men of Judah retorted, "Because the king is related to us, that's why! But why make a scene? You don't see us getting treated special because of it, do you?"

The men of Israel shot back, "We have ten shares in the king to your one. Besides we're the firstborn—so why are we having to play second fiddle? It was our idea to bring him back."

But the men of Judah took a harder line than the men of Israel.

20 Just then a good-for-nothing named Sheba son of Bicri the Benjaminite blew a blast on the ram's horn trumpet, calling out,

We've got nothing to do with David,
    there's no future for us with the son of Jesse!
Let's get out of here, Israel—head for your tents!

So all the men of Israel deserted David and followed Sheba son of Bicri. But the men of Judah stayed committed, sticking with their king all the way from the Jordan to Jerusalem. When David arrived home in Jerusalem, the king took the ten concubines he had left to watch the palace and placed them in seclusion, under guard. He provided for their needs but didn't visit them. They were virtual prisoners until they died, widows as long as they lived.

The king ordered Amasa, "Muster the men of Judah for me in three days; then report in." Amasa went to carry out his orders, but he was late reporting back. So David told Abishai, "Sheba son of Bicri is going to hurt us even worse than Absalom did. Take your master's servants and hunt him down before he gets holed up in some fortress city where we can't get to him." So under Abishai's command, all the best men — Joab's men and the Kerethites and Pelethites — left Jerusalem to hunt down Sheba son of Bicri. They were near the boulder at Gibeon when Amasa came their way. Joab was wearing a tunic with a sheathed sword strapped on his waist, but the sword slipped out and fell to the ground. Joab greeted Amasa, "How are you, brother?" and took Amasa's beard in his right hand as if to kiss him. Amasa didn't notice the sword in Joab's other hand. Joab stuck him in the belly and his guts spilled to the ground. A second blow wasn't needed; he was dead. Then Joab and his brother Abishai continued to chase Sheba son of Bicri.

One of Joab's soldiers took up his post over the body and called out, "Everyone who sides with Joab and supports David, follow Joab!" Amasa was lying in a pool of blood in the middle of the road; the man realized that the whole army was going to stop and take a look, so he pulled Amasa's corpse off the road into the field and threw a blanket over him so it wouldn't collect spectators. As soon as he'd gotten him off the road, the traffic flowed normally, following Joab in the chase after Sheba son of Bicri. Sheba passed through all the tribes of Israel as far as Abel Beth Maacah; all the Bicrites clustered and followed him into the city.

Joab's army arrived and laid siege to Sheba in Abel Beth Maacah. They built a siege-ramp up against the city's fortification. The plan was to knock down the wall.

But a shrewd woman called out from the city, "Listen, everybody! Please tell Joab to come close so I can talk to him." When he had come, the woman said, "Are you Joab?"

He said, "I am."

"Then," she said, "listen to what I have to say."

He said, "I'm listening."

"There's an old saying in these parts: 'If it's answers you want, come to Abel and get it straight.' We're a peaceful people here, and reliable. And here you are, trying to tear down one of Israel's mother cities. Why would you want to mess with GOD's legacy like that?"

Joab protested, "Believe me, you've got me all wrong. I'm not here to hurt anyone or destroy anything — not on your life! But a man from the hill country of Ephraim, Sheba son of Bicri by name, revolted against King David; hand him over, him only, and we'll get out of here."

The woman told Joab, "Sounds good. His head will be tossed to you from the wall."

The woman presented her strategy to the whole city and they did it: They cut off the head of Sheba son of Bicri and tossed it down to Joab. He then blew a blast on the ram's horn trumpet and the soldiers all went home. Joab returned to the king in Jerusalem.

Joab was again commander of the whole army of Israel. Benaiah son of Jehoiada was over the Kerethites and Pelethites; Adoniram over the work crews; Jehoshaphat son of Ahilud was clerk; Sheva was historian; Zadok and Abiathar were priests; Ira the Jairite was David's chaplain.

FAMINE AND WAR

21 There was a famine in David's time. It went on year after year after year — three years. David went to GOD seeking the reason.

GOD said, "This is because there is blood on Saul and his house, from the time he massacred the Gibeonites."

So the king called the Gibeonites together for consultation. (The Gibeonites were not part of Israel; they were what was left of the Amorites, and protected by a treaty with Israel. But Saul, a fanatic for the honor of Israel and Judah, tried to kill them off.)

David addressed the Gibeonites: "What can I do for you? How can I compensate you so that you will bless GOD's legacy of land and people?"

The Gibeonites replied, "We don't want any money from Saul and his family. And it's not up to us to put anyone in Israel to death."

But David persisted: "What are you saying I should do for you?"

Then they told the king, "The man who tried to get rid of us, who schemed to wipe us off the map of Israel — well, let seven of his sons be handed over to us to be executed — hanged before GOD at Gibeah of Saul, the holy mountain."

And David agreed, "I'll hand them over to you."

The king spared Mephibosheth son of Jonathan, the son of Saul, because of the promise David and Jonathan had spoken before GOD. But the king selected Armoni and Mephibosheth, the two sons that Rizpah daughter of Aiah had borne to Saul, plus the five sons that Saul's daughter

Merab had borne to Adriel son of Barzillai the Meholathite. He turned them over to the Gibeonites who hanged them on the mountain before GOD—all seven died together. Harvest was just getting underway, the beginning of the barley harvest, when they were executed.

Rizpah daughter of Aiah took rough burlap and spread it out for herself on a rock from the beginning of the harvest until the heavy rains started. She kept the birds away from the bodies by day and the wild animals by night.

David was told what she had done, this Rizpah daughter of Aiah and concubine of Saul. He then went and got the remains of Saul and Jonathan his son from the leaders at Jabesh Gilead (who had rescued them from the town square at Beth Shan where the Philistines had hung them after striking them down at Gilboa). He gathered up their remains and brought them together with the dead bodies of the seven who had just been hanged. The bodies were taken back to the land of Benjamin and given a decent burial in the tomb of Kish, Saul's father.

They did everything the king ordered to be done. That cleared things up: from then on God responded to Israel's prayers for the land.

War broke out again between the Philistines and Israel. David and his men went down to fight. David became exhausted. Ishbi-Benob, a warrior descended from Rapha, with a spear weighing nearly eight pounds and outfitted in brand-new armor, announced that he'd kill David. But Abishai son of Zeruiah came to the rescue, struck the Philistine, and killed him.

Then David's men swore to him, "No more fighting on the front-lines for you! Don't snuff out the lamp of Israel!"

Later there was another skirmish with the Philistines at Gob. That time Sibbecai the Hushathite killed Saph, another of the warriors descended from Rapha.

At yet another battle with the Philistines at Gob, Elhanan son of Jaar, the weaver of Bethlehem, killed Goliath the Gittite whose spear was as big as a flagpole.

Still another fight broke out in Gath. There was a giant there with six fingers on his hands and six toes on his feet—twenty-four fingers and toes! He was another of those descended from Rapha. He insulted Israel, and Jonathan son of Shimeah, David's brother, killed him.

These four were descended from Rapha in Gath. And they all were killed by David and his soldiers.

22 David prayed to GOD the words of this song after GOD saved him from all his enemies and from Saul.

GOD is bedrock under my feet,
    the castle in which I live,
    my rescuing knight.
My God—the high crag
    where I run for dear life,
    hiding behind the boulders,
    safe in the granite hideout;
My mountaintop refuge,
    he saves me from ruthless men.

I sing to GOD the Praise-Lofty,
    and find myself safe and saved.

The waves of death crashed over me,
    devil waters rushed over me.
Hell's ropes cinched me tight;
    death traps barred every exit.

A hostile world! I called to GOD,
    to my God I cried out.
From his palace he heard me call;
    my cry brought me right into his presence—
    a private audience!

Earth wobbled and lurched;
    the very heavens shook like leaves,
Quaked like aspen leaves
    because of his rage.
His nostrils flared, billowing smoke;
    his mouth spit fire.
Tongues of fire darted in and out;
    he lowered the sky.
He stepped down;
    under his feet an abyss opened up.
He rode a winged creature,
    swift on wind-wings.

He wrapped himself
    in a trenchcoat of black rain-cloud darkness.
But his cloud-brightness burst through,
    a grand comet of fireworks.
Then GOD thundered out of heaven;
    the High God gave a great shout.
God shot his arrows—pandemonium!
    He hurled his lightnings—a rout!
The secret sources of ocean were exposed,
    the hidden depths of earth lay uncovered
The moment GOD roared in protest,
    let loose his hurricane anger.

But me he caught—reached all the way
    from sky to sea; he pulled me out
Of that ocean of hate, that enemy chaos,
    the void in which I was drowning.
They hit me when I was down,
    but GOD stuck by me.
He stood me up on a wide-open field;
    I stood there saved—surprised to be loved!

GOD made my life complete
    when I placed all the pieces before him.
When I cleaned up my act,
    he gave me a fresh start.
Indeed, I've kept alert to GOD's ways;
    I haven't taken God for granted.
Every day I review the ways he works,
    I try not to miss a trick.
I feel put back together,
    and I'm watching my step.
GOD rewrote the text of my life
    when I opened the book of my heart to his eyes.

You stick by people who stick with you,
    you're straight with people who're straight with you,
You're good to good people,
    you shrewdly work around the bad ones.

You take the side of the down-and-out,
    but the stuck-up you take down a peg.

Suddenly, GOD, your light floods my path,
    GOD drives out the darkness.
I smash the bands of marauders,
    I vault the high fences.
What a God! His road
    stretches straight and smooth.
Every GOD-direction is road-tested.
    Everyone who runs toward him
Makes it.

Is there any god like GOD?
    Are we not at bedrock?
Is not this the God who armed me well,
    then aimed me in the right direction?
Now I run like a deer;
    I'm king of the mountain.
He shows me how to fight;
    I can bend a bronze bow!
You protect me with salvation-armor;
    you touch me and I feel ten feet tall.
You cleared the ground under me
    so my footing was firm.
When I chased my enemies I caught them;
    I didn't let go till they were dead men.
I nailed them; they were down for good;
    then I walked all over them.
You armed me well for this fight;
    you smashed the upstarts.
You made my enemies turn tail,
    and I wiped out the haters.
They cried "uncle"
    but Uncle didn't come;
They yelled for GOD
    and got no for an answer.
I ground them to dust; they gusted in the wind.
    I threw them out, like garbage in the gutter.

You rescued me from a squabbling people;
   you made me a leader of nations.
People I'd never heard of served me;
   the moment they got wind of me they submitted.
They gave up; they came trembling from their hideouts.

Live, GOD! Blessing to my Rock,
   my towering Salvation-God!
This God set things right for me
   and shut up the people who talked back.
He rescued me from enemy anger.
   You pulled me from the grip of upstarts,
You saved me from the bullies.
   That's why I'm thanking you, GOD,
   all over the world.
That's why I'm singing songs
   that rhyme your name.
God's king takes the trophy;
   God's chosen is beloved.
I mean David and all his children —
   always.

23 These are David's last words:

The voice of the son of Jesse,
   the voice of the man God took to the top,
Whom the God of Jacob made king,
   and Israel's most popular singer!

GOD's Spirit spoke through me,
   his words took shape on my tongue.
The God of Israel spoke to me,
   Israel's Rock-Mountain said,
"Whoever governs fairly and well,
   who rules in the Fear-of-God,
Is like first light at daybreak
   without a cloud in the sky,
Like green grass carpeting earth,
   glistening under fresh rain."

And this is just how my regime has been,
    for God guaranteed his covenant with me,
Spelled it out plainly
    and kept every promised word—
My entire salvation,
    my every desire.
But the devil's henchmen are like thorns
    culled and piled as trash;
Better not try to touch them;
    keep your distance with a rake or hoe.
They'll make a glorious bonfire!

⁘

This is the listing of David's top men.

Josheb-Basshebeth, the Tahkemonite. He was chief of the Three. He once put his spear to work against eight hundred—killed them all in a day.

Eleazar son of Dodai the Ahohite was the next of the elite Three. He was with David when the Philistines poked fun at them at Pas Dammim. When the Philistines drew up for battle, Israel retreated. But Eleazar stood his ground and killed Philistines right and left until he was exhausted—but he never let go of his sword! A big win for GOD that day. The army then rejoined Eleazar, but all there was left to do was the clean-up.

Shammah son of Agee the Hararite was the third of the Three. The Philistines had mustered for battle at Lehi, where there was a field full of lentils. Israel fled before the Philistines, but Shammah took his stand at the center of the field, successfully defended it, and routed the Philistines. Another great victory for GOD!

One day during harvest, the Three parted from the Thirty and joined David at the Cave of Adullam. A squad of Philistines had set up camp in the Valley of Rephaim. While David was holed up in the Cave, the Philistines had their base camp in Bethlehem. David had a sudden craving and said, "Would I ever like a drink of water from the well at the gate of Bethlehem!" So the Three penetrated the Philistine lines, drew water from the well at the gate of Bethlehem, and brought it back to David. But David wouldn't drink it; he poured it out as an offering to GOD, saying, "There is no way, GOD, that I'll drink this! This isn't mere water, it's their life-blood—they risked their very lives to bring it!" So David refused to drink it.

This is the sort of thing that the Three did.

Abishai brother of Joab and son of Zeruiah was the head of the Thirty. He once got credit for killing three hundred with his spear, but he was never named in the same breath as the Three. He was the most respected of the Thirty and was their captain, but never got included among the Three.

Benaiah son of Jehoiada from Kabzeel was a vigorous man who accomplished a great deal. He once killed two lion cubs in Moab. Another time, on a snowy day, he climbed down into a pit and killed a lion. Another time he killed a formidable Egyptian. The Egyptian was armed with a spear and Benaiah went against him with nothing but a walking stick; he seized the spear from his grip and killed him with his own spear.

These are the things that Benaiah son of Jehoiada is famous for. But neither did he ever get ranked with the Three. He was held in greatest respect among the Thirty, but he never got included with the Three. David put him in charge of his bodyguard.

THE THIRTY

"The Thirty" consisted of:
    Asahel brother of Joab;
    Elhanan son of Dodo of Bethlehem;
    Shammah the Harodite;
    Elika the Harodite;
    Helez the Paltite;
    Ira son of Ikkesh the Tekoite;
    Abiezer the Anathothite;
    Sibbecai the Hushathite;
    Zalmon the Ahohite;
    Maharai the Netophathite;
    Heled son of Baanah the Netophathite;
    Ithai son of Ribai from Gibeah of the Benjaminites;
    Benaiah the Pirathonite;
    Hiddai from the badlands of Gaash;
    Abi-Albon the Arbathite;
    Azmaveth the Barhumite;
    Eliahba the Shaalbonite;
    Jashen the Gizonite;

Jonathan son of Shammah the Hararite;
Ahiam son of Sharar the Urite;
Eliphelet son of Ahasbai the Maacathite;
Eliam son of Ahithophel the Gilonite;
Hezro the Carmelite;
Paarai the Arbite;
Igal son of Nathan, commander of the army of Hagrites;
Zelek the Ammonite;
Naharai the Beerothite, weapon bearer of Joab son of Zeruiah;
Ira the Ithrite;
Gareb the Ithrite;
Uriah the Hittite.
Thirty-seven, all told.

24 Once again GOD's anger blazed out against Israel. He tested David by telling him, "Go and take a census of Israel and Judah." So David gave orders to Joab and the army officers under him, "Canvass all the tribes of Israel, from Dan to Beersheba, and get a count of the population. I want to know the number."

But Joab resisted the king: "May your GOD multiply people by the hundreds right before the eyes of my master the king, but why on earth would you do a thing like this?"

Nevertheless, the king insisted, and so Joab and the army officers left the king to take a census of Israel. They crossed the Jordan and began with Aroer and the town in the canyon of the Gadites near Jazer, proceeded through Gilead, passed Hermon, then on to Dan, but detoured Sidon. They covered Fort Tyre and all the Hivite and Canaanite cities, and finally reached the Negev of Judah at Beersheba. They canvassed the whole country and after nine months and twenty days arrived back in Jerusalem. Joab gave the results of the census to the king: 800,000 able-bodied fighting men in Israel; in Judah 500,000.

But when it was all done, David was overwhelmed with guilt because he had counted the people, replacing trust with statistics. And David prayed to GOD, "I have sinned badly in what I have just done. But now GOD forgive my guilt—I've been really stupid."

When David got up the next morning, the word of GOD had already come to Gad the prophet, David's spiritual advisor, "Go and give David this message: 'GOD has spoken thus: There are three things I can do to you; choose one out of the three and I'll see that it's done.'"

Gad came to deliver the message: "Do you want three years of famine in the land, or three months of running from your enemies while they chase you down, or three days of an epidemic on the country? Think it over and make up your mind. What shall I tell the one who sent me?"

David told Gad, "They're all terrible! But I'd rather be punished by GOD, whose mercy is great, than fall into human hands."

So GOD let loose an epidemic from morning until suppertime. From Dan to Beersheba seventy thousand people died. But when the angel reached out over Jerusalem to destroy it, GOD felt the pain of the terror and told the angel who was spreading death among the people, "Enough's enough! Pull back!"

The angel of GOD had just reached the threshing floor of Araunah the Jebusite. David looked up and saw the angel hovering between earth and sky, sword drawn and about to strike Jerusalem. David and the elders bowed in prayer and covered themselves with rough burlap.

When David saw the angel about to destroy the people, he prayed, "Please! I'm the one who sinned; I, the shepherd, did the wrong. But these sheep, what did they do wrong? Punish me and my family, not them."

That same day Gad came to David and said, "Go and build an altar on the threshing floor of Araunah the Jebusite." David did what Gad told him, what GOD commanded.

Araunah looked up and saw David and his men coming his way; he met them, bowing deeply, honoring the king and saying, "Why has my master the king come to see me?"

"To buy your threshing floor," said David, "so I can build an altar to GOD here and put an end to this disaster."

"Oh," said Araunah, "let my master the king take and sacrifice whatever he wants. Look, here's an ox for the burnt offering and threshing paddles and ox-yokes for fuel—Araunah gives it all to the king! And may GOD, your God, act in your favor."

But the king said to Araunah, "No. I've got to buy it from you for a good price; I'm not going to offer GOD, my God, sacrifices that are no sacrifice."

So David bought the threshing floor and the ox, paying out fifty shekels of silver. He built an altar to GOD there and sacrificed burnt offerings and peace offerings. GOD was moved by the prayers and that was the end of the disaster.

1-2 KINGS

Sovereignty, *God's* sovereignty, is one of the most difficult things for people of faith to live out in everyday routines. But we have no choice: God is Sovereign. God rules. Not only in our personal affairs, but in the cosmos. Not only in our times and places of worship, but in office buildings, political affairs, factories, universities, hospitals—yes, even behind the scenes in saloons and rock concerts. It's a wild and extravagant notion, to be sure. But nothing in our Scriptures is attested to more frequently or emphatically.

Yet not much in our daily experience confirms it. Impersonal forces and arrogant egos compete for the last word in power. Most of us are knocked around much of the time by forces and wills that give no hint of God. Still, generation after generation, men and women of sound mind continue to give sober witness to God's sovereign rule. One of the enduring titles given to Jesus is "King."

So how do we manage to live believingly and obediently in and under this revealed sovereignty in a world that is mostly either ignorant or defiant of it?

Worship shaped by an obedient reading of Scripture is basic. We submit to having our imaginations and behaviors conditioned by the reality of God rather than by what is handed out in school curricula and media reporting. In the course of this worshipful listening, the Books of Kings turn out to provide essential data on what we can expect as we live under God's sovereign rule.

The story of our ancestors, the Hebrew kings, began in the Books of Samuel. This story makes it clear that it was not God's idea that the Hebrews have a king, but since they insisted, he let them have their way. But God never abdicated his sovereignty to any of the Hebrew kings; the idea was that they would represent *his* sovereignty, not that he would delegate his sovereignty to them.

But it never worked very well. After five hundred years and something over forty kings, there was not much to show for it. Even the bright spots—David and Hezekiah and Josiah—were not *very* bright. Human beings, no matter how well intentioned or gifted, don't seem to be able to represent God's rule anywhere close to satisfactory. The Books of Kings, in that light, are a relentless exposition of failure—a relentless five-hundred-year documentation proving that the Hebrew demand of God to "have a king" was about the worst thing they could have asked for.

But through the centuries, readers of this text have commonly realized something else: In the midst of the incredible mess these kings are making of God's purposes, God continues to work his purposes and *uses them* in the work—doesn't discard them, doesn't detour around them; he uses them. They are part of his sovereign rule, whether they want to be or not, whether they know it or not. God's purposes are worked out in confrontation and revelation, in judgment and salvation, but they *are* worked out. God's rule is not imposed in the sense that he forces each man and woman into absolute conformity to justice and truth and righteousness. The rule is worked from within, much of the time invisible and unnoticed, but always patiently and resolutely *there*. The Books of Kings provide a premier witness to the sovereignty of God carried out among some of the most unlikely and uncooperative people who have ever lived.

The benefit of reading these books is enormous. To begin with, our understanding and experience of God's sovereignty develops counter to all power-based and piety-based assumptions regarding God's effective rule. We quit spinning our wheels on utopian projects and dreams. Following that, we begin to realize that if God's sovereignty is never canceled out by the so deeply sin-flawed leaders ("kings") in both our culture and our church, we can quite cheerfully exult in God's sovereignty as it is being exercised (though often silently and hiddenly) in all the circumstantial details of the actual present.

1 KINGS

David

1 King David grew old. The years had caught up with him. Even though they piled blankets on him, he couldn't keep warm. So his servants said to him, "We're going to get a young virgin for our master the king to be at his side and look after him; she'll get in bed with you and arouse our master the king." So they searched the country of Israel for the most ravishing girl they could find; they found Abishag the Shunammite and brought her to the king. The girl was stunningly beautiful; she stayed at his side and looked after the king, but the king did not have sex with her.

At this time Adonijah, whose mother was Haggith, puffed himself up saying, "I'm the next king!" He made quite a splash, with chariots and riders and fifty men to run ahead of him. His father had spoiled him rotten as a child, never once reprimanding him. Besides that, he was very good-looking and the next in line after Absalom.

Adonijah talked with Joab son of Zeruiah and with Abiathar the priest, and they threw their weight on his side. But neither the priest Zadok, nor Benaiah son of Jehoiada, nor Nathan the prophet, nor Shimei and Rei, nor David's personal bodyguards supported Adonijah.

Next Adonijah held a coronation feast, sacrificing sheep, cattle, and grain-fed heifers at the Stone of Zoheleth near the Rogel Spring. He invited all his brothers, the king's sons, and everyone in Judah who had position and influence—but he did not invite the prophet Nathan, Benaiah, the bodyguards, or his brother Solomon.

Nathan went to Bathsheba, Solomon's mother, "Did you know that Adonijah, Haggith's son, has taken over as king, and our master David doesn't know a thing about it? Quickly now, let me tell you how you can save both your own life and Solomon's. Go immediately to King David. Speak up: 'Didn't you, my master the king, promise me, "Your son Solomon will be king after me and sit on my throne"? So why is Adonijah now king?' While you're there talking with the king, I'll come in and corroborate your story."

Bathsheba went at once to the king in his palace bedroom. He was so old! Abishag was at his side making him comfortable. As Bathsheba bowed low, honoring the king, he said, "What do you want?"

"My master," she said, "you promised me in GOD's name, 'Your son Solomon will be king after me and sit on my throne.' And now look what's happened—Adonijah has taken over as king, and my master the king doesn't even know it! He has thrown a huge coronation feast—cattle and grain-fed heifers and sheep—inviting all the king's sons, the priest Abiathar, and Joab head of the army. But your servant Solomon was *not* invited. My master the king, every eye in Israel is watching you to see what you'll do—to see who will sit on the throne of my master the king after him. If you fail to act, the moment you're buried my son Solomon and I are as good as dead."

Abruptly, while she was telling the king all this, Nathan the prophet came in and was announced: "Nathan the prophet is here." He came before the king, honoring him by bowing deeply, his face touching the ground.

"My master the king," Nathan began, "did you say, 'Adonijah shall be king after me and sit on my throne'? Because that's what's happening. He's thrown a huge coronation feast—cattle, grain-fed heifers, sheep—inviting all the king's sons, the army officers, and Abiathar the priest. They're having a grand time, eating and drinking and shouting, 'Long live King Adonijah!' But I wasn't invited, nor was the priest Zadok, nor Benaiah son of Jehoiada, nor your servant Solomon. Is this something that my master the king has done behind our backs, not telling your servants who you intended to be king after you?"

King David took action: "Get Bathsheba back in here." She entered and stood before the king.

The king solemnly promised, "As GOD lives, the God who delivered me from every kind of trouble, I'll do exactly what I promised in GOD's name, the God of Israel: Your son Solomon will be king after me and take my place on the throne. And I'll make sure it happens this very day."

Bathsheba bowed low, her face to the ground. Kneeling in reverence before the king she said, "Oh, may my master, King David, live forever!"

King David said, "Call Zadok the priest, Nathan the prophet, and Benaiah son of Jehoiada." They came to the king.

Then he ordered, "Gather my servants, then mount my son Solomon on my royal mule and lead him in procession down to Gihon. When you get there, Zadok the priest and Nathan the prophet will anoint him king over Israel. Then blow the ram's horn trumpet and shout, 'Long live King Solomon!' You will then accompany him as he enters and takes his place on my throne, succeeding me as king. I have named him ruler over Israel and Judah."

Benaiah son of Jehoiada backed the king: "Yes! And may GOD, the God of my master the king, confirm it! Just as GOD has been with my master the king, may he also be with Solomon and make his rule even greater than that of my master King David!"

Then Zadok the priest, Nathan the prophet, Benaiah son of Jehoiada, and the king's personal bodyguard (the Kerethites and Pelethites) went down, mounted Solomon on King David's mule, and paraded with him to Gihon. Zadok the priest brought a flask of oil from the sanctuary and anointed Solomon. They blew the ram's horn trumpet and everyone shouted, "Long live King Solomon!" Everyone joined the fanfare, the band playing and the people singing, the very earth reverberating to the sound.

Adonijah and his retinue of guests were just finishing their "coronation" feast when they heard it. When Joab heard the blast of the ram's horn trumpet he said, "What's going on here? What's all this uproar?"

Suddenly, in the midst of the questioning, Jonathan son of Abiathar the priest, showed up. Adonijah said, "Welcome! A brave and good man like you must have good news."

But Jonathan answered, "Hardly! Our master King David has just made Solomon king! And the king has surrounded him with Zadok the priest, Nathan the prophet, Benaiah son of Jehoiada, with the Kerethites and Pelethites; and they've mounted Solomon on the royal mule. Zadok the priest and Nathan the prophet have anointed him king at Gihon and the parade is headed up this way singing—a great fanfare! The city is rocking! That's what you're hearing. Here's the crowning touch— Solomon is seated on the throne of the kingdom! And that's not all: The king's servants have come to give their blessing to our master King David saying, 'God make Solomon's name even more honored than yours, and make his rule greater than yours!' On his death bed the king worshiped God and prayed, 'Blessed be GOD, Israel's God, who has provided a successor to my throne, and I've lived to see it!'"

Panicked, Adonijah's guests got out of there, scattering every which way. But Adonijah himself, afraid for his life because of Solomon, fled to the sanctuary and grabbed the horns of the Altar.

Solomon was told, "Adonijah, fearful of King Solomon, has taken sanctuary and seized the horns of the Altar and is saying, 'I'm not leaving until King Solomon promises that he won't kill me.'"

Solomon then said, "If he proves to be a man of honor, not a hair of his head will be hurt; but if there is evil in him, he'll die." Solomon summoned him and they brought him from the Altar. Adonijah came and bowed down, honoring the king. Solomon dismissed him, "Go home."

2 When David's time to die approached, he charged his son Solomon, saying, "I'm about to go the way of all the earth, but you—be strong; show what you're made of! Do what GOD tells you. Walk in the paths he shows you: Follow the life-map absolutely, keep an eye out for the signposts, his course for life set out in the revelation to Moses; then you'll get on well in whatever you do and wherever you go. Then GOD will confirm what he promised me when he said, 'If your sons watch their step, staying true to me heart and soul, you'll always have a successor on Israel's throne.'

"And don't forget what Joab son of Zeruiah did to the two commanders of Israel's army, to Abner son of Ner and to Amasa son of Jether. He murdered them in cold blood, acting in peacetime as if he were at war, and has been stained with that blood ever since. Do what you think best with him, but by no means let him get off scot-free— make him pay.

"But be generous to the sons of Barzillai the Gileadite—extend every hospitality to them; that's the way they treated me when I was running for my life from Absalom your brother.

"You also will have to deal with Shimei son of Gera the Benjaminite from Bahurim, the one who cursed me so viciously when I was on my way to Mahanaim. Later, when he welcomed me back at the Jordan, I promised him under GOD, 'I won't put you to death.' But neither should you treat him as if nothing ever happened. You're wise, you know how to handle these things. You'll know what to do to make him pay before he dies."

✠

Then David joined his ancestors. He was buried in the City of David. David ruled Israel for forty years—seven years in Hebron and another thirty-three in Jerusalem. Solomon took over on the throne of his father David; he had a firm grip on the kingdom.

SOLOMON

Adonijah son of Haggith came to Bathsheba, Solomon's mother. She said, "Do you come in peace?"

He said, "In peace." And then, "May I say something to you?"
"Go ahead," she said, "speak."

"You know that I had the kingdom right in my hands and every-one expected me to be king, and then the whole thing backfired and the kingdom landed in my brother's lap—GOD's doing. So now I have one request to ask of you; please don't refuse me."

"Go ahead, ask," she said.

"Ask King Solomon—he won't turn *you* down—to give me Abishag the Shunammite as my wife."

"Certainly," said Bathsheba. "I'll speak to the king for you."

Bathsheba went to King Solomon to present Adonijah's request. The king got up and welcomed her, bowing respectfully, and returned to his throne. Then he had a throne put in place for his mother, and she sat at his right hand.

She said, "I have a small favor to ask of you. Don't refuse me."

The king replied, "Go ahead, Mother; of course I won't refuse you."

She said, "Give Abishag the Shunammite to your brother Adonijah as his wife."

King Solomon answered his mother, "What kind of favor is this, asking that Abishag the Shunammite be given to Adonijah? Why don't you just ask me to hand over the whole kingdom to him on a platter since he *is* my older brother and has Abiathar the priest and Joab son of Zeruiah on his side!"

Then King Solomon swore under GOD, "May God do his worst to me if Adonijah doesn't pay for this with his life! As surely as GOD lives, the God who has set me firmly on the throne of my father David and has put me in charge of the kingdom just as he promised, Adonijah will die for this—today!"

King Solomon dispatched Benaiah son of Jehoiada; he struck Adonijah and he died.

The king then told Abiathar the priest, "You're exiled to your place in Anathoth. You deserve death but I'm not going to kill you—for now anyway—because you were in charge of the Chest of our ruling GOD in the company of David my father, and because you shared all the hard times with my father."

Solomon stripped Abiathar of his priesthood, fulfilling GOD's word at Shiloh regarding the family of Eli.

When this news reached Joab, this Joab who had conspired with Adonijah (although he had remained loyal in the Absalom affair), he took refuge in the sanctuary of GOD, seizing the horns of the Altar and holding on for dear life. King Solomon was told that Joab had escaped to the sanctuary of GOD and was clinging to the Altar; he immediately sent Benaiah son of Jehoiada with orders, "Kill him."

Benaiah went to the sanctuary of GOD and said, "King's orders: Come out."

He said, "No—I'll die right here."

Benaiah went back to the king and reported, "This was Joab's answer."

The king said, "Go ahead then, do what he says: Kill him and bury him. Absolve me and my father's family of the guilt from Joab's senseless murders. GOD is avenging those bloody murders on Joab's head. Two men he murdered, men better by far than he ever was: Behind my father's back he brutally murdered Abner son of Ner, commander of Israel's army, and Amasa son of Jether, commander of Judah's army. Responsibility for their murders is forever fixed on Joab and his descendants; but for David and his descendants, his family and kingdom, the final verdict is GOD's peace."

So Benaiah son of Jehoiada went back, struck Joab, and killed him. He was buried in his family plot out in the desert. The king appointed Benaiah son of Jehoiada over the army in place of Joab, and replaced Abiathar with Zadok the priest.

The king next called in Shimei and told him, "Build yourself a house in Jerusalem and live there, but you are not to leave the area. If you so much as cross the Brook Kidron, you're as good as dead—you will have decreed your own death sentence."

Shimei answered the king, "Oh, thank you! Your servant will do exactly as my master the king says." Shimei lived in Jerusalem a long time.

But it so happened that three years later, two of Shimei's slaves ran away to Achish son of Maacah, king of Gath. Shimei was told, "Your slaves are in Gath." Shimei sprang into action, saddled his donkey, and went to Achish in Gath looking for his slaves. And then he came back, bringing his slaves.

Solomon was told, "Shimei left Jerusalem for Gath, and now he's back."

Solomon then called for Shimei and said, "Didn't I make you promise me under GOD, and give you a good warning besides, that you would not leave this area? That if you left you would have decreed your own death sentence? And didn't you say, 'Oh, thank you—I'll do exactly as you say'? So why didn't you keep your sacred promise and do what I ordered?"

Then the king told Shimei, "Deep in your heart you know all the evil that you did to my father David; GOD will now avenge that evil on you. But King Solomon will be blessed and the rule of David will be a sure thing under GOD forever."

The king then gave orders to Benaiah son of Jehoiada; he went out and struck Shimei dead.

The kingdom was now securely in Solomon's grasp.

3 Solomon arranged a marriage contract with Pharaoh, king of Egypt. He married Pharaoh's daughter and brought her to the City of David until he had completed building his royal palace and GOD's Temple and the wall around Jerusalem. Meanwhile, the people were worshiping at local shrines because at that time no temple had yet been built to the Name of GOD. Solomon loved GOD and continued to live in the God-honoring ways of David his father, except that he also worshiped at the local shrines, offering sacrifices and burning incense.

The king went to Gibeon, the most prestigious of the local shrines, to worship. He sacrificed a thousand Whole-Burnt-Offerings on that altar. That night, there in Gibeon, GOD appeared to Solomon in a dream: God said, "What can I give you? Ask."

Solomon said, "You were extravagantly generous in love with David my father, and he lived faithfully in your presence, his relationships were just and his heart right. And you have persisted in this great and generous love by giving him—and this very day!—a son to sit on his throne.

"And now here I am: GOD, my God, you have made me, your servant, ruler of the kingdom in place of David my father. I'm too young for this, a mere child! I don't know the ropes, hardly know the 'ins' and 'outs' of this job. And here I am, set down in the middle of the people you've chosen, a great people—far too many to ever count.

"Here's what I want: Give me a God-listening heart so I can lead your people well, discerning the difference between good and evil. For who on their own is capable of leading your glorious people?"

God, the Master, was delighted with Solomon's response. And God said to him, "Because you have asked for this and haven't grasped after a long life, or riches, or the doom of your enemies, but you have asked for the ability to lead and govern well, I'll give you what you've asked for—I'm giving you a wise and mature heart. There's never been one like you before; and there'll be no one after. As a bonus, I'm giving you both the wealth and glory you didn't ask for—there's not a king anywhere who will come up to your mark. And if you stay on course, keeping your eye on the life-map and the God-signs as your father David did, I'll also give you a long life."

Solomon woke up—what a dream! He returned to Jerusalem, took his place before the Chest of the Covenant of God, and worshiped by sacrificing Whole-Burnt-Offerings and Peace-Offerings. Then he laid out a banquet for everyone in his service.

The very next thing, two prostitutes showed up before the king. The one woman said, "My master, this woman and I live in the same house. While we were living together, I had a baby. Three days after I gave birth, this woman also had a baby. We were alone—there wasn't anyone else in the house except for the two of us. The infant son of this woman died one night when she rolled over on him in her sleep. She got up in the middle of the night and took my son—I was sound asleep, mind you!—and put him at her breast and put her dead son at my breast. When I got up in the morning to nurse my son, here was this dead baby! But when I looked at him in the morning light, I saw immediately that he wasn't my baby."

"Not so!" said the other woman. "The living one's mine; the dead one's yours."

The first woman countered, "No! Your son's the dead one; mine's the living one."

They went back and forth this way in front of the king.

The king said, "What are we to do? This woman says, 'The living son is mine and the dead one is yours,' and this woman says, 'No, the dead one's yours and the living one's mine.'"

After a moment the king said, "Bring me a sword." They brought the sword to the king.

Then he said, "Cut the living baby in two—give half to one and half to the other."

The real mother of the living baby was overcome with emotion for her son and said, "Oh no, master! Give her the whole baby alive; don't kill him!"

But the other one said, "If I can't have him, you can't have him—cut away!"

The king gave his decision: "Give the living baby to the first woman. Nobody is going to kill this baby. She is the real mother."

The word got around—everyone in Israel heard of the king's judgment. They were all in awe of the king, realizing that it was God's wisdom that enabled him to judge truly.

4 King Solomon was off to a good start ruling Israel. These were the leaders in his government:

Azariah son of Zadok—the priest;
Elihoreph and Ahijah, sons of Shisha—secretaries;
Jehoshaphat son of Ahilud—historian;
Benaiah son of Jehoiada—commander of the army;
Zadok and Abiathar—priests;
Azariah son of Nathan—in charge of the regional managers;
Zabud son of Nathan—priest and friend to the king;
Ahishar—manager of the palace;
Adoniram son of Abda—manager of the slave labor.

Solomon had twelve regional managers distributed throughout Israel. They were responsible for supplying provisions for the king and his administration. Each was in charge of bringing supplies for one month of the year. These are the names:
Ben-Hur in the Ephraim hills;
Ben-Deker in Makaz, Shaalbim, Beth Shemesh, and Elon Bethhanan;
Ben-Hesed in Arubboth—this included Socoh and all of Hepher;
Ben-Abinadab in Naphoth Dor (he was married to Solomon's daughter Taphath);
Baana son of Ahilud in Taanach and Megiddo, all of Beth Shan next to Zarethan below Jezreel, and from Beth Shan to Abel Meholah over to Jokmeam;
Ben-Geber in Ramoth Gilead—this included the villages of Jair son of Manasseh in Gilead and the region of Argob in Bashan with its sixty large walled cities with bronze-studded gates;
Ahinadab son of Iddo in Mahanaim;
Ahimaaz in Naphtali (he was married to Solomon's daughter Basemath);
Baana son of Hushai in Asher and Aloth;
Jehoshaphat son of Paruah in Issachar;
Shimei son of Ela in Benjamin;

Geber son of Uri in Gilead—this was the country of Sihon king
of the Amorites and also of Og king of Bashan; he managed
the whole district by himself.

SOLOMON'S PROSPERITY

Judah and Israel were densely populated—like sand on an ocean
beach! All their needs were met; they ate and drank and were happy.
Solomon was sovereign over all the kingdoms from the River Euphrates
in the east to the country of the Philistines in the west, all the way to
the border of Egypt. They brought tribute and were vassals of Solomon
all his life.

One day's food supply for Solomon's household was:
185 bushels of fine flour
375 bushels of meal
10 grain-fed cattle
20 range cattle
100 sheep
and miscellaneous deer, gazelles, roebucks, and choice fowl.

Solomon was sovereign over everything, countries and kings, west
of the River Euphrates from Tiphsah to Gaza. Peace reigned everywhere. Throughout Solomon's life, everyone in Israel and Judah lived
safe and sound, all of them from Dan in the north to Beersheba in the
south—content with what they had.

Solomon had forty thousand stalls for chariot horses and twelve
thousand horsemen. The district managers, each according to his
assigned month, delivered food supplies for King Solomon and all who
sat at the king's table; there was always plenty. They also brought to the
designated place their assigned quota of barley and straw for the horses.

God gave Solomon wisdom—the deepest of understanding and
the largest of hearts. There was nothing beyond him, nothing he
couldn't handle. Solomon's wisdom outclassed the vaunted wisdom
of wise men of the East, outshone the famous wisdom of Egypt. He was
wiser than anyone—wiser than Ethan the Ezrahite, wiser than Heman,
wiser than Calcol and Darda the sons of Mahol. He became famous
among all the surrounding nations. He created three thousand
proverbs; his songs added up to 1,005. He knew all about plants, from
the huge cedar that grows in Lebanon to the tiny hyssop that grows

in the cracks of a wall. He understood everything about animals and birds, reptiles and fish. Sent by kings from all over the earth who had heard of his reputation, people came from far and near to listen to the wisdom of Solomon.

INTERNATIONAL FAME

5 Hiram king of Tyre sent ambassadors to Solomon when he heard that he had been crowned king in David's place. Hiram had loved David his whole life. Solomon responded, saying, "You know that David my father was not able to build a temple in honor of GOD because of the wars he had to fight on all sides, until GOD finally put them down. But now GOD has provided peace all around—no one against us, nothing at odds with us.

"Now here is what I want to do: Build a temple in honor of GOD, *my* God, following the promise that GOD gave to David my father, namely, 'Your son whom I will provide to succeed you as king, he will build a house in my honor.' And here is how you can help: Give orders for cedars to be cut from the Lebanon forest; my loggers will work alongside yours and I'll pay your men whatever wage you set. We both know that there is no one like you Sidonians for cutting timber."

When Hiram got Solomon's message, he was delighted, exclaiming, "Blessed be GOD for giving David such a wise son to rule this flourishing people!"

Then he sent this message to Solomon: "I received your request for the cedars and cypresses. It's as good as done—your wish is my command. My lumberjacks will haul the timbers from the Lebanon forest to the sea, assemble them into log rafts, float them to the place you set, then have them disassembled for you to haul away. All I want from you is that you feed my crew."

In this way Hiram supplied all the cedar and cypress timber that Solomon wanted. In his turn, Solomon gave Hiram 125,000 bushels of wheat and 115,000 gallons of virgin olive oil. He did this every year. And GOD, for his part, gave Solomon wisdom, just as he had promised. The healthy peace between Hiram and Solomon was formalized by a treaty.

THE TEMPLE WORK BEGINS

King Solomon raised a workforce of 30,000 men from all over Israel. He sent them in shifts of 10,000 each month to the Lebanon forest; they would work a month in Lebanon and then be at home two months. Adoniram was in charge of the work crew. Solomon also had

70,000 unskilled workers and another 80,000 stonecutters up in the hills — plus 3,300 foremen managing the project and supervising the work crews. Following the king's orders, they quarried huge blocks of the best stone — dressed stone for the foundation of The Temple. Solomon and Hiram's construction workers, assisted by the men of Gebal, cut and prepared the timber and stone for building The Temple.

6 Four hundred and eighty years after the Israelites came out of Egypt, in the fourth year of Solomon's rule over Israel, in the month of Ziv, the second month, Solomon started building The Temple of GOD. The Temple that King Solomon built to GOD was ninety feet long, thirty feet wide, and forty-five feet high. There was a porch across the thirty-foot width of The Temple that extended out fifteen feet. Within The Temple he made narrow, deep-silled windows. Against the outside walls he built a supporting structure in which there were smaller rooms: The lower floor was seven and a half feet wide, the middle floor nine feet, and the third floor ten and a half feet. He had projecting ledges built into the outside Temple walls to support the buttressing beams.

The stone blocks for the building of The Temple were all dressed at the quarry so that the building site itself was reverently quiet — no noise from hammers and chisels and other iron tools.

The entrance to the ground floor was at the south end of The Temple; stairs led to the second floor and then to the third. Solomon built and completed The Temple, finishing it off with roof beams and planks of cedar. The supporting structure along the outside walls was attached to The Temple with cedar beams and the rooms in it were seven and a half feet tall.

The word of GOD came to Solomon saying, "About this Temple you are building — what's important is that you *live* the way I've set out for you and *do* what I tell you, following my instructions carefully and obediently. Then I'll complete in you the promise I made to David your father. I'll personally take up my residence among the Israelites — I won't desert my people Israel."

Solomon built and completed The Temple. He paneled the interior walls from floor to ceiling with cedar planks; for flooring he used cypress. The thirty feet at the rear of The Temple he made into an Inner Sanctuary, cedar planks from floor to ceiling — the Holy of Holies. The Main Sanctuary area in front was sixty feet long. The entire interior of The Temple was cedar, with carvings of fruits and flowers. All cedar — none of the stone was exposed.

The Inner Sanctuary within The Temple was for housing the Chest of the Covenant of God. This Inner Sanctuary was a cube, thirty feet each way, all plated with gold. The Altar of cedar was also gold-plated. Everywhere you looked there was pure gold: gold chains strung in front of the gold-plated Inner Sanctuary—gold everywhere—walls, ceiling, floor, and Altar. Dazzling!

Then he made two cherubim, gigantic angel-like figures, from olivewood. Each was fifteen feet tall. The outstretched wings of the cherubim (they were identical in size and shape) measured another fifteen feet. He placed the two cherubim, their wings spread, in the Inner Sanctuary. The combined wingspread stretched the width of the room, the wing of one cherub touched one wall, the wing of the other the other wall, and the wings touched in the middle. The cherubim were gold plated.

He then carved engravings of cherubim, palm trees, and flower blossoms on all the walls of both the Inner and the Main Sanctuary. And all the floors of both inner and outer rooms were gold plated.

He constructed doors of olivewood for the entrance to the Inner Sanctuary; the lintel and doorposts were five-sided. The doors were also carved with cherubim, palm trees, and flowers, and then covered with gold leaf.

Similarly, he built the entrance to the Main Sanctuary using olivewood for the doorposts but these doorposts were four-sided. The doors were of cypress, split into two panels, each panel swinging separately. These also were carved with cherubim, palm trees, and flowers, and plated with finely hammered gold leaf.

He built the inner court with three courses of dressed stones topped with a course of planed cedar timbers.

The foundation for GOD's Temple was laid in the fourth year in the month of Ziv. It was completed in the eleventh year in the month of Bul (the eighth month) down to the last detail, just as planned. It took Solomon seven years to build it.

✢

7 It took Solomon another thirteen years to finish building his own palace complex. He built the Palace of the Forest of Lebanon a hundred and fifty feet long, seventy-five feet wide, and forty-five feet high. There were four rows of cedar columns supporting forty-five cedar beams, fifteen in each row, and then roofed with cedar. Windows in groupings of three were set high in the walls on either side. All the

doors were rectangular and arranged symmetrically.

He built a colonnaded courtyard seventy-five feet long and forty-five wide. It had a roofed porch at the front with ample eaves.

He built a court room, the Hall of Justice, where he would decide judicial matters, and paneled it with cedar.

He built his personal residence behind the Hall on a similar plan. Solomon also built another one just like it for Pharaoh's daughter, whom he had married.

No expense was spared—everything here, inside and out, from foundation to roof was constructed using high-quality stone, accurately cut and shaped and polished. The foundation stones were huge, ranging in size from twelve to fifteen feet, and of the very best quality. The finest stone was used above the foundation, shaped to size and trimmed with cedar. The courtyard was enclosed with a wall made of three layers of stone and topped with cedar timbers, just like the one in the porch of The Temple of GOD.

✠

King Solomon sent to Tyre and asked Hiram (not the king; another Hiram) to come. Hiram's mother was a widow from the tribe of Naphtali. His father was a Tyrian and a master worker in bronze. Hiram was a real artist—he could do anything with bronze. He came to King Solomon and did all the bronze work.

First he cast two pillars in bronze, each twenty-seven feet tall and eighteen feet in circumference. He then cast two capitals in bronze to set on the pillars; each capital was seven and a half feet high and flared at the top in the shape of a lily. Each capital was dressed with an elaborate filigree of seven braided chains and a double row of two hundred pomegranates, setting the pillars off magnificently. He set the pillars up in the entrance porch to The Temple; the pillar to the south he named Security (Jachin) and the pillar to the north Stability (Boaz). The capitals were in the shape of lilies.

When the pillars were finished, Hiram's next project was to make the Sea—an immense round basin of cast metal fifteen feet in diameter, seven and a half feet tall, and forty-five feet in circumference. Just under the rim there were two bands of decorative gourds, ten gourds to each foot and a half. The gourds were cast in one piece with the Sea.

The Sea was set on twelve bulls, three facing north, three facing west, three facing south, and three facing east; the bulls faced outward supporting the Sea on their hindquarters. The Sea was three inches thick and flared at the rim like a cup, or like a lily. It held about 11,500 gallons.

Hiram also made ten washstands of bronze. Each was six feet square and four and a half feet tall. They were made like this: Panels were fastened to the uprights. Lions, bulls, and cherubim were represented on the panels and uprights. Beveled wreath-work bordered the lions and bulls above and below. Each stand was mounted on four bronze wheels with bronze axles. The uprights were cast with decorative relief work. Each stand held a basin on a circular engraved support a foot and a half deep set on a pedestal two and a quarter feet square. The washstand itself was square. The axles were attached under the stand and the wheels fixed to them. The wheels were twenty-seven inches in diameter; they were designed like chariot wheels. Everything—axles, rims, spokes, and hubs—was of cast metal.

There was a handle at the four corners of each washstand, the handles cast in one piece with the stand. At the top of the washstand there was a ring about nine inches deep. The uprights and handles were cast with the stand. Everything and every available surface was engraved with cherubim, lions, and palm trees, bordered by arabesques. The washstands were identical, all cast in the same mold.

He also made ten bronze washbasins, each six feet in diameter with a capacity of 230 gallons, one basin for each of the ten washstands. He arranged five stands on the south side of The Temple and five on the north. The Sea was placed at the southeast corner of The Temple. Hiram then fashioned the various utensils: buckets and shovels and bowls.

Hiram completed all the work he set out to do for King Solomon on The Temple of GOD:

> two pillars;
> two capitals on top of the pillars;
> two decorative filigrees for the capitals;
> four hundred pomegranates for the two filigrees
> (a double row of pomegranates for each filigree);
> ten washstands each with its washbasin;
> one Sea;
> twelve bulls under the Sea;
> miscellaneous buckets, shovels, and bowls.

All these artifacts that Hiram made for King Solomon for The Temple of GOD were of burnished bronze. He cast them in clay in a foundry on the Jordan plain between Succoth and Zarethan. These artifacts were never weighed—there were far too many! Nobody has any idea how much bronze was used.

Solomon was also responsible for all the furniture and accessories in The Temple of GOD:

the gold Altar;
the gold Table that held the Bread of the Presence;
the pure gold candelabras, five to the right and five to the
    left in front of the Inner Sanctuary;
the gold flowers, lamps, and tongs;
the pure gold dishes, wick trimmers, sprinkling bowls, ladles,
    and censers;
the gold sockets for the doors of the Inner Sanctuary, the Holy of
    Holies, used also for the doors of the Main Sanctuary.

That completed all the work King Solomon did on The Temple of GOD. He then brought in the items consecrated by his father David, the silver and the gold and the artifacts. He placed them all in the treasury of GOD's Temple.

⊹

8 Bringing all this to a climax, King Solomon called in the leaders of Israel, all the heads of the tribes and the family patriarchs, to bring up the Chest of the Covenant of GOD from Zion, the City of David. And they came, all Israel before King Solomon in the month of Ethanim, the seventh month, for the great autumn festival.

With all Israel's leaders present, the priests took up the Chest of GOD and carried up the Chest and the Tent of Meeting and all the holy vessels that went with the Tent. King Solomon and the entire congregation of Israel were there at the Chest worshiping and sacrificing huge numbers of sheep and cattle—so many that no one could keep track.

Then the priests brought the Chest of the Covenant of GOD to its place in the Inner Sanctuary, the Holy of Holies, under the wings of the cherubim. The outspread wings of the cherubim stretched over the Chest and its poles. The poles were so long that their ends could be seen from the entrance to the Inner Sanctuary, but were not noticeable farther out. They're still there today. There was nothing in the Chest but the two stone tablets that Moses had placed in it at Horeb where GOD made a covenant with Israel after bringing them up from Egypt.

THE TEMPLE FINISHED, DEDICATED, FILLED

When the priests left the Holy Place, a cloud filled The Temple of GOD. The priests couldn't carry out their priestly duties because of the cloud—the glory of GOD filled The Temple of GOD!

Then Solomon spoke:

GOD has told us that he lives in the dark
    where no one can see him;
I've built this splendid Temple, O God,
    to mark your invisible presence forever.

The king then turned to face the congregation and blessed them: "Blessed be GOD, the God of Israel, who spoke personally to my father David. Now he has kept the promise he made when he said, 'From the day I brought my people Israel from Egypt, I haven't set apart one city among the tribes of Israel to build a Temple to fix my Name there. But I did choose David to rule my people Israel.'

"My father David had it in his heart to build a Temple honoring the Name of GOD, the God of Israel. But GOD told him 'It was good that you wanted to build a Temple in my honor—most commendable! But you are not the one to do it—your son will build it to honor my Name.'

"GOD has done what he said he would do: I have succeeded David my father and ruled over Israel just as GOD promised; and now I've built a Temple to honor GOD, the God of Israel, and I've secured a place for the Chest that holds the covenant of GOD, the covenant that he made with our ancestors when he brought them up from the land of Egypt."

✠

Before the entire congregation of Israel, Solomon took a position before the Altar, spread his hands out before heaven, and prayed,

O GOD, God of Israel, there is no God like you in the skies
    above or on the earth below who unswervingly keeps covenant

with his servants and relentlessly loves them as they sincerely live in obedience to your way. You kept your word to David my father, your personal word. You did exactly what you promised—every detail. The proof is before us today!

Keep it up, GOD, O God of Israel! Continue to keep the promises you made to David my father when you said, "You'll always have a descendant to represent my rule on Israel's throne, on the condition that your sons are as careful to live obediently in my presence as you have."

O God of Israel, let this all happen;
confirm and establish it!

Can it be that God will actually move into our neighborhood? Why, the cosmos itself isn't large enough to give you breathing room, let alone this Temple I've built. Even so, I'm bold to ask: Pay attention to these my prayers, both intercessory and personal, O GOD, my God. Listen to my prayers, energetic and devout, that I'm setting before you right now. Keep your eyes open to this Temple night and day, this place of which you said, "My Name will be honored there," and listen to the prayers that I pray at this place.

Listen from your home in heaven
and when you hear, forgive.

When someone hurts a neighbor and promises to make things right, and then comes and repeats the promise before your Altar in this Temple, listen from heaven and act accordingly: Judge your servants, making the offender pay for his offense and setting the offended free of any charges.

When your people Israel are beaten by an enemy because they've sinned against you, but then turn to you and acknowledge your rule in prayers desperate and devout in this Temple,

Listen from your home in heaven,
forgive the sin of your people Israel,
return them to the land you gave their ancestors.

227

When the skies shrivel up and there is no rain because your people have sinned against you, but then they pray at this place, acknowledging your rule and quitting their sins because you have scourged them,

> Listen from your home in heaven,
> forgive the sins of your servants, your people Israel.

Then start over with them: Train them to live right and well; send rain on the land you gave your people as an inheritance.

When disasters strike, famine or catastrophe, crop failure or disease, locust or beetle, or when an enemy attacks their defenses—calamity of any sort—any prayer that's prayed from anyone at all among your people Israel, hearts penetrated by the disaster, hands and arms thrown out to this Temple for help,

> Listen from your home in heaven.

Forgive and go to work on us. Give what each deserves, for you know each life from the inside (you're the only one with such "inside knowledge"!) so that they'll live before you in life-long reverent and believing obedience on this land you gave our ancestors.

And don't forget the foreigner who is not a member of your people Israel but has come from a far country because of your reputation. People *are* going to be attracted here by your great reputation, your wonder-working power, who come to pray at this Temple.

> Listen from your home in heaven.

Honor the prayers of the foreigner so that people all over the world will know who you are and what you're like and will live in reverent obedience before you, just as your own people Israel do; so they'll know that you personally make this Temple that I've built what it is.

When your people go to war against their enemies at the time and place you send them and they pray to GOD toward the city you chose and this Temple I've built to honor your Name,

Listen from heaven to what they pray and ask for,
and do what's right for them.

When they sin against you—and they certainly will; there's
no one without sin!—and in anger you turn them over to the
enemy and they are taken captive to the enemy's land, whether
far or near, but repent in the country of their captivity and pray
with changed hearts in their exile, "We've sinned; we've done
wrong; we've been most wicked," and turn back to you heart
and soul in the land of the enemy who conquered them, and
pray to you toward their homeland, the land you gave their
ancestors, toward the city you chose, and this Temple I have
built to the honor of your Name,

Listen from your home in heaven
to their prayers desperate and devout
and do what is best for them.

Forgive your people who have sinned against you; forgive their
gross rebellions and move their captors to treat them with compassion. They are, after all, your people and your precious
inheritance whom you rescued from the heart of that iron-
smelting furnace, Egypt!

O be alert and attentive to the needy prayers of me, your
servant, and your dear people Israel; listen every time they cry
out to you! You handpicked them from all the peoples on earth
to be your very own people, as you announced through your
servant Moses when you, O GOD, in your masterful rule, delivered our ancestors from Egypt.

✛

Having finished praying to GOD—all these bold and passionate
prayers—Solomon stood up before GOD's Altar where he had been
kneeling all this time, his arms stretched upward to heaven. Standing,
he blessed the whole congregation of Israel, blessing them at the top
of his lungs:
"Blessed be GOD, who has given peace to his people Israel just as he
said he'd do. Not one of all those good and wonderful words that he

spoke through Moses has misfired. May GOD, our very own God, continue to be with us just as he was with our ancestors—may he never give up and walk out on us. May he keep us centered and devoted to him, following the life path he has cleared, watching the signposts, walking at the pace and rhythms he laid down for our ancestors.

"And let these words that I've prayed in the presence of GOD be always right there before him, day and night, so that he'll do what is right for me, to guarantee justice for his people Israel day after day after day. Then all the people on earth will know GOD is the true God; there is no other God. And *you*, your lives must be totally obedient to GOD, our personal God, following the life path he has cleared, alert and attentive to everything he has made plain this day."

✠

The king and all Israel with him then worshiped, offering sacrifices to GOD. Solomon offered Peace-Offerings, sacrificing to GOD twenty-two thousand cattle, a hundred and twenty thousand sheep. This is how the king and all Israel dedicated The Temple of GOD.

That same day, the king set apart the central area of the Courtyard in front of GOD's Temple for sacred use and there sacrificed the Whole-Burnt-Offerings, Grain-Offerings, and fat from the Peace-Offerings—the bronze Altar was too small to handle all these offerings.

This is how Solomon kept the great autumn feast, and all Israel with him, people there all the way from the far northeast (the Entrance to Hamath) to the far southwest (the Brook of Egypt)—a huge congregation. They started out celebrating for seven days—and then did it another seven days! Two solid weeks of celebration! Then he dismissed them. They blessed the king and went home, exuberant with heartfelt gratitude for all the good GOD had done for his servant David and for his people Israel.

✠

9 After Solomon had completed building The Temple of GOD and his own palace, all the projects he had set his heart on doing, GOD appeared to Solomon again, just as he had appeared to him at Gibeon.

And GOD said to him, "I've listened to and received all your prayers, your ever-so-passionate prayers. I've sanctified this Temple that you have built: My Name is stamped on it forever; my eyes are on it and my heart in it always. As for you, if you live in my presence as your father

David lived, pure in heart and action, living the life I've set out for you, attentively obedient to my guidance and judgments, then I'll back your kingly rule over Israel, make it a sure thing on a solid foundation. The same guarantee I gave David your father I'm giving you: 'You can count on always having a descendant on Israel's throne.'

"But if you or your sons betray me, ignoring my guidance and judgments, taking up with alien gods by serving and worshiping them, then the guarantee is off: I'll wipe Israel right off the map and repudiate this Temple I've just sanctified to honor my Name. And Israel will become nothing but a bad joke among the peoples of the world. And this Temple, splendid as it now is, will become an object of contempt; visitors will shake their heads, saying, 'Whatever happened here? What's the story behind these ruins?' Then they'll be told, 'The people who used to live here betrayed their GOD, the very God who rescued their ancestors from Egypt; they took up with alien gods, worshiping and serving them. That's what's behind this GOD-visited devastation.'"

✛

At the end of twenty years, having built the two buildings, The Temple of GOD and his personal palace, Solomon rewarded Hiram king of Tyre with a gift of twenty villages in the district of Galilee. Hiram had provided him with all the cedar and cypress and gold that he had wanted. But when Hiram left Tyre to look over the villages that Solomon had given him, he didn't like what he saw.

He said, "What kind of reward is this, my friend? Twenty backwoods hick towns!" People still refer to them that way. This is all Hiram got from Solomon in exchange for four and a half tons of gold!

✛

This is the work record of the labor force that King Solomon raised to build The Temple of GOD, his palace, the defense complex (the Millo), the Jerusalem wall, and the fortified cities of Hazor, Megiddo, and Gezer.

Pharaoh king of Egypt had come up and captured Gezer, torched it, and killed all the Canaanites who lived there. He gave it as a wedding present to his daughter, Solomon's wife. So Solomon rebuilt Gezer.

He also built Lower Beth Horon, Baalath, and Tamar in the desert, back-country storehouse villages, and villages for chariots and horses. Solomon built widely and extravagantly in Jerusalem, in Lebanon, and wherever he fancied.

The remnants from the original inhabitants of the land (Amorites, Hittites, Perizzites, Hivites, and Jebusites—all non-Israelites), survivors of the holy wars, were rounded up by Solomon for his gangs of slave labor, a policy still in effect. But true Israelites were not treated this way; they were used in his army and administration—government leaders and commanders of his chariots and charioteers. They were also the project managers responsible for Solomon's building operations—550 of them in charge of the workforce.

It was after Pharaoh's daughter ceremonially ascended from the City of David and took up residence in the house built especially for her that Solomon built the defense complex (the Millo).

Three times a year Solomon worshiped at the Altar of GOD, sacrificing Whole-Burnt-Offerings and Peace-Offerings, and burning incense in the presence of GOD. Everything that had to do with The Temple he did generously and well; he didn't skimp.

And ships! King Solomon also built ships at Ezion Geber, located near Elath in Edom on the Red Sea. Hiram sent seaworthy sailors to assist Solomon's men with the fleet. They embarked for Ophir, brought back sixteen tons of gold, and presented it to King Solomon.

✠

THE QUEEN OF SHEBA VISITS

10 The queen of Sheba heard about Solomon and his connection with the Name of GOD. She came to put his reputation to the test by asking tough questions. She made a grand and showy entrance into Jerusalem—camels loaded with spices, a huge amount of gold, and precious gems. She came to Solomon and talked about all the things that she cared about, emptying her heart to him. Solomon answered everything she put to him—nothing stumped him. When the queen of Sheba experienced for herself Solomon's wisdom and saw with her own eyes the palace he had built, the meals that were served, the impressive array of court officials and sharply dressed waiters, the lavish crystal, and the elaborate worship extravagant with Whole-Burnt-Offerings at the steps leading up to The Temple of GOD, it took her breath away.

She said to the king, "It's all true! Your reputation for accomplishment and wisdom that reached all the way to my country is confirmed. I wouldn't have believed it if I hadn't seen it for myself; they didn't exaggerate! Such wisdom and elegance—far more than I could ever have imagined. Lucky the men and women who work for you, getting to be around you every day and hear your wise words firsthand! And blessed be God, your God, who took such a liking to you and made you king. Clearly, God's love for Israel is behind this, making you king to keep a just order and nurture a God-pleasing people."

She then gave the king four and a half tons of gold, and also sack after sack of spices and expensive gems. There hasn't been a cargo of spices like that since that shipload the queen of Sheba brought to King Solomon.

The ships of Hiram also imported gold from Ophir along with tremendous loads of fragrant sandalwood and expensive gems. The king used the sandalwood for fine cabinetry in The Temple of God and the palace complex, and for making harps and dulcimers for the musicians. Nothing like that shipment of sandalwood has been seen since.

King Solomon for his part gave the queen of Sheba all her heart's desire—everything she asked for, on top of what he had already so generously given her. Satisfied, she returned home with her train of servants.

✠

Solomon received twenty-five tons of gold in tribute annually. This was above and beyond the taxes and profit on trade with merchants and assorted kings and governors.

King Solomon crafted two hundred body-length shields of hammered gold—seven and a half pounds of gold to each shield—and three hundred smaller shields about half that size. He stored the shields in the House of the Forest of Lebanon.

The king built a massive throne of ivory accented with a veneer of gold. The throne had six steps leading up to it, its back shaped like an arch. The armrests on each side were flanked by lions. Lions, twelve of them, were placed at either end of the six steps. There was no throne like it in any of the surrounding kingdoms.

King Solomon's chalices and tankards were made of gold and all the dinnerware and serving utensils in the House of the Forest of Lebanon were pure gold—nothing was made of silver; silver was considered common and cheap.

The king had a fleet of ocean-going ships at sea with Hiram's ships. Every three years the fleet would bring in a cargo of gold, silver, and ivory, and apes and peacocks.

King Solomon was wiser and richer than all the kings of the earth—he surpassed them all. People came from all over the world to be with Solomon and drink in the wisdom God had given him. And everyone who came brought gifts—artifacts of gold and silver, fashionable robes and gowns, the latest in weapons, exotic spices, and horses and mules—parades of visitors, year after year.

Solomon collected chariots and horses: fourteen hundred chariots and twelve thousand horses! He stabled them in the special chariot cities as well as in Jerusalem. The king made silver as common as rocks and cedar as common as the fig trees in the lowland hills. His horses were brought in from Egypt and Cilicia, specially acquired by the king's agents. Chariots from Egypt went for fifteen pounds of silver and a horse for about three and three-quarter pounds of silver. Solomon carried on a brisk horse-trading business with the Hittite and Aramean royal houses.

11 King Solomon was obsessed with women. Pharaoh's daughter was only the first of the many foreign women he loved—Moabite, Ammonite, Edomite, Sidonian, and Hittite. He took them from the surrounding pagan nations of which GOD had clearly warned Israel, "You must not marry them; they'll seduce you into infatuations with their gods." Solomon fell in love with them anyway, refusing to give them up. He had seven hundred royal wives and three hundred concubines—a thousand women in all! And they did seduce him away from God. As Solomon grew older, his wives beguiled him with their alien gods and he became unfaithful—he didn't stay true to his GOD as his father David had done. Solomon took up with Ashtoreth, the whore goddess of the Sidonians, and Molech, the horrible god of the Ammonites.

Solomon openly defied GOD; he did not follow in his father David's footsteps. He went on to build a sacred shrine to Chemosh, the horrible god of Moab, and to Molech, the horrible god of the Ammonites, on a hill just east of Jerusalem. He built similar shrines for all his foreign wives, who then polluted the countryside with the smoke and stench of their sacrifices.

GOD was furious with Solomon for abandoning the GOD of Israel, the God who had twice appeared to him and had so clearly commanded him not to fool around with other gods. Solomon faithlessly disobeyed GOD's orders.

GOD said to Solomon, "Since this is the way it is with you, that you have no intention of keeping faith with me and doing what I have commanded, I'm going to rip the kingdom from you and hand it over to someone else. But out of respect for your father David I won't do it in your lifetime. It's your son who will pay—I'll rip it right out of his grasp. Even then I won't take it all; I'll leave him one tribe in honor of my servant David and out of respect for my chosen city Jerusalem."

GOD incited Hadad, a descendant of the king of Edom, into hostile actions against Solomon. Years earlier, when David devastated Edom, Joab, commander of the army, on his way to bury the dead, massacred all the men of Edom. Joab and his army stayed there for six months, making sure they had killed every man in Edom. Hadad, just a boy at the time, had escaped with some of the Edomites who had worked for his father. Their escape route took them through Midian to Paran. They picked up some men in Paran and went on to Egypt and to Pharaoh king of Egypt, who gave Hadad a house, food, and even land. Pharaoh liked him so well that he gave him the sister of his wife, Queen Tahpenes, in marriage. She bore Hadad a son named Genubath who was raised like one of the royal family. Genubath grew up in the palace with Pharaoh's children.

While living in Egypt, Hadad heard that both David and Joab, commander of the army, were dead. He approached Pharaoh and said, "Send me off with your blessing—I want to return to my country."

"But why?" said Pharaoh. "Why would you want to leave here? Hasn't everything been to your liking?"

"Everything has been just fine," said Hadad, "but I want to go home—give me a good send-off!"

✠

Then God incited another adversary against Solomon, Rezon son of Eliada, who had deserted from his master, Hadadezer king of Zobah. After David's slaughter of the Arameans, Rezon collected a band of outlaws and became their leader. They later settled in Damascus, where Rezon eventually took over as king. Like Hadad, Rezon was a thorn in Israel's side all of Solomon's life. He was king over Aram, and he hated Israel.

ADVERSARIES ARISE

And then, the last straw: Jeroboam son of Nebat rebelled against the king. He was an Ephraimite from Zeredah, his mother a widow named Zeruah. He served in Solomon's administration.

This is why he rebelled. Solomon had built the outer defense system (the Millo) and had restored the fortifications that were in disrepair from the time of his father David. Jeroboam stood out during the construction as strong and able. When Solomon observed what a good worker he was, he put the young man in charge of the entire workforce of the tribe of Joseph.

One day Jeroboam was walking down the road out of Jerusalem. Ahijah the prophet of Shiloh, wearing a brand-new cloak, met him. The two of them were alone on that remote stretch of road. Ahijah took off the new cloak that he was wearing and ripped it into twelve pieces.

Then he said to Jeroboam, "Take ten of these pieces for yourself; this is by order of the GOD of Israel: See what I'm doing—I'm ripping the kingdom out of Solomon's hands and giving you ten of the tribes. In honor of my servant David and out of respect for Jerusalem, the city I especially chose, he will get one tribe. And here's the reason: He faithlessly abandoned me and went off worshiping Ashtoreth goddess of the Sidonians, Chemosh god of the Moabites, and Molech god of the Ammonites. He hasn't lived the way I have shown him, hasn't done what I have wanted, and hasn't followed directions or obeyed orders as his father David did.

"Still, I won't take the whole kingdom away from him. I'll stick with him through his lifetime because of my servant David whom I chose and who did follow my directions and obey my orders. But after that I'll remove the kingdom from his son's control and give you ten tribes. I'll leave one tribe to his son, to maintain a witness to my servant David in Jerusalem, the city I chose as a memorial to my Name.

"But I have taken you in hand. Rule to your heart's content! You are to be the king of Israel. If you listen to what I tell you and live the way I show you and do what pleases me, following directions and obeying orders as my servant David did, I'll stick with you no matter what. I'll build you a kingdom as solid as the one I built for David. Israel will be yours! I am bringing pain and trouble on David's descendants, but the trials won't last forever."

Solomon ordered the assassination of Jeroboam, but he got away to Egypt and found asylum there with King Shishak. He remained in exile there until Solomon died.

The rest of Solomon's life and rule, his work and his wisdom, you can read for yourself in *The Chronicles of Solomon*. Solomon ruled in Jerusalem over all Israel for forty years. He died and was buried in the City of David his father. His son Rehoboam was the next king.

REHOBOAM

12 Rehoboam traveled to Shechem where all Israel had gathered to inaugurate him as king. Jeroboam had been in Egypt, where he had taken asylum from King Solomon; when he got the report of Solomon's death he had come back.

Rehoboam assembled Jeroboam and all the people. They said to Rehoboam, "Your father made life hard for us—worked our fingers to the bone. Give us a break; lighten up on us and we'll willingly serve you."

"Give me three days to think it over, then come back," Rehoboam said.

King Rehoboam talked it over with the elders who had advised his father when he was alive: "What's your counsel? How do you suggest that I answer the people?"

They said, "If you will be a servant to this people, be considerate of their needs and respond with compassion, work things out with them, they'll end up doing anything for you."

But he rejected the counsel of the elders and asked the young men he'd grown up with who were now currying his favor, "What do you think? What should I say to these people who are saying, 'Give us a break from your father's harsh ways—lighten up on us'?"

The young turks he'd grown up with said, "These people who complain, 'Your father was too hard on us; lighten up'—well, tell them this: 'My little finger is thicker than my father's waist. If you think life under my father was hard, you haven't seen the half of it. My father thrashed you with whips; I'll beat you bloody with chains!'"

Three days later Jeroboam and the people showed up, just as Rehoboam had directed when he said, "Give me three days to think it over, then come back." The king's answer was harsh and rude. He spurned the counsel of the elders and went with the advice of the younger set, "If you think life under my father was hard, you haven't seen the half of it. My father thrashed you with whips; I'll beat you bloody with chains!"

Rehoboam turned a deaf ear to the people. GOD was behind all this, confirming the message that he had given to Jeroboam son of Nebat through Ahijah of Shiloh.

When all Israel realized that the king hadn't listened to a word they'd said, they stood up to him and said,

Get lost, David!
We've had it with you, son of Jesse!

Let's get out of here, Israel, and fast!
From now on, David, mind your own business.

And with that, they left. But Rehoboam continued to rule those who lived in the towns of Judah.

✠

When King Rehoboam next sent out Adoniram, head of the workforce, the Israelites ganged up on him, pelted him with stones, and killed him. King Rehoboam jumped in his chariot and fled to Jerusalem as fast as he could. Israel has been in rebellion against the Davidic regime ever since.

JEROBOAM OF ISRAEL

When the word was out that Jeroboam was back and available, the assembled people invited him and inaugurated him king over all Israel. The only tribe left to the Davidic dynasty was Judah.

When Rehoboam got back to Jerusalem, he called up the men of Judah and the tribe of Benjamin, a hundred and eighty thousand of their best soldiers, to go to war against Israel and recover the kingdom for Rehoboam son of Solomon.

At this time the word of God came to Shemaiah, a man of God: "Tell this to Rehoboam son of Solomon king of Judah, along with everyone in Judah and Benjamin and anyone else who is around: This is GOD's word: Don't march out; don't fight against your brothers the Israelites; go back home, every last one of you; *I'm* in charge here." And they did it; they did what GOD said and went home.

✠

Jeroboam made a fort at Shechem in the hills of Ephraim, and made that his headquarters. He also built a fort at Penuel.

But then Jeroboam thought, "It won't be long before the kingdom is reunited under David. As soon as these people resume worship at The Temple of GOD in Jerusalem, they'll start thinking of Rehoboam king of Judah as their ruler. They'll then kill me and go back to King Rehoboam."

So the king came up with a plan: He made two golden calves. Then he announced, "It's too much trouble for you to go to Jerusalem to worship. Look at these—the gods who brought you out of Egypt!" He put one calf in Bethel; the other he placed in Dan. This was blatant sin. Think of it—people traveling all the way to Dan to worship a calf!

And that wasn't the end of it. Jeroboam built forbidden shrines all over the place and recruited priests from wherever he could find them, regardless of whether they were fit for the job or not. To top it off, he created a holy New Year festival to be held on the fifteenth day of the eighth month to replace the one in Judah, complete with worship offered on the Altar at Bethel and sacrificing before the calves he had set up there. He staffed Bethel with priests from the local shrines he had made. This was strictly his own idea to compete with the feast in Judah; and he carried it off with flair, a festival exclusively for Israel, Jeroboam himself leading the worship at the Altar.

13 And then this happened: Just as Jeroboam was at the Altar, about to make an offering, a holy man came from Judah by GOD's command and preached (these were GOD's orders) to the Altar: "Altar, Altar! GOD's message! 'A son will be born into David's family named Josiah. The priests from the shrines who are making offerings on you, he will sacrifice—on you! Human bones burned on you!'" At the same time he announced a sign: "This is the proof GOD gives—the Altar will split into pieces and the holy offerings spill into the dirt."

When the king heard the message the holy man preached against the Altar at Bethel, he reached out to grab him, yelling, "Arrest him!" But his arm was paralyzed and hung useless. At the same time the Altar broke apart and the holy offerings all spilled into the dirt—the very sign the holy man had announced by GOD's command.

The king pleaded with the holy man, "Help me! Pray to your GOD for the healing of my arm." The holy man prayed for him and the king's arm was healed—as good as new!

Then the king invited the holy man, "Join me for a meal; I have a gift for you."

The holy man told the king, "Not on your life! You couldn't pay me enough to get me to sit down with you at a meal in this place. I'm here under GOD's orders, and he commanded, 'Don't eat a crumb, don't drink a drop, and don't go back the way you came.'" Then he left by a different road than the one on which he had walked to Bethel.

There was an old prophet who lived in Bethel. His sons came and told him the story of what the holy man had done that day in Bethel, told him everything that had happened and what the holy man had said to the king.

Their father said, "Which way did he go?" His sons pointed out the road that the holy man from Judah had taken.

He told his sons, "Saddle my donkey." When they had saddled it, he got on and rode after the holy man. He found him sitting under an oak tree.

He asked him, "Are you the holy man who came from Judah?"

"Yes, I am," he said.

"Well, come home with me and have a meal."

"Sorry, I can't do that," the holy man said. "I can neither go back with you nor eat with you in this country. I'm under strict orders from GOD: 'Don't eat a crumb; don't drink a drop; and don't come back the way you came.'"

But he said, "I am also a prophet, just like you. And an angel came to me with a message from GOD: 'Bring him home with you, and give him a good meal!'" But the man was lying. So the holy man went home with him and they had a meal together.

There they were, sitting at the table together, when the word of GOD came to the prophet who had brought him back. He confronted the holy man who had come from Judah: "GOD's word to you: You disobeyed GOD's command; you didn't keep the strict orders your GOD gave you; you came back and sat down to a good meal in the very place GOD told you, 'Don't eat a crumb; don't drink a drop.' For that you're going to die far from home and not be buried in your ancestral tomb."

When the meal was over, the prophet who had brought him back saddled his donkey for him. Down the road a way, a lion met him and killed him. His corpse lay crumpled on the road, the lion on one side and the donkey on the other. Some passersby saw the corpse in a heap on the road, with the lion standing guard beside it. They went to the village where the old prophet lived and told what they had seen.

When the prophet who had gotten him off track heard it, he said, "It's the holy man who disobeyed GOD's strict orders. GOD turned him over to the lion who knocked him around and killed him, just as GOD had told him."

The prophet told his sons, "Saddle my donkey." They did it. He rode out and found the corpse in a heap in the road, with the lion and the donkey standing there. The lion hadn't bothered either the corpse or the donkey. The old prophet loaded the corpse of the holy man on his donkey and returned it to his own town to give it a decent burial. He placed the body in his own tomb. The people mourned, saying, "A sad day, brother!"

After the funeral, the prophet said to his sons, "When I die, bury me in the same tomb where the holy man is buried, my bones alongside his bones. The message that he preached by GOD's command against the Altar at Bethel and against all the sex-and-religion shrines in the towns of Samaria will come true."

After this happened, Jeroboam kept right on doing evil, recruiting priests for the forbidden shrines indiscriminately—anyone who wanted to could be a priest at one of the local shrines. This was the root sin of Jeroboam's government. And it was this that ruined him.

☩

14 At about this time Jeroboam's son Abijah came down sick. Jeroboam said to his wife, "Do something. Disguise yourself so no one will know you are the queen and go to Shiloh. Ahijah the prophet lives there, the same Ahijah who told me I'd be king over this people. Take along ten loaves of bread, some sweet rolls, and a jug of honey. Make a visit to him and he'll tell you what's going on with our boy."

Jeroboam's wife did as she was told; she went straight to Shiloh and to Ahijah's house. Ahijah was an old man at this time, and blind, but GOD had warned Ahijah, "Jeroboam's wife is on her way to consult with you regarding her sick son; tell her this and this and this."

When she came in she was disguised. Ahijah heard her come through the door and said, "Welcome, wife of Jeroboam! But why the deception? I've got bad news for you. Go and deliver this message I received firsthand from GOD, the God of Israel, to Jeroboam: I raised you up from obscurity and made you the leader of my people Israel. I ripped the kingdom from the hands of David's family and gave it to you, but you weren't at all like my servant David who did what I told him and lived from his undivided heart, pleasing me. Instead you've set a new record in works of evil by making alien gods—tin gods! Pushing me aside and turning your back—you've made me mighty angry.

"And I'll not put up with it: I'm bringing doom on the household of Jeroboam, killing the lot of them right down to the last male wretch in Israel, whether slave or free. They've become nothing but garbage and I'm getting rid of them. The ones who die in the city will be eaten by stray dogs; the ones who die out in the country will be eaten by carrion crows. GOD's decree!

"And that's it. Go on home—the minute you step foot in town, the boy will die. Everyone will come to his burial, mourning his death. He is the only one in Jeroboam's family who will get a decent burial; he's the only one for whom GOD, the God of Israel, has a good word to say.

"Then GOD will appoint a king over Israel who will wipe out Jeroboam's family, wipe them right off the map—doomsday for Jeroboam! He will hit Israel hard, as a storm slaps reeds about; he'll pull them up by the roots from this good land of their inheritance, weeding them out, and then scatter them to the four winds. And why? Because they made GOD so angry with Asherah sex-and-religion shrines. He'll wash his hands of Israel because of Jeroboam's sins, which have led Israel into a life of sin."

Jeroboam's wife left and went home to Tirzah. The moment she stepped through the door, the boy died. They buried him and everyone mourned his death, just as GOD had said through his servant the prophet Ahijah.

The rest of Jeroboam's life, the wars he fought and the way he ruled, is written in *The Chronicles of the Kings of Israel*. He ruled for twenty-two years. He died and was buried with his ancestors. Nadab his son was king after him.

⊁

Rehoboam son of Solomon was king in Judah. He was forty-one years old when he took the throne and was king for seventeen years in Jerusalem, the city GOD selected from all the tribes of Israel for the worship of his Name. Rehoboam's mother was Naamah, an Ammonite. Judah was openly wicked before GOD, making him very angry. They set new records in sin, surpassing anything their ancestors had done. They built Asherah sex-and-religion shrines and set up sacred stones all over the place—on hills, under trees, wherever you looked. Worse, they had male sacred prostitutes, polluting the country outrageously—all the stuff that GOD had gotten rid of when he brought Israel into the land.

In the fifth year of King Rehoboam's rule, Shishak king of Egypt made war against Jerusalem. He plundered The Temple of GOD and the royal palace of their treasures, cleaned them out—even the gold shields that Solomon had made. King Rehoboam replaced them with bronze shields and outfitted the royal palace guards with them. Whenever the king went to God's Temple, the guards carried the shields but always returned them to the guardroom.

The rest of Rehoboam's life, what he said and did, is all written in *The Chronicles of the Kings of Judah*. There was war between Rehoboam and Jeroboam the whole time. Rehoboam died and was buried with his ancestors in the City of David. His mother was Naamah, an Ammonite. His son Abijah ruled after him.

ABIJAH OF JUDAH

15 In the eighteenth year of the rule of Jeroboam son of Nebat, Abijah took over the throne of Judah. He ruled in Jerusalem three years. His mother was Maacah daughter of Absalom. He continued to sin just like his father before him. He was not truehearted to God as his grandfather David had been. But despite that, out of respect for David, his God graciously gave him a lamp, a son to follow him and keep Jerusalem secure. For David had lived an exemplary life before God all his days, not going off on his own in willful defiance of God's clear directions (except for that time with Uriah the Hittite). But war continued between Abijah and Jeroboam the whole time.

The rest of Abijah's life, everything he did, is written in *The Chronicles of the Kings of Judah*. But the war with Jeroboam was the dominant theme. Abijah died and was buried with his ancestors in the City of David. His son Asa was king after him.

ASA OF JUDAH

In the twentieth year of Jeroboam king of Israel, Asa began his rule over Judah. He ruled for forty-one years in Jerusalem. His grandmother's name was Maacah.

Asa conducted himself well before God, reviving the ways of his ancestor David. He cleaned house: He got rid of the sacred prostitutes and threw out all the idols his predecessors had made. Asa spared nothing and no one; he went so far as to remove Queen Maacah from her position because she had built a shockingly obscene memorial to the whore goddess Asherah. Asa tore it down and burned it up in the Kidron Valley. Unfortunately, he didn't get rid of the local sex-and-religion shrines. But he was well-intentioned—his heart was in the right place, in tune with God. All the gold and silver vessels and artifacts that he and his father had consecrated for holy use he installed in The Temple.

But through much of his reign there was war between Asa and Baasha king of Israel. Baasha king of Israel started it by building a fort at Ramah and closing the border between Israel and Judah so no one could enter or leave Judah.

Asa took all the silver and gold that was left in the treasuries of The Temple of GOD and the royal palace, gave it to his servants, and sent them to Ben-Hadad son of Tabrimmon, the son of Hezion king of Aram, who was ruling in Damascus, with this message: "Let's make a treaty like the one between our fathers. I'm showing my good faith with this gift of silver and gold. Break your deal with Baasha king of Israel so he'll quit fighting against me."

Ben-Hadad went along with King Asa and sent out his troops against the towns of Israel. He attacked Ijon, Dan, Abel Beth Maacah, and the entire region of Kinnereth, including Naphtali. When Baasha got the report he quit fortifying Ramah and pulled back to Tirzah.

Then King Asa issued orders to everyone in Judah—no exemptions—to haul away the logs and stones Baasha had used in the fortification of Ramah and use them to fortify Geba in Benjamin and Mizpah.

A full account of Asa's life, all the great things he did and the fortifications he constructed, is written in *The Chronicles of the Kings of Judah*. In his old age he developed severe gout. Then Asa died and was buried with his ancestors in the City of David. His son Jehoshaphat became king after him.

NADAB OF ISRAEL

Nadab son of Jeroboam became king over Israel in the second year of Asa's rule in Judah. He was king of Israel two years. He was openly evil before GOD—he followed in the footsteps of his father who both sinned and made Israel sin.

Baasha son of Ahijah of the tribe of Issachar ganged up on him and attacked him at the Philistine town of Gibbethon while Nadab and the Israelites were doing battle there. Baasha killed Nadab in the third year of Asa king of Judah and became Israel's next king.

As soon as he was king he killed everyone in Jeroboam's family. There wasn't a living soul left to the name of Jeroboam; Baasha wiped them out totally, just as GOD's servant Ahijah of Shiloh had prophesied—punishment for Jeroboam's sins and for making Israel sin, for making the GOD of Israel thoroughly angry.

The rest of Nadab's life, everything else he did, is written in *The Chronicles of the Kings of Israel*. There was continuous war between Asa and Baasha king of Israel.

BAASHA OF ISRAEL

In the third year of Asa king of Judah, Baasha son of Ahijah became king in Tirzah over all Israel. He ruled twenty-four years. He was openly evil before GOD, walking in the footsteps of Jeroboam, who both sinned and made Israel sin.

16 The word of GOD came to Jehu son of Hanani with this message for Baasha: "I took you from nothing—a complete nobody—and set you up as the leader of my people Israel, but you plodded along in the rut of Jeroboam, making my people Israel sin and making me seethe over their sin. And now the consequences—I will burn Baasha and his regime to cinders, the identical fate of Jeroboam son of Nebat. Baasha's people who die in the city will be eaten by scavenger dogs; carrion crows will eat the ones who die in the country."

The rest of Baasha's life, the record of his regime, is written in *The Chronicles of the Kings of Israel*. Baasha died and was buried with his ancestors in Tirzah. His son Elah was king after him.

That's the way it was with Baasha: Through the prophet Jehu son of Hanani, GOD's word came to him and his regime because of his life of open evil before GOD and his making GOD so angry—a chip off the block of Jeroboam, even though GOD had destroyed him.

ELAH OF ISRAEL

In the twenty-sixth year of Asa king of Judah, Elah son of Baasha began his rule. He was king in Tirzah only two years. One day when he was at the house of Arza the palace manager, drinking himself drunk, Zimri, captain of half his chariot-force, conspired against him. Zimri slipped in, knocked Elah to the ground, and killed him. This happened in the twenty-seventh year of Asa king of Judah. Zimri then became the king.

Zimri had no sooner become king than he killed everyone connected with Baasha, got rid of them all like so many stray dogs—relatives and friends alike. Zimri totally wiped out the family of Baasha, just as GOD's word delivered by the prophet Jehu had said—wages for the sins of Baasha and his son Elah; not only for their sins but for dragging Israel into their sins and making the GOD of Israel angry with their stupid idols.

The rest of Elah's life, what he said and did, is written in *The Chronicles of the Kings of Israel.*

ZIMRI OF ISRAEL

Zimri was king in Tirzah for all of seven days during the twenty-seventh year of the reign of Asa king of Judah. The Israelite army was on maneuvers near the Philistine town of Gibbethon at the time. When they got the report, "Zimri has conspired against the king and killed him," right there in the camp they made Omri, commander of the army, king. Omri and the army immediately left Gibbethon and attacked Tirzah. When Zimri saw that he was surrounded and as good as dead, he entered the palace citadel, set the place on fire, and died. It was a fit end for his sins, for living a flagrantly evil life before GOD, walking in the footsteps of Jeroboam, sinning and then dragging Israel into his sins.

As for the rest of Zimri's life, along with his infamous conspiracy, it's all written in *The Chronicles of the Kings of Israel.*

OMRI OF ISRAEL

After that the people of Israel were split right down the middle: Half favored Tibni son of Ginath as king, and half wanted Omri. Eventually the Omri side proved stronger than the Tibni side. Tibni ended up dead and Omri king.

Omri took over as king of Israel in the thirty-first year of the reign of Asa king of Judah. He ruled for twelve years, the first six in Tirzah. He then bought the hill Samaria from Shemer for 150 pounds of silver. He developed the hill and named the city that he built Samaria, after its original owner Shemer.

But as far as GOD was concerned, Omri lived an evil life—set new records in evil. He walked in the footsteps of Jeroboam son of Nebat, who not only sinned but dragged Israel into his sins, making GOD angry—such an empty-headed, empty-hearted life!

The rest of Omri's life, the mark he made on his times, is written in *The Chronicles of the Kings of Israel.* Omri died and was buried in Samaria. His son Ahab was the next king after him.

AHAB OF ISRAEL

Ahab son of Omri became king of Israel in the thirty-eighth year of Asa king of Judah. Ahab son of Omri was king over Israel for twenty-two years. He ruled from Samaria. Ahab son of Omri did even more open evil before GOD than anyone yet—a new champion in evil! It wasn't enough for him to copy the sins of Jeroboam son of Nebat; no, he went all out, first by marrying Jezebel daughter of Ethbaal king of the Sidonians, and then by serving and worshiping the god Baal. He built a temple for Baal in Samaria, and then furnished it with an altar for Baal. Worse, he went on and built a shrine to the sacred whore Asherah. He made the GOD of Israel angrier than all the previous kings of Israel put together.

It was under Ahab's rule that Hiel of Bethel refortified Jericho, but at a terrible cost: He ritually sacrificed his firstborn son Abiram at the laying of the foundation, and his youngest son Segub at the setting up of the gates. This is exactly what Joshua son of Nun said would happen.

17 And then this happened: Elijah the Tishbite, from among the settlers of Gilead, confronted Ahab: "As surely as GOD lives, the God of Israel before whom I stand in obedient service, the next years are going to see a total drought—not a drop of dew or rain unless I say otherwise."

GOD then told Elijah, "Get out of here, and fast. Head east and hide out at the Kerith Ravine on the other side of the Jordan River. You can drink fresh water from the brook; I've ordered the ravens to feed you."

Elijah obeyed GOD's orders. He went and camped in the Kerith canyon on the other side of the Jordan. And sure enough, ravens brought him his meals, both breakfast and supper, and he drank from the brook.

Eventually the brook dried up because of the drought. Then GOD spoke to him: "Get up and go to Zarephath in Sidon and live there. I've instructed a woman who lives there, a widow, to feed you."

So he got up and went to Zarephath. As he came to the entrance of the village he met a woman, a widow, gathering firewood. He asked her, "Please, would you bring me a little water in a jug? I need a drink." As she went to get it, he called out, "And while you're at it, would you bring me something to eat?"

She said, "I swear, as surely as your GOD lives, I don't have so much as a biscuit. I have a handful of flour in a jar and a little oil in a bottle; you found me scratching together just enough firewood to make a last meal for my son and me. After we eat it, we'll die."

Elijah said to her, "Don't worry about a thing. Go ahead and do what you've said. But first make a small biscuit for me and bring it back here. Then go ahead and make a meal from what's left for you and your son. This is the word of the GOD of Israel: 'The jar of flour will not run out and the bottle of oil will not become empty before GOD sends rain on the land and ends this drought.'"

And she went right off and did it, did just as Elijah asked. And it turned out as he said—daily food for her and her family. The jar of meal didn't run out and the bottle of oil didn't become empty: GOD's promise fulfilled to the letter, exactly as Elijah had delivered it!

Later on the woman's son became sick. The sickness took a turn for the worse—and then he stopped breathing.

The woman said to Elijah, "Why did you ever show up here in the first place—a holy man barging in, exposing my sins, and killing my son?"

Elijah said, "Hand me your son."

He then took him from her bosom, carried him up to the loft where he was staying, and laid him on his bed. Then he prayed, "O GOD, my God, why have you brought this terrible thing on this widow who has opened her home to me? Why have you killed her son?"

Three times he stretched himself out full-length on the boy, praying with all his might, "GOD, my God, put breath back into this boy's body!" GOD listened to Elijah's prayer and put breath back into his body—he was alive! Elijah picked the boy up, carried him downstairs from the loft, and gave him to his mother. "Here's your son," said Elijah, "alive!"

The woman said to Elijah, "I see it all now—you *are* a holy man. When you speak, GOD speaks—a true word!"

18 A long time passed. Then GOD's word came to Elijah. The drought was now in its third year. The message: "Go and present yourself to Ahab; I'm about to make it rain on the country." Elijah set out to present himself to Ahab. The drought in Samaria at the time was most severe.

Ahab called for Obadiah, who was in charge of the palace. Obadiah feared GOD—he was very devout. Earlier, when Jezebel had tried to kill off all the prophets of GOD, Obadiah had hidden away a hundred of them in two caves, fifty in a cave, and then supplied them with food and water.

Ahab ordered Obadiah, "Go through the country; locate every spring and every stream. Let's see if we can find enough grass to keep our horses and mules from dying." So they divided the country between them for the search—Ahab went one way, Obadiah the other.

Obadiah went his way and suddenly there he was—Elijah! Obadiah fell on his knees, bowing in reverence, and exclaimed, "Is it really you—my master Elijah?"

"Yes," said Elijah, "the real me. Now go and tell your boss, 'I've seen Elijah.'"

Obadiah said, "But what have I done to deserve this? Ahab will kill me. As surely as your GOD lives, there isn't a country or kingdom where my master hasn't sent out search parties looking for you. And if they said, 'We can't find him; we've looked high and low,' he would make that country or kingdom swear that you were not to be found. And now you're telling me, 'Go and tell your master Elijah's found!' The minute I leave you the Spirit of GOD will whisk you away to who knows where. Then when I report to Ahab, you'll have disappeared and Ahab will kill me. And I've served GOD devoutly since I was a boy! Hasn't anyone told you what I did when Jezebel was out to kill the prophets of GOD, how I risked my life by hiding a hundred of them, fifty to a cave, and made sure they got food and water? And now you're telling me to draw attention to myself by announcing to my master, 'Elijah's been found.' Why, he'll kill me for sure."

Elijah said, "As surely as GOD-of-the-Angel-Armies lives, and before whom I take my stand, I'll meet with your master face to face this very day."

So Obadiah went straight to Ahab and told him. And Ahab went out to meet Elijah.

The moment Ahab saw Elijah he said, "So it's you, old troublemaker!"

"It's not I who has caused trouble in Israel," said Elijah, "but you and your government—you've dumped GOD's ways and commands and run off after the local gods, the Baals. Here's what I want you to do: Assemble everyone in Israel at Mount Carmel. And make sure that the special pets of Jezebel, the four hundred and fifty prophets of the local gods, the Baals, and the four hundred prophets of the whore goddess Asherah, are there."

So Ahab summoned everyone in Israel, particularly the prophets, to Mount Carmel.

Elijah challenged the people: "How long are you going to sit on the fence? If GOD is the real God, follow him; if it's Baal, follow him. Make up your minds!"

Nobody said a word; nobody made a move.

Then Elijah said, "I'm the only prophet of GOD left in Israel; and there are four hundred and fifty prophets of Baal. Let the Baal prophets bring up two oxen; let them pick one, butcher it, and lay it out on an altar on firewood—but don't ignite it. I'll take the other ox, cut it up, and lay it on the wood. But neither will I light the fire. Then you pray to your gods and I'll pray to GOD. The god who answers with fire will prove to be, in fact, God."

All the people agreed: "A good plan—do it!"

Elijah told the Baal prophets, "Choose your ox and prepare it. You go first, you're the majority. Then pray to your god, but don't light the fire."

So they took the ox he had given them, prepared it for the altar, then prayed to Baal. They prayed all morning long, "Oh Baal, answer us!" But nothing happened—not so much as a whisper of breeze. Desperate, they jumped and stomped on the altar they had made.

By noon, Elijah had started making fun of them, taunting, "Call a little louder—he is a god, after all. Maybe he's off meditating somewhere or other, or maybe he's gotten involved in a project, or maybe he's on vacation. You don't suppose he's overslept, do you, and needs to be waked up?" They prayed louder and louder, cutting themselves with swords and knives—a ritual common to them—until they were covered with blood.

This went on until well past noon. They used every religious trick and strategy they knew to make something happen on the altar, but nothing happened—not so much as a whisper, not a flicker of response.

Then Elijah told the people, "Enough of that—it's my turn. Gather around." And they gathered. He then put the altar back together for by now it was in ruins. Elijah took twelve stones, one for each of the tribes of Jacob, the same Jacob to whom GOD had said, "From now on your name is Israel." He built the stones into the altar in honor of GOD. Then Elijah dug a fairly wide trench around the altar. He laid firewood on the altar, cut up the ox, put it on the wood, and said, "Fill four buckets with water and drench both the ox and the firewood." Then he said, "Do it again," and they did it. Then he said, "Do it a third time," and they did it a third time. The altar was drenched and the trench was filled with water.

When it was time for the sacrifice to be offered, Elijah the prophet came up and prayed, "O GOD, God of Abraham, Isaac, and Israel, make it known right now that you are God in Israel, that I am your servant, and that I'm doing what I'm doing under your orders. Answer me, GOD; O answer me and reveal to this people that you are GOD, the true God, and that you are giving these people another chance at repentance."

Immediately the fire of G OD fell and burned up the offering, the wood, the stones, the dirt, and even the water in the trench.

All the people saw it happen and fell on their faces in awed worship, exclaiming, "G OD is the true God! G OD is the true God!"

Elijah told them, "Grab the Baal prophets! Don't let one get away!"

They grabbed them. Elijah had them taken down to the Brook Kishon and they massacred the lot.

Elijah said to Ahab, "Up on your feet! Eat and drink—celebrate! Rain is on the way; I hear it coming."

Ahab did it: got up and ate and drank. Meanwhile, Elijah climbed to the top of Carmel, bowed deeply in prayer, his face between his knees. Then he said to his young servant, "On your feet now! Look toward the sea."

He went, looked, and reported back, "I don't see a thing."

"Keep looking," said Elijah, "seven times if necessary."

And sure enough, the seventh time he said, "Oh yes, a cloud! But very small, no bigger than someone's hand, rising out of the sea."

"Quickly then, on your way. Tell Ahab, 'Saddle up and get down from the mountain before the rain stops you.'"

Things happened fast. The sky grew black with wind-driven clouds, and then a huge cloudburst of rain, with Ahab hightailing it in his chariot for Jezreel. And G OD strengthened Elijah mightily. Pulling up his robe and tying it around his waist, Elijah ran in front of Ahab's chariot until they reached Jezreel.

R EVENGE FROM J EZEBEL

19 Ahab reported to Jezebel everything that Elijah had done, including the massacre of the prophets. Jezebel immediately sent a messenger to Elijah with her threat: "The gods will get you for this and I'll get even with you! By this time tomorrow you'll be as dead as any one of those prophets."

When Elijah saw how things were, he ran for dear life to Beersheba, far in the south of Judah. He left his young servant there and then went on into the desert another day's journey. He came to a lone broom bush and collapsed in its shade, wanting in the worst way to be done with it all—to just die: "Enough of this, G OD! Take my life—I'm ready to join my ancestors in the grave!" Exhausted, he fell asleep under the lone broom bush.

Suddenly an angel shook him awake and said, "Get up and eat!"

He looked around and, to his surprise, right by his head were a loaf of bread baked on some coals and a jug of water. He ate the meal and went back to sleep.

The angel of GOD came back, shook him awake again, and said, "Get up and eat some more—you've got a long journey ahead of you."

He got up, ate and drank his fill, and set out. Nourished by that meal, he walked forty days and nights, all the way to the mountain of God, to Horeb. When he got there, he crawled into a cave and went to sleep.

Then the word of GOD came to him: "So Elijah, what are you doing here?"

"I've been working my heart out for the GOD-of-the-Angel-Armies," said Elijah. "The people of Israel have abandoned your covenant, destroyed the places of worship, and murdered your prophets. I'm the only one left, and now they're trying to kill me."

Then he was told, "Go, stand on the mountain at attention before GOD. GOD will pass by."

A hurricane wind ripped through the mountains and shattered the rocks before GOD, but GOD wasn't to be found in the wind; after the wind an earthquake, but GOD wasn't in the earthquake; and after the earthquake fire, but GOD wasn't in the fire; and after the fire a gentle and quiet whisper.

When Elijah heard the quiet voice, he muffled his face with his great cloak, went to the mouth of the cave, and stood there. A quiet voice asked, "So Elijah, now tell me, what are you doing here?" Elijah said it again, "I've been working my heart out for GOD, the GOD-of-the-Angel-Armies, because the people of Israel have abandoned your covenant, destroyed your places of worship, and murdered your prophets. I'm the only one left, and now they're trying to kill me."

GOD said, "Go back the way you came through the desert to Damascus. When you get there anoint Hazael; make him king over Aram. Then anoint Jehu son of Nimshi; make him king over Israel. Finally, anoint Elisha son of Shaphat from Abel Meholah to succeed you as prophet. Anyone who escapes death by Hazael will be killed by Jehu; and anyone who escapes death by Jehu will be killed by Elisha. Meanwhile, I'm preserving for myself seven thousand souls: the knees that haven't bowed to the god Baal, the mouths that haven't kissed his image."

Elijah went straight out and found Elisha son of Shaphat in a field where there were twelve pairs of yoked oxen at work plowing; Elisha was in charge of the twelfth pair. Elijah went up to him and threw his cloak over him.

Elisha deserted the oxen, ran after Elijah, and said, "Please! Let me kiss my father and mother good-bye—then I'll follow you."

"Go ahead," said Elijah, "but, mind you, don't forget what I've just done to you."

So Elisha left; he took his yoke of oxen and butchered them. He made a fire with the plow and tackle and then boiled the meat—a true farewell meal for the family. Then he left and followed Elijah, becoming his right-hand man.

20 At about this same time Ben-Hadad king of Aram mustered his troops. He recruited in addition thirty-two local sheiks, all outfitted with horses and chariots. He set out in force and surrounded Samaria, ready to make war. He sent an envoy into the city to set his terms before Ahab king of Israel: "Ben-Hadad lays claim to your silver and gold, and to the pick of your wives and sons."

The king of Israel accepted the terms: "As you say, distinguished lord; I and everything I have is yours."

But then the envoy returned a second time, saying, "On second thought, I want it all—your silver and gold and *all* your wives and sons. Hand them over—the whole works. I'll give you twenty-four hours; then my servants will arrive to search your palace and the houses of your officials and loot them; anything that strikes their fancy, they'll take."

The king of Israel called a meeting of all his tribal elders. He said, "Look at this—outrageous! He's just looking for trouble. He means to clean me out, demanding all my women and children. And after I already agreed to pay him off handsomely!"

The elders, backed by the people, said, "Don't cave in to him. Don't give an inch."

So he sent an envoy to Ben-Hadad, "Tell my distinguished lord, 'I agreed to the terms you delivered the first time, but this I can't do—this I *won't* do!'"

The envoy went back and delivered the answer.

Ben-Hadad shot back his response: "May the gods do their worst to me, and then worse again, if there'll be anything left of Samaria but rubble."

The king of Israel countered, "Think about it—it's easier to start a fight than end one."

It happened that when Ben-Hadad heard this retort he was into some heavy drinking, boozing it up with the sheiks in their field shelters. Drunkenly, he ordered his henchmen, "Go after them!" And they attacked the city.

Just then a lone prophet approached Ahab king of Israel and said, "GOD's word: Have you taken a good look at this mob? Well, look again—I'm turning it over to you this very day. And you'll know, beyond the shadow of a doubt, that I am GOD."

Ahab said, "Really? And who is going to make this happen?"

GOD said, "The young commandos of the regional chiefs."

"And who," said Ahab, "will strike the first blow?"

GOD said, "You."

Ahab looked over the commandos of the regional chiefs; he counted 232. Then he assessed the available troops—7,000.

At noon they set out after Ben-Hadad who, with his allies, the thirty-two sheiks, was busy at serious drinking in the field shelters. The commandos of the regional chiefs made up the vanguard.

A report was brought to Ben-Hadad: "Men are on their way from Samaria."

He said, "If they've come in peace, take them alive as hostages; if they've come to fight, the same—take them alive as hostages."

The commandos poured out of the city with the full army behind them. They hit hard in hand-to-hand combat. The Arameans scattered from the field, with Israel hard on their heels. But Ben-Hadad king of Aram got away on horseback, along with his cavalry.

The king of Israel cut down both horses and chariots—an enormous defeat for Aram.

Sometime later the prophet came to the king of Israel and said, "On the alert now—build up your army, assess your capabilities, and see what has to be done. Before the year is out, the king of Aram will be back in force."

Meanwhile the advisors to the king of Aram said, "Their god is a god of the mountains—we don't stand a chance against them there. So let's engage them on the plain where we'll have the advantage. Here's the strategy: Remove each sheik from his place of leadership and replace him with a seasoned officer. Then recruit a fighting force equivalent in size to the army that deserted earlier—horse for horse, chariot for chariot. And we'll fight them on the plain—we're sure to prove stronger than they are."

It sounded good to the king; he did what they advised.

As the new year approached, Ben-Hadad rallied Aram and they went up to Aphek to make war on Israel. The Israelite army prepared to fight and took the field to meet Aram. They moved into battle formation before Aram in two camps, like two flocks of goats. The plain was seething with Arameans.

Just then a holy man approached the king of Israel saying, "This is GOD's word: Because Aram said, 'GOD is a god of the mountains and not a god of the valleys,' I'll hand over this huge mob of an army to you. Then you'll know that I am GOD."

The two armies were poised in a standoff for seven days. On the seventh day fighting broke out. The Israelites killed 100,000 of the Aramean infantry in one day. The rest of the army ran for their lives back to the city, Aphek, only to have the city wall fall on 27,000 of the survivors.

Ben-Hadad escaped into the city and hid in a closet. Then his advisors told him, "Look, we've heard that the kings of Israel play by the rules; let's dress in old gunnysacks, carry a white flag of truce, and present ourselves to the king of Israel on the chance that he'll let you live."

So that's what they did. They dressed in old gunnysacks and carried a white flag, and came to the king of Israel saying, "Your servant Ben-Hadad said, 'Please let me live.'"

Ahab said, "You mean to tell me that he's still alive? If he's alive, he's my brother."

The men took this as a good sign and concluded that everything was going to be all right: "Ben-Hadad is most certainly your brother!"

The king said, "Go and get him." They went and brought him back by chariot.

Ahab said, "I am prepared to return the cities that my father took from your father. And you can set up your headquarters in Damascus just as my father did in Samaria; I'll send you home under safe conduct." Then he made a covenant with him and sent him off.

A man who was one of the prophets said to a bystander, "Hit me; wound me. Do it for GOD's sake—it's his command. Hit me; wound me." But the man wouldn't do it.

So he told him, "Because you wouldn't obey GOD's orders, as soon as you leave me a lion will attack you." No sooner had the man left his side than a lion met him and attacked.

He then found another man and said, "Hit me; wound me." That man did it—hit him hard in the face, drawing blood.

Then the prophet went and took a position along the road, with a bandage over his eyes, waiting for the king. It wasn't long before the king happened by. The man cried out to the king, "Your servant was in the thick of the battle when a man showed up and turned over a prisoner to me, saying, 'Guard this man with your life; if he turns up missing you'll pay dearly.' But I got busy doing one thing after another and the next time I looked he was gone."

The king of Israel said, "You've just pronounced your own verdict."

At that, the man ripped the bandage off his eyes and the king recognized who he was—one of the prophets!

The man said to the king, "GOD's word: Because you let a man go who was under sentence by GOD, it's now your life for his, your people for his."

The king of Israel went home in a sulk. He arrived in Samaria in a very bad mood.

21 And then, to top it off, came this: Naboth the Jezreelite owned a vineyard in Jezreel that bordered the palace of Ahab king of Samaria. One day Ahab spoke to Naboth, saying, "Give me your vineyard so I can use it as a kitchen garden; it's right next to my house—so convenient. In exchange I'll give you a far better vineyard, or if you'd prefer I'll pay you money for it."

But Naboth told Ahab, "Not on your life! So help me GOD, I'd never sell the family farm to you!" Ahab went home in a black mood, sulking over Naboth the Jezreelite's words, "I'll never turn over my family inheritance to you." He went to bed, stuffed his face in his pillow, and refused to eat.

Jezebel his wife came to him. She said, "What's going on? Why are you so out of sorts and refusing to eat?"

He told her, "Because I spoke to Naboth the Jezreelite. I said, 'Give me your vineyard—I'll pay you for it or, if you'd rather, I'll give you another vineyard in exchange.' And he said, 'I'll never give you my vineyard.'"

Jezebel said, "Is this any way for a king of Israel to act? Aren't you the boss? On your feet! Eat! Cheer up! I'll take care of this; I'll get the vineyard of this Naboth the Jezreelite for you."

She wrote letters over Ahab's signature, stamped them with his official seal, and sent them to the elders in Naboth's city and to the civic leaders. She wrote "Call for a fast day and put Naboth at the head table. Then seat a couple of stool pigeons across from him who, in front of everybody will say, 'You! You blasphemed God and the king!' Then they'll throw him out and stone him to death."

And they did it. The men of the city—the elders and civic leaders—followed Jezebel's instructions that she wrote in the letters sent to them. They called for a fast day and seated Naboth at the head table. Then they brought in two stool pigeons and seated them opposite Naboth. In front of everybody the two degenerates accused him, "He blasphemed God and the king!" The company threw him out in the street, stoned him mercilessly, and he died.

When Jezebel got word that Naboth had been stoned to death, she told Ahab, "Go for it, Ahab—take the vineyard of Naboth the Jezreelite for your own, the vineyard he refused to sell you. Naboth is no more; Naboth is dead."

The minute Ahab heard that Naboth was dead, he set out for the vineyard of Naboth the Jezreelite and claimed it for his own.

Then GOD stepped in and spoke to Elijah the Tishbite, "On your feet; go down and confront Ahab of Samaria, king of Israel. You'll find him in the vineyard of Naboth; he's gone there to claim it as his own. Say this to him: 'GOD's word: What's going on here? First murder, then theft?' Then tell him, 'GOD's verdict: The very spot where the dogs lapped up Naboth's blood, they'll lap up your blood—that's right, *your* blood.'"

Ahab answered Elijah, "My enemy! So, you've run me down!"

"Yes, I've found you out," said Elijah. "And because you've bought into the business of evil, defying GOD. 'I will most certainly bring doom upon you, make mincemeat of your descendants, kill off every sorry male wretch who's even remotely connected with the name Ahab. And I'll bring down on you the same fate that fell on Jeroboam son of Nebat and Baasha son of Ahijah—you've made me *that* angry by making Israel sin.'"

As for Jezebel, GOD said, "Dogs will fight over the flesh of Jezebel all over Jezreel. Anyone tainted by Ahab who dies in the city will be eaten by stray dogs; corpses in the country will be eaten by carrion crows."

Ahab, pushed by his wife Jezebel and in open defiance of GOD, set an all-time record in making big business of evil. He indulged in outrageous obscenities in the world of idols, copying the Amorites whom GOD had earlier kicked out of Israelite territory.

When Ahab heard what Elijah had to say, he ripped his clothes to shreds, dressed in penitential rough burlap, and fasted. He even slept in coarse burlap pajamas. He tiptoed around, quiet as a mouse.

Then GOD spoke to Elijah the Tishbite: "Do you see how penitently submissive Ahab has become to me? Because of his repentance I'll not bring the doom during his lifetime; Ahab's son, though, will get it."

22 They enjoyed three years of peace—no fighting between Aram and Israel. In the third year, Jehoshaphat king of Judah had a meeting with the king of Israel. Israel's king remarked to his aides, "Do you realize that Ramoth Gilead belongs to us, and we're sitting around on our hands instead of taking it back from the king of Aram?"

He turned to Jehoshaphat and said, "Will you join me in fighting for Ramoth Gilead?"

Jehoshaphat said, "You bet. I'm with you all the way—my troops are your troops, my horses are your horses." He then continued, "But before you do anything, ask GOD for guidance."

The king of Israel got the prophets together—all four hundred of them—and put the question to them: "Should I attack Ramoth Gilead? Or should I hold back?"

"Go for it," they said. "GOD will hand it over to the king."

But Jehoshaphat dragged his heels: "Is there still another prophet of GOD around here we can consult?"

The king of Israel told Jehoshaphat, "As a matter of fact, there is still one such man. But I hate him. He never preaches anything good to me, only doom, doom, doom—Micaiah son of Imlah."

"The king shouldn't talk about a prophet like that," said Jehoshaphat.

So the king of Israel ordered one of his men, "On the double! Get Micaiah son of Imlah."

Meanwhile, the king of Israel and Jehoshaphat were seated on their thrones, dressed in their royal robes, resplendent in front of the Samaria city gates. All the prophets were staging a prophecy-performance for their benefit. Zedekiah son of Kenaanah had even made a set of iron horns, and brandishing them called out, "GOD's word! With these horns you'll gore Aram until there's nothing left of him!" All the prophets chimed in, "Yes! Go for Ramoth Gilead! An easy victory! GOD's gift to the king!"

The messenger who went to get Micaiah said, "The prophets have all said Yes to the king. Make it unanimous—vote Yes!"

But Micaiah said, "As surely as GOD lives, what GOD says, I'll say."

With Micaiah before him, the king asked him, "So Micaiah—do we attack Ramoth Gilead, or do we hold back?"

"Go ahead," he said. "An easy victory. GOD's gift to the king."

"Not so fast," said the king. "How many times have I made you promise under oath to tell me the truth and nothing but the truth?"

"All right," said Micaiah, "since you insist.

I saw all of Israel scattered over the hills,
    sheep with no shepherd.
Then GOD spoke: 'These poor people
    have no one to tell them what to do.
Let them go home and do
    the best they can for themselves.'"

Then the king of Israel turned to Jehoshaphat, "See! What did I tell you? He never has a good word for me from GOD, only doom."

Micaiah kept on: "I'm not done yet; listen to GOD's word:

I saw GOD enthroned,
    and all the angel armies of heaven
Standing at attention
    ranged on his right and his left.
And GOD said, 'How can we seduce Ahab
    into attacking Ramoth Gilead?'
Some said this,
    and some said that.
Then a bold angel stepped out,
    stood before GOD, and said,
'I'll seduce him.'
    'And how will you do it?' said GOD.
'Easy,' said the angel,
    'I'll get all the prophets to lie.'
'That should do it,' said GOD.
    'On your way—seduce him!'

"And that's what has happened. GOD filled the mouths of your puppet prophets with seductive lies. GOD has pronounced your doom."

Just then Zedekiah son of Kenaanah came up and punched Micaiah in the nose, saying, "Since when did the Spirit of GOD leave me and take up with you?"

Micaiah said, "You'll know soon enough; you'll know it when you're frantically and futilely looking for a place to hide."

The king of Israel had heard enough: "Get Micaiah out of here! Turn him over to Amon the city magistrate and to Joash the king's son with this message, 'King's orders: Lock him up in jail; keep him on bread and water until I'm back in one piece.'"

Micaiah said, "If you ever get back in one piece, I'm no prophet of GOD."

He added, "When it happens, O people, remember where you heard it!"

The king of Israel and Jehoshaphat king of Judah attacked Ramoth Gilead. The king of Israel said to Jehoshaphat, "Wear my kingly robe; I'm going into battle disguised." So the king of Israel entered the battle in disguise.

Meanwhile, the king of Aram had ordered his chariot commanders (there were thirty-two of them): "Don't bother with anyone, whether small or great; go after the king of Israel and him only."

When the chariot commanders saw Jehoshaphat they said, "There he is! The king of Israel!" and took after him. Jehoshaphat yelled out, and the chariot commanders realized they had the wrong man—it wasn't the king of Israel after all. They let him go.

Just then someone, without aiming, shot an arrow randomly into the crowd and hit the king of Israel in the chink of his armor. The king told his charioteer, "Turn back! Get me out of here—I'm wounded."

All day the fighting continued, hot and heavy. Propped up in his chariot, the king watched from the sidelines. He died that evening. Blood from his wound pooled in the chariot. As the sun went down, shouts reverberated through the ranks, "Abandon camp! Head for home! The king is dead!"

The king was brought to Samaria and there they buried him. They washed down the chariot at the pool of Samaria where the town whores bathed, and the dogs lapped up the blood, just as GOD's word had said.

The rest of Ahab's life—everything he did, the ivory palace he built, the towns he founded, and the defense system he built up—is all written up in *The Chronicles of the Kings of Israel*. He was buried in the family cemetery and his son Ahaziah was the next king.

JEHOSHAPHAT OF JUDAH

Jehoshaphat son of Asa became king of Judah in the fourth year of Ahab king of Israel. Jehoshaphat was thirty-five years old when he became king and he ruled for twenty-five years in Jerusalem. His mother was Azubah daughter of Shilhi. He continued the kind of life characteristic of his father Asa—no detours, no dead ends—pleasing GOD with his life. But he failed to get rid of the neighborhood sex-and-religion shrines. People continued to pray and worship at these idolatrous shrines. And he kept on good terms with the king of Israel.

The rest of Jehoshaphat's life, his achievements and his battles, is all written in *The Chronicles of the Kings of Judah*. Also, he got rid of the sacred prostitutes left over from the days of his father Asa.

Edom was kingless during his reign; a deputy was in charge.

Jehoshaphat built ocean-going ships to sail to Ophir for gold. But they never made it; they shipwrecked at Ezion Geber. During that time Ahaziah son of Ahab proposed a joint shipping venture, but Jehoshaphat wouldn't go in with him.

Then Jehoshaphat died and was buried in the family cemetery in the City of David his ancestor. Jehoram his son was the next king.

AHAZIAH OF ISRAEL

Ahaziah son of Ahab became king over Israel in Samaria in the seventeenth year of Jehoshaphat king of Judah. He ruled Israel for two years. As far as GOD was concerned, he lived an evil life, reproducing the bad life of his father and mother, repeating the pattern set down by Jeroboam son of Nebat, who led Israel into a life of sin. Worshiping at the Baal shrines, he made GOD, the God of Israel, angry, oh, so angry. If anything, he was worse than his father.

2 KINGS

1 After Ahab died, Moab rebelled against Israel.
One day Ahaziah fell through the balcony railing on the rooftop of his house in Samaria and was injured. He sent messengers off to consult Baal-Zebub, the god of Ekron, "Am I going to recover from this accident?"

GOD's angel spoke to Elijah the Tishbite: "Up on your feet! Go out and meet the messengers of the king of Samaria with this word, 'Is it because there's no God in Israel that you're running off to consult Baal-Zebub god of Ekron?' Here's a message from the GOD you've tried to bypass: 'You're not going to get out of that bed you're in—you're as good as dead already.'" Elijah delivered the message and was gone.

The messengers went back. The king said, "So why are you back so soon—what's going on?"

They told him, "A man met us and said, 'Turn around and go back to the king who sent you; tell him, GOD's message: Is it because there's no God in Israel that you're running off to consult Baal-Zebub god of Ekron? You needn't bother. You're not going to get out of that bed you're in—you're as good as dead already.'"

The king said, "Tell me more about this man who met you and said these things to you. What was he like?"

"Shaggy," they said, "and wearing a leather belt."

He said, "That has to be Elijah the Tishbite!"

The king sent a captain with fifty men to Elijah. Meanwhile Elijah was sitting, big as life, on top of a hill. The captain said, "O Holy Man! King's orders: Come down!"

Elijah answered the captain of the fifty, "If it's true that I'm a 'holy man,' lightning strike you and your fifty men!" Out of the blue lightning struck and incinerated the captain and his fifty.

The king sent another captain with his fifty men, "O Holy Man! King's orders: Come down. And right now!"

Elijah answered, "If it's true that I'm a 'holy man,' lightning strike you and your fifty men!" Immediately a divine lightning bolt struck and incinerated the captain and his fifty.

The king then sent a third captain with his fifty men. For a third time, a captain with his fifty approached Elijah. This one fell on his knees in supplication: "O Holy Man, have respect for my life and the souls of these fifty men! Twice now lightning from out of the blue has struck and incinerated captains with their fifty men; please, I beg you, respect my life!"

The angel of GOD told Elijah, "Go ahead; and don't be afraid." Elijah got up and went down with him to the king.

Elijah told him, "GOD's word: Because you sent messengers to consult Baal-Zebub the god of Ekron, as if there were no God in Israel to whom you could pray, you'll never get out of that bed alive—already you're as good as dead."

And he died, exactly as GOD's word spoken by Elijah had said.

Because Ahaziah had no son, his brother Joram became the next king. The succession took place in the second year of the reign of Jehoram son of Jehoshaphat king of Judah.

The rest of Ahaziah's life is recorded in *The Chronicles of the Kings of Israel.*

2 Just before GOD took Elijah to heaven in a whirlwind, Elijah and Elisha were on a walk out of Gilgal. Elijah said to Elisha, "Stay here. GOD has sent me on an errand to Bethel."

Elisha said, "Not on your life! I'm not letting you out of my sight!" So they both went to Bethel.

The guild of prophets at Bethel met Elisha and said, "Did you know that GOD is going to take your master away from you today?"

"Yes," he said, "I know it. But keep it quiet."

Then Elijah said to Elisha, "Stay here. GOD has sent me on an errand to Jericho."

Elisha said, "Not on your life! I'm not letting you out of my sight!" So they both went to Jericho.

The guild of prophets at Jericho came to Elisha and said, "Did you know that GOD is going to take your master away from you today?"

"Yes," he said, "I know it. But keep it quiet."

Then Elijah said to Elisha, "Stay here. GOD has sent me on an errand to the Jordan."

Elisha said, "Not on your life! I'm not letting you out of my sight!" And so the two of them went their way together.

Meanwhile, fifty men from the guild of prophets gathered some distance away while the two of them stood at the Jordan.

Elijah took his cloak, rolled it up, and hit the water with it. The river divided and the two men walked through on dry land.

When they reached the other side, Elijah said to Elisha, "What can I do for you before I'm taken from you? Ask anything."

Elisha said, "Your life repeated in my life. I want to be a holy man just like you."

"That's a hard one!" said Elijah. "But if you're watching when I'm taken from you, you'll get what you've asked for. But only if you're watching."

And so it happened. They were walking along and talking. Suddenly a chariot and horses of fire came between them and Elijah went up in a whirlwind to heaven. Elisha saw it all and shouted, "My father, my father! You—the chariot and cavalry of Israel!" When he could no longer see anything, he grabbed his robe and ripped it to pieces. Then he picked up Elijah's cloak that had fallen from him, returned to the shore of the Jordan, and stood there. He took Elijah's cloak—all that was left of Elijah!—and hit the river with it, saying, "Now where is the GOD of Elijah? Where is he?"

When he struck the water, the river divided and Elisha walked through.

The guild of prophets from Jericho saw the whole thing from where they were standing. They said, "The spirit of Elijah lives in Elisha!" They welcomed and honored him.

They then said, "We're at your service. We have fifty reliable men here; let's send them out to look for your master. Maybe GOD's spirit has swept him off to some mountain or dropped him into a remote ravine."

Elisha said, "No. Don't send them."

But they pestered him until he caved in: "Go ahead then. Send them."

So they sent the fifty men off. For three days they looked, searching high and low. Nothing.

Finally, they returned to Elisha in Jericho. He told them, "So there—didn't I tell you?"

One day the men of the city said to Elisha, "You can see for yourself, master, how well our city is located. But the water is polluted and nothing grows."

He said, "Bring me a brand-new bowl and put some salt in it." They brought it to him.

He then went to the spring, sprinkled the salt into it, and proclaimed, "GOD's word: I've healed this water. It will no longer kill you or poison your land." And sure enough, the water was healed—and remains so to this day, just as Elisha said.

Another time, Elisha was on his way to Bethel and some little kids came out from the town and taunted him, "What's up, old baldhead! Out of our way, skinhead!"

Elisha turned, took one look at them, and cursed them in the name of GOD. Two bears charged out of the underbrush and knocked them about, ripping them limb from limb—forty-two children in all!

Elisha went on to Mount Carmel, and then returned to Samaria.

JORAM OF ISRAEL

3 Joram son of Ahab began his rule over Israel in Samaria in the eighteenth year of Jehoshaphat king of Judah. He was king for twelve years. In GOD's sight he was a bad king. But he wasn't as bad as his father and mother—to his credit he destroyed the obscene Baal stone that his father had made. But he hung on to the sinful practices of Jeroboam son of Nebat, the ones that had corrupted Israel for so long. He wasn't about to give them up.

King Mesha of Moab raised sheep. He was forced to give the king of Israel one hundred thousand lambs and another hundred thousand rams. When Ahab died, the king of Moab rebelled against the king of Israel. So King Joram set out from Samaria and prepared Israel for war. His first move was to send a message to Jehoshaphat king of Judah: "The king of Moab has rebelled against me. Would you join me and fight him?"

"I'm with you all the way," said Jehoshaphat. "My troops are your troops, my horses are your horses. Which route shall we take?"

"Through the badlands of Edom."

The king of Israel, the king of Judah, and the king of Edom started out on what proved to be a looping detour. After seven days they had run out of water for both army and animals.

The king of Israel said, "Bad news! GOD has gotten us three kings out here to dump us into the hand of Moab."

But Jehoshaphat said, "Isn't there a prophet of GOD anywhere around through whom we can consult GOD?"

One of the servants of the king of Israel said, "Elisha son of Shaphat is around somewhere—the one who was Elijah's right-hand man."

Jehoshaphat said, "Good! A man we can trust!" So the three of them—the king of Israel, Jehoshaphat, and the king of Edom—went to meet him.

Elisha addressed the king of Israel, "What do you and I have in common? Go consult the puppet-prophets of your father and mother."

"Never!" said the king of Israel. "It's GOD who has gotten us into this fix, dumping all three of us kings into the hand of Moab."

Elisha said, "As GOD-of-the-Angel-Armies lives, and before whom I stand ready to serve, if it weren't for the respect I have for Jehoshaphat king of Judah, I wouldn't give you the time of day. But considering— bring me a minstrel." (When a minstrel played, the power of GOD came on Elisha.)

He then said, "GOD's word: Dig ditches all over this valley. Here's what will happen—you won't hear the wind, you won't see the rain, but this valley is going to fill up with water and your army and your animals will drink their fill. This is easy for GOD to do; he will also hand over Moab to you. You will ravage the country: Knock out its fortifications, level the key villages, clear-cut the orchards, clog the springs, and litter the cultivated fields with stones."

In the morning—it was at the hour of morning sacrifice—the water had arrived, water pouring in from the west, from Edom, a flash-flood filling the valley with water.

By this time everyone in Moab had heard that the kings had come up to make war against them. Everyone who was able to handle a sword was called into service and took a stand at the border. They were up and ready early in the morning when the sun rose over the water. From where the Moabites stood, the water reflecting the sun looked red, like blood.

"Blood! Look at the blood!" they said. "The kings must have fought each other—a bloody massacre! Go for the loot, Moab!"

When Moab entered the camp of Israel, the Israelites were up on their feet killing Moabites right and left, the Moabites running for their lives, Israelites relentless in pursuit—a slaughter. They leveled the towns, littered the cultivated fields with rocks, clogged the springs, and clear-cut the orchards. Only the capital, Kir Hareseth, was left intact, and that not for long; it too was surrounded and attacked with thrown and flung rocks.

When the king of Moab realized that he was fighting a losing battle, he took seven hundred swordsmen to hack a corridor past the king of Edom, but they didn't make it. Then he took his son, his firstborn

who would succeed him as king, and sacrificed him on the city wall.
That set off furious anger against Israel. Israel pulled back and returned
home.

4 One day the wife of a man from the guild of prophets called out to
Elisha, "Your servant my husband is dead. You well know what a
good man he was, devoted to GOD. And now the man to whom he was
in debt is on his way to collect by taking my two children as slaves."

Elisha said, "I wonder how I can be of help. Tell me, what do you
have in your house?"

"Nothing," she said. "Well, I do have a little oil."

"Here's what you do," said Elisha. "Go up and down the street and
borrow jugs and bowls from all your neighbors. And not just a few—
all you can get. Then come home and lock the door behind you, you and
your sons. Pour oil into each container; when each is full, set it aside."

She did what he said. She locked the door behind her and her sons;
as they brought the containers to her, she filled them. When all the
jugs and bowls were full, she said to one of her sons, "Another jug,
please."

He said, "That's it. There are no more jugs."

Then the oil stopped.

She went and told the story to the man of God. He said, "Go sell
the oil and make good on your debts. Live, both you and your sons, on
what's left."

✠

One day Elisha passed through Shunem. A leading lady of the town
talked him into stopping for a meal. And then it became his custom:
Whenever he passed through, he stopped by for a meal.

"I'm certain," said the woman to her husband, "that this man who
stops by with us all the time is a holy man of God. Why don't we add
on a small room upstairs and furnish it with a bed and desk, chair and
lamp, so that when he comes by he can stay with us?"

And so it happened that the next time Elisha came by he went to
the room and lay down for a nap.

Then he said to his servant Gehazi, "Tell the Shunammite woman
I want to see her." He called her and she came to him.

Through Gehazi Elisha said, "You've gone far beyond the call of
duty in taking care of us; what can we do for you? Do you have a

request we can bring to the king or to the commander of the army?"

She replied, "Nothing. I'm secure and satisfied in my family."

Elisha conferred with Gehazi: "There's got to be something we can do for her. But what?"

Gehazi said, "Well, she has no son, and her husband is an old man."

"Call her in," said Elisha. He called her and she stood at the open door.

Elisha said to her, "This time next year you're going to be nursing an infant son."

"O my master, O Holy Man," she said, "don't play games with me, teasing me with such fantasies!"

The woman conceived. A year later, just as Elisha had said, she had a son.

The child grew up. One day he went to his father, who was working with the harvest hands, complaining, "My head, my head!"

His father ordered a servant, "Carry him to his mother."

The servant took him in his arms and carried him to his mother. He lay on her lap until noon and died.

She took him up and laid him on the bed of the man of God, shut him in alone, and left.

She then called her husband, "Get me a servant and a donkey so I can go to the Holy Man; I'll be back as soon as I can."

"But why today? This isn't a holy day—it's neither New Moon nor Sabbath."

She said, "Don't ask questions; I need to go right now. Trust me."

She went ahead and saddled the donkey, ordering her servant, "Take the lead—and go as fast as you can; I'll tell you if you're going too fast." And so off she went. She came to the Holy Man at Mount Carmel.

The Holy Man, spotting her while she was still a long way off, said to his servant Gehazi, "Look out there; why, it's the Shunammite woman! Quickly now. Ask her, 'Is something wrong? Are you all right? Your husband? Your child?'"

She said, "Everything's fine."

But when she reached the Holy Man at the mountain, she threw herself at his feet and held tightly to him.

Gehazi came up to pull her away, but the Holy Man said, "Leave her alone—can't you see that she's in distress? But GOD hasn't let me in on why; I'm completely in the dark."

Then she spoke up: "Did I ask for a son, master? Didn't I tell you,

'Don't tease me with false hopes'?"

He ordered Gehazi, "Don't lose a minute—grab my staff and run as fast as you can. If you meet anyone, don't even take time to greet him, and if anyone greets you, don't even answer. Lay my staff across the boy's face."

The boy's mother said, "As sure as GOD lives and you live, you're not leaving me behind." And so Gehazi let her take the lead, and followed behind.

But Gehazi arrived first and laid the staff across the boy's face. But there was no sound—no sign of life. Gehazi went back to meet Elisha and said, "The boy hasn't stirred."

Elisha entered the house and found the boy stretched out on the bed dead. He went into the room and locked the door—just the two of them in the room—and prayed to GOD. He then got into bed with the boy and covered him with his body, mouth on mouth, eyes on eyes, hands on hands. As he was stretched out over him like that, the boy's body became warm. Elisha got up and paced back and forth in the room. Then he went back and stretched himself upon the boy again. The boy started sneezing—seven times he sneezed!—and opened his eyes.

He called Gehazi and said, "Get the Shunammite woman in here!" He called her and she came in.

Elisha said, "Embrace your son!"

She fell at Elisha's feet, face to the ground in reverent awe. Then she embraced her son and went out with him.

Elisha went back down to Gilgal. There was a famine there. While he was consulting with the guild of prophets, he told his servant, "Put a large pot on the fire and cook up some stew for the prophets."

One of the men went out into the field to get some herbs; he came across a wild vine and picked gourds from it, filling his gunnysack. He brought them back, sliced them up, and put them in the stew, even though no one knew what kind of plant it was. The stew was then served up for the men to eat. They started to eat, and then exclaimed, "Death in the pot, O man of God! Death in the pot!" Nobody could eat it.

Elisha ordered, "Get me some meal." Then he sprinkled it into the stew pot.

"Now serve it up to the men," he said. They ate it, and it was just fine—nothing wrong with *that* stew!

One day a man arrived from Baal Shalishah. He brought the man of God twenty loaves of fresh baked bread from the early harvest, along with a few apples from the orchard.

Elisha said, "Pass it around to the people to eat."

His servant said, "For a hundred men? There's not nearly enough!"

Elisha said, "Just go ahead and do it. GOD says there's plenty."

And sure enough, there was. He passed around what he had—they not only ate, but had leftovers.

5 Naaman was general of the army under the king of Aram. He was important to his master, who held him in the highest esteem because it was by him that GOD had given victory to Aram: a truly great man, but afflicted with a grievous skin disease. It so happened that Aram, on one of its raiding expeditions against Israel, captured a young girl who became a maid to Naaman's wife. One day she said to her mistress, "Oh, if only my master could meet the prophet of Samaria, he would be healed of his skin disease."

Naaman went straight to his master and reported what the girl from Israel had said.

"Well then, go," said the king of Aram. "And I'll send a letter of introduction to the king of Israel."

So he went off, taking with him about 750 pounds of silver, 150 pounds of gold, and ten sets of clothes.

Naaman delivered the letter to the king of Israel. The letter read, "When you get this letter, you'll know that I've personally sent my servant Naaman to you; heal him of his skin disease."

When the king of Israel read the letter, he was terribly upset, ripping his robe to pieces. He said, "Am I a god with the power to bring death or life that I get orders to heal this man from his disease? What's going on here? That king's trying to pick a fight, that's what!"

Elisha the man of God heard what had happened, that the king of Israel was so distressed that he'd ripped his robe to shreds. He sent word to the king, "Why are you so upset, ripping your robe like this? Send him to me so he'll learn that there's a prophet in Israel."

So Naaman with his horses and chariots arrived in style and stopped at Elisha's door.

Elisha sent out a servant to meet him with this message: "Go to the River Jordan and immerse yourself seven times. Your skin will be healed and you'll be as good as new."

Naaman lost his temper. He turned on his heel saying, "I thought he'd personally come out and meet me, call on the name of GOD, wave his hand over the diseased spot, and get rid of the disease. The Damascus rivers, Abana and Pharpar, are cleaner by far than any of the rivers in Israel. Why not bathe in them? I'd at least get clean." He stomped off, mad as a hornet.

But his servants caught up with him and said, "Father, if the prophet had asked you to do something hard and heroic, wouldn't you have done it? So why not this simple 'wash and be clean'?"

So he did it. He went down and immersed himself in the Jordan seven times, following the orders of the Holy Man. His skin was healed; it was like the skin of a little baby. He was as good as new.

He then went back to the Holy Man, he and his entourage, stood before him, and said, "I now know beyond a shadow of a doubt that there is no God anywhere on earth other than the God of Israel. In gratitude let me give you a gift."

"As GOD lives," Elisha replied, "the God whom I serve, I'll take nothing from you." Naaman tried his best to get him to take something, but he wouldn't do it.

"If you won't take anything," said Naaman, "let me ask you for something: Give me a load of dirt, as much as a team of donkeys can carry, because I'm never again going to worship any god other than GOD. But there's one thing for which I need GOD's pardon: When my master, leaning on my arm, enters the shrine of Rimmon and worships there, and I'm with him there, worshiping Rimmon, may you see to it that GOD forgive me for this."

Elisha said, "Everything will be all right. Go in peace."

But he hadn't gone far when Gehazi, servant to Elisha the Holy Man, said to himself, "My master has let this Aramean Naaman slip through his fingers without so much as a thank-you. By the living GOD, I'm going after him to get something or other from him!" And Gehazi took off after Naaman.

Naaman saw him running after him and jumped down from his chariot to greet him, "Is something wrong?"

"Nothing's wrong, but something's come up. My master sent me to tell you: 'Two young men just showed up from the hill country of Ephraim, brothers from the guild of the prophets. Supply their needs with a gift of seventy-five pounds of silver and a couple of sets of clothes.'"

Naaman said, "Of course, how about a hundred and fifty pounds?" Naaman insisted. He tied up the money in two sacks and gave him the two sets of clothes; he even gave him two servants to carry the gifts back with him.

When they got to the fort on the hill, Gehazi took the gifts from the servants, stored them inside, then sent the servants back.

He returned and stood before his master. Elisha said, "So what have you been up to, Gehazi?"

"Nothing much," he said.

Elisha said, "Didn't you know I was with you in spirit when that man stepped down from his chariot to greet you? Tell me, is this a time to look after yourself, lining your pockets with gifts? Naaman's skin disease will now infect you and your family, with no relief in sight."

Gehazi walked away, his skin flaky and white like snow.

6 One day the guild of prophets came to Elisha and said, "You can see that this place where we're living under your leadership is getting cramped—we have no elbow room. Give us permission to go down to the Jordan where each of us will get a log. We'll build a roomier place."

Elisha said, "Go ahead."

One of them then said, "Please! Come along with us!"

He said, "Certainly."

He went with them. They came to the Jordan and started chopping down trees. As one of them was felling a timber, his axhead flew off and sank in the river.

"Oh no, master!" he cried out. "And it was borrowed!"

The Holy Man said, "Where did it sink?"

The man showed him the place.

He cut off a branch and tossed it at the spot. The axhead floated up. "Grab it," he said. The man reached out and took it.

One time when the king of Aram was at war with Israel, after consulting with his officers, he said, "At such and such a place I want an ambush set."

The Holy Man sent a message to the king of Israel: "Watch out when you're passing this place, because Aram has set an ambush there."

So the king of Israel sent word concerning the place of which the Holy Man had warned him.

This kind of thing happened all the time.

The king of Aram was furious over all this. He called his officers together and said, "Tell me, who is leaking information to the king of Israel? Who is the spy in our ranks?"

But one of his men said, "No, my master, dear king. It's not any of us. It's Elisha the prophet in Israel. He tells the king of Israel everything you say, even what you whisper in your bedroom."

The king said, "Go and find out where he is. I'll send someone and capture him."

The report came back, "He's in Dothan."

Then he dispatched horses and chariots, an impressive fighting force. They came by night and surrounded the city.

Early in the morning a servant of the Holy Man got up and went out. Surprise! Horses and chariots surrounding the city! The young man exclaimed, "Oh, master! What shall we do?"

He said, "Don't worry about it—there are more on our side than on their side."

Then Elisha prayed, "O GOD, open his eyes and let him see."

The eyes of the young man were opened and he saw. A wonder! The whole mountainside full of horses and chariots of fire surrounding Elisha!

When the Arameans attacked, Elisha prayed to GOD, "Strike these people blind!" And GOD struck them blind, just as Elisha said.

Then Elisha called out to them, "Not that way! Not this city! Follow me and I'll lead you to the man you're looking for." And he led them into Samaria.

As they entered the city, Elisha prayed, "O GOD, open their eyes so they can see where they are." GOD opened their eyes. They looked around—they were trapped in Samaria!

When the king of Israel saw them, he said to Elisha, "Father, shall I massacre the lot?"

"Not on your life!" said Elisha. "You didn't lift a hand to capture them, and now you're going to kill them? No sir, make a feast for them and send them back to their master."

So he prepared a huge feast for them. After they ate and drank their fill he dismissed them. Then they returned home to their master. The raiding bands of Aram didn't bother Israel anymore.

At a later time, this: Ben-Hadad king of Aram pulled together his troops and launched a siege on Samaria. This brought on a terrible famine, so bad that food prices soared astronomically. Eighty shekels for a donkey's head! Five shekels for a bowl of field greens!

One day the king of Israel was walking along the city wall. A woman cried out, "Help! Your majesty!"

He answered, "If GOD won't help you, where on earth can *I* go for help? To the granary? To the dairy?"

The king continued, "Tell me your story."

She said, "This woman came to me and said, 'Give up your son and we'll have him for today's supper; tomorrow we'll eat my son.' So we cooked my son and ate him. The next day I told her, 'Your turn — bring your son so we can have him for supper.' But she had hidden her son away."

When the king heard the woman's story he ripped apart his robe. Since he was walking on the city wall, everyone saw that next to his skin he was wearing coarse burlap. And he called out, "God do his worst to me — and more — if Elisha son of Shaphat still has a head on his shoulders at this day's end."

Elisha was sitting at home, the elders sitting with him. The king had already dispatched an executioner, but before the man arrived Elisha spoke to the elders: "Do you know that this murderer has just now sent a man to take off my head? Look, when the executioner arrives, shut the door and lock it. Don't I even now hear the footsteps of his master behind him?"

While he was giving his instructions, the king showed up, accusing, "This trouble is directly from GOD! And what's next? I'm fed up with GOD!"

7 Elisha said, "Listen! GOD's word! The famine's over. This time tomorrow food will be plentiful — a handful of meal for a shekel; two handfuls of grain for a shekel. The market at the city gate will be buzzing."

The attendant on whom the king leaned for support said to the Holy Man, "You expect us to believe that? Trapdoors opening in the sky and food tumbling out?"

"You'll watch it with your own eyes," he said, "but *you* will not eat so much as a mouthful!"

It happened that four lepers were sitting just outside the city gate. They said to one another, "What are we doing sitting here at death's door? If we enter the famine-struck city we'll die; if we stay here we'll die. So let's take our chances in the camp of Aram and throw ourselves on their mercy. If they receive us we'll live, if they kill us we'll die. We've got nothing to lose."

So after the sun went down they got up and went to the camp of Aram. When they got to the edge of the camp, surprise! Not a man in the camp! The Master had made the army of Aram hear the sound of horses and a mighty army on the march. They told one another, "The king of Israel hired the kings of the Hittites and the kings of Egypt to attack us!" Panicked, they ran for their lives through the darkness, abandoning tents, horses, donkeys—the whole camp just as it was—running for dear life. These four lepers entered the camp and went into a tent. First they ate and drank. Then they grabbed silver, gold, and clothing, and went off and hid it. They came back, entered another tent, and looted it, again hiding their plunder.

Finally they said to one another, "We shouldn't be doing this! This is a day of good news and we're making it into a private party! If we wait around until morning we'll get caught and punished. Come on! Let's go tell the news to the king's palace!"

So they went and called out at the city gate, telling what had happened: "We went to the camp of Aram and, surprise!—the place was deserted. Not a soul, not a sound! Horses and donkeys left tethered and tents abandoned just as they were."

The gatekeepers got the word to the royal palace, giving them the whole story. Roused in the middle of the night, the king told his servants, "Let me tell you what Aram has done. They knew that we were starving, so they left camp and have hid in the field, thinking, 'When they come out of the city, we'll capture them alive and take the city.'"

One of his advisors answered, "Let some men go and take five of the horses left behind. The worst that can happen is no worse than what could happen to the whole city. Let's send them and find out what's happened."

They took two chariots with horses. The king sent them after the army of Aram with the orders, "Scout them out; find out what happened."

They went after them all the way to the Jordan. The whole way was strewn with clothes and equipment that Aram had dumped in their panicked flight. The scouts came back and reported to the king.

The people then looted the camp of Aram. Food prices dropped overnight—a handful of meal for a shekel; two handfuls of grain for a shekel—GOD's word to the letter!

The king ordered his attendant, the one he leaned on for support, to be in charge of the city gate. The people, turned into a mob, poured through the gate, trampling him to death. It was exactly what the Holy Man had said when the king had come to see him.

Every word of the Holy Man to the king—"A handful of meal for a shekel, two handfuls of grain for a shekel this time tomorrow in the gate of Samaria," with the attendant's sarcastic reply to the Holy Man, "You expect us to believe that? Trapdoors opening in the sky and food tumbling out?" followed by the response, "You'll watch it with your own eyes, but you won't eat so much as a mouthful"—proved true. The final stroke came when the people trampled the man to death at the city gate.

8 Years before, Elisha had told the woman whose son he had brought to life, "Leave here and go, you and your family, and live someplace else. GOD has ordered a famine in the land; it will last for seven years." The woman did what the Holy Man told her and left. She and her family lived as aliens in the country of Philistia for seven years. Then, when the seven years were up, the woman and her family came back. She went directly to the king and asked for her home and farm.

The king was talking with Gehazi, servant to the Holy Man, saying, "Tell me some stories of the great things Elisha did." It so happened that as he was telling the king the story of the dead person brought back to life, the woman whose son was brought to life showed up asking for her home and farm.

Gehazi said, "My master the king, this is the woman! And this is her son whom Elisha brought back to life!"

The king wanted to know all about it, and so she told him the story. The king assigned an officer to take care of her, saying, "Make sure she gets everything back that's hers, plus all profits from the farm from the time she left until now."

Elisha traveled to Damascus. Ben-Hadad, king of Aram, was sick at the time. He was told, "The Holy Man is in town."

The king ordered Hazael, "Take a gift with you and go meet the Holy Man. Ask GOD through him, 'Am I going to recover from this sickness?'"

Hazael went and met with Elisha. He brought with him every choice thing he could think of from Damascus—forty camel-loads of items! When he arrived he stood before Elisha and said, "Your son

Ben-Hadad, king of Aram, sent me here to ask you, 'Am I going to recover from this sickness?'"

Elisha answered, "Go and tell him, 'Don't worry; you'll live.' The fact is, though—GOD showed me—that he's doomed to die." Elisha then stared hard at Hazael, reading his heart. Hazael felt exposed and dropped his eyes. Then the Holy Man wept.

Hazael said, "Why does my master weep?"

"Because," said Elisha, "I know what you're going to do to the children of Israel:

burn down their forts,
murder their youth,
smash their babies,
rip open their pregnant women."

Hazael said, "Am I a mongrel dog that I'd do such a horrible thing?"

"GOD showed me," said Elisha, "that you'll be king of Aram."

Hazael left Elisha and returned to his master, who asked, "So, what did Elisha tell you?"

"He told me, 'Don't worry; you'll live.'"

But the very next day, someone took a heavy quilt, soaked it in water, covered the king's face, and suffocated him.

Now Hazael was king.

JEHORAM OF JUDAH

In the fifth year of the reign of Joram son of Ahab king of Israel, Jehoram son of Jehoshaphat king of Judah became king. He was thirty-two years old when he began his rule, and was king for eight years in Jerusalem. He copied the way of life of the kings of Israel, marrying into the Ahab family and continuing the Ahab line of sin—from GOD's point of view, an evil man living an evil life. But despite that, because of his servant David, GOD was not ready to destroy Judah. He had, after all, promised to keep a lamp burning through David's descendants.

During Jehoram's reign, Edom revolted against Judah's rule and set up their own king. Jehoram responded by taking his army of chariots to Zair.

Edom surrounded him, but in the middle of the night he and his charioteers broke through the lines and hit Edom hard. But his infantry deserted him.

Edom continues in revolt against Judah right up to the present. Even little Libnah revolted at that time.

The rest of the life and times of Jehoram, the record of his rule, is written in *The Chronicles of the Kings of Judah*. Jehoram died and was buried in the family grave in the City of David. His son Ahaziah succeeded him as king.

Ahaziah of Judah

In the twelfth year of the reign of Joram son of Ahab king of Israel, Ahaziah son of Jehoram king of Judah began his reign. Ahaziah was twenty-two years old when he became king; he ruled only a year in Jerusalem. His mother was Athaliah, granddaughter of Omri king of Israel. He lived and ruled just like the Ahab family had done, continuing the same evil-in-God's-sight line of sin, related by both marriage and sin to the Ahab clan.

He joined Joram son of Ahab king of Israel in a war against Hazael king of Aram at Ramoth Gilead. The archers wounded Joram. Joram pulled back to Jezreel to convalesce from the injuries he had received in the fight with Hazael. Ahaziah son of Jehoram king of Judah paid a visit to Joram son of Ahab on his sickbed in Jezreel.

Jehu of Israel

9 One day Elisha the prophet ordered a member of the guild of prophets, "Get yourself ready, take a flask of oil, and go to Ramoth Gilead. Look for Jehu son of Jehoshaphat son of Nimshi. When you find him, get him away from his companions and take him to a back room. Take your flask of oil and pour it over his head and say, 'God's word: I anoint you king over Israel.' Then open the door and get out of there as fast as you can. Don't wait around."

The young prophet went to Ramoth Gilead. On arrival he found the army officers all sitting around. He said, "I have a matter of business with you, officer."

Jehu said, "Which one of us?"

"With you, officer."

He got up and went inside the building. The young prophet poured the oil on his head and said, "God's word, the God of Israel: I've anointed you to be king over the people of God, over Israel. Your assignment is to attack the regime of Ahab your master. I am avenging the massacre of my servants the prophets—yes, the Jezebel-massacre of all the prophets of God. The entire line of Ahab is doomed. I'm wiping

278

out the entire bunch of that sad lot. I'll see to it that the family of Ahab experiences the same fate as the family of Jeroboam son of Nebat and the family of Baasha son of Ahijah. As for Jezebel, the dogs will eat her carcass in the open fields of Jezreel. No burial for her!" Then he opened the door and made a run for it.

Jehu went back out to his master's officers. They asked, "Is everything all right? What did that crazy fool want with you?"

He said, "You know that kind of man—all talk."

"That's a lie!" they said. "Tell us what's going on."

He said, "He told me this and this and this—in effect, 'God's word: I anoint you king of Israel!'"

They sprang into action. Each man grabbed his robe; they piled them at the top of the steps for a makeshift throne. Then they blew the trumpet and declared, "Jehu is king!"

That ignited the conspiracy of Jehu son of Jehoshaphat son of Nimshi against Joram.

Meanwhile, Joram and the entire army were defending Ramoth Gilead against Hazael king of Aram. Except that Joram had pulled back to Jezreel to convalesce from the injuries he got from the Arameans in the battle with Hazael king of Aram.

Jehu said, "If you really want me as king, don't let anyone sneak out of the city and blab the news in Jezreel."

Then Jehu mounted a chariot and rode to Jezreel, where Joram was in bed, resting. King Ahaziah of Judah had come down to visit Joram.

A sentry standing duty on the watchtower in Jezreel saw the company of Jehu arrive. He said, "I see a band of men."

Joram said, "Get a horseman and send him out to meet them and inquire, 'Is anything wrong?'"

The horseman rode out to meet Jehu and said, "The king wants to know if there's anything wrong."

Jehu said, "What's it to you whether things are right or wrong? Fall in behind me."

The sentry said, "The messenger reached them, but he's not returning."

The king then sent a second horseman. When he reached them he said, "The king wants to know if there's anything wrong."

Jehu said, "What's it to you whether things are right or wrong? Fall in behind me."

The sentry said, "The messenger reached them, but he's not returning. The driving is like the driving of Jehu son of Nimshi—crazy!"

Joram ordered, "Get my chariot ready!" They hitched up his chariot. Joram king of Israel and Ahaziah king of Judah, each in his own chariot, drove out to meet Jehu. They met in the field of Naboth of Jezreel.

When Joram saw Jehu he called out, "Good day, Jehu!"

Jehu answered, "What's good about it? How can there be anything good about it as long as the promiscuous whoring and sorceries of your mother Jezebel pollute the country?"

Joram wheeled his chariot around and fled, yelling to Ahaziah, "It's a trap, Ahaziah!"

Jehu pulled on his bow and released an arrow; it hit Joram between the shoulder blades and went right through his heart. He slumped to his knees in his chariot.

Jehu ordered Bidkar, his lieutenant, "Quick—throw him into the field of Naboth of Jezreel. Remember when you and I were driving our chariots behind Ahab his father? That's when GOD pronounced this doom upon him: 'As surely as I saw the blood of murdered Naboth and his sons yesterday, you'll pay for it on this exact piece of ground. GOD's word!' So take him and throw him out in the field. GOD's instructions carried out to the letter!"

Ahaziah king of Judah saw what was going on and made his escape on the road toward Beth Haggan. Jehu chased him, yelling out, "Get him, too!" Jehu's troops shot and wounded him in his chariot on the hill up to Gur, near Ibleam. He was able to make it as far as Megiddo; there he died.

His aides drove on to Jerusalem. They buried him in the family plot in the City of David.

In the eleventh year of the reign of Joram son of Ahab, Ahaziah had become king of Judah.

When Jezebel heard that Jehu had arrived in Jezreel, she made herself up—put on eyeshadow and arranged her hair—and posed seductively at the window. When Jehu came through the city gate, she called down, "So, how are things, 'Zimri,' you dashing king-killer?"

Jehu looked up at the window and called, "Is there anybody up there on my side?" Two or three palace eunuchs looked out.

He ordered, "Throw her down!" They threw her out the window.

Her blood spattered the wall and the horses, and Jehu trampled her under his horse's hooves.

Then Jehu went inside and ate his lunch. During lunch he gave orders, "Take care of that damned woman; give her a decent burial— she is, after all, a king's daughter."

They went out to bury her, but there was nothing left of her but skull, feet, and hands. They came back and told Jehu. He said, "It's GOD's word, the word spoken by Elijah the Tishbite:

In the field of Jezreel,
    dogs will eat Jezebel;
The body of Jezebel will be like
    dog-droppings on the ground in Jezreel.
Old friends and lovers will say,
    'I wonder, is *this* Jezebel?'"

10 Ahab had seventy sons still living in Samaria. Jehu wrote letters addressed to the officers of Jezreel, the city elders, and those in charge of Ahab's sons, and posted them to Samaria. The letters read:

This letter is fair warning. You're in charge of your master's children, chariots, horses, fortifications, and weapons. Pick the best and most capable of your master's sons and put him on the throne. Prepare to fight for your master's position.

They were absolutely terrified at the letter. They said, "Two kings have already been wiped out by him; what hope do we have?"

So they sent the warden of the palace, the mayor of the city, the elders, and the guardians to Jehu with this message: "We are your servants. Whatever you say, we'll do. We're not making anyone king here. You're in charge—do what you think best."

Then Jehu wrote a second letter:

If you are on my side and are willing to follow my orders, here's what you do: Decapitate the sons of your master and bring the heads to me by this time tomorrow in Jezreel.

The king's sons numbered seventy. The leaders of the city had taken responsibility for them. When they got the letter, they took the king's sons and killed all seventy. Then they put the heads in baskets and sent them to Jehu in Jezreel.

A messenger reported to Jehu: "They've delivered the heads of the king's sons."

He said, "Stack them in two piles at the city gate until morning."

In the morning Jehu came out, stood before the people, and addressed them formally: "Do you realize that this very day you are participants in GOD's righteous workings? True, I am the one who conspired against my master and assassinated him. But who, do you suppose, is responsible for this pile of skulls? Know this for certain: Not a single syllable that GOD spoke in judgment on the family of Ahab is canceled; you're seeing it with your own eyes—GOD doing what, through Elijah, he said he'd do."

Then Jehu proceeded to kill everyone who had anything to do with Ahab's family in Jezreel—leaders, friends, priests. He wiped out the entire lot.

That done, he brushed himself off and set out for Samaria. Along the way, at Beth Eked (Binding House) of the Shepherds, he met up with some relatives of Ahaziah king of Judah.

Jehu said, "Who are you?"

They said, "We're relatives of Ahaziah and we've come down to a reunion of the royal family."

"Grab them!" ordered Jehu. They were taken and then massacred at the well of Beth Eked. Forty-two of them—no survivors.

He went on from there and came upon Jehonadab the Recabite who was on his way to meet him. Greeting him, he said, "Are we together and of one mind in this?"

Jehonadab said, "We are—count on me."

"Then give me your hand," said Jehu.

They shook hands on it and Jehonadab stepped up into the chariot with Jehu.

"Come along with me," said Jehu, "and witness my zeal for GOD." Together they proceeded in the chariot.

When they arrived in Samaria, Jehu massacred everyone left in Samaria who was in any way connected with Ahab—a mass execution, just as GOD had told Elijah.

Next, Jehu got all the people together and addressed them:

Ahab served Baal small-time;
Jehu will serve him big-time.

"Get all the prophets of Baal here—everyone who served him, all his priests. Get everyone here; don't leave anyone out. I have a great sacrifice to offer Baal. If you don't show up, you won't live to tell about it." (Jehu was lying, of course. He planned to destroy all the worshipers of Baal.)

Jehu ordered, "Make preparation for a holy convocation for Baal." They did and posted the date.

Jehu then summoned everyone in Israel. They came in droves—every worshiper of Baal in the country. Nobody stayed home. They came and packed the temple of Baal to capacity.

Jehu directed the keeper of the wardrobe, "Get robes for all the servants of Baal." He brought out their robes.

Jehu and Jehonadab the Recabite now entered the temple of Baal and said, "Double-check and make sure that there are no worshipers of GOD in here; only Baal-worshipers are allowed." Then they launched the worship, making the sacrifices and burnt offerings.

Meanwhile, Jehu had stationed eighty men outside with orders: "Don't let a single person escape; if you do, it's your life for his life."

When Jehu had finished with the sacrificial solemnities, he signaled to the officers and guards, "Enter and kill! No survivors!"

And the bloody slaughter began. The officers and guards threw the corpses outside and cleared the way to enter the inner shrine of Baal. They hauled out the sacred phallic stone from the temple of Baal and pulverized it. They smashed the Baal altars and tore down the Baal temple. It's been a public toilet ever since.

And that's the story of Jehu's wasting of Baal in Israel.

But for all that, Jehu didn't turn back from the sins of Jeroboam son of Nebat, the sins that had dragged Israel into a life of sin—the golden calves in Bethel and Dan stayed.

GOD commended Jehu: "You did well to do what I saw was best. You did what I ordered against the family of Ahab. As reward, your sons will occupy the throne of Israel for four generations."

Even then, though, Jehu wasn't careful to walk in GOD's ways and honor the God of Israel from an undivided heart. He didn't turn back from the sins of Jeroboam son of Nebat, who led Israel into a life of sin.

It was about this time that GOD began to shrink Israel. Hazael hacked away at the borders of Israel from the Jordan to the east—

all the territory of Gilead, Gad, Reuben, and Manasseh from Aroer near the Brook Arnon. In effect, all Gilead and Bashan.

The rest of the life and times of Jehu, his accomplishments and fame, are written in *The Chronicles of the Kings of Israel.* Jehu died and was buried in the family plot in Samaria. His son Jehoahaz was the next king. Jehu ruled Israel from Samaria for twenty-eight years.

ATHALIAH OF JUDAH

11 Athaliah was the mother of Ahaziah. When she saw that her son was dead, she took over. She began by massacring the entire royal family. But Jehosheba, daughter of King Joram and sister of Ahaziah, took Ahaziah's son Joash and kidnapped him from among the king's sons slated for slaughter. She hid him and his nurse in a private room away from Athaliah. He didn't get killed. He was there with her, hidden away for six years in The Temple of GOD. Athaliah, oblivious to his existence, ruled the country.

In the seventh year Jehoiada sent for the captains of the bodyguards and the Palace Security Force. They met him in The Temple of GOD. He made a covenant with them, swore them to secrecy, and only then showed them the young prince.

Then he commanded them, "These are your instructions: Those of you who come on duty on the Sabbath and guard the palace, and those of you who go off duty on the Sabbath and guard The Temple of GOD, are to join forces at the time of the changing of the guard and form a ring around the young king, weapons at the ready. Kill anyone who tries to break through your ranks. Your job is to stay with the king at all times and places, coming and going."

The captains obeyed the orders of Jehoiada the priest. Each took his men, those who came on duty on the Sabbath and those who went off duty on the Sabbath, and presented them to Jehoiada the priest. The priest armed the officers with spears and shields originally belonging to King David, stored in The Temple of GOD. Well-armed, the guards took up their assigned positions for protecting the king, from one end of The Temple to the other, surrounding both Altar and Temple.

Then the priest brought the prince into view, crowned him, handed him the scroll of God's covenant, and made him king. As they anointed him, everyone applauded and shouted, "Long live the king!"

Athaliah heard the shouting of guards and people and came to the crowd gathered at The Temple of GOD. Astonished, she saw the king standing beside the throne, flanked by the captains and heralds, with everybody beside themselves with joy, trumpets blaring. Athaliah ripped her robes in dismay and shouted, "Treason! Treason!"

Jehoiada the priest ordered the military officers, "Drag her outside and kill anyone who tries to follow her!" (The priest had said, "Don't kill her inside The Temple of GOD.") So they dragged her out to the palace's horse corral; there they killed her.

Jehoiada now made a covenant between GOD and the king and the people: They were GOD's people. Another covenant was made between the king and the people.

The people poured into the temple of Baal and tore it down, smashing altar and images to smithereens. They killed Mattan the priest in front of the altar.

Jehoiada then stationed sentries in The Temple of GOD. He arranged for the officers of the bodyguard and the palace security, along with the people themselves, to escort the king down from The Temple of GOD through the Gate of the Guards and into the palace. There he sat on the royal throne. Everybody celebrated the event. And the city was safe and undisturbed—they had killed Athaliah with the royal sword.

Joash was seven years old when he became king.

JOASH OF JUDAH

12 In the seventh year of Jehu, Joash began his kingly rule. He was king for forty years in Jerusalem. His mother's name was Gazelle. She was from Beersheba.

Taught and trained by Jehoiada the priest, Joash did what pleased GOD for as long as he lived. (Even so, he didn't get rid of the sacred fertility shrines—people still frequented them, sacrificing and burning incense.)

Joash instructed the priests: "Take the money that is brought into The Temple of GOD for holy offerings—both mandatory offerings and freewill offerings—and, keeping a careful accounting, use them to renovate The Temple wherever it has fallen into disrepair."

But by the twenty-third year of Joash's rule, the priests hadn't done one thing—The Temple was as dilapidated as ever.

King Joash called Jehoiada the priest and the company of priests and said, "Why haven't you renovated this sorry-looking Temple? You are forbidden to take any more money for Temple repairs—from now on, hand over everything you get."

The priests agreed not to take any more money or to be involved in The Temple renovation.

Then Jehoiada took a single chest and bored a hole in the lid and placed it to the right of the main entrance into The Temple of GOD. All the offerings that were brought to The Temple of GOD were placed in the chest by the priests who guarded the entrance. When they saw that a large sum of money had accumulated in the chest, the king's secretary and the chief priest would empty the chest and count the offerings. They would give the money accounted for to the managers of The Temple project; they in turn would pay the carpenters, construction workers, masons, stoneworkers, and the buyers of timber and quarried stone for the repair and renovation of The Temple of GOD—any expenses connected with fixing up The Temple. But none of the money brought into The Temple of GOD was used for liturgical "extras" (silver chalices, candle snuffers, trumpets, various gold and silver vessels, etc.). It was given to the workmen to pay for their repairing GOD's Temple. And no one even had to check on the men who handled the money given for the project—they were honest men. Offerings designated for Compensation Offerings and Absolution Offerings didn't go into the building project—those went directly to the priests.

Around this time Hazael king of Aram ventured out and attacked Gath, and he captured it. Then he decided to try for Jerusalem. Joash king of Judah countered by gathering up all the sacred memorials—gifts dedicated for holy use by his ancestors, the kings of Judah, Jehoshaphat, Jehoram, and Ahaziah, along with the holy memorials he himself had received, plus all the gold that he could find in the temple and palace storerooms—and sent it to Hazael king of Aram. Appeased, Hazael went on his way and didn't bother Jerusalem.

The rest of the life and times of Joash and all that he did are written in *The Chronicles of the Kings of Judah*. At the last his palace staff formed a conspiracy and assassinated Joash as he was strolling along the ramp of the fortified outside city wall. Jozabad son of Shimeath and Jehozabad son of Shomer were the assassins. And so Joash died and was buried in the family plot in the City of David. His son Amaziah was king after him.

JEHOAHAZ OF ISRAEL

13 In the twenty-third year of Joash son of Ahaziah king of Judah, Jehoahaz son of Jehu became king of Israel in Samaria—a rule of seventeen years. He lived an evil life before GOD, walking step for step in the tracks of Jeroboam son of Nebat who led Israel into a life of sin, swerving neither left or right. Exasperated, GOD was furious with Israel and turned them over to Hazael king of Aram and Ben-Hadad son of Hazael. This domination went on for a long time.

Then Jehoahaz prayed for a softening of GOD's anger, and GOD listened. He realized how wretched Israel had become under the brutalities of the king of Aram. So GOD provided a savior for Israel who brought them out from under Aram's oppression. The children of Israel were again able to live at peace in their own homes. But it didn't make any difference: They didn't change their lives, didn't turn away from the Jeroboam-sins that now characterized Israel, including the sex-and-religion shrines of Asherah still flourishing in Samaria.

Nothing was left of Jehoahaz's army after Hazael's oppression except for fifty cavalry, ten chariots, and ten thousand infantry. The king of Aram had decimated the rest, leaving behind him mostly chaff.

The rest of the life and times of Jehoahaz, the record of his accomplishments, are written in *The Chronicles of the Kings of Israel*. Jehoahaz died and was buried with his ancestors in Samaria. His son Jehoash succeeded him as king.

JEHOASH OF ISRAEL

In the thirty-seventh year of Joash king of Judah, Jehoash son of Jehoahaz became king of Israel in Samaria—a reign of sixteen years. In GOD's eyes he lived an evil life. He didn't deviate one bit from the sins of Jeroboam son of Nebat, who led Israel into a life of sin. He plodded along in the same tracks, step after step.

The rest of the life and times of Jehoash, the record of his accomplishments and his war against Amaziah king of Judah, are written in *The Chronicles of the Kings of Israel*. Jehoash died and joined his ancestors. Jeroboam took over his throne. Jehoash was buried in Samaria in the royal cemetery.

Elisha came down sick. It was the sickness of which he would soon die. Jehoash king of Israel paid him a visit. When he saw him he wept openly, crying, "My father, my father! Chariot and horsemen of Israel!"

Elisha told him, "Go and get a bow and some arrows." The king brought him the bow and arrows.

Then he told the king, "Put your hand on the bow." He put his hand on the bow. Then Elisha put his hand over the hand of the king.

Elisha said, "Now open the east window." He opened it.

Then he said, "Shoot!" And he shot.

"The arrow of GOD's salvation!" exclaimed Elisha. "The arrow of deliverance from Aram! You will do battle against Aram until there's nothing left of it."

"Now pick up the other arrows," said Elisha. He picked them up. Then he said to the king of Israel, "Strike the ground."

The king struck the ground three times and then quit.

The Holy Man became angry with him: "Why didn't you hit the ground five or six times? Then you would beat Aram until he was finished. As it is, you'll defeat him three times only."

Then Elisha died and they buried him.

Some time later, raiding bands of Moabites, as they often did, invaded the country. One day, some men were burying a man and spotted the raiders. They threw the man into Elisha's tomb and got away. When the body touched Elisha's bones, the man came alive, stood up, and walked out on his own two feet.

Hazael king of Aram badgered and bedeviled Israel all through the reign of Jehoahaz. But GOD was gracious and showed mercy to them. He stuck with them out of respect for his covenant with Abraham, Isaac, and Jacob. He never gave up on them, never even considered discarding them, even to this day. Hazael king of Aram died. His son Ben-Hadad was the next king.

Jehoash son of Jehoahaz turned things around and took back the cities that Ben-Hadad son of Hazael had taken from his father Jehoahaz. Jehoash went to war three times and defeated him each time, recapturing the cites of Israel.

AMAZIAH OF JUDAH

14 In the second year of Jehoash son of Jehoahaz king of Israel, Amaziah son of Joash became king of Judah. He was twenty-five years old when he became king and he reigned for twenty-nine years in Jerusalem. His mother's name was Jehoaddin. She was from Jerusalem.

He lived the way GOD wanted and did the right thing. But he didn't come up to the standards of his ancestor David; instead he lived pretty much as his father Joash had; the local sex-and-religion shrines continued to stay in business with people frequenting them.

When he had the affairs of the kingdom well in hand, he executed the palace guard that had assassinated his father the king. But he didn't kill the sons of the assassins. He was obedient to what GOD commanded, written in the Word revealed to Moses, that parents shouldn't be executed for their children's sins, nor children for those of their parents. We each pay personally for our sins.

Amaziah roundly defeated Edom in the Valley of Salt to the tune of ten thousand dead. In another battle he took The Rock and renamed it Joktheel, the name it still bears.

One day Amaziah sent envoys to Jehoash son of Jehoahaz, the son of Jehu, king of Israel, challenging him to a fight: "Come and meet with me—I dare you. Let's have it out face to face!"

Jehoash king of Israel replied to Amaziah king of Judah, "One day a thistle in Lebanon sent word to a cedar in Lebanon, 'Give your daughter to my son in marriage.' But then a wild animal of Lebanon passed by and stepped on the thistle, crushing it. Just because you've defeated Edom in battle, you now think you're a big shot. Go ahead and be proud, but stay home. Why press your luck? Why bring defeat on yourself and Judah?"

Amaziah wouldn't take No for an answer. So Jehoash king of Israel gave in and agreed to a battle between him and Amaziah king of Judah. They met at Beth Shemesh, a town of Judah.

Judah was thoroughly beaten by Israel—all their soldiers ran home in defeat.

Jehoash king of Israel captured Amaziah king of Judah, the son of Joash, the son of Ahaziah, at Beth Shemesh. But Jehoash didn't stop there; he went on to attack Jerusalem. He demolished the wall of Jerusalem all the way from the Ephraim Gate to the Corner Gate—a stretch of about 600 feet. He looted the gold, silver, and furnishings—anything he found that was worth taking—from both the palace and

The Temple of GOD. And, for good measure, he took hostages. Then he returned to Samaria.

The rest of the life and times of Jehoash, his significant accomplishments and the fight with Amaziah king of Judah, are all written in *The Chronicles of the Kings of Israel*. Jehoash died and was buried in Samaria in the cemetery of the kings of Israel. His son Jeroboam became the next king.

Amaziah son of Joash king of Judah continued as king fifteen years after the death of Jehoash son of Jehoahaz king of Israel. The rest of the life and times of Amaziah is written in *The Chronicles of the Kings of Judah*.

At the last they cooked up a plot against Amaziah in Jerusalem and he had to flee to Lachish. But they tracked him down in Lachish and killed him there. They brought him back on horseback and buried him in Jerusalem, with his ancestors in the City of David.

Azariah—he was only sixteen years old at the time—was the unanimous choice of the people of Judah to succeed his father Amaziah as king. Following his father's death, he rebuilt and restored Elath to Judah.

JEROBOAM II OF ISRAEL

In the fifteenth year of Amaziah son of Joash king of Judah, Jeroboam son of Jehoash became king of Israel in Samaria. He ruled for forty-one years. As far as GOD was concerned he lived an evil life, never deviating an inch from all the sin of Jeroboam son of Nebat, who led Israel into a life of sin. But he did restore the borders of Israel to Lebo Hamath in the far north and to the Dead Sea in the south, matching what GOD, the God of Israel, had pronounced through his servant Jonah son of Amittai, the prophet from Gath Hepher.

GOD was fully aware of the trouble in Israel, its bitterly hard times. No one was exempt, whether slave or citizen, and no hope of help anywhere was in sight. But GOD wasn't yet ready to blot out the name of Israel from history, so he used Jeroboam son of Jehoash to save them.

The rest of the life and times of Jeroboam, his victories in battle and how he recovered for Israel both Damascus and Hamath which had belonged to Judah, these are all written in *The Chronicles of the Kings of Israel*. Jeroboam died and was buried with his ancestors in the royal cemetery. His son Zechariah became the next king.

AZARIAH (UZZIAH) OF JUDAH

15 In the twenty-seventh year of Jeroboam king of Israel, Azariah son of Amaziah became king in Judah. He was sixteen years old when he began his rule and he was king for fifty-two years in Jerusalem. His mother's name was Jecoliah. She was from Jerusalem. He did well in the eyes of GOD, following in the footsteps of his father Amaziah. But he also failed to get rid of the local sex-and-religion shrines; they continued to be popular with the people. GOD afflicted the king with a bad skin disease until the day of his death. He lived in the palace but no longer acted as king; his son Jotham ran the government and ruled the country.

The rest of the life and times of Azariah, everything he accomplished, is written in *The Chronicles of the Kings of Judah.* Azariah died and was buried with his ancestors in the City of David. Jotham his son was king after him.

ZECHARIAH OF ISRAEL

In the thirty-eighth year of Azariah king of Judah, Zechariah son of Jeroboam became king over Israel in Samaria. He lasted only six months. He lived a bad life before GOD, no different from his ancestors. He continued in the line of Jeroboam son of Nebat who led Israel into a life of sin.

Shallum son of Jabesh conspired against him, assassinated him in public view, and took over as king.

The rest of the life and times of Zechariah is written plainly in *The Chronicles of the Kings of Israel.* That completed the word of GOD that was given to Jehu, namely, "For four generations your sons will sit on the throne of Israel." Zechariah was the fourth.

SHALLUM OF ISRAEL

Shallum son of Jabesh became king in the thirty-ninth year of Azariah king of Judah. He was king in Samaria for only a month.

Menahem son of Gadi came up from Tirzah to Samaria. He attacked Shallum son of Jabesh and killed him. He then became king.

The rest of the life and times of Shallum and the account of the conspiracy are written in *The Chronicles of the Kings of Israel.*

MENAHEM OF ISRAEL

Using Tirzah as his base, Menahem opened his reign by smashing Tiphsah, devastating both the town and its suburbs because they didn't welcome him with open arms. He savagely ripped open all the pregnant women.

In the thirty-ninth year of Azariah king of Judah, Menahem son of Gadi became king over Israel. He ruled from Samaria for ten years. As far as GOD was concerned he lived an evil life. Sin for sin, he repeated the sins of Jeroboam son of Nebat, who led Israel into a life of sin.

Then Tiglath-Pileser III king of Assyria showed up and attacked the country. But Menahem made a deal with him: He bought his support by handing over about thirty-seven tons of silver. He raised the money by making every landowner in Israel pay fifty shekels to the king of Assyria. That satisfied the king of Assyria, and he left the country.

The rest of the life and times of Menahem, everything he did, is written in *The Chronicles of the Kings of Israel*. Menahem died and joined his ancestors. His son Pekahiah became the next king.

PEKAHIAH OF ISRAEL

In the fiftieth year of Azariah king of Judah, Pekahiah son of Menahem became king of Israel. He ruled in Samaria for two years. In GOD's eyes he lived an evil life. He stuck to the old sin tracks of Jeroboam son of Nebat, who led Israel into a life of sin.

And then his military aide Pekah son of Remaliah conspired against him—killed him in cold blood while he was in his private quarters in the royal palace in Samaria. He also killed Argob and Arieh. Fifty Gadites were in on the conspiracy with him. After the murder he became the next king.

The rest of the life and times of Pekahiah, everything he did, is written in *The Chronicles of the Kings of Israel*.

PEKAH OF ISRAEL

In the fifty-second year of Azariah king of Judah, Pekah son of Remaliah became king of Israel in Samaria. He ruled for twenty years. In GOD's view he lived an evil life; he didn't deviate so much as a hair's breadth from the path laid down by Jeroboam son of Nebat, who led Israel into a life of sin.

During the reign of Pekah king of Israel, Tiglath-Pileser III king of Assyria invaded the country. He captured Ijon, Abel Beth Maacah, Janoah, Kedesh, Hazor, Gilead, Galilee—the whole country of Naphtali—and took everyone captive to Assyria.

But then Hoshea son of Elah mounted a conspiracy against Pekah son of Remaliah. He assassinated him and took over as king. This was in the twentieth year of Jotham son of Uzziah.

The rest of the life and times of Pekah, everything he did, is written in *The Chronicles of the Kings of Israel.*

JOTHAM OF JUDAH

In the second year of Pekah son of Remaliah king of Israel, Jotham son of Uzziah became king in Judah. He was twenty-five years old when he became king and reigned sixteen years in Jerusalem. His mother's name was Jerusha daughter of Zadok. He acted well in GOD's eyes, following in the steps of his father Uzziah. But he didn't interfere with the traffic to the neighborhood sex-and-religion shrines; they continued, as popular as ever. The construction of the High Gate to The Temple of GOD was his work.

The rest of the life and times of Jotham, the record of his work, is written in *The Chronicles of the Kings of Judah.* It was during these years that GOD began sending Rezin king of Aram and Pekah son of Remaliah to attack Judah. Jotham died and joined his ancestors. They buried him in the family cemetery in the City of David. His son Ahaz was the next king.

AHAZ OF JUDAH

16 In the seventeenth year of Pekah son of Remaliah, Ahaz son of Jotham became king of Judah. Ahaz was twenty years old when he became king and he ruled for sixteen years in Jerusalem. He didn't behave in the eyes of his GOD; he wasn't at all like his ancestor David. Instead he followed in the track of the kings of Israel. He even indulged in the outrageous practice of "passing his son through the fire"—a truly abominable act he picked up from the pagans GOD had earlier thrown out of the country. He also participated in the activities of the neighborhood sex-and-religion shrines that flourished all over the place.

Then Rezin king of Aram and Pekah son of Remaliah king of Israel ganged up against Jerusalem, throwing a siege around the city, but they couldn't make further headway against Ahaz.

At about this same time and on another front, the king of Edom recovered the port of Elath and expelled the men of Judah. The Edomites occupied Elath and have been there ever since.

Ahaz sent envoys to Tiglath-Pileser king of Assyria with this message: "I'm your servant and your son. Come and save me from the heavy-handed invasion of the king of Aram and the king of Israel. They're attacking me right now." Then Ahaz robbed the treasuries of the palace and The Temple of GOD of their gold and silver and sent them to the king of Assyria as a bribe.

The king of Assyria responded to him. He attacked and captured Damascus. He deported the people to Nineveh as exiles. Rezin he killed.

King Ahaz went to meet Tiglath-Pileser king of Assyria in Damascus. The altar in Damascus made a great impression on him. He sent back to Uriah the priest a drawing and set of blueprints of the altar. Uriah the priest built the altar to the specifications that King Ahaz had sent from Damascus. By the time the king returned from Damascus, Uriah had completed the altar.

The minute the king saw the altar he approached it with reverence and arranged a service of worship with a full course of offerings: Whole-Burnt-Offerings with billows of smoke, Grain-Offerings, libations of Drink-Offerings, the sprinkling of blood from the Peace-Offerings—the works. But the old bronze Altar that signaled the presence of GOD he displaced from its central place and pushed it off to the side of his new altar.

Then King Ahaz ordered Uriah the priest: "From now on offer all the sacrifices on the new altar, the great altar: morning Whole-Burnt-Offerings, evening Grain-Offerings, the king's Whole-Burnt-Offerings and Grain-Offerings, the people's Whole-Burnt-Offerings and Grain-Offerings, and also their Drink-Offerings. Splash all the blood from the burnt offerings and sacrifices against this altar. The old bronze Altar will be for my personal use.

The priest Uriah followed King Ahaz's orders to the letter.

Then King Ahaz proceeded to plunder The Temple furniture of all its bronze. He stripped the bronze from The Temple furnishings, even salvaged the four bronze oxen that supported the huge basin, The Sea, and set The Sea unceremoniously on the stone pavement. Finally, he removed any distinctive features from within The Temple that were offensive to the king of Assyria.

The rest of the life and times of Ahaz is written in *The Chronicles of the Kings of Judah*. Ahaz died and was buried with his ancestors in the City of David. His son Hezekiah became the next king.

HOSHEA OF ISRAEL

17 In the twelfth year of Ahaz king of Judah, Hoshea son of Elah became king of Israel. He ruled in Samaria for nine years. As far as GOD was concerned, he lived a bad life, but not nearly as bad as the kings who had preceded him.

Then Shalmaneser king of Assyria attacked. Hoshea was already a puppet of the Assyrian king and regularly sent him tribute, but Shalmaneser discovered that Hoshea had been operating traitorously behind his back—having worked out a deal with King So of Egypt. And, adding insult to injury, Hoshea was way behind on his annual payments of tribute to Assyria. So the king of Assyria arrested him and threw him in prison, then proceeded to invade the entire country. He attacked Samaria and threw up a siege against it. The siege lasted three years.

In the ninth year of Hoshea's reign the king of Assyria captured Samaria and took the people into exile in Assyria. He relocated them in Halah, in Gozan along the Habor River, and in the towns of the Medes.

The exile came about because of sin: The children of Israel sinned against GOD, their God, who had delivered them from Egypt and the brutal oppression of Pharaoh king of Egypt. They took up with other gods, fell in with the ways of life of the pagan nations GOD had chased off, and went along with whatever their kings did. They did all kinds of things on the sly, things offensive to their GOD, then openly and shamelessly built local sex-and-religion shrines at every available site. They set up their sex-and-religion symbols at practically every cross-roads. Everywhere you looked there was smoke from their pagan offerings to the deities—the identical offerings that had gotten the pagan nations off into exile. They had accumulated a long list of evil actions and GOD was fed up, fed up with their persistent worship of gods carved out of deadwood or shaped out of clay, even though GOD had plainly said, "Don't do this—ever!"

GOD had taken a stand against Israel and Judah, speaking clearly through countless holy prophets and seers time and time again, "Turn away from your evil way of life. Do what I tell you and have been telling you in The Revelation I gave your ancestors and of which I've kept reminding you ever since through my servants the prophets."

But they wouldn't listen. If anything, they were even more bull-headed than their stubborn ancestors, if that's possible. They were contemptuous of his instructions, the solemn and holy covenant he had made with their ancestors, and of his repeated reminders and warnings. They lived a "nothing" life and became "nothings"—just like the pagan peoples all around them. They were well-warned: GOD said, "Don't!" but they did it anyway.

They threw out everything GOD, their God, had told them, and replaced him with two statue-gods shaped like bull-calves and then a phallic pole for the whore goddess Asherah. They worshiped cosmic forces—sky gods and goddesses—and frequented the sex-and-religion shrines of Baal. They even sank so low as to offer their own sons and daughters as sacrificial burnt offerings! They indulged in all the black arts of magic and sorcery. In short, they prostituted themselves to every kind of evil available to them. And GOD had had enough.

GOD was so thoroughly angry that he got rid of them, got them out of the country for good until only one tribe was left—Judah. (Judah, actually, wasn't much better, for Judah also failed to keep GOD's commands, falling into the same way of life that Israel had adopted.) GOD rejected everyone connected with Israel, made life hard for them, and permitted anyone with a mind to exploit them to do so. And then this final No as he threw them out of his sight.

Back at the time that God ripped Israel out of their place in the family of David, they had made Jeroboam son of Nebat king. Jeroboam debauched Israel—turned them away from serving GOD and led them into a life of total sin. The children of Israel went along with all the sins that Jeroboam did, never murmured so much as a word of protest. In the end, GOD spoke a final No to Israel and turned his back on them. He had given them fair warning, and plenty of time, through the preaching of all his servants the prophets. Then he exiled Israel from her land to Assyria. And that's where they are now.

The king of Assyria brought in people from Babylon, Cuthah, Avva, Hamath, and Sepharvaim, and relocated them in the towns of Samaria, replacing the exiled Israelites. They moved in as if they owned the place and made themselves at home. When the Assyrians first moved in, GOD was just another god to them; they neither honored nor worshiped him. Then GOD sent lions among them and people were mauled and killed.

This message was then sent back to the king of Assyria: "The people you brought in to occupy the towns of Samaria don't know what's expected of them from the god of the land, and now he's sent lions and they're killing people right and left because nobody knows what the god of the land expects of them."

The king of Assyria ordered, "Send back some priests who were taken into exile from there. They can go back and live there and instruct the people in what the god of the land expects of them."

One of the priests who had been exiled from Samaria came back and moved into Bethel. He taught them how to honor and worship GOD.

But each people that Assyria had settled went ahead anyway making its own gods and setting them up in the neighborhood sex-and-religion shrines that the citizens of Samaria had left behind—a local custom-made god for each people:

for Babylon, Succoth Benoth;
for Cuthah, Nergal;
for Hamath, Ashima;
for Avva, Nibhaz and Tartak;
for Sepharvaim, Adrammelech and Anammelech (people burned their children in sacrificial offerings to these gods!).

They honored and worshiped GOD, but not exclusively—they also appointed all sorts of priests, regardless of qualification, to conduct a variety of rites at the local fertility shrines. They honored and worshiped GOD, but they also kept up their devotions to the old gods of the places they had come from.

And they're still doing it, still worshiping any old god that has nostalgic appeal to them. They don't really worship GOD—they don't take seriously what he says regarding how to behave and what to believe, what he revealed to the children of Jacob whom he named Israel. GOD made a covenant with his people and ordered them, "Don't honor other gods: Don't worship them, don't serve them, don't offer sacrifices to them. Worship GOD, the God who delivered you from Egypt in great and personal power. Reverence and fear him. Worship him. Sacrifice to him. And only him! All the things he had written down for you, directing you in what to believe and how to behave—well, do them for as long as you live. And whatever you do, *don't worship other gods*! And the covenant he made with you, don't forget your part in that. *And don't worship other gods*! Worship GOD, and GOD only—he's the one who will save your from enemy oppression."

But they didn't pay any attention. They kept doing what they'd always done. As it turned out, all the time these people were putting on a front of worshiping GOD, they were at the same time involved with their local idols. And they're still doing it. Like father, like son.

HEZEKIAH OF JUDAH

18In the third year of Hoshea son of Elah king of Israel, Hezekiah son of Ahaz began his rule over Judah. He was twenty-five years old when he became king and he ruled for twenty-nine years in Jerusalem. His mother's name was Abijah daughter of Zechariah. In GOD's opinion he was a good king; he kept to the standards of his ancestor David. He got rid of the local fertility shrines, smashed the phallic stone monuments, and cut down the sex-and-religion Asherah groves. As a final stroke he pulverized the ancient bronze serpent that Moses had made; at that time the Israelites had taken up the practice of sacrificing to it—they had even dignified it with a name, Nehushtan (The Old Serpent).

Hezekiah put his whole trust in the GOD of Israel. There was no king quite like him, either before or after. He held fast to GOD—never loosened his grip—and obeyed to the letter everything GOD had commanded Moses. And GOD, for his part, held fast to him through all his adventures.

He revolted against the king of Assyria; he refused to serve him one more day. And he drove back the Philistines, whether in sentry outposts or fortress cities, all the way to Gaza and its borders.

In the fourth year of Hezekiah and the seventh year of Hoshea son of Elah king of Israel, Shalmaneser king of Assyria attacked Samaria. He threw a siege around it and after three years captured it. It was in the sixth year of Hezekiah and the ninth year of Hoshea that Samaria fell to Assyria. The king of Assyria took Israel into exile and relocated them in Halah, in Gozan on the Habor River, and in towns of the Medes.

All this happened because they wouldn't listen to the voice of their GOD and treated his covenant with careless contempt. They refused either to listen or do a word of what Moses, the servant of GOD, commanded.

In the fourteenth year of King Hezekiah, Sennacherib king of Assyria attacked all the outlying fortress cities of Judah and captured them. King Hezekiah sent a message to the king of Assyria at his headquarters in Lachish: "I've done wrong; I admit it. Pull back your army; I'll pay whatever tribute you set."

The king of Assyria demanded tribute from Hezekiah king of Judah—eleven tons of silver and a ton of gold. Hezekiah turned over all the silver he could find in The Temple of GOD and in the palace treasuries. Hezekiah even took down the doors of The Temple of GOD and the doorposts that he had overlaid with gold and gave them to the king of Assyria.

So the king of Assyria sent his top three military chiefs (the Tartan, the Rabsaris, and the Rabshakeh) from Lachish with a strong military force to King Hezekiah in Jerusalem. When they arrived at Jerusalem, they stopped at the aqueduct of the Upper Pool on the road to the laundry commons.

They called loudly for the king. Eliakim son of Hilkiah who was in charge of the palace, Shebna the royal secretary, and Joah son of Asaph the court historian went out to meet them.

The third officer, the Rabshakeh, was spokesman. He said, "Tell Hezekiah: A message from The Great King, the king of Assyria: You're living in a world of make-believe, of pious fantasy. Do you think that mere words are any substitute for military strategy and troops? Now that you've revolted against me, who can you expect to help you? You thought Egypt would, but Egypt's nothing but a paper tiger—one puff of wind and she collapses; Pharaoh king of Egypt is nothing but bluff and bluster. Or are you going to tell me, 'We rely on GOD'? But Hezekiah has just eliminated most of the people's access to God by getting rid of all the local God-shrines, ordering everyone in Judah and Jerusalem, 'You must worship at the Jerusalem altar only.'

"So be reasonable. Make a deal with my master, the king of Assyria. I'll give you two thousand horses if you think you can provide riders for them. You can't do it? Well, then, how do you think you're going to turn back even one raw buck private from my master's troops? How long are you going to hold on to that figment of your imagination, these hoped-for Egyptian chariots and horses?

"Do you think I've come up here to destroy this country without the express approval of GOD? The fact is that GOD expressly ordered me, 'Attack and destroy this country!'"

Eliakim son of Hilkiah and Shebna and Joah said to the Rabshakeh, "Please, speak to us in the Aramaic language. We understand Aramaic. Don't speak in Hebrew—everyone crowded on the city wall can hear you."

But the Rabshakeh said, "We weren't sent with a private message to your master and you; this is public—a message to everyone within earshot. After all, they're involved in this as well as you; if you don't come to terms, they'll be eating their own turds and drinking their own pee right along with you."

Then he stepped forward and spoke in Hebrew loud enough for everyone to hear, "Listen carefully to the words of The Great King, the king of Assyria: Don't let Hezekiah fool you; he can't save you. And don't let Hezekiah give you that line about trusting in GOD, telling you, 'GOD will save us—this city will never be abandoned to the king of Assyria.' Don't listen to Hezekiah—he doesn't know what he's talking about. Listen to the king of Assyria—deal with me and live the good life; I'll guarantee everyone your own plot of ground—a garden and a well! I'll take you to a land sweeter by far than this one, a land of grain and wine, bread and vineyards, olive orchards and honey. You only live once—so live, really live!

"No. Don't listen to Hezekiah. Don't listen to his lies, telling you 'GOD will save us.' Has there ever been a god anywhere who delivered anyone from the king of Assyria? Where are the gods of Hamath and Arpad? Where are the gods of Sepharvaim, Hena, and Ivvah? And Samaria—did their gods save them? Can you name a god who saved anyone anywhere from me, the king of Assyria? So what makes you think that GOD can save Jerusalem from me?"

The people were silent. No one spoke a word for the king had ordered, "Don't anyone say a word—not one word!"

Then Eliakim son of Hilkiah, the palace administrator, and Shebna the royal secretary, and Joah son of Asaph the court historian went back to Hezekiah. They had ripped their robes in despair; they reported to Hezekiah the speech of the Rabshakeh.

19 When Hezekiah heard it all, he too ripped his robes apart and dressed himself in rough burlap. Then he went into The Temple of GOD. He sent Eliakim, who was in charge of the palace, Shebna the secretary, and the senior priests, all of them dressed in rough burlap, to the prophet Isaiah son of Amoz. They said to him, "A message from Hezekiah: 'This is a black day, a terrible day—doomsday!

> Babies poised to be born,
> No strength to birth them.

"'Maybe GOD, your God, has been listening to the blasphemous speech of the Rabshakeh who was sent by the king of Assyria, his master, to humiliate the living God; maybe GOD, your God, won't let him get by with such talk; and you, maybe you will lift up prayers for what's left of these people.'"

That's the message King Hezekiah's servants delivered to Isaiah.

Isaiah answered them, "Tell your master, 'GOD's word: Don't be at all concerned about what you've heard from the king of Assyria's bootlicking errand boys—these outrageous blasphemies. Here's what I'm going to do: Afflict him with self-doubt. He's going to hear a rumor and, frightened for his life, retreat to his own country. Once there, I'll see to it that he gets killed.'"

The Rabshakeh left and found that the king of Assyria had pulled up stakes from Lachish and was now fighting against Libnah. Then Sennacherib heard that Tirhakah king of Cush was on his way to fight against him. So he sent another envoy with orders to deliver this message to Hezekiah king of Judah: "Don't let that god that you think so much of keep stringing you along with the line, 'Jerusalem will never fall to the king of Assyria.' That's a barefaced lie. You know the track record of the kings of Assyria—country after country laid waste, devastated. And what makes you think you'll be an exception? Take a good look at these wasted nations, destroyed by my ancestors; did their gods do them any good? Look at Gozan, Haran, Rezeph, the people of Eden at Tel Assar. Ruins. And what's left of the king of Hamath, the king of Arpad, the king of Sepharvaim, of Hena, of Ivvah? Bones."

Hezekiah took the letter from the envoy and read it. He went to The Temple of GOD and spread it out before GOD. And Hezekiah prayed—oh, how he prayed!

GOD, God of Israel, seated
    in majesty on the cherubim-throne.
You are the one and only God,
    sovereign over all kingdoms on earth,
Maker of heaven,
    maker of earth.
Open your ears, GOD, and listen,
    open your eyes and look.
Look at this letter Sennacherib has sent,
    a brazen insult to the living God!
The facts are true, O GOD: The kings of Assyria
    have laid waste countries and kingdoms.
Huge bonfires they made of their gods, their
    no-gods hand-made from wood and stone.
But now O GOD, *our* God,
    save us from raw Assyrian power;

Make all the kingdoms on earth know
    that you are GOD, the one and only God.

It wasn't long before Isaiah son of Amoz sent word to Hezekiah:

GOD'S word: You've prayed to me regarding Sennacherib king of
Assyria; I've heard your prayer. This is my response to him:

The Virgin Daughter of Zion
    holds you in utter contempt;
Daughter Jerusalem
    thinks you're nothing but scum.
Who do you think it is you've insulted?
    Who do you think you've been bad-mouthing?
Before whom do you suppose you've been strutting?
    The Holy One of Israel, that's who!
You dispatched your errand boys
    to humiliate the Master.
You bragged, "With my army of chariots
    I've climbed the highest mountains,
    snow-peaked alpine Lebanon mountains!
I've cut down its giant cedars,
    chopped down its prize pine trees.
I've traveled the world,
    visited the finest forest retreats.
I've dug wells in faraway places
    and drunk their exotic waters;
I've waded and splashed barefoot
    in the rivers of Egypt."

Did it never occur to you
    that I'm behind all this?
Long, long ago I drew up the plans,
    and now I've gone into action,
Using you as a doomsday weapon,
    reducing proud cities to piles of rubble,
Leaving their people dispirited,
    slumped shoulders, limp souls.

Useless as weeds, fragile as grass,
  insubstantial as wind-blown chaff.
I know when you sit down, when you come
  and when you go;
And, yes, I've marked every one
  of your temper tantrums against me.
It's because of your temper,
  your blasphemous foul temper,
That I'm putting my hook in your nose
  and my bit in your mouth
And turning you back
  to where you came from.

And this, Hezekiah, will be for you the confirming sign:

This year you'll eat the gleanings, next year
  whatever you can beg, borrow, or steal;
But the third year you'll sow and harvest,
  plant vineyards and eat grapes.
A remnant of the family of Judah yet again
  will sink down roots and raise up fruit.
The remnant will come from Jerusalem,
  the survivors from Mount Zion.
The Zeal of GOD
  will make it happen.

To sum up, this is what GOD says regarding the king of Assyria:

He won't enter this city,
  nor shoot so much as a single arrow there;
Won't brandish a shield,
  won't even begin to set siege;
He'll go home by the same road he came;
  he won't enter this city. GOD's word!
I'll shield this city, I'll save this city,
  for my sake and for David's sake.

And it so happened that that very night an angel of GOD came and massacred a hundred and eighty-five thousand Assyrians. When the people of Jerusalem got up next morning, there it was—a whole camp of corpses!

Sennacherib king of Assyria got out of there fast, headed straight home for Nineveh, and stayed put. One day when he was worshiping in the temple of his god Nisroch, his sons Adrammelech and Sharezer murdered him and then escaped to the land of Ararat. His son Esarhaddon became the next king.

20 Some time later Hezekiah became deathly sick. The prophet Isaiah son of Amoz paid him a visit and said, "Put your affairs in order; you're about to die—you haven't long to live."

Hezekiah turned from Isaiah and faced GOD, praying:

> Remember, O GOD, who I am, what I've done!
> I've lived an honest life before you,
> My heart's been true and steady,
> I've lived to please you; lived for your approval.

And then the tears flowed. Hezekiah wept.

Isaiah, leaving, was not halfway across the courtyard when the word of GOD stopped him: "Go back and tell Hezekiah, prince of my people, 'GOD's word, Hezekiah! From the God of your ancestor David: I've listened to your prayer and I've observed your tears. I'm going to heal you. In three days you will walk on your own legs into The Temple of GOD. I've just added fifteen years to your life; I'm saving you from the king of Assyria, and I'm covering this city with my shield—for my sake and my servant David's sake.'"

Isaiah then said, "Prepare a plaster of figs."

They prepared the plaster, applied it to the boil, and Hezekiah was on his way to recovery.

Hezekiah said to Isaiah, "How do I know whether this is of GOD and not just the fig plaster? What confirming sign is there that GOD is healing me and that in three days I'll walk into The Temple of GOD on my own legs?"

"This will be your sign from GOD," said Isaiah, "that GOD is doing what he said he'd do: Do you want the shadow to advance ten degrees on the sundial or go back ten degrees? You choose."

Hezekiah said, "It would be easy to make the sun's shadow advance ten degrees. Make it go back ten degrees."

So Isaiah called out in prayer to GOD, and the shadow went back ten degrees on Ahaz's sundial.

Shortly after this, Merodach-Baladan, the son of Baladan king of Babylon, having heard that the king was sick, sent a get-well card and a gift to Hezekiah. Hezekiah was pleased and showed the messengers around the place—silver, gold, spices, aromatic oils, his stockpile of weapons—a guided tour of all his prized possessions. There wasn't a thing in his palace or kingdom that Hezekiah didn't show them.

And then Isaiah the prophet showed up: "And just what were these men doing here? Where did they come from and why?"

Hezekiah said, "They came from far away—from Babylon."

"And what did they see in your palace?"

"Everything," said Hezekiah. "There isn't anything I didn't show them—I gave them the grand tour."

Then Isaiah spoke to Hezekiah, "Listen to what GOD has to say about this: The day is coming when everything you own and everything your ancestors have passed down to you, right down to the last cup and saucer, will be cleaned out of here—plundered and packed off to Babylon. GOD's word! Worse yet, your sons, the progeny of sons you've begotten, will end up as eunuchs in the palace of the king of Babylon."

Hezekiah said to Isaiah, "If GOD says it, it must be good." But he was thinking to himself, "It won't happen during my lifetime—I'll enjoy peace and security as long as I live."

The rest of the life and times of Hezekiah, along with his projects, especially the way he engineered the Upper Pool and brought water into the city, are written in *The Chronicles of the Kings of Judah*. Hezekiah died and was buried with his ancestors. His son Manasseh became the next king.

MANASSEH OF JUDAH

21 Manasseh was twelve years old when he became king. He ruled for fifty-five years in Jerusalem. His mother's name was Hephzibah. In GOD's judgment he was a bad king—an evil king. He reintroduced all the moral rot and spiritual corruption that had been scoured from the country when GOD dispossessed the pagan nations in favor of the children of Israel. He rebuilt all the sex-and-religion shrines that his father Hezekiah had torn down, and he built altars and phallic

images for the sex god Baal and sex goddess Asherah, exactly what Ahaz king of Israel had done. He worshiped the cosmic powers, taking orders from the constellations. He even built these pagan altars in The Temple of GOD, the very Jerusalem Temple dedicated exclusively by GOD's decree ("in Jerusalem I place my Name") to GOD's Name. And he built shrines to the cosmic powers and placed them in both courtyards of The Temple of GOD. He burned his own son in a sacrificial offering. He practiced black magic and fortune-telling. He held séances and consulted spirits from the underworld. Much evil—in GOD's judgment, a career in evil. And GOD was angry.

As a last straw he placed the carved image of the sex goddess Asherah in The Temple of GOD, a flagrant and provocative violation of GOD's well-known statement to both David and Solomon, "In this Temple and in this city Jerusalem, my choice out of all the tribes of Israel, I place my Name—exclusively and forever. Never again will I let my people Israel wander off from this land I gave to their ancestors. But here's the condition: They must keep everything I've commanded in the instructions my servant Moses passed on to them."

But the people didn't listen. Manasseh led them off the beaten path into practices of evil even exceeding the evil of the pagan nations that GOD had earlier destroyed.

GOD, thoroughly fed up, sent word through his servants the prophets: "Because Manasseh king of Judah has committed these outrageous sins, eclipsing the sin-performance of the Amorites before him, setting new records in evil, using foul idols to debase Judah into a nation of sinners, this is my judgment, GOD's verdict: I, the God of Israel, will visit catastrophe on Jerusalem and Judah, a doom so terrible that when people hear of it they'll shake their heads in disbelief, saying, 'I can't believe it!'

"I'll visit the fate of Samaria on Jerusalem, a rerun of Ahab's doom. I'll wipe out Jerusalem as you would wipe out a dish, wiping it out and turning it over to dry. I'll get rid of what's left of my inheritance, dumping them on their enemies. If their enemies can salvage anything from them, they're welcome to it. They've been nothing but trouble to me from the day their ancestors left Egypt until now. They pushed me to my limit; I won't put up with their evil any longer."

The final word on Manasseh was that he was an indiscriminate murderer. He drenched Jerusalem with the innocent blood of his victims.

That's on top of all the sins in which he involved his people. As far as GOD was concerned, he'd turned them into a nation of sinners.

The rest of the life and times of Manasseh, everything he did and his sorry record of sin, is written in *The Chronicles of the Kings of Judah.* Manasseh died and joined his ancestors. He was buried in the palace garden, the Garden of Uzza. His son Amon became the next king.

AMON OF JUDAH

Amon was twenty-two years old when he became king. He was king for two years in Jerusalem. His mother's name was Meshullemeth, the daughter of Haruz. She was from Jotbah. In GOD's opinion he lived an evil life, just like his father Manasseh. He followed in the footsteps of his father, serving and worshiping the same foul gods his father had served. He totally deserted the GOD of his ancestors; he did not live GOD's way.

Amon's servants revolted and assassinated him, killing the king right in his own palace. But the people, in their turn, killed the conspirators against King Amon and then crowned Josiah, Amon's son, as king.

The rest of the life and times of Amon is written in *The Chronicles of the Kings of Judah.* They buried Amon in his burial plot in the Garden of Uzza. His son Josiah became the next king.

JOSIAH OF JUDAH

22 Josiah was eight years old when he became king. He ruled for thirty-one years in Jerusalem. His mother's name was Jedidah daughter of Adaiah; she was from Bozkath. He lived the way GOD wanted. He kept straight on the path blazed by his ancestor David, not one step to either left or right.

One day in the eighteenth year of his kingship, King Josiah sent the royal secretary Shaphan son of Azaliah, the son of Meshullam, to The Temple of GOD with instructions: "Go to Hilkiah the high priest and have him count the money that has been brought to The Temple of GOD that the doormen have collected from the people. Have them turn it over to the foremen who are managing the work on The Temple of GOD so they can pay the workers who are repairing GOD's Temple, all the carpenters, construction workers, and masons. Also, authorize them to buy the lumber and dressed stone for The Temple repairs. You don't need to get a receipt for the money you give them—they're all honest men."

307

The high priest Hilkiah reported to Shaphan the royal secretary, "I've just found the Book of GOD's Revelation, instructing us in GOD's ways. I found it in The Temple!" He gave it to Shaphan and Shaphan read it.

Then Shaphan the royal secretary came back to the king and gave him an account of what had gone on: "Your servants have bagged up the money that has been collected for The Temple; they have given it to the foremen to pay The Temple workers."

Then Shaphan the royal secretary told the king, "Hilkiah the priest gave me a book." Shaphan proceeded to read it to the king.

When the king heard what was written in the book, God's Revelation, he ripped his robes in dismay. And then he called for Hilkiah the priest, Ahikam son of Shaphan, Acbor son of Micaiah, Shaphan the royal secretary, and Asaiah the king's personal aide. He ordered them all: "Go and pray to GOD for me and for this people—for all Judah! Find out what we must do in response to what is written in this book that has just been found! GOD's anger must be burning furiously against us—our ancestors haven't obeyed a thing written in this book, followed none of the instructions directed to us."

Hilkiah the priest, Ahikam, Acbor, Shaphan, and Asaiah went straight to Huldah the prophetess. She was the wife of Shallum son of Tikvah, the son of Harhas, who was in charge of the palace wardrobe. She lived in Jerusalem in the Second Quarter. The five men consulted with her. In response to them she said, "GOD's word, the God of Israel: Tell the man who sent you here that I'm on my way to bring the doom of judgment on this place and this people. Every word written in the book read by the king of Judah will happen. And why? Because they've deserted me and taken up with other gods, made me thoroughly angry by setting up their god-making businesses. My anger is raging white-hot against this place and nobody is going to put it out.

"And also tell the king of Judah, since he sent you to ask GOD for direction; tell him this, GOD's comment on what he read in the book: 'Because you took seriously the doom of judgment I spoke against this place and people, and because you responded in humble repentance, tearing your robe in dismay and weeping before me, I'm taking you seriously. GOD's word: I'll take care of you. You'll have a quiet death and be buried in peace. You won't be around to see the doom that I'm going to bring upon this place.'"

The men took her message back to the king.

23 The king acted immediately, assembling all the elders of Judah and Jerusalem. Then the king proceeded to The Temple of GOD, bringing everyone in his train—priests and prophets and people ranging from the famous to the unknown. Then he read out publicly everything written in the Book of the Covenant that was found in The Temple of GOD. The king stood by the pillar and before GOD solemnly committed them all to the covenant: to follow GOD believingly and obediently; to follow his instructions, heart and soul, on what to believe and do; to put into practice the entire covenant, all that was written in the book. The people stood in affirmation; their commitment was unanimous.

Then the king ordered Hilkiah the high priest, his associate priest, and The Temple sentries to clean house—to get rid of everything in The Temple of GOD that had been made for worshiping Baal and Asherah and the cosmic powers. He had them burned outside Jerusalem in the fields of Kidron and then disposed of the ashes in Bethel. He fired the pagan priests whom the kings of Judah had hired to supervise the local sex-and-religion shrines in the towns of Judah and neighborhoods of Jerusalem. In a stroke he swept the country clean of the polluting stench of the round-the-clock worship of Baal, sun and moon, stars—all the so-called cosmic powers. He took the obscene phallic Asherah pole from The Temple of GOD to the Valley of Kidron outside Jerusalem, burned it up, then ground up the ashes and scattered them in the cemetery. He tore out the rooms of the male sacred prostitutes that had been set up in The Temple of GOD; women also used these rooms for weavings for Asherah. He swept the outlying towns of Judah clean of priests and smashed the sex-and-religion shrines where they worked their trade from one end of the country to the other—all the way from Geba to Beersheba. He smashed the sex-and-religion shrine that had been set up just to the left of the city gate for the private use of Joshua, the city mayor. Even though these sex-and-religion priests did not defile the Altar in The Temple itself, they were part of the general priestly corruption and had to go.

Then Josiah demolished the Topheth, the iron furnace griddle set up in the Valley of Ben Hinnom for sacrificing children in the fire. No longer could anyone burn son or daughter to the god Molech. He hauled off the horse statues honoring the sun god that the kings of Judah had set up near the entrance to The Temple. They were in the courtyard next to the office of Nathan-Melech, the warden. He burned up the sun-chariots as so much rubbish.

The king smashed all the altars to smithereens—the altar on the roof shrine of Ahaz, the various altars the kings of Judah had made, the altars of Manasseh that littered the courtyard of The Temple—he smashed them all, pulverized the fragments, and scattered their dust in the Valley of Kidron. The king proceeded to make a clean sweep of all the sex-and-religion shrines that had proliferated east of Jerusalem on the south slope of Abomination Hill, the ones Solomon king of Israel had built to the obscene Sidonian sex goddess Ashtoreth, to Chemosh the dirty-old-god of the Moabites, and to Milcom the depraved god of the Ammonites. He tore apart the altars, chopped down the phallic Asherah-poles, and scattered old bones over the sites. Next, he took care of the altar at the shrine in Bethel that Jeroboam son of Nebat had built—the same Jeroboam who had led Israel into a life of sin. He tore apart the altar, burned down the shrine leaving it in ashes, and then lit fire to the phallic Asherah-pole.

As Josiah looked over the scene, he noticed the tombs on the hillside. He ordered the bones removed from the tombs and had them cremated on the ruined altars, desacralizing the evil altars. This was a fulfillment of the word of GOD spoken by the Holy Man years before when Jeroboam had stood by the altar at the sacred convocation.

Then the king said, "And *that* memorial stone—whose is that?"

The men from the city said, "That's the grave of the Holy Man who spoke the message against the altar at Bethel that you have just fulfilled."

Josiah said, "Don't trouble his bones." So they left his bones undisturbed, along with the bones of the prophet from Samaria.

But Josiah hadn't finished. He now moved through all the towns of Samaria where the kings of Israel had built neighborhood sex-and-religion shrines, shrines that had so angered GOD. He tore the shrines down and left them in ruins—just as at Bethel. He killed all the priests who had conducted the sacrifices and cremated them on their own altars, thus desacralizing the altars. Only then did Josiah return to Jerusalem.

The king now commanded the people, "Celebrate the Passover to GOD, your God, exactly as directed in this Book of the Covenant."

This commanded Passover had not been celebrated since the days that the judges judged Israel—none of the kings of Israel and Judah had celebrated it. But in the eighteenth year of the rule of King Josiah this very Passover was celebrated to GOD in Jerusalem.

Josiah scrubbed the place clean and trashed spirit-mediums, sorcerers, domestic gods, and carved figures—all the vast accumulation of foul and obscene relics and images on display everywhere you looked in Judah and Jerusalem. Josiah did this in obedience to the words of GOD's Revelation written in the book that Hilkiah the priest found in The Temple of GOD.

There was no king to compare with Josiah—neither before nor after—a king who turned in total and repentant obedience to GOD, heart and mind and strength, following the instructions revealed to and written by Moses. The world would never again see a king like Josiah.

But despite Josiah, GOD's hot anger did not cool; the raging anger ignited by Manasseh burned unchecked. And GOD, not swerving in his judgment, gave sentence: "I'll remove Judah from my presence in the same way I removed Israel. I'll turn my back on this city, Jerusalem, that I chose, and even from this Temple of which I said, 'My Name lives here.'"

The rest of the life and times of Josiah is written in *The Chronicles of the Kings of Judah*. Josiah's death came about when Pharaoh Neco king of Egypt marched out to join forces with the king of Assyria at the Euphrates River. When King Josiah intercepted him at the Plain of Megiddo, Neco killed him. Josiah's servants took his body in a chariot, returned him to Jerusalem, and buried him in his own tomb. By popular choice Jehoahaz son of Josiah was anointed and succeeded his father as king.

JEHOAHAZ OF JUDAH

Jehoahaz was twenty-three years old when he began to rule. He was king in Jerusalem for a mere three months. His mother's name was Hamutal daughter of Jeremiah. She came from Libnah.

In GOD's opinion, he was an evil king, reverting to the evil ways of his ancestors.

Pharaoh Neco captured Jehoahaz at Riblah in the country of Hamath and put him in chains, preventing him from ruling in Jerusalem. He demanded that Judah pay tribute of nearly four tons of silver and seventy-five pounds of gold. Then Pharaoh Neco made Eliakim son of Josiah the successor to Josiah, but changed his name to Jehoiakim. Jehoahaz was carted off to Egypt and eventually died there.

Meanwhile Jehoiakim, like a good puppet, dutifully paid out the silver and gold demanded by Pharaoh. He scraped up the money by gouging the people, making everyone pay an assessed tax.

JEHOIAKIM OF JUDAH

Jehoiakim was twenty-five years old when he began to rule; he was king for eleven years in Jerusalem. His mother's name was Zebidah daughter of Pedaiah. She had come from Rumah. In GOD's opinion he was an evil king, picking up on the evil ways of his ancestors.

24 It was during his reign that Nebuchadnezzar king of Babylon invaded the country. Jehoiakim became his puppet. But after three years he had had enough and revolted.

GOD dispatched a succession of raiding bands against him: Babylonian, Aramean, Moabite, and Ammonite. The strategy was to destroy Judah. Through the preaching of his servants and prophets, GOD had said he would do this, and now he was doing it. None of this was by chance—it was GOD's judgment as he turned his back on Judah because of the enormity of the sins of Manasseh—Manasseh, the killer-king, who made the Jerusalem streets flow with the innocent blood of his victims. GOD wasn't about to overlook such crimes.

The rest of the life and times of Jehoiakim is written in *The Chronicles of the Kings of Judah*. Jehoiakim died and was buried with his ancestors. His son Jehoiachin became the next king.

The threat from Egypt was now over—no more invasions by the king of Egypt—for by this time the king of Babylon had captured all the land between the Brook of Egypt and the Euphrates River, land formerly controlled by the king of Egypt.

JEHOIACHIN OF JUDAH

Jehoiachin was eighteen years old when he became king. His rule in Jerusalem lasted only three months. His mother's name was Nehushta daughter of Elnathan; she was from Jerusalem. In GOD's opinion he also was an evil king, no different from his father.

The next thing to happen was that the officers of Nebuchadnezzar king of Babylon attacked Jerusalem and put it under siege. While his officers were laying siege to the city, Nebuchadnezzar king of Babylon paid a personal visit. And Jehoiachin king of Judah, along with his mother, officers, advisors, and government leaders, surrendered.

In the eighth year of his reign Jehoiachin was taken prisoner by the king of Babylon. Nebuchadnezzar emptied the treasuries of both The Temple of GOD and the royal palace and confiscated all the gold furnishings that Solomon king of Israel had made for The Temple of GOD. This should have been no surprise—GOD had said it would happen. And then he emptied Jerusalem of people—all its leaders and soldiers, all its craftsmen and artisans. He took them into exile, something like ten thousand of them! The only ones he left were the very poor.

He took Jehoiachin into exile to Babylon. With him he took the king's mother, his wives, his chief officers, the community leaders, anyone who was anybody—in round numbers, seven thousand soldiers plus another thousand or so craftsmen and artisans, all herded off into exile in Babylon.

Then the king of Babylon made Jehoiachin's uncle, Mattaniah, his puppet king, but changed his name to Zedekiah.

ZEDEKIAH OF JUDAH

Zedekiah was twenty-one years old when he started out as king. He was king in Jerusalem for eleven years. His mother's name was Hamutal the daughter of Jeremiah. Her home town was Libnah.

As far as GOD was concerned Zedekiah was just one more evil king, a carbon copy of Jehoiakim.

The source of all this doom to Jerusalem and Judah was GOD's anger—GOD turned his back on them as an act of judgment. And then Zedekiah revolted against the king of Babylon.

25 The revolt dates from the ninth year and tenth month of Zedekiah's reign. Nebuchadnezzar set out for Jerusalem immediately with a full army. He set up camp and sealed off the city by building siege mounds around it. The city was under siege for nineteen months (until the eleventh year of Zedekiah). By the fourth month of Zedekiah's eleventh year, on the ninth day of the month, the famine was so bad that there wasn't so much as a crumb of bread for anyone. Then there was a breakthrough. At night, under cover of darkness, the entire army escaped through an opening in the wall (it was the gate between the two walls above the King's Garden). They slipped through the lines of the Babylonians who surrounded the city and headed for the Jordan on the Arabah Valley road. But the Babylonians were in pursuit of the

king and they caught up with him in the Plains of Jericho. By then Zedekiah's army had deserted and was scattered. The Babylonians took Zedekiah prisoner and marched him off to the king of Babylon at Riblah, then tried and sentenced him on the spot. Zedekiah's sons were executed right before his eyes; the summary murder of his sons was the last thing he saw, for they then blinded him. Securely handcuffed, he was hauled off to Babylon.

In the nineteenth year of Nebuchadnezzar king of Babylon, on the seventh day of the fifth month, Nebuzaradan, the king of Babylon's chief deputy, arrived in Jerusalem. He burned The Temple of GOD to the ground, went on to the royal palace, and then finished off the city—burned the whole place down. He put the Babylonian troops he had with him to work knocking down the city walls. Finally, he rounded up everyone left in the city, including those who had earlier deserted to the king of Babylon, and took them off into exile. He left a few poor dirt farmers behind to tend the vineyards and what was left of the fields.

The Babylonians broke up the bronze pillars, the bronze washstands, and the huge bronze basin (the Sea) that were in The Temple of GOD and hauled the bronze off to Babylon. They also took the various bronze-crafted liturgical accessories used in the services of Temple worship, as well as the gold and silver censers and sprinkling bowls. The king's deputy didn't miss a thing—he took every scrap of precious metal he could find.

The amount of bronze they got from the two pillars, the Sea, and all the washstands that Solomon had made for The Temple of GOD was enormous—they couldn't weigh it all! Each pillar stood twenty-seven feet high, plus another four and a half feet for an ornate capital of bronze filigree and decorative fruit.

The king's deputy took a number of special prisoners: Seraiah the chief priest, Zephaniah the associate priest, three wardens, the chief remaining army officer, five of the king's counselors, the accountant, the chief recruiting officer for the army, and sixty men of standing from among the people. Nebuzaradan the king's deputy marched them all off to the king of Babylon at Riblah. And there at Riblah, in the land of Hamath, the king of Babylon killed the lot of them in cold blood.

Judah went into exile, orphaned from her land.

Regarding the common people who were left behind in Judah, this: Nebuchadnezzar king of Babylon appointed Gedaliah son of Ahikam, the son of Shaphan, as their governor. When veteran army officers among the people heard that the king of Babylon had appointed Gedaliah, they came to Gedaliah at Mizpah. Among them were Ishmael son of Nethaniah, Johanan son of Kareah, Seraiah son of Tanhumeth the Netophathite, Jaazaniah the son of the Maacathite, and some of their followers.

Gedaliah assured the officers and their men, giving them his word, "Don't be afraid of the Babylonian officials. Go back to your farms and families and respect the king of Babylon. Trust me, everything is going to be all right."

Some time later—it was in the seventh month—Ishmael son of Nethaniah, the son of Elishama (he had royal blood in him), came back with ten men and killed Gedaliah, the traitor Jews, and the Babylonian officials who were stationed at Mizpah—a bloody massacre.

But then, afraid of what the Babylonians would do, they all took off for Egypt, leaders and people, small and great.

When Jehoiachin king of Judah had been in exile for thirty-seven years, Evil-Merodach became king in Babylon and let Jehoiachin out of prison. This release took place on the twenty-seventh day of the twelfth month. The king treated him most courteously and gave him preferential treatment beyond anything experienced by the other political prisoners held in Babylon. Jehoiachin took off his prison garb and for the rest of his life ate his meals in company with the king. The king provided everything he needed to live comfortably.

1-2 CHRONICLES

There is always more than one way to tell a story. The story of Israel's kings is first narrated in the Books of Samuel and Kings. Here is another telling of the same story, a hundred or so years later, by another voice and from another perspective: Chronicles. Some of the earlier narrative is omitted and there are substantial additions but it is recognizably the same story. But Israel's fortunes have changed considerably since the earlier authoritative writing (Genesis through Kings); God's people are in danger of losing touch with what made them God's people in the first place. In retrospect, from the low point in their history in which they now find themselves, it looks very much like a succession of world powers; Assyria and Egypt, Babylon and Persia, have been calling all the shots. The People of Israel are swamped by alien influences; they are also, it seems, mired in internal religious pettiness; will they be obliterated?

A new writer (it may have been Ezra) took it in hand to tell the old and by now familiar story but with a new slant. His task was to recover and restore Israel's confidence and obedience as God's people. Remarkably—and improbably, considering the political and cultural conditions of the time—this writer insisted, with very little "hometown" support, on the core identity of Israel as a worshiping people in the Davidic tradition. And he did it all by writing the book you are about to read. Israel did not finally disappear into the ancient Near East melting pot of violence and sex and religion.

Names launch this story, hundreds and hundreds of names, lists of names, page after page of names, *personal* names. There is no true story-telling without names, and this immersion in names calls attention to the individual, the unique, the personal, which is inherent in all spirituality. Name lists (genealogies) occur in other places in Scripture (Genesis, Numbers, Matthew, Luke) but none as extravagantly copious as here. Holy history is not constructed from impersonal forces or abstract ideas; it is woven from names—persons, each one unique. Chronicles erects a solid defense against depersonalized religion.

And Chronicles provides a witness to the essential and primary place of accurate worship in human life. The narrative backbone of Chronicles is worship—the place of worship (the Jerusalem Temple), the ministers of worship (the priests and Levites), the musical components of worship (both vocal and instrumental), and the authoritative role of King David, the master of worship, who maintains faithfulness and integrity in worship.

In the way this story of Israel's past is told, nothing takes precedence over worship in nurturing and protecting our identity as a people of God—not politics, not economics, not family life, not art. And nothing in the preparation for and conduct of worship is too small to be left to whim or chance—nothing in architecture, personnel, music, or theology.

Earlier threats to Israel's identity and survival as a people of God frequently came in the form of hostile outsiders—Egyptians, Canaanites, Philistines, Amalekites, and others; but in this assessment of what matters, right and faithful worship turns out to be what counts most of all. The people of God are not primarily a political entity or a military force or an economic power; they are a holy congregation diligent in worship. To lose touch with the Davidic (and Moses-based) life of worship is to disintegrate as a holy people. To be seduced by the popular pagan worship of the surrounding culture is to be obliterated as a holy people.

Not many readers of this text will find their names in the lists of names in this book. Few worshiping congregations will recognize architectural continuities between The Temple and their local church sanctuaries. Not many communities have access to a pool of Levites from which to recruit choirs and appoint leaders of worship. So, what's left?

Well, worship is left—and names. Accurate worship, defined and fed by the God who reveals himself in Jesus Christ. And personal names that add up to a people of God, a holy congregation. Christians have characteristically read and prayed themselves into Chronicles in order to stay alert to the irreducibly personal in all matters of faith and practice, and to maintain a critical awareness that the worship of God is the indispensable foundation for living whole and redeemed lives.

1 CHRONICLES

ISRAEL'S FAMILY TREE: THE TRUNK

1 Adam
Seth
Enosh
Kenan
Mahalalel
Jared
Enoch
Methuselah
Lamech
Noah
Shem, Ham, and Japheth.

THE JAPHETH BRANCH

Japheth had Gomer, Magog, Madai, Javan, Tubal, Meshech, and Tiras.
Gomer had Ashkenaz, Riphath, and Togarmah.
Javan had Elishah, Tarshish, Kittim, and Rodanim.

THE HAM BRANCH

Ham had Cush, Mizraim, Put, and Canaan.
Cush had Seba, Havilah, Sabta, Raamah, and Sabteca.
Raamah had Sheba and Dedan.
Cush had Nimrod, the first great hero on earth.
Mizraim was ancestor to the Ludim, the Anamim, the Lehabim, the Naphtuhim, the Pathrusim, the Casluhim, and the Caphtorim from whom the Philistines descended.
Canaan had Sidon (his firstborn) and Heth, and was ancestor to the Jebusites, the Amorites, the Girgashites, the Hivites, the Arkites, the Sinites, the Arvadites, the Zemarites, and the Hamathites.

THE SHEM BRANCH

Shem had Elam, Asshur, Arphaxad, Lud, Aram, Uz, Hul, Gether, and Meshech.
Arphaxad had Shelah and Shelah had Eber. Eber had two sons:

318

Peleg (Division) because in his time the earth was divided up; his brother was Joktan.

Joktan had Almodad, Sheleph, Hazarmaveth, Jerah, Hadoram, Uzal, Diklah, Ebal, Abimael, Sheba, Ophir, Havilah, and Jobab—all sons of Joktan.

The three main branches in summary: Shem, Arphaxad, Shelah, Eber, Peleg, Reu, Serug, Nahor, Terah, and Abram (Abraham). And Abraham had Isaac and Ishmael.

THE FAMILY OF ABRAHAM

Abraham's family tree developed along these lines: Ishmael had Nebaioth (his firstborn), then Kedar, Adbeel, Mibsam, Mishma, Dumah, Massa, Hadad, Tema, Jetur, Naphish, and Kedemah—the Ishmael branch.

Keturah, Abraham's concubine, gave birth to Zimran, Jokshan, Medan, Midian, Ishbak, and Shuah. Then Jokshan had Sheba and Dedan. And Midian had Ephah, Epher, Hanoch, Abida, and Eldaah. These made up the Keturah branch.

Abraham had Isaac, and Isaac had Esau and Israel (Jacob). Esau had Eliphaz, Reuel, Jeush, Jalam, and Korah. Eliphaz had Teman, Omar, Zepho, Gatam, Kenaz, Timna, and Amalek. And Reuel had Nahath, Zerah, Shammah, and Mizzah.

Seir then had Lotan, Shobal, Zibeon, Anah, Dishon, Ezer, and Dishan. Lotan had Hori and Homam. Timna was Lotan's sister. Shobal had Alian, Manahath, Ebal, Shepho, and Onam. Zibeon had Aiah and Anah. Anah had Dishon. Dishon had Hemdan, Eshban, Ithran, and Keran. Ezer had Bilhan, Zaavan, and Akan. And Dishan had Uz and Aran.

THE EDOMITE KING LIST

A list of the kings who ruled in the country of Edom before Israel had a king:

Bela son of Beor; his city was Dinhabah.

Bela died; Jobab son of Zerah from Bozrah was the next king.

Jobab died; Husham from the country of the Temanites was the next king.

Husham died; Hadad son of Bedad, who defeated Midian in the country of Moab, was the next king; his city was Avith.

Hadad died; Samlah from Masrekah was the next king.

Samlah died; Shaul from Rehoboth-by-the-River was the next king.

Shaul died; Baal-Hanan son of Acbor was the next king.

Baal-Hanan died; Hadad was the next king; his city was Pau and his wife was Mehetabel daughter of Matred, the daughter of Me-Zahab. Last of all Hadad died.

The chieftains of Edom after that were Chief Timna, Chief Alvah, Chief Jetheth, Chief Oholibamah, Chief Elah, Chief Pinon, Chief Kenaz, Chief Teman, Chief Mibzar, Chief Magdiel, and Chief Iram. These were the chieftains of Edom.

THE FAMILY OF ISRAEL (JACOB)

2 Israel's (that is, Jacob's) sons: Reuben, Simeon, Levi, Judah, Issachar, Zebulun, Dan, Joseph, Benjamin, Naphtali, Gad, and Asher.

Judah had Er, Onan, and Shelah; their mother was Bathshua the Canaanite. Er, Judah's firstborn, was so bad before GOD that GOD killed him. Judah also had Perez and Zerah by his daughter-in-law Tamar — a total of five sons. Perez had Hezron and Hamul; Zerah had Zimri, Ethan, Heman, Calcol, and Darda — five sons. Carmi had Achar, who brought doom on Israel when he violated a holy ban. Ethan's son was Azariah. And Hezron had Jerahmeel, Ram, and Chelubai.

Ram had Amminadab and Amminadab had Nahshon, a prominent leader in the Judah family. Nahshon had Salmon and Salmon had Boaz. Boaz had Obed and Obed had Jesse. Jesse's firstborn was Eliab, followed by Abinadab, Shimea, Nethanel, Raddai, Ozem, and finally David; David was the seventh. Their sisters were Zeruiah and Abigail. Zeruiah gave birth to three sons: Abishai, Joab, and Asahel; Abigail was the mother of Amasa (the father was Jether the Ishmaelite).

THE FAMILY OF CALEB

Caleb son of Hezron had children by his wife Azubah and also by Jerioth. Azubah's sons were Jesher, Shobab, and Ardon. After Azubah died, Caleb married Ephrath, who gave birth to Hur. Hur had Uri and Uri had Bezalel. Some time later Hezron married the daughter of Makir the father of Gilead; he was sixty years old when he married her; she gave birth to Segub. Then Segub had Jair who owned twenty-three cities in the land of Gilead. Geshur and Aram captured the nomadic villages of Jair and Kenath and their satellite settlements — sixty towns. These all belonged to Makir the father of Gilead. After the death of Hezron, Caleb married Ephrathah the wife of his father Hezron; she then gave birth to Ashhur the father of Tekoa.

THE FAMILY OF JERAHMEEL

The sons of Jerahmeel, Hezron's firstborn: Ram his firstborn, followed by Bunah, Oren, Ozem, and Ahijah. Jerahmeel had another wife whose name was Atarah; she gave birth to Onam.

The sons of Ram, Jerahmeel's firstborn: Maaz, Jamin, and Eker.

The sons of Onam: Shammai and Jada.

The sons of Shammai: Nadab and Abishur. Abishur's wife was Abihail; she gave birth to Ahban and Molid.

Nadab had Seled and Appaim. Seled died leaving no sons.

Appaim had Ishi; Ishi had Sheshan; and Sheshan had Ahlai.

Jada, Shammai's brother, had Jether and Jonathan. Jether died leaving no sons.

Jonathan had Peleth and Zaza.

This is the family tree of the sons of Jerahmeel.

✜

Sheshan had no sons, only daughters. But Sheshan had an Egyptian servant, Jarha. Sheshan married his daughter to Jarha and she gave birth to Attai. Attai had Nathan, Nathan had Zabad, Zabad had Ephlal, Ephlal had Obed, Obed had Jehu, Jehu had Azariah, Azariah had Helez, Helez had Eleasah, Eleasah had Sismai, Sismai had Shallum, Shallum had Jekamiah, and Jekamiah had Elishama.

✜

Jerahmeel's brother Caleb had a son, his firstborn, named Mesha; Mesha had Ziph; Ziph's son was Mareshah the father of Hebron.

The sons of Hebron: Korah, Tappuah, Rekem, and Shema. Shema had Raham the father of Jorkeam; Rekem had Shammai.

Shammai's son was Maon and Maon was the father of Beth Zur.

Caleb's concubine Ephah gave birth to Haran, Moza, and Gazez; Haran had Gazez.

The sons of Jahdai: Regem, Jotham, Geshan, Pelet, Ephah, and Shaaph.

Another concubine of Caleb, Maacah, gave birth to Sheber and Tirhanah. She also bore Shaaph the father of Madmannah and Sheva the father of Macbenah and Gibea. Caleb's daughter was Acsah. These made up the Caleb branch of the family tree.

The sons of Hur, Ephrathah's firstborn: Shobal who had Kiriath Jearim, Salma who had Bethlehem, and Hareph father of Beth Gader.

The family of Shobal, father of Kiriath Jearim: Haroeh, half of the population of Manahath, the families of Kiriath Jearim, the Ithrites, the Puthites, the Shumathites, and the Mishraites. The Zorathites and Eshtaolites also came from this line.

The sons of Salma: Bethlehem, the Netophathites, Atroth Beth Joab, half of the Manahathites, the Zorites, and the families of Sopherim who lived at Jabez—the Tirathites, the Shimeathites, and the Sucathites. They made up the Kenites who came from Hammath the father of the house of Recab.

THE FAMILY OF DAVID

3 These are the sons that David had while he lived at Hebron:
His firstborn was Amnon by Ahinoam of Jezreel;
second, Daniel by Abigail of Carmel;
third, Absalom born of Maacah, daughter of Talmai king of Geshur;
fourth, Adonijah born of Haggith;
fifth, Shephatiah born of Abital;
sixth, Ithream born of his wife Eglah.

He had these six sons while he was in Hebron; he was king there for seven years and six months.

He went on to be king in Jerusalem for another thirty-three years. These are the sons he had in Jerusalem: first Shammua, then Shobab, Nathan, and Solomon. Bathsheba daughter of Ammiel was the mother of these four. And then there were another nine sons: Ibhar, Elishua, Eliphelet, Nogah, Nepheg, Japhia, Elishama, Eliada, Eliphelet—David's sons, plus Tamar their sister. There were other sons by his concubines.

In the next generation Solomon had Rehoboam, who had Abijah, who had Asa, who had Jehoshaphat, who had Jehoram, who had Ahaziah, who had Joash, who had Amaziah, who had Azariah, who had Jotham, who had Ahaz, who had Hezekiah, who had Manasseh, who had Amon, who had Josiah.

Josiah's firstborn was Johanan, followed by Jehoiakim, then Zedekiah, and finally Shallum.

Jehoiakim's sons were Jeconiah (Jehoiachin) and Zedekiah.

The sons of Jeconiah born while he was captive in Babylon: Shealtiel, Malkiram, Pedaiah, Shenazzar, Jekamiah, Hoshama, and Nedabiah.

Pedaiah had Zerubbabel and Shimei; Zerubbabel had Meshullam and Hananiah. Shelomith was their sister. And then five more—Hashubah, Ohel, Berekiah, Hasadiah, and Jushab-Hesed.

Hananiah's sons were Pelatiah and Jeshaiah. There were also sons of Rephaiah, sons of Arnan, sons of Obadiah, and sons of Shecaniah.

Shecaniah had Shemaiah who in his turn had Hattush, Igal, Bariah, Neariah, and Shaphat—six of them.

Neariah had three sons: Elioenai, Hizkiah, and Azrikam.

And Elioenai had seven sons: Hodaviah, Eliashib, Pelaiah, Akkub, Johanan, Delaiah, and Anani.

An Appendix to the Family of Judah

4 Sons of Judah: Perez, Hezron, Carmi, Hur, and Shobal. Reaiah, Shobal's son, had Jahath; and Jahath had Ahumai and Lahad. These made up the families of the Zorathites.

Sons of Etam: Jezreel, Ishma, and Idbash. Their sister was named Hazzelelponi. Penuel had Gedor and Ezer had Hushah. These were the sons of Hur, firstborn son of Ephrathah, who was the father of Bethlehem.

Ashhur the father of Tekoa had two wives, Helah and Naarah. Naarah gave birth to Ahuzzam, Hepher, Temeni, and Haahashtari—Naarah's children. Helah's sons were Zereth, Zohar, Ethnan, and Koz, who had Anub, Hazzobebah, and the families of Aharhel son of Harum.

⊹

Jabez was a better man than his brothers, a man of honor. His mother had named him Jabez (Oh, the pain!), saying, "A painful birth! I bore him in great pain!" Jabez prayed to the God of Israel: "Bless me, O bless me! Give me land, large tracts of land. And provide your personal protection—don't let evil hurt me." God gave him what he asked.

⊹

Kelub, Shuhah's brother, had Mehir; Mehir had Eshton; Eshton had Beth Rapha, Paseah, and Tehinnah, who founded Ir Nahash (City of Smiths). These were known as the men of Recah.

The sons of Kenaz: Othniel and Seraiah.

The sons of Othniel: Hathath and Meonothai.

Meonothai had Ophrah; Seraiah had Joab, the founder of Ge Harashim (Colony of Artisans).

The sons of Caleb son of Jephunneh: Iru, Elah, and Naam.

The son of Elah: Kenaz.

The sons of Jehallelel: Ziph, Ziphah, Tiria, and Asarel.

The sons of Ezrah: Jether, Mered, Epher, and Jalon. One of Mered's wives, Pharaoh's daughter Bithiah, gave birth to Miriam, Shammai, and Ishbah the father of Eshtemoa. His Judean wife gave birth to Jered father of Gedor, Heber father of Soco, and Jekuthiel father of Zanoah.

The sons of Hodiah's wife, Naham's sister: the father of Keilah the Garmite, and Eshtemoa the Maacathite.

The sons of Shimon: Amnon, Rinnah, Ben-Hanan, and Tilon.

The sons of Ishi: Zoheth and Ben-Zoheth.

The sons of Shelah son of Judah: Er the father of Lecah, Laadah the father of Mareshah and the family of linen workers at Beth Ashbea, Jokim, the men of Cozeba, and Joash and Saraph, who ruled in Moab and Jashubi Lehem. (These records are from very old traditions.) They were the potters who lived at Netaim and Gederah, resident potters who worked for the king.

THE FAMILY OF SIMEON

The Simeon family tree: Nemuel, Jamin, Jarib, Zerah, and Shaul; Shaul had Shallum, Shallum had Mibsam, and Mibsam had Mishma.

The sons of Mishma: Hammuel had Zaccur and Zaccur had Shimei.

Shimei had sixteen sons and six daughters, but his brothers were not nearly as prolific and never became a large family like Judah. They lived in Beersheba, Moladah, Hazar Shual, Bilhah, Ezem, Tolad, Bethuel, Hormah, Ziklag, Beth Marcaboth, Hazar Susim, Beth Biri, and Shaaraim. They lived in these towns until David became king. Other settlements in the vicinity were the five towns of Etam, Ain, Rimmon, Token, and Ashan, and all the villages around these towns as far as Baalath. These were their settlements. And they kept good family records.

Meshobab; Jamlech; Joshah the son of Amaziah; Joel; Jehu the son of Joshibiah, the son of Seraiah, the son of Asiel; Elioenai; Jaakobah; Jeshohaiah; Asaiah; Adiel; Jesimiel; Benaiah; and Ziza the son of Shiphi, the son of Allon, the son of Jedaiah, the son of Shimri, the son of Shemaiah—all these were the leaders in their families. They prospered and increased in numbers so that they had to go as far as Gedor (Gerar) to the east of the valley looking for pasture for their flocks. And they found it—lush pasture, lots of elbow room, peaceful and quiet.

Some Hamites had lived there in former times. But the men in these family trees came when Hezekiah was king of Judah and attacked the Hamites, tearing down their tents and houses. There was nothing left of them, as you can see today. Then they moved in and took over because of the great pastureland. Five hundred of these Simeonites went on and invaded the hill country of Seir, led by Pelatiah, Neariah, Rephaiah, and Uzziel, the sons of Ishi. They killed all the escaped Amalekites who were still around. And they still live there.

5 The family of Reuben the firstborn of Israel: Though Reuben was Israel's firstborn, after he slept with his father's concubine, a defiling act, his rights as the firstborn were passed on to the sons of Joseph son of Israel. He lost his "firstborn" place in the family tree. And even though Judah became the strongest of his brothers and King David eventually came from that family, the firstborn rights stayed with Joseph.

The sons of Reuben, firstborn of Israel: Hanoch, Pallu, Hezron, and Carmi.

The descendants of Joel: Shemaiah his son, Gog his son, Shimei his son, Micah his son, Reaiah his son, Baal his son, and Beerah his son, whom Tiglath-Pileser king of Assyria took into exile. Beerah was the prince of the Reubenites.

Beerah's brothers are listed in the family tree by families: first Jeiel, followed by Zechariah: then Bela son of Azaz, the son of Shema, the son of Joel. Joel lived in the area from Aroer to Nebo and Baal Meon. His family occupied the land up to the edge of the desert that goes all the way to the Euphrates River, since their growing herds of livestock spilled out of Gilead. During Saul's reign they fought and defeated the Hagrites; they then took over their tents and lived in them on the eastern frontier of Gilead.

✠

The family of Gad were their neighbors in Bashan, as far as Salecah: Joel was the chief, Shapham the second-in-command, and then Janai, the judge in Bashan.

Their brothers, by families, were Michael, Meshullam, Sheba, Jorai, Jacan, Zia, and Eber—seven in all. These were the sons of Abihail son of Huri, the son of Jaroah, the son of Gilead, the son of Michael, the son of Jeshishai, the son of Jahdo, the son of Buz. Ahi son of Abdiel, the son of Guni, was head of their family.

The family of Gad lived in Gilead and Bashan, including the outlying villages and extending as far as the pastures of Sharon.

They were all written into the official family tree during the reigns of Jotham king of Judah and Jeroboam king of Israel.

✛

The families of Reuben, Gad, and the half-tribe of Manasseh had 44,760 men trained for war—physically fit and skilled in handling shield, sword, and bow. They fought against the Hagrites, Jetur, Naphish, and Nodab. God helped them as they fought. God handed the Hagrites and all their allies over to them, because they cried out to him during the battle. God answered their prayers because they trusted him. They plundered the Hagrite herds and flocks: 50,000 camels, 250,000 sheep, and 2,000 donkeys. They also captured 100,000 people. Many were killed, because the battle was God's. They lived in that country until the exile.

✛

The half-tribe of Manasseh had a large population. They occupied the land from Bashan to Baal Hermon, that is, to Senir (Mount Hermon). The heads of their families were Epher, Ishi, Eliel, Azriel, Jeremiah, Hodaviah, and Jahdiel—brave warriors, famous, and heads of their families. But they were not faithful to the God of their ancestors. They took up with the ungodly gods of the peoples of the land whom God had gotten rid of before they arrived. So the God of Israel stirred up the spirit of Pul king of Assyria (Tiglath-Pileser king of Assyria) to take the families of Reuben, Gad, and the half-tribe of Manasseh into exile. He deported them to Halah, Habor, Hara, and the river of Gozan. They've been there ever since.

THE FAMILY OF LEVI

6 The sons of Levi were Gershon, Kohath, and Merari. The sons of Kohath were Amram, Izhar, Hebron, and Uzziel. The children of Amram were Aaron, Moses, and Miriam. The sons of Aaron were Nadab, Abihu, Eleazar, and Ithamar. Eleazar had Phinehas, Phinehas had Abishua, Abishua had Bukki, Bukki had Uzzi, Uzzi had Zerahiah, Zerahiah had Meraioth, Meraioth had Amariah, Amariah had Ahitub, Ahitub had Zadok, Zadok had Ahimaaz, Ahimaaz had Azariah, Azariah had Johanan, and Johanan had Azariah (who served as priest in the temple Solomon built in Jerusalem). Azariah had Amariah, Amariah had Ahitub, Ahitub had Zadok, Zadok had Shallum, Shallum had Hilkiah, Hilkiah had Azariah, Azariah had Seraiah, and Seraiah had Jehozadak.

Jehozadak went off to exile when GOD used Nebuchadnezzar to take Judah and Jerusalem into exile.

✝

The sons of Levi were Gershon, Kohath, and Merari. These are the names of the sons of Gershon: Libni and Shimei. The sons of Kohath were Amram, Izhar, Hebron, and Uzziel. The sons of Merari were Mahli and Mushi. These are the Levitical clans according to families: the sons of Gershon were Libni his son, Jehath his son, Zimmah his son, Joah his son, Iddo his son, Zerah his son, and Jeatherai his son. The sons of Kohath were Amminadab his son, Korah his son, Assir his son, Elkanah his son, Ebiasaph his son, Assir his son, Tahath his son, Uriel his son, Uzziah his son, and Shaul his son. The sons of Elkanah were Amasai and Ahimoth, Elkanah his son, Zophai his son, Nahath his son, Eliab his son, Jeroham his son, and Elkanah his son. The sons of Samuel were Joel his firstborn son and Abijah his second. The sons of Merari were Mahli, Libni his son, Shimei his son, Uzzah his son, Shimea his son, Haggiah his son, and Asaiah his son.

DAVID'S WORSHIP LEADERS

These are the persons David appointed to lead the singing in the house of GOD after the Chest was placed there. They were the ministers of music in the place of worship, which was the Tent of Meeting until Solomon built The Temple of GOD in Jerusalem. As they carried out their work, they followed the instructions given to them.

These are the persons, together with their sons, who served by preparing for and directing worship: from the family of the Kohathites was Heman the choirmaster, the son of Joel, the son of Samuel, the son of Elkanah, the son of Jeroham, the son of Eliel, the son of Toah, the son of Zuph, the son of Elkanah, the son of Mahath, the son of Amasai, the son of Elkanah, the son of Joel, the son of Azariah, the son of Zephaniah, the son of Tahath, the son of Assir, the son of Ebiasaph, the son of Korah, the son of Izhar, the son of Kohath, the son of Levi, the son of Israel.

Heman's associate Asaph stood at his right hand. Asaph was the son of Berekiah, the son of Shimea, the son of Michael, the son of Baaseiah, the son of Malkijah, the son of Ethni, the son of Zerah, the son of Adaiah, the son of Ethan, the son of Zimmah, the son of Shimei, the son of Jahath, the son of Gershon, the son of Levi.

Of the sons of Merari, the associates who stood at his left hand, was Ethan the son of Kishi, the son of Abdi, the son of Malluch, the son of Hashabiah, the son of Amaziah, the son of Hilkiah, the son of Amzi, the son of Bani, the son of Shemer, the son of Mahli, the son of Mushi, the son of Merari, the son of Levi.

The rest of the Levites were assigned to all the other work in the place of worship, the house of God.

✝

Aaron and his sons offered the sacrifices on the Altar of Burnt Offering and the Altar of Incense; they were in charge of all the work surrounding the Holy of Holies. They made atonement for Israel following the instructions commanded by Moses, servant of God.

These are the sons of Aaron: Eleazar his son, Phinehas his son, Abishua his son, Bukki his son, Uzzi his son, Zerahiah his son, Meraioth his son, Amariah his son, Ahitub his son, Zadok his son, and Ahimaaz his son.

THE PRIESTLY CITIES

And these are the places where the priestly families were assigned to live. The first assignment went by lot to the sons of Aaron of the Kohathite family; they were given Hebron in the land of Judah and all the neighboring pastures. Caleb the son of Jephunneh got the fields and villages around the city. The family of Aaron was also given the cities of refuge, with pastures included: Hebron, Libnah, Jattir, Eshtemoa, Hilen, Debir, Ashan, and Beth Shemesh. They were also given Geba from the tribe of Benjamin, Alemeth, and Anathoth, all with pastures included. In all, thirteen cities were distributed among the Kohathite families. The rest of the Kohathites were given another ten cities, distributed by lot from the half-tribe of Manasseh. The sons of Gershon were given, family by family, thirteen cities from the tribes of Issachar, Asher, Naphtali, and Manasseh in Bashan. The sons of Merari, family by family, were assigned by lot twelve cities from the tribes of Reuben, Gad, and Zebulun. The sons of Israel gave the Levites both the cities and their pastures. They also distributed by lot cities from the tribes of Judah, Simeon, and Benjamin. Some of the Kohath families were given their cities from the tribe of Ephraim, cities of refuge: Shechem in the hill country of Ephraim, Gezer, Jokmeam, Beth Horon, Aijalon, and Gath Rimmon—all with their pastures. The rest of the sons of Kohath were given Aner and Bileam with their pastures from the half-tribe of Manasseh. The sons of Gershon were given, family by family, from the half-tribe of Manasseh, Golan in Bashan and Ashtaroth; from the tribe of Issachar, Kedesh, Daberath, Ramoth, and

Anem; from the tribe of Asher, Mashal, Abdon, Hukok, and Rehob; from the tribe of Naphtali, Kedesh in Galilee, Hammon, and Kiriathaim. The rest of the sons of Merari got Rimmono and Tabor from the tribe of Zebulun; Bezer in the desert, Jahzah, Kedemoth, and Mephaath from the tribe of Reuben to the east of the Jordan; and Ramoth in Gilead, Mahanaim, Heshbon, and Jazer from the tribe of Gad. Pastures were included in all these towns.

THE FAMILY OF ISSACHAR

7 The sons of Issachar were Tola, Puah, Jashub, and Shimron—four sons. The sons of Tola were Uzzi, Rephaiah, Jeriel, Jahmai, Ibsam, and Samuel—the chiefs of their families. During David's reign, the Tola family counted 22,600 warriors in their lineage. The son of Uzzi was Izrahiah; the sons of Izrahiah were Michael, Obadiah, Joel, and Isshiah—five sons and all of them chiefs. They counted 36,000 warriors in their lineage because they had more wives and sons than their brothers. The extended families of Issachar accounted for 87,000 warriors—all of them listed in the family tree.

THE FAMILY OF BENJAMIN

Benjamin had three sons: Bela, Beker, and Jediael. Bela had five: Ezbon, Uzzi, Uzziel, Jerimoth, and Iri, all of them chiefs and warriors. They counted 22,034 names in their family tree. Beker's sons were Zemirah, Joash, Eliezer, Elioenai, Omri, Jeremoth, Abijah, Anathoth, and Alemeth. Through these chiefs their family tree listed 20,200 warriors. Jediael's son was Bilhan and the sons of Bilhan were Jeush, Benjamin, Ehud, Kenaanah, Zethan, Tarshish, and Ahishahar—all sons of Jediael and family chiefs; they counted 17,200 combat-ready warriors. Shuppim and Huppim were the sons of Ir; Hushim were from the family of Aher.

THE FAMILY OF NAPHTALI

The sons of Naphtali were Jahziel, Guni, Jezer, and Shallum; they are listed under the maternal line of Bilhah, their grandfather's concubine.

THE FAMILY OF MANASSEH

Manasseh's sons, born of his Aramean concubine, were Asriel and Makir the father of Gilead. Makir got his wife from the Huppites and Shuppites. His sister's name was Maacah. Another son, Zelophehad, had only daughters. Makir's wife Maacah bore a son whom she named Peresh; his brother's name was Sheresh and his sons were Ulam and Rakem. Ulam's son was Bedan. This accounts for the sons of Gilead son of Makir, the son of Manasseh. His sister Hammoleketh gave birth to Ishdod, Abiezer, and Mahlah. The sons of Shemida were Ahian, Shechem, Likhi, and Aniam.

THE FAMILY OF EPHRAIM

The sons of Ephraim were Shuthelah, Bered his son, Tahath his son, Eleadah his son, Tahath his son, Zabad his son, Shuthelah his son, and Ezer and Elead, cattle-rustlers, killed on one of their raids by the natives of Gath. Their father Ephraim grieved a long time and his family gathered to give him comfort. Then he slept with his wife again. She conceived and produced a son. He named him Beriah (Unlucky), because of the bad luck that had come to his family. His daughter was Sheerah. She built Lower and Upper Beth Horon and Uzzen Sheerah.

Rephah was Ephraim's son and also Resheph; Telah was his son, Tahan his son, Ladan his son, Ammihud his son, Elishama his son, Nun his son, and Joshua his son. They occupied Bethel and the neighboring country from Naaran on the east to Gezer and its villages on the west, along with Shechem and its villages, and extending as far as Ayyah and its villages. Stretched along the borders of Manasseh were Beth Shan, Taanach, Megiddo, and Dor, together with their satellite villages. The families descended from Joseph son of Israel lived in all these places.

THE FAMILY OF ASHER

The sons of Asher were Imnah, Ishvah, Ishvi, and Beriah; Serah was their sister. The sons of Beriah were Heber and Malkiel, who had Birzaith. Heber had Japhlet, Shomer, Hotham, and Shua their sister.

Japhlet had Pasach, Bimhal, and Ashvath. His brother Shomer had Rohgah, Hubbah, and Aram. His brother Helem had Zophah, Imna, Shelesh, and Amal. Zophah had Suah, Harnepher, Shual, Beri, Imrah, Bezer, Hod, Shamma, Shilshah, Ithran, and Beera. Jether had Jephunneh, Pispah, and Ara. Ulla had Arah, Hanniel, and Rizia. These were Asher's sons, all of them responsible, excellent in character, and brave in battle—good leaders. They listed 26,000 combat-ready men in their family tree.

THE FAMILY OF BENJAMIN (CONTINUED)

8 Benjamin's firstborn son was Bela, followed by Ashbel, Aharah, Nohah, and Rapha—five in all. Bela's sons were Addar, Gera,

Abihud, Abishua, Naaman, Ahoah, Gera, Shephuphan, and Huram. These are the families of Ehud that lived in Geba and were exiled to Manahath: Naaman, Ahijah, and Gera, who led them to exile and had Uzza and Ahihud.

In the land of Moab, Shaharaim had children after he divorced his wives Hushim and Baara. From his new wife Hodesh he had Jobab, Zibia, Mesha, Malcam, Jeuz, Sakia, and Mirmah—sons who became heads of families. From his earlier wife Hushim he had Abitub and Elpaal. Elpaal's sons were Eber, Misham, and Shemed, who built Ono and Lod with all their villages.

Beriah and Shema were family chiefs who lived at Aijalon. They drove out the citizens of Gath. Their brothers were Shashak and Jeremoth. The sons of Beriah were Zebadiah, Arad, Eder, Michael, Ishpah, and Joha. The sons of Elpaal were Zebadiah, Meshullam, Hizki, Heber, Ishmerai, Izliah, and Jobab. The sons of Shimei were Jakim, Zicri, Zabdi, Elienai, Zillethai, Eliel, Adaiah, Beraiah, and Shimrath. The sons of Shashak were Ishpan, Eber, Eliel, Abdon, Zicri, Hanan, Hananiah, Elam, Anthothijah, Iphdeiah, and Penuel. The sons of Jeroham were Shamsherai, Shehariah, Athaliah, Jaareshiah, Elijah, and Zicri. These were the chiefs of the families as listed in their family tree. They lived in Jerusalem.

Jeiel the father of Gibeon lived in Gibeon. His wife's name was Maacah. Abdon was his firstborn son, followed by Zur, Kish, Baal, Nadab, Gedor, Ahio, Zeker, and Mikloth. Mikloth had Shimeah. They lived in the neighborhood of their extended families in Jerusalem.

Ner had Kish, Kish had Saul, and Saul had Jonathan, Malki-Shua, Abinadab, and Esh-Baal. Jonathan had Merib-Baal, and Merib-Baal had Micah. Micah's sons were Pithon, Melech, Tarea, and Ahaz. Ahaz had Jehoaddah and Jehoaddah had Alemeth, Azmaveth, and Zimri. Zimri had Moza and Moza had Binea. Raphah was his son, Eleasah his son, and Azel his son. Azel had six sons named Azrikam, Bokeru, Ishmael, Sheariah, Obadiah, and Hanan. His brother Eshek's sons were Ulam his firstborn, followed by Jeush and Eliphelet. Ulam's sons were warriors well known as archers. They had lots of sons and grandsons—at least 150. These were all in Benjamin's family tree.

9 This is the complete family tree for all Israel, recorded in the *Royal Annals of the Kings of Israel and Judah* at the time they were exiled to Babylon because of their unbelieving and disobedient lives.

THE BACK-FROM-EXILE COMMUNITY IN JERUSALEM

The first Israelites to return from exile to their homes and cities were the priests, the Levites, and the temple support staff.

Returning to Jerusalem from the families of Judah, Benjamin, Ephraim, and Manasseh were the following: Uthai son of Ammihud, the son of Omri, the son of Imri, the son of Bani, from the line of Perez son of Judah; from the Shilonites were Asaiah the firstborn and his sons; from the family of Zerah there was Jeuel. There were 690 in the Judah group.

From the family of Benjamin were Sallu son of Meshullam, the son of Hodaviah, the son of Hassenuah, and Ibneiah son of Jeroham, and Elah son of Uzzi, the son of Micri, and Meshullam son of Shephatiah, the son of Reuel, the son of Ibnijah. There were 956 in the Benjamin group. All these named were heads of families.

From the company of priests there were Jedaiah; Jehoiarib; Jakin; Azariah son of Hilkiah, the son of Meshullam, the son of Zadok, the son of Meraioth, the son of Ahitub, who was in charge of taking care of the house of God; Adaiah son of Jeroham, the son of Pashhur, the son of Malkijah; also Maasai son of Adiel, the son of Jahzerah, the son of Meshullam, the son of Meshillemith, the son of Immer. The priests, all of them heads of families, numbered 1,760, skilled and seasoned servants in the work of worshiping God.

From the Levites were Shemaiah son of Hasshub, the son of Azrikam, the son of Hashabiah, a Merarite; then Bakbakkar, Heresh, Galal, Mattaniah son of Mica, the son of Zicri, the son of Asaph; also Obadiah son of Shemaiah, the son of Galal, the son of Jeduthun; and finally Berekiah son of Asa, the son of Elkanah, who lived in the villages of the Netophathites.

The security guards were Shallum, Akkub, Talmon, Ahiman, and their brothers. Shallum was the chief and up to now the security guard at the King's Gate on the east. They also served as security guards at the camps of Levite families.

Shallum son of Kore, the son of Ebiasaph, the son of Korah, along with his brothers in the Korahite family, were in charge of the services of worship as doorkeepers of the Tent, as their ancestors had guarded the entrance to the camp of God. In the early days, Phinehas son of Eleazar was in charge of the security guards—God be with him! Now Zechariah son of Meshelemiah was the security guard at the entrance of the Tent of Meeting. The number of those who had been chosen to be security guards was 212—they were officially registered in their own camps. David and Samuel the seer handpicked them for their dependability. They and their sons had the permanent responsibility for guarding the gates of God's house, the house of worship; the main security guards were posted at the four entrances, east, west, north, and south; their brothers in the villages were scheduled to give them relief weekly—the four main security guards were responsible for round-the-clock surveillance.

Being Levites, they were responsible for the security of all supplies and valuables in the house of God. They kept watch all through the night and had the key to open the doors each morning. Some were in charge of the articles used in The Temple worship—they counted them both when they brought them in and when they took them out. Others were in charge of supplies in the sanctuary—flour, wine, oil, incense, and spices. And some of the priests were assigned to mixing the oils for the perfume. The Levite Mattithiah, the firstborn son of Shallum the Korahite, was responsible for baking the bread for the services of worship. Some of the brothers, sons of the Kohathites, were assigned to preparing the bread set out on the table each Sabbath.

And then there were the musicians, all heads of Levite families. They had permanent living quarters in The Temple; because they were on twenty-four-hour duty, they were exempt from all other duties. These were the heads of Levite families as designated in their family tree. They lived in Jerusalem.

THE FAMILY OF SAUL

Jeiel the father of Gibeon lived at Gibeon; his wife was Maacah. His firstborn son was Abdon, followed by Zur, Kish, Baal, Ner, Nadab, Gedor, Ahio, Zechariah, and Mikloth. Mikloth had Shimeam. They lived in the same neighborhood as their relatives in Jerusalem.

Ner had Kish, Kish had Saul, Saul had Jonathan, Malki-Shua, Abinadab, and Esh-Baal. Merib-Baal was the son of Jonathan and Merib-Baal had Micah. Micah's sons were Pithon, Melech, and Tahrea. Ahaz had Jarah, Jarah had Alemeth, Azmaveth, and Zimri; Zimri had Moza, Moza had Binea, Rephaiah was his son, Eleasah was his son, and Azel was his son. Azel had six sons: Azrikam, Bokeru, Ishmael, Sheariah, Obadiah, and Hanan—the sons of Azel.

✠

10 The Philistines went to war against Israel; the Israelites ran for their lives from the Philistines but fell, slaughtered on Mount Gilboa. The Philistines zeroed in on Saul and his sons and killed his sons Jonathan, Abinadab, and Malki-Shua. The battle went hard against Saul—the archers found him and wounded him. Saul said to his armor bearer, "Draw your sword and finish me off before these pagan pigs get to me and make a sport of my body." But his armor bearer, restrained by both reverence and fear, wouldn't do it. So Saul took his own sword and killed himself. The armor bearer, panicked because Saul was dead, then killed himself.

So Saul and his three sons—all four the same day—died. When all the Israelites in the valley saw that the army had fled and that Saul and his sons were dead, they abandoned their cities and ran off; the Philistines came and moved in.

The next day the Philistines came to plunder the dead bodies and found Saul and his sons dead on Mount Gilboa. They stripped Saul, removed his head and his armor, and put them on exhibit throughout Philistia, reporting the victory news to their idols and the people. Then they put Saul's armor on display in the temple of their gods and placed his skull as a trophy in the temple of their god Dagon.

The people of Jabesh Gilead heard what the Philistines had done to Saul. All of their fighting men went into action—retrieved the bodies of Saul and his sons and brought them to Jabesh, gave them a dignified burial under the oak at Jabesh, and mourned their deaths for seven days.

Saul died in disobedience, disobedient to GOD. He didn't obey GOD's words. Instead of praying, he went to a witch to seek guidance. Because he didn't go to GOD for help, GOD took his life and turned the kingdom over to David son of Jesse.

KING DAVID

11 Then all Israel assembled before David at Hebron. "Look at us," they said. "We're your very flesh and blood. In the past, yes, even while Saul was king, you were the real leader of Israel. GOD told you, 'You will shepherd my people Israel; you are to be the ruler of my people Israel.'" When all the elders of Israel came to the king at Hebron, David made a covenant with them in the presence of GOD at Hebron. Then they anointed David king over Israel exactly as GOD had commanded through Samuel.

David and all Israel went to Jerusalem (it was the old Jebus, where the Jebusites lived). The citizens of Jebus told David, "No trespassing—you can't come here." David came on anyway and captured the fortress of Zion, the City of David. David had said, "The first person to kill a Jebusite will be commander-in-chief." Joab son of Zeruiah was the first; and he became the chief.

David took up residence in the fortress city; that's how it got its name, "City of David." David fortified the city all the way around, both the outer bulwarks (the Millo) and the outside wall. Joab rebuilt the city gates. David's stride became longer, his embrace larger—yes, GOD-of-the-Angel-Armies was with him!

DAVID'S MIGHTY MEN

These are the chiefs of David's Mighty Men, the ones who linked arms with him as he took up his kingship, with all Israel joining in, helping him become king in just the way GOD had spoken regarding Israel. The list of David's Mighty Men:

Jashobeam son of Hacmoni was chief of the Thirty. Singlehandedly he killed three hundred men, killed them all in one skirmish.

Next was Eleazar son of Dodai the Ahohite, one of the Big Three of the Mighty Men. He was with David at Pas Dammim, where the Philistines had mustered their troops for battle. It was an area where there was a field of barley. The army started to flee from the Philistines and then took its stand right in that field—and turned the tide! They slaughtered the Philistines, GOD helping them—a huge victory.

The Big Three from the Thirty made a rocky descent to David at the Cave of Adullam while a company of Philistines was camped in the Valley of Rephaim. David was holed up in the Cave while the Philistines were prepared for battle at Bethlehem. David had a sudden craving: "What I wouldn't give for a drink of water from the well in Bethlehem, the one at the gate!" The Three penetrated the Philistine camp, drew water from the well at the Bethlehem gate, shouldered it, and brought it to David. And then David wouldn't drink it! He poured it out as a sacred offering to GOD, saying, "I'd rather be damned by God than drink this! It would be like drinking the lifeblood of these men—they risked their lives to bring it." So he refused to drink it. These are the kinds of things that the Big Three of the Mighty Men did.

Abishai brother of Joab was the chief of the Thirty. Singlehandedly he fought three hundred men, and killed the lot, but he never made it into the circle of the Three. He was highly honored by the Thirty—he was their chief—still, he didn't measure up to the Three.

Benaiah son of Jehoiada was a Mighty Man from Kabzeel with many exploits to his credit: he killed two famous Moabites; he climbed down into a pit and killed a lion on a snowy day; and he killed an Egyptian, a giant seven and a half feet tall. The Egyptian had a spear like a ship's boom but Benaiah went at him with a mere club, tore the spear from the Egyptian's hand, and killed him with it. These are some of the things Benaiah son of Jehoiada did. But he was never included with the Three. He was highly honored among the Thirty, but didn't measure up to the Three. David put him in charge of his personal bodyguard.

The Mighty Men of the military were Asahel brother of Joab, Elhanan son of Dodo of Bethlehem, Shammoth the Harorite, Helez the Pelonite, Ira son of Ikkesh the Tekoite, Abiezer the Anathothite, Sibbecai the Hushathite, Ilai the Ahohite, Maharai the Netophathite, Heled son of Baanah the Netophathite, Ithai son of Ribai from Gibeah of the Benjaminite, Benaiah the Pirathonite, Hurai from the ravines of Gaash, Abiel the Arbathite, Azmaveth the Baharumite, Eliahba the Shaalbonite, the sons of Hashem the Gizonite, Jonathan son of Shagee the Hararite, Ahiam son of Sacar the Haranite, Eliphal son of Ur, Hepher the Mekerathite, Ahijah the Pelonite, Hezro the Carmelite, Naarai son of Ezbai, Joel brother of Nathan, Mibhar son of Hagri, Zelek the Ammonite, Naharai the Berothite, the armor bearer of Joab son of Zeruiah, Ira the Ithrite, Gareb the Ithrite, Uriah the Hittite, Zabad son of Ahlai, Adina son of Shiza the Reubenite, the Reubenite chief of the Thirty, Hanan son of Maacah, Joshaphat the Mithnite, Uzzia the Ashterathite, Shama and Jeiel the sons of Hotham the Aroerite, Jediael son of Shimri, Joha the Tizite his brother, Eliel the Mahavite, Jeribai and Joshaviah the sons of Elnaam, Ithmah the Moabite, Eliel, Obed, and Jaasiel the Mezobaite.

12 These are the men who joined David in Ziklag; it was during the time he was banished by Saul the son of Kish; they were among the Mighty Men, good fighters. They were armed with bows and could sling stones and shoot arrows either right- or left-handed. They hailed from Saul's tribe, Benjamin.

The first was Ahiezer; then Joash son of Shemaah the Gibeathite; Jeziel and Pelet the sons of Azmaveth; Beracah; Jehu the Anathothite; Ishmaiah the Gibeonite, a Mighty Man among the Thirty, a leader of the

Thirty; Jeremiah; Jahaziel; Johanan; Jozabad the Gederathite; Eluzai; Jerimoth; Bealiah; Shemariah; Shephatiah the Haruphite; Elkanah; Isshiah; Azarel; Joezer; Jashobeam; the Korahites; and Joelah and Zebadiah, the sons of Jeroham from Gedor.

There were some Gadites there who had defected to David at his wilderness fortress; they were seasoned and eager fighters who knew how to handle shield and spear. They were wild in appearance, like lions, but as agile as gazelles racing across the hills. Ezer was the first, then Obadiah, Eliab, Mishmannah, Jeremiah, Attai, Eliel, Johanan, Elzabad, Jeremiah, and Macbannai—eleven of them. These Gadites were the cream of the crop—any one of them was worth a hundred lesser men, and the best of them were worth a thousand. They were the ones who crossed the Jordan when it was at flood stage in the first month, and put everyone in the lowlands to flight, both east and west.

There were also men from the tribes of Benjamin and Judah who joined David in his wilderness fortress. When David went out to meet them, this is what he said: "If you have come in peace and to help me, you are most welcome to join this company; but if you have come to betray me to my enemies, innocent as I am, the God of our ancestors will see through you and bring judgment on you."

Just then Amasai chief of the Thirty, moved by God's Spirit, said,

We're on your side, O David,
    We're committed, O son of Jesse;
All is well, yes, all is well with you,
    And all's well with whoever helps you.
Yes, for your God has helped and does help you.

So David took them on and assigned them a place under the chiefs of the raiders.

Some from the tribe of Manasseh also defected to David when he started out with the Philistines to go to war against Saul. In the end, they didn't actually fight because the Philistine leaders, after talking it over, sent them home, saying, "We can't trust them with our lives—they'll betray us to their master Saul."

The men from Manasseh who defected to David at Ziklag were Adnah, Jozabad, Jediael, Michael, Jozabad, Elihu, and Zillethai, all leaders among the families of Manasseh. They helped David in his raids against the desert bandits; they were all stalwart fighters and good leaders among his raiders.

Hardly a day went by without men showing up to help—it wasn't long before his band seemed as large as God's own army!

✠

Here are the statistics on the battle-seasoned warriors who came down from the north to David at Hebron to hand over Saul's kingdom, in accord with GOD's word: from Judah, carrying shield and spear, 6,800 battle-ready; from Simeon, 7,100 stalwart fighters; from Levi, 4,600, which included Jehoiada leader of the family of Aaron, bringing 3,700 men and the young and stalwart Zadok with twenty-two leaders from his family; from Benjamin, Saul's family, 3,000, most of whom had stuck it out with Saul until now; from Ephraim, 20,800, fierce fighters and famous in their home towns; from the half-tribe of Manasseh, 18,000 elected to come and make David king; from Issachar, men who understood both the times and Israel's duties, 200 leaders with their families; from Zebulun, 50,000 well-equipped veteran warriors, unswervingly loyal; from Naphtali, 1,000 chiefs leading 37,000 men heavily armed; from Dan, 28,600 battle-ready men; from Asher, 40,000 veterans, battle-ready; and from East of Jordan, men from Reuben, Gad, and the half-tribe of Manasseh, heavily armed, 120,000.

All these soldiers came to David at Hebron, ready to fight if necessary; they were both united and determined to make David king over all Israel. And everyone else in Israel was of the same mind—"Make David king!" They were with David for three days of feasting celebration, with food and drink supplied by their families. Neighbors ranging from as far north as Issachar, Zebulun, and Naphtali arrived with donkeys, camels, mules, and oxen loaded down with food for the party: flour, fig cakes, raisin cakes, wine, oil, cattle, and sheep—joy in Israel!

DAVID GOES TO GET THE CHEST OF GOD

13 David consulted with all of his leaders, the commanders of thousands and of hundreds. Then David addressed the entire assembly of Israel, "If it seems right to you, and it is GOD's will, let's invite all our relatives wherever they are throughout Israel, along with their relatives, including their priests and Levites from their cities and surrounding pastures, to join us. And let's bring the Chest of our God back—the Chest that was out of sight, out of mind during the days of Saul." The entire assembly of Israel agreed—everybody agreed that it was the right thing to do. So David gathered all Israel together, from Egypt's Pond of

Horus in the southwest to the Pass of Hamath in the northeast, to go and get the Chest of God from Kiriath Jearim. Then David and all Israel went to Baalah (Kiriath Jearim) in Judah to bring back the Chest of God, the "Cherubim-Throne-of-GOD," where GOD's Name is invoked. They moved the Chest of God on a brand-new cart from the house of Abinadab with Uzzah and Ahio in charge. In procession with the Chest of God, David and all Israel worshiped exuberantly in song and dance, with a marching band of all kinds of instruments. When they were at the threshing floor of Kidon, the oxen stumbled and Uzzah grabbed the Chest to keep it from falling off. GOD erupted in anger against Uzzah and killed him because he grabbed the Chest. He died on the spot—in the presence of God. David lost his temper, angry because GOD exploded against Uzzah; the place is still called Perez Uzzah (Exploded Uzzah). David was terrified of God that day; he said, "How can I possibly continue this parade with the Chest of God?" So David called off the parade of the Chest to the City of David; instead he stored it in the house of Obed-Edom the Gittite. The Chest of God was in storage in the house of Obed-Edom for three months. GOD blessed the family of Obed-Edom and everything around him.

DAVID BUILDS

14 King Hiram of Tyre sent an envoy to David, along with cedar lumber, masons, and carpenters to build him a royal palace. Then David knew for sure that GOD had confirmed him as king over Israel, because of the rising reputation that GOD was giving his kingdom for the benefit of his people Israel. David married more wives and had more children in Jerusalem. His children born in Jerusalem were Shammua, Shobab, Nathan, Solomon, Ibhar, Elishua, Elpelet, Nogah, Nepheg, Japhia, Elishama, Beeliada, and Eliphelet.

✠

The minute the Philistines heard that David had been made king over a united Israel, they went out in force to capture David. When David got the report, he marched out to confront them. On their way, the Philistines stopped off to plunder the Valley of Rephaim.

David prayed to God: "Is this the right time to attack the Philistines? Will you give me the victory?"

GOD answered, "Attack; I'll give you the victory."

David attacked at Baal Perazim and slaughtered them. David said,

"God exploded my enemies, as water explodes from a burst pipe." That's how the place got its name, Baal Perazim (Baal-Explosion). The Philistines left their gods behind and David ordered that they be burned up.

And then the Philistines were back at it again, plundering in the valley. David again prayed to God. God answered, "This time don't attack head-on; circle around and come at them out of the balsam grove. When you hear a sound like shuffling feet in the tops of the balsams, attack; God will be two steps ahead of you, slaughtering the Philistines."

David did exactly as God commanded, slaughtering Philistines all the way from Gibeon to Gezer.

David was soon famous all over the place, far and near; and GOD put the fear of God into the godless nations.

DAVID WORSHIPS

15 After David built houses for himself in the City of David, he cleared a place for the Chest and pitched a tent for it. Then David gave orders: "No one carries the Chest of God except the Levites; GOD designated them and them only to carry the Chest of GOD and be available full time for service in the work of worship."

David then called everyone in Israel to assemble in Jerusalem to bring up the Chest of GOD to its specially prepared place. David also called in the family of Aaron and the Levites. From the family of Kohath, Uriel the head with 120 relatives; from the family of Merari, Asaiah the head with 220 relatives; from the family of Gershon, Joel the head with 130 relatives; from the family of Elizaphan, Shemaiah the head with 200 relatives; from the family of Hebron, Eliel the head with 80 relatives; from the family of Uzziel, Amminadab the head with 112 relatives.

Then David called in Zadok and Abiathar the priests, and Uriel, Asaiah, Joel, Shemaiah, Eliel, and Amminadab the Levites. He said, "You are responsible for the Levitical families; now consecrate yourselves, both you and your relatives, and bring up the Chest of the GOD of Israel to the place I have set aside for it. The first time we did this, you Levites did not carry it properly, and GOD exploded in anger at us because we didn't make proper preparation and follow instructions."

So the priests and Levites consecrated themselves to bring up the Chest of the GOD of Israel. The Levites carried the Chest of God exactly as Moses, instructed by GOD, commanded—carried it with poles on their shoulders, careful not to touch it with their hands.

David ordered the heads of the Levites to assign their relatives to sing in the choir, accompanied by a well-equipped marching band, and fill the air with joyful sound.

The Levites assigned Heman son of Joel, and from his family, Asaph son of Berekiah, then Ethan son of Kushaiah from the family of Merari, and after them in the second rank their brothers Zechariah, Jaaziel, Shemiramoth, Jehiel, Unni, Eliab, Benaiah, Maaseiah, Mattithiah, Eliphelehu, Mikneiah, Obed-Edom, and Jeiel as security guards.

The members of the choir and marching band were: Heman, Asaph, and Ethan with bronze cymbals; Zechariah, Aziel, Shemiramoth, Jehiel, Unni, Eliab, Maaseiah, and Benaiah with lyres carrying the melody; Mattithiah, Eliphelehu, Mikneiah, Obed-Edom, Jeiel, and Azaziah with harps filling in the harmony; Kenaniah, the Levite in charge of music, a very gifted musician, was music director.

Berekiah and Elkanah were porters for the Chest. The priests Shebaniah, Joshaphat, Nethanel, Amasai, Zechariah, Benaiah, and Eliezer blew the trumpets before the Chest of God. Obed-Edom and Jehiah were also porters for the Chest.

Now they were ready. David, the elders of Israel, and the commanders of thousands started out to get the Chest of the Covenant of GOD and bring it up from the house of Obed-Edom. And they went rejoicing. Because God helped the Levites, strengthening them as they carried the Chest of the Covenant of GOD, they paused to worship by sacrificing seven bulls and seven rams. They were all dressed in elegant linen—David, the Levites carrying the Chest, the choir and band, and Kenaniah who was directing the music. David also wore a linen prayer shawl (called an ephod). On they came, all Israel on parade bringing up the Chest of the Covenant of GOD, shouting and cheering, playing every kind of brass and percussion and string instrument.

When the Chest of the Covenant of GOD entered the City of David, Michal, Saul's daughter, was watching from a window. When she saw King David dancing ecstatically she was filled with contempt.

✝

16 They brought the Chest of God and placed it right in the center of the tent that David had pitched for it; then they worshiped by presenting burnt offerings and peace offerings to God. When David had completed the offerings of worship, he blessed the people in the name of GOD. Then he passed around to every one there, men and women alike, a loaf of bread, a slice of barbecue, and a raisin cake.

Then David assigned some of the Levites to the Chest of GOD to lead worship—to intercede, give thanks, and praise the GOD of Israel. Asaph was in charge; under him were Zechariah, Jeiel, Shemiramoth, Jehiel, Mattithiah, Eliab, Benaiah, Obed-Edom, and Jeiel, who played the musical instruments. Asaph was on percussion. The priests Benaiah and Jahaziel blew the trumpets before the Chest of the Covenant of God at set times through the day.

That was the day that David inaugurated regular worship of praise to GOD, led by Asaph and his company.

Thank GOD! Call out his Name!
    Tell the whole world who he is and what he's done!
Sing to him! Play songs for him!
    Broadcast all his wonders!
Revel in his holy Name,
    GOD-seekers, be jubilant!
Study GOD and his strength,
    seek his presence day and night;
Remember all the wonders he performed,
    the miracles and judgments that came out of his mouth.
Seed of Israel his servant!
    Children of Jacob, his first choice!
He is GOD, *our* God;
    wherever you go you come on his judgments and decisions.
He keeps his commitments across thousands
    of generations, the covenant he commanded,
The same one he made with Abraham,
    the very one he swore to Isaac;
He posted it in big block letters to Jacob,
    this eternal covenant with Israel:
"I give you the land of Canaan,
    this is your inheritance;
Even though you're not much to look at,
    a few straggling strangers."

They wandered from country to country,
    camped out in one kingdom after another;
But he didn't let anyone push them around,
    he stood up for them against bully-kings:

"Don't you dare touch my anointed ones,
　　don't lay a hand on my prophets."

Sing to GOD, everyone and everything!
　　Get out his salvation news every day!
Publish his glory among the godless nations,
　　his wonders to all races and religions.
And why? Because GOD is great—well worth praising!
　　No god or goddess comes close in honor.
All the popular gods are stuff and nonsense,
　　but GOD made the cosmos!
Splendor and majesty flow out of him,
　　strength and joy fill his place.

Shout Bravo! to GOD, families of the peoples,
　　in awe of the Glory, in awe of the Strength: Bravo!
Shout Bravo! to his famous Name,
　　lift high an offering and enter his presence!
Stand resplendent in his robes of holiness!

God is serious business, take him seriously;
　　he's put the earth in place and it's not moving.
So let heaven rejoice, let earth be jubilant,
　　and pass the word among the nations, "GOD reigns!"
Let Ocean, all teeming with life, bellow,
　　let Field and all its creatures shake the rafters;
Then the trees in the forest will add their applause
　　to all who are pleased and present before GOD
　　　　—he's on his way to set things right!

Give thanks to GOD—he is good
　　and his love never quits.
Say, "Save us, Savior God,
　　round us up and get us out of these godless places,
So we can give thanks to your holy Name,
　　and bask in your life of praise."
Blessed be GOD, the God of Israel,
　　from everlasting to everlasting.

Then everybody said, "Yes! Amen!" and "Praise GOD!"

⊹

David left Asaph and his coworkers with the Chest of the Covenant of GOD and in charge of the work of worship; they were responsible for the needs of worship around the clock. He also assigned Obed-Edom and his sixty-eight relatives to help them. Obed-Edom son of Jeduthun and Hosah were in charge of the security guards. The priest Zadok and his family of priests were assigned to the Tent of GOD at the sacred mound at Gibeon to make sure that the services of morning and evening worship were conducted daily, complete with Whole-Burnt-Offerings offered on the Altar of Burnt Offering, as ordered in the Law of GOD, which was the norm for Israel. With them were Heman, Jeduthun, and others specifically named, with the job description: "Give thanks to GOD, for his love never quits!" Heman and Jeduthun were also well equipped with trumpets, cymbals, and other instruments for accompanying sacred songs. The sons of Jeduthun formed the security guard.

Arrangements completed, the people all left for home. And David went home to bless his family.

DAVID SUBMITS AND PRAYS

17 After the king had made himself at home, he said to Nathan the prophet, "Look at this: Here I am comfortable in a luxurious palace of cedar and the Chest of the Covenant of GOD sits under a tent."

Nathan told David, "Whatever is on your heart, go and do it; God is with you."

But that night, the word of God came to Nathan, saying, "Go and tell my servant David, This is GOD's word on the matter: You will not build me a 'house' to live in. Why, I haven't lived in a 'house' from the time I brought up the children of Israel from Egypt till now; I've gone from one tent and makeshift shelter to another. In all my travels with all Israel, did I ever say to any of the leaders I commanded to shepherd Israel, 'Why haven't you built me a house of cedar?'

"So here is what you are to tell my servant David: The GOD-of-the-Angel-Armies has this word for you: I took you from the pasture, tagging after sheep, and made you prince over my people Israel. I was with you everywhere you went and mowed your enemies down before you; and now I'm about to make you famous, ranked with the great names on earth. I'm going to set aside a place for my people Israel and plant them there so they'll have their own home and not be knocked around anymore; nor will evil nations afflict them as they always have, even during the days I set judges over my people Israel. And finally, I'm going to conquer all your enemies.

"And now I'm telling you this: GOD himself will build *you* a house! When your life is complete and you're buried with your ancestors, then I'll raise up your child to succeed you, a child from your own body, and I'll firmly establish his rule. *He* will build a house to honor me, and I will guarantee his kingdom's rule forever. I'll be a father to him, and he'll be a son to me. I will never remove my gracious love from him as I did from the one who preceded you. I will set him over my house and my kingdom forever; his throne will always be there, rock solid."

Nathan gave David a complete and accurate report of everything he heard and saw in the vision.

King David went in, took his place before GOD, and prayed:

Who am I, my Master GOD, and what is my family, that you have brought me to this place in life? But that's nothing compared to what's coming, for you've also spoken of my family far into the future, given me a glimpse into tomorrow and looked on me, Master GOD, as a Somebody. What's left for David to say to this—to your honoring your servant, even though you know me, just as I am? O GOD, out of the goodness of your heart, you've taken your servant to do this great thing and put your great work on display. There's none like you, GOD, no *God* but you, nothing to compare with what we've heard with our own ears. And who is like your people, like Israel, a nation unique on earth, whom God set out to redeem as his own people (and became most famous for it), performing great and fearsome acts, throwing out nations and their gods left and right as you saved your people from Egypt? You established for yourself a people—your very own Israel!— your people forever. And you, GOD, became their God.

So now, great GOD, this word that you have spoken to me and my family, guarantee it forever! Do exactly what you've promised! Then your reputation will be confirmed and flourish always as people exclaim, "The GOD-of-the-Angel-Armies, the God over Israel, is Israel's God!" And the house of your servant

David will remain rock solid under your watchful presence. You, my God, have told me plainly, "I will build you a house." That's how I was able to find the courage to pray this prayer to you. GOD, being the God you are, you have spoken all these wonderful words to me. As if that weren't enough, you've blessed my family so that it will continue in your presence always. Because you have blessed it, GOD, it's *really* blessed—blessed for good!

DAVID FIGHTS

18 In the days that followed, David struck hard at the Philistines, bringing them to their knees, captured Gath, and took control of the surrounding countryside.

He also fought and defeated Moab. The Moabites came under David's rule and paid regular tribute.

On his way to restore his sovereignty at the Euphrates River, David defeated Hadadezer king of Zobah (over toward Hamath). David captured a thousand chariots, 7,000 cavalry, and 20,000 infantry from him. He hamstrung all the chariot horses, but saved back a hundred.

When the Arameans from Damascus came to the aid of Hadadezer king of Zobah, David killed 22,000 of them. David set up a puppet government in Aram-Damascus. The Arameans became subjects of David and were forced to bring tribute. GOD gave victory to David wherever he marched.

David plundered the gold shields that belonged to the servants of Hadadezer and brought them to Jerusalem. He also looted Tebah and Cun, cities of Hadadezer, of a huge quantity of bronze that Solomon later used to make the Great Bronze Sea, the Pillars, and bronze equipment in The Temple.

Tou king of Hamath heard that David had struck down the entire army of Hadadezer king of Zobah. He sent his son Hadoram to King David to greet and congratulate him for fighting and defeating Hadadezer. Tou and Hadadezer were old enemies. Hadoram brought David various things made of silver, gold, and bronze. King David consecrated these things along with the silver and gold that he had plundered from other nations: Edom, Moab, the Ammonites, the Philistines, and Amalek.

Abishai son of Zeruiah fought and defeated the Edomites in the Valley of Salt—18,000 of them. He set up a puppet government in Edom and the Edomites became subjects under David.

GOD gave David victory wherever he marched.

✠

Thus David ruled over all of Israel. He ruled well, fair and evenhanded in all his duties and relationships.

Joab son of Zeruiah was head of the army;

Jehoshaphat son of Ahilud was in charge of public records;

Zadok son of Ahitub and Abimelech son of Abiathar were priests;

Shavsha was secretary;

Benaiah son of Jehoiada was over the special forces, the Kerethites and Pelethites;

And David's sons held high positions, close to the king.

✠

19Some time after this Nahash king of the Ammonites died and his son succeeded him as king. David said, "I'd like to show some kindness to Hanun son of Nahash—treat him as well and as kindly as his father treated me." So David sent condolences about his father's death.

But when David's servants arrived in Ammonite country and came to Hanun to bring condolences, the Ammonite leaders warned Hanun, "Do you for a minute suppose that David is honoring your father by sending you comforters? Don't you know that he's sent these men to snoop around the city and size it up so that he can capture it?"

So Hanun seized David's men, shaved them clean, cut off their robes half way up their buttocks, and sent them packing.

When this was all reported to David, he sent someone to meet them, for they were seriously humiliated. The king told them, "Stay in Jericho until your beards grow out; only then come back."

When it dawned on the Ammonites that as far as David was concerned, they stank to high heaven, they hired, at a cost of a thousand talents of silver (thirty-seven and a half tons!), chariots and horsemen from the Arameans of Naharaim, Maacah, and Zobah—32,000 chariots and drivers; plus the king of Maacah with his troops who came and set up camp at Medeba; the Ammonites, too, were mobilized from their cities and got ready for battle.

When David heard this, he dispatched Joab with his strongest fighters in full force.

The Ammonites marched out and spread out in battle formation at the city gate; the kings who had come as allies took up a position in the open fields. When Joab saw that he had two fronts to fight, before and behind, he took his pick of the best of Israel and deployed them to confront the Arameans. The rest of the army he put under the command of Abishai, his brother, and deployed them to deal with the Ammonites. Then he said, "If the Arameans are too much for me, you help me; and if the Ammonites prove too much for you, I'll come and help you. Courage! We'll fight might and main for our people and for the cities of our God. And GOD will do whatever he sees needs doing!"

But when Joab and his soldiers moved in to fight the Arameans, they ran off in full retreat. Then the Ammonites, seeing the Arameans run for dear life, took to their heels and ran from Abishai into the city. So Joab withdrew from the Ammonites and returned to Jerusalem.

When the Arameans saw how badly they'd been beaten by Israel, they picked up the pieces and regrouped; they sent for the Arameans who were across the river; Shophach, commander of Hadadezer's army, led them.

When all this was reported to David, he mustered all Israel, crossed the Jordan, advanced, and prepared to fight. The Arameans went into battle formation, ready for David, and the fight was on. But the Arameans again scattered before Israel. David killed 7,000 chariot drivers and 40,000 infantry. He also killed Shophach, the army commander. When all the kings who were vassals of Hadadezer saw that they had been routed by Israel, they made peace with David and served him. The Arameans were afraid to help the Ammonites ever again.

20 That spring, the time when kings usually go off to war, Joab led the army out and ravaged the Ammonites. He then set siege to Rabbah. David meanwhile was back in Jerusalem. Joab hit Rabbah hard and left it in ruins. David took the crown off the head of their king. Its weight was found to be a talent of gold and set with a precious stone. It was placed on David's head. He hauled great quantities of loot from the city and put the people to hard labor with saws and picks and axes. This is what he did to all the Ammonites. Then David and his army returned to Jerusalem.

Later war broke out with the Philistines at Gezer. That was the time Sibbecai the Hushathite killed Sippai of the clan of giants. The Philistines had to eat crow. In another war with the Philistines, Elhanan son of Jair killed Lahmi, the brother of Goliath the Gittite whose spear was like a ship's boom. And then there was the war at Gath that featured a hulking giant who had twenty-four fingers and toes, six on each hand and foot—yet another from the clan of giants. When he mocked Israel, Jonathan son of Shimea, David's brother, killed him. These came from the clan of giants and were killed by David and his men.

DAVID, SATAN, AND ARAUNAH

21 Now Satan entered the scene and seduced David into taking a census of Israel. David gave orders to Joab and the army officers under him, "Canvass all the tribes of Israel, from Dan to Beersheba, and get a count of the population. I want to know the number."

Joab resisted: "May GOD multiply his people by hundreds! Don't they all belong to my master the king? But why on earth would you do a thing like this—why risk getting Israel into trouble with God?"

But David wouldn't take no for an answer, so Joab went off and did it—canvassed the country and then came back to Jerusalem and reported the results of the census: There were 1,100,000 fighting men; of that total, Judah accounted for 470,000. Joab, disgusted by the command—it, in fact, turned his stomach!—protested by leaving Levi and Benjamin out of the census-taking. And God, offended by the whole thing, punished Israel.

Then David prayed, "I have sinned badly in what I have just done, substituting statistics for trust; forgive my sin—I've been really stupid."

GOD answered by speaking to Gad, David's pastor: "Go and give David this message: 'GOD's word: You have your choice of three punishments; choose one and I'll do the rest.'"

Gad delivered the message to David: "Do you want three years of famine, three months of running from your enemies while they chase you down, or three days of the sword of GOD—an epidemic unleashed on the country by an angel of GOD? Think it over and make up your mind. What shall I tell the One who sent me?"

David told Gad, "They're all terrible! But I'd rather be punished by GOD whose mercy is great, than fall into human hands."

So GOD unleashed an epidemic in Israel—70,000 Israelites died. God then sent the angel to Jerusalem but when he saw the destruction about to begin, he compassionately changed his mind and ordered the death angel, "Enough's enough! Pull back!"

The angel of GOD had just reached the threshing floor of Araunah the Jebusite. David looked up and saw the angel hovering between earth and sky, sword drawn and about to strike Jerusalem. David and the elders bowed in prayer and covered themselves with rough burlap.

David prayed, "Please! I'm the one who sinned; I'm the one at fault. But these sheep, what did they do wrong? Punish me, not them, me and my family; don't take it out on them."

The angel of GOD ordered Gad to tell David to go and build an altar to GOD on the threshing floor of Araunah the Jebusite. David did what Gad told him in obedience to GOD's command.

Meanwhile Araunah had quit threshing the wheat and was watching the angel; his four sons took cover and hid. David came up to Araunah. When Araunah saw David, he left the threshing floor and bowed deeply before David, honoring the king.

David said to Araunah, "Give me the site of the threshing floor so I can build an altar to GOD. Charge me the market price; we're going to put an end to this disaster."

"O master, my king," said Araunah, "just take it; do whatever you want with it! Look, here's an ox for the burnt offering and threshing paddles for the fuel and wheat for the meal offering—it's all yours!"

David replied to Araunah, "No. I'm *buying* it from you, and at the full market price. I'm not going to offer GOD sacrifices that are no sacrifice." So David bought the place from Araunah for 600 shekels of gold. He built an altar to GOD there and sacrificed Whole-Burnt-Offerings and Peace-Offerings. He called out to GOD and GOD answered by striking the altar of Whole-Burnt-Offering with lightning. Then GOD told the angel to put his sword back into its scabbard.

And that's the story of what happened when David saw that GOD answered him on the threshing floor of Araunah the Jebusite at the time he offered the sacrifice.

✟

At this time the Tabernacle that Moses had constructed in the desert, and with it the Altar of Burnt Offering, were set up at the worship center at Gibeon. But David, terrified by the angel's sword, wouldn't go there to pray to God anymore. So David declared, "From now on, *this* is the site for the worship of GOD; *this* is the place for Israel's Altar of Burnt Offering."

DAVID CHARGES SOLOMON TO BUILD THE TEMPLE

22 David ordered all the resident aliens in the land to come together; he sent them to the stone quarries to cut dressed stone to build The Temple of God. He also stockpiled a huge quantity of iron for nails

and bracings for the doors of the gates, more bronze than could be weighed, and cedar logs past counting (the Sidonians and Tyrians shipped in huge loads of cedar logs for David).

David was thinking, "My son Solomon is too young to plan ahead for this. But the sanctuary that is to be built for GOD has to be the greatest, the talk of all the nations; so I'll get the construction materials together." That's why David prepared this huge stockpile of building materials before he died. Then he called in Solomon his son and commanded him to build a sanctuary for the GOD of Israel.

David said to Solomon, "I wanted in the worst way to build a sanctuary to honor my GOD. But GOD prevented me, saying, 'You've killed too many people, fought too many wars. You are not the one to honor me by building a sanctuary—you've been responsible for too much killing, too much bloodshed. But you are going to have a son and he will be a quiet and peaceful man, and I will calm his enemies down on all sides. His very name will speak peace—that is, Solomon, which means Peace—and I'll give peace and rest under his rule. He will be the one to build a sanctuary in my honor. He'll be my royal adopted son and I'll be his father; and I'll make sure that the authority of his kingdom over Israel lasts forever.'

"So now, son, GOD be with you. GOD-speed as you build the sanctuary for your GOD, the job God has given you. And may GOD also give you discernment and understanding when he puts you in charge of Israel so that you will rule in reverent obedience under GOD's Revelation. That's what will make you successful, following the directions and doing the things that GOD commanded Moses for Israel. Courage! Take charge! Don't be timid; don't hold back. Look at this—I've gone to a lot of trouble to stockpile materials for the sanctuary of GOD: 100,000 talents (3,775 tons) of gold, a million talents (37,750 tons) of silver, tons of bronze and iron—too much to weigh—and all this timber and stone. And you're free to add more. And workers both plentiful and prepared: stonecutters, masons, carpenters, artisans in gold and silver, bronze and iron. You're all set—get to work! And GOD-speed!"

David gave orders to all of Israel's leaders to help his son Solomon, saying, "Isn't it obvious that your GOD is present with you; that he has given you peaceful relations with everyone around? My part in this was to put down the enemies, subdue the land to GOD and his people; your part is to give yourselves, heart and soul, to praying to your GOD. So get moving—build the sacred house of worship to GOD! Then bring the Chest of the Covenant of GOD and all the holy furnishings for the worship of God into the sanctuary built in honor of GOD."

PREPARATIONS FOR WORSHIP

23 When David got to be an old man, he made his son Solomon king over Israel.

At the same time he brought together all the leaders of Israel, the priests, and the Levites. The Levites thirty years and older were counted; the total was 38,000. David sorted them into work groups: "24,000 are in charge of administering worship in the sanctuary; 6,000 are officials and judges; 4,000 are security guards; and 4,000 are to serve in the orchestra, praising GOD with instruments that I have provided for praise."

David then divided the Levites into groupings named after the sons of Levi: Gershon, Kohath, and Merari.

The Gershonites: Ladan and Shimei. The three sons of Ladan: Jehiel, Zetham, and Joel. The three sons of Shimei: Shelomoth, Haziel, and Haran, all heads of the families of Ladan. The four sons of Shimei: Jahath, Ziza, Jeush, and Beriah. Jahath came first, followed by Ziza. Jeush and Beriah did not have many sons so they were counted as one family with one task.

The four sons of Kohath: Amram, Izhar, Hebron, and Uzziel. The sons of Amram: Aaron and Moses. Aaron was especially ordained to work in the Holy of Holies, to burn incense before GOD, to serve God and bless his Name always. This was a permanent appointment for Aaron and his sons. Moses and his sons were counted in the tribe of Levi.

The sons of Moses: Gershom and Eliezer. Shubael was the first son of Gershom. Rehabiah was the first and only son of Eliezer; but though Eliezer had no other sons, Rehabiah had many sons.

Shelomith was the first son of Izhar. Hebron had four sons: Jeriah, Amariah, Jahaziel, and Jekameam. Uzziel had two sons: Micah and Isshiah. The sons of Merari: Mahli and Mushi. The sons of Mahli: Eleazar and Kish. Eleazar died without any sons, only daughters. Their cousins, the sons of Kish, married the daughters. Mushi had three sons: Mahli, Eder, and Jerimoth.

These are the sons of Levi twenty years and older, divided up according to families and heads of families and listed in the work groups that took care of the worship in the sanctuary of GOD.

David said, "Now that the GOD of Israel has given rest to his people and made Jerusalem his permanent home, the Levites no longer have to carry the Tabernacle and all the furniture required for the work of worship." These last words of David referred only to Levites twenty years old and above.

From now on the assigned work of the Levites was to assist Aaron's sons in the work of worship in GOD's house: maintain courtyards and closets, keep the furniture and utensils of worship clean, take care of any extra work needed in the work of worship, and provide bread for the table and flour for the Meal Offerings and the unraised wafers— all baking and mixing, all measuring and weighing. Also they were to be present for morning prayers, thanking and praising GOD, for evening prayers, and at the service of Whole-Burnt-Offerings to GOD on Sabbath, at New Moons, and at all festivals. They were on regular duty to serve GOD according to their assignment and the required number.

In short, the Levites, with the sons of Aaron as their companions in the ministry of holy worship, were responsible for everything that had to do with worship: the place and times and ordering of worship.

24 The family of Aaron was grouped as follows: Aaron's sons were Nadab, Abihu, Eleazar, and Ithamar. Nadab and Abihu died before their father and left no sons. So Eleazar and Ithamar filled the office of priest. David assigned Zadok from the family of Eleazar and Ahimelech from the family of Ithamar and assigned them to separate divisions for carrying out their appointed ministries. It turned out that there were more leaders in Eleazar's family than in Ithamar's and so they divided them proportionately: sixteen clan leaders from Eleazar's family and eight clan leaders from Ithamar's family. They assigned the leaders by lot, treating both families alike, for there were officials of the sanctuary and officials of God among both the Eleazar and Ithamar families.

The secretary Shemaiah son of Nethanel, a Levite, wrote down their names in the presence of the king, the officials, Zadok the priest, Ahimelech son of Abiathar, and the leaders of the priestly and Levitical families. They took turns: One family was selected from Eleazar and then one from Ithamar.

The first lot fell to Jehoiarib,
the second to Jedaiah,
the third to Harim,
the fourth to Seorim,
the fifth to Malkijah,
the sixth to Mijamin,

the seventh to Hakkoz,
    the eighth to Abijah,
the ninth to Jeshua,
    the tenth to Shecaniah,
the eleventh to Eliashib,
    the twelfth to Jakim,
the thirteenth to Huppah,
    the fourteenth to Jeshebeab,
the fifteenth to Bilgah,
    the sixteenth to Immer,
the seventeenth to Hezir,
    the eighteenth to Happizzez,
the nineteenth to Pethahiah,
    the twentieth to Jehezkel,
the twenty-first to Jakin,
    the twenty-second to Gamul,
the twenty-third to Delaiah,
    and the twenty-fourth to Maaziah.

They served in this appointed order when they entered The Temple of GOD, following the procedures laid down by their ancestor Aaron as GOD, the God of Israel, had commanded him.

The rest of the Levites are as follows:

From the sons of Amram: Shubael; from the sons of Shubael: Jehdeiah.

Concerning Rehabiah: from his sons, Isshiah was the first.

From the Izharites: Shelomoth; from the sons of Shelomoth: Jahath.

The sons of Hebron: Jeriah the first, Amariah the second, Jahaziel the third, and Jekameam the fourth.

The son of Uzziel: Micah, and from the sons of Micah: Shamir. The brother of Micah was Isshiah, and from the sons of Isshiah: Zechariah.

The sons of Merari: Mahli and Mushi. The son of Jaaziah: Beno. The sons of Merari from Jaaziah: Beno, Shoham, Zaccur, and Ibri.

From Mahli: Eleazar, who had no sons.

From Kish: Jerahmeel, the son of Kish.

And from the sons of Mushi: Mahli, Eder, and Jerimoth.

These were the Levites by their families. They also cast lots, the same as their kindred the sons of Aaron had done, in the presence of

David the king, Zadok, Ahimelech, and the leaders of the priestly and Levitical families. The families of the oldest and youngest brothers were treated the same.

THE MUSICIANS FOR WORSHIP

25 Next David and the worship leaders selected some from the family of Asaph, Heman, and Jeduthun for special service in preaching and music. Here is the roster of names and assignments: From the family of Asaph: Zaccur, Joseph, Nethaniah, and Asarelah; they were supervised by Asaph, who spoke for GOD backed up by the king's authority. From the family of Jeduthun there were six sons: Gedaliah, Zeri, Jeshaiah, Shimei, Hashabiah, and Mattithiah; they were supervised by their father Jeduthun, who preached and accompanied himself with the zither—he was responsible for leading the thanks and praise to GOD. From the family of Heman: Bukkiah, Mattaniah, Uzziel, Shubael, Jerimoth, Hananiah, Hanani, Eliathah, Giddalti, Romamti-Ezer, Joshbekashah, Mallothi, Hothir, and Mahazioth. These were the sons of Heman the king's seer; they supported and assisted him in his divinely appointed work. God gave Heman fourteen sons and three daughters. Under their father's supervision they were in charge of leading the singing and providing musical accompaniment in the work of worship in the sanctuary of God (Asaph, Jeduthun, and Heman took their orders directly from the king). They were well-trained in the sacred music, all of them masters. There were 288 of them.

They drew names at random to see who would do what. Nobody, whether young or old, teacher or student, was given preference or advantage over another.

The first name from Asaph's family was Joseph and his twelve sons and brothers; second, Gedaliah and his twelve sons and brothers; third, Zaccur and his twelve sons and brothers; fourth, Izri and his twelve sons and brothers; fifth, Nethaniah and his twelve sons and brothers; sixth, Bukkiah and his twelve sons and brothers; seventh, Jesarelah and his twelve sons and brothers; eighth, Jeshaiah and his twelve sons and brothers; ninth, Mattaniah and his twelve sons and brothers; tenth, Shimei and his twelve sons and brothers; eleventh, Azarel and his twelve sons and brothers; twelfth, Hashabiah and his twelve sons and brothers; thirteenth, Shubael and his twelve sons and brothers; fourteenth, Mattithiah and his twelve sons and brothers; fifteenth, Jerimoth and his twelve sons and brothers; sixteenth, Hananiah and his twelve sons and brothers; seventeenth, Joshbekashah and his twelve sons and brothers; eighteenth, Hanani and his twelve sons and brothers; nineteenth, Mallothi and his twelve sons and brothers; twentieth, Eliathah and his twelve sons and brothers; twenty-first, Hothir and his twelve sons and brothers; twenty-second, Giddalti and his twelve sons and brothers; twenty-third, Mahazioth and his twelve sons and brothers; twenty-fourth, Romamti-Ezer and his twelve sons and brothers.

THE SECURITY GUARDS

26 The teams of security guards were from the family of Korah: Meshelemiah son of Kore (one of the sons of Asaph). Meshelemiah's sons were Zechariah, the firstborn, followed by Jediael, Zebadiah, Jathniel, Elam, Jehohanan, and Eliehoenai—seven sons. Obed-Edom's sons were Shemaiah, the firstborn, followed by Jehozabad, Joah, Sacar, Nethanel, Ammiel, Issachar, and Peullethai—God blessed him with eight sons. His son Shemaiah had sons who provided outstanding leadership in the family: Othni, Rephael, Obed, and Elzabad; his relatives Elihu and Semakiah were also exceptional. These all came from the line of Obed-Edom—all of them outstanding and strong. There were sixty-two of them. Meshelemiah had eighteen sons and relatives who were outstanding. The sons of Hosah the Merarite were Shimri (he was not the firstborn but his father made him first), then Hilkiah, followed by Tabaliah and Zechariah. Hosah accounted for thirteen.

These teams of security guards, supervised by their leaders, kept order in The Temple of God, keeping up the traditions of their ancestors. They were all assigned to their posts by the same method regardless of the prominence of their families—each picked his gate assignment from a hat. Shelemiah was assigned to the East Gate; his son Zechariah, a shrewd counselor, got the North Gate. Obed-Edom got the South Gate; and his sons pulled duty at the storehouse. Shuppim and Hosah were posted to the West Gate and the Shalleketh Gate on the high road.

The guards stood shoulder to shoulder: six Levites per day on the east, four per day on the north and on the south, and two at a time at the storehouse. At the open court to the west, four guards were posted on the road and two at the court.

These are the teams of security guards from the sons of Korah and Merari.

FINANCIAL AFFAIRS: ACCOUNTANTS AND BOOKKEEPERS

Other Levites were put in charge of the financial affairs of The Temple of God. From the family of Ladan (all Gershonites) came Jehieli, and the sons of Jehieli, Zetham and his brother Joel. They supervised the finances of the sanctuary of GOD.

From the Amramites, the Izharites, the Hebronites, and the Uzzielites: Shubael, descended from Gershom the son of Moses, was the chief financial officer. His relatives through Eliezer: his son Rehabiah, his son Jeshaiah, his son Joram, his son Zicri, and his son Shelomith. Shelomith and his relatives were in charge of valuables consecrated by David the king, family heads, and various generals and commanders from the army. They dedicated the plunder that they had gotten in war to the work of the worship of GOD. In addition, everything that had been dedicated by Samuel the seer, Saul son of Kish, Abner son of Ner, and Joab son of Zeruiah—anything that had been dedicated, ever, was the responsibility of Shelomith and his family.

From the family of the Izharites, Kenaniah and sons were appointed as officials and judges responsible for affairs outside the work of worship and sanctuary. From the family of the Hebronites, Hashabiah and his relatives—1,700 well-qualified men—were responsible for administration of matters related to the worship of GOD and the king's work in the territory west of the Jordan.

According to the family tree of the Hebronites, Jeriah held pride of place. In the fortieth year of David's reign (his last), the Hebron family tree was researched and outstanding men were found at Jazer in Gilead, namely, Jeriah and 2,700 men of his extended family: David the king made them responsible for administration of matters related to the worship of God and the work of the king in the territory east of the Jordan— the Reubenites, the Gadites, and the half-tribe of Manasseh.

MILITARY ORGANIZATION

27 Here is the listing of the sons of Israel by family heads, commanders and captains, and other officers who served the king in everything military. Army divisions were on duty a month at a time for the twelve months of the year. Each division comprised 24,000 men.

First division, first month: Jashobeam son of Zabdiel was in charge with 24,000 men. He came from the line of Perez. He was over all the army officers during the first month.

The division for the second month: Dodai the Ahohite was in charge: 24,000 men; Mikloth was the leader of his division.

Commander for the third month: Benaiah son of Jehoiada the priest with 24,000 men. This was the same Benaiah who was a Mighty Man among the Thirty and their chief. His son Ammizabad was in charge of the division.

Fourth division for the fourth month: Asahel brother of Joab; his son Zebadiah succeeded him: 24,000 men.

Fifth division, fifth month: commander Shamhuth the Izrahite: 24,000 men.

Sixth division, sixth month: Ira son of Ikkesh the Tekoite: 24,000 men.

Seventh division, seventh month: Helez the Pelonite, an Ephraimite: 24,000 men.

Eighth division, eighth month: Sibbecai the Hushathite, a Zerahite: 24,000 men.

Ninth division, ninth month: Abiezer the Anathothite, a Benjaminite: 24,000 men.

Tenth division, tenth month: Maharai the Netophathite, a Zerahite: 24,000 men.

Eleventh division, eleventh month: Benaiah the Pirathomite, an Ephraimite: 24,000 men.

Twelfth division, twelfth month: Heldai the Netophathite from the family of Othniel: 24,000 men.

TRIBAL ADMINISTRATORS

Administrators of the affairs of the tribes:
for Reuben: Eliezer son of Zicri;
for Simeon: Shephatiah son of Maacah;
for Levi: Hashabiah son of Kemuel;
for Aaron: Zadok;
for Judah: Elihu, David's brother;
for Issachar: Omri son of Michael;
for Zebulun: Ishmaiah son of Obadiah;
for Naphtali: Jerimoth son of Azriel;
for Ephraim: Hoshea son of Azaziah;
for one half-tribe of Manasseh: Joel son of Pedaiah;
for the half-tribe of Manasseh in Gilead: Iddo son of Zechariah;
for Benjamin: Jaasiel son of Abner;
for Dan: Azarel son of Jeroham.

These are the administrative officers assigned to the tribes of Israel. David didn't keep a count of men under the age of twenty, because GOD had promised to give Israel a population as numerous as the stars in the sky. Joab son of Zeruiah started out counting the men, but he never finished. God's anger broke out on Israel because of the counting. As it turned out, the numbers were never entered into the court records of King David.

SUPPLY OFFICERS

The king's storage facilities were supervised by Azmaveth son of Adiel. Jonathan son of Uzziah was responsible for the warehouses in the outlying areas.

Ezri son of Kelub was in charge of the field workers on the farms.

Shimei the Ramathite was in charge of the vineyards and Zabdi the Shiphmite was in charge of grapes for the wine vats.

Baal-Hanan the Gederite was in charge of the olive and sycamore-fig trees in the western hills, and Joash was in charge of the olive oil.

Shitrai the Sharonite was in charge of herds grazing in Sharon and Shaphat son of Adlai was in charge of herds in the valley.

Obil the Ismaelite was in charge of the camels, Jehdeiah the Meronothite was in charge of the donkeys, and Jaziz the Hagrite was in charge of the flocks.

These were the ones responsible for taking care of King David's property.

DAVID'S COUNSELORS

Jonathan, David's uncle, a wise and literate counselor, and Jehiel son of Hacmoni, were responsible for rearing the king's sons.

Ahithophel was the king's counselor; Hushai the Arkite was the king's friend. Ahithophel was later replaced by Jehoiada son of Benaiah and by Abiathar.

Joab was commander of the king's army.

DAVID'S VALEDICTORY ADDRESS

28 David called together all the leaders of Israel—tribal administrators, heads of various governmental operations, military commanders and captains, stewards in charge of the property and livestock belonging to the king and his sons—everyone who held responsible positions in the kingdom.

King David stood tall and spoke: "Listen to me, my people: I fully intended to build a permanent structure for the Chest of the Covenant of GOD, God's footstool. But when I got ready to build it, God said to me, 'You may not build a house to honor me—you've done too much fighting—killed too many people.' GOD chose me out of my family to be king over Israel forever. First he chose Judah as the lead tribe, then he narrowed it down to my family, and finally he picked me from my father's sons, pleased to make me the king over all Israel. And then from all my sons—and GOD gave me many!—he chose my son Solomon to sit on the throne of GOD's rule over Israel. He went on to say, 'Your son Solomon will build my house and my courts: I have chosen him to be my royal adopted son; and I will be to him a father. I will guarantee that his kingdom will last if he continues to be as strong-minded in doing what I command and carrying out my decisions as he is doing now.'

"And now, in this public place, all Israel looking on and God listening in, as GOD's people, obey and study every last one of the commandments of your GOD so that you can make the most of living in this good land and pass it on intact to your children, insuring a good future.

"And you, Solomon my son, get to know well your father's God; serve him with a whole heart and eager mind, for GOD examines every heart and sees through every motive. If you seek him, he'll make sure you find him, but if you abandon him, he'll leave you for good. Look sharp now! GOD has chosen *you* to build his holy house. Be brave, determined! And do it!"

Then David presented his son Solomon with the plans for The Temple complex: porch, storerooms, meeting rooms, and the place for atoning sacrifice. He turned over the plans for everything that God's Spirit had brought to his mind: the design of the courtyards, the arrangements of rooms, and the closets for storing all the holy things. He gave him his plan for organizing the Levites and priests in their work of leading and ordering worship in the house of God, and for caring for the liturgical furnishings. He provided exact specifications for how much gold and silver was needed for each article used in the services of worship: the gold and silver Lampstands and lamps, the gold tables for consecrated bread, the silver tables, the gold forks, the bowls and the jars, and the incense altar. And he gave him the plan for sculpting the cherubs with their wings outstretched over the Chest of the Covenant of GOD—the cherubim throne. "Here are the blueprints for the whole project as GOD gave me to understand it," David said.

David continued to address Solomon: "Take charge! Take heart! Don't be anxious or get discouraged. GOD, my God, is with you in this; he won't walk off and leave you in the lurch. He's at your side until every last detail is completed for conducting the worship of GOD. You have all the priests and Levites standing ready to pitch in, and skillful craftsmen and artisans of every kind ready to go to work. Both leaders and people are ready. Just say the word."

THEY GET READY TO BUILD

29 Then David the king addressed the congregation: "My son Solomon was singled out and chosen by God to do this. But he's young and untested and the work is huge—this is not just a place for people to meet each other, but a house for GOD to meet us. I've done my best to get everything together for building this house for my God, all the materials necessary: gold, silver, bronze, iron, lumber, precious and varicolored stones, and building stones—vast stockpiles. Furthermore, because my heart is in this, in addition to and beyond what I have gathered, I'm turning over my personal fortune of gold and silver for making this place of worship for my God: 3,000 talents (about 113 tons) of gold—all from Ophir, the best—and 7,000 talents (214 tons) of silver for covering the walls of the buildings, and for the gold and silver work by craftsmen and artisans.

"And now, how about you? Who among you is ready and willing to join in the giving?"

Ready and willing, the heads of families, leaders of the tribes of Israel, commanders and captains in the army, stewards of the king's affairs, stepped forward and gave willingly. They gave 5,000 talents (188 tons) and 10,000 darics (185 pounds) of gold, 10,000 talents of silver (377 tons), 18,000 talents of bronze (679 tons), and 100,000 talents (3,775 tons) of iron. Anyone who had precious jewels put them in the treasury for the building of The Temple of GOD in the custody of Jehiel the Gershonite.

And the people were full of a sense of celebration—all that giving! And all given willingly, freely! King David was exuberant.

David blessed GOD in full view of the entire congregation:

Blessed are you, GOD of Israel, our father
 from of old and forever.

361

To you, O GOD, belong the greatness and the might,
    the glory, the victory, the majesty, the splendor;
Yes! Everything in heaven, everything on earth;
    the kingdom all yours! You've raised yourself high over all.
Riches and glory come from you,
    you're ruler over all;
You hold strength and power in the palm of your hand
    to build up and strengthen all.
And here we are, O God, our God, giving thanks to you,
    praising your splendid Name.

"But me—who am I, and who are these my people, that we should presume to be giving something to you? Everything comes from you; all we're doing is giving back what we've been given from your generous hand. As far as you're concerned, we're homeless, shiftless wanderers like our ancestors, our lives mere shadows, hardly anything to us. GOD, our God, all these materials—these piles of stuff for building a house of worship for you, honoring your Holy Name—it all came from you! It was all yours in the first place! I know, dear God, that you care nothing for the surface—you want *us,* our true selves—and so I have given from the heart, honestly and happily. And now see all these people doing the same, giving freely, willingly—what a joy! O GOD, God of our fathers Abraham, Isaac, and Israel, keep this generous spirit alive forever in these people always, keep their hearts set firmly in you. And give my son Solomon an uncluttered and focused heart so that he can obey what you command, live by your directions and counsel, and carry through with building The Temple for which I have provided."

David then addressed the congregation: "Bless GOD, your God!" And they did it, blessed GOD, the God of their ancestors, and worshiped reverently in the presence of GOD and the king.

The very next day they butchered the sacrificial animals and offered in the worship of Israel to GOD a thousand bulls, a thousand rams, a thousand sheep, and in addition drink offerings and many other sacrifices. They feasted all day, eating and drinking before GOD, exuberant with joy.

Then they ceremonially reenacted Solomon's coronation, anointing David's son before GOD as their leader, and Zadok as priest. Solomon sat on the throne of GOD as king in place of David his father. And everything went well; all Israel obeyed him. All the leaders of the people, including all the sons of King David, accepted Solomon as their king and promised their loyalty. Solomon rode high on a crest of popular acclaim—it was all GOD's doing. GOD gave him position and honor beyond any king in Israel before him.

⁜

David son of Jesse ruled over all Israel. He was king for forty years. He ruled from Hebron seven years and from Jerusalem thirty-three. He died at a ripe old age, full of days, wealth, and glory. His son Solomon ruled after him. The history of David the king, from start to finish, is written in the chronicles of Samuel the seer, Nathan the prophet, and Gad the seer, including a full account of his rule, his exploits, and the times through which he and Israel and the surrounding kingdoms passed.

2 CHRONICLES

KING SOLOMON

1 Solomon son of David took a firm grip on the reins of his kingdom. GOD was with him and gave him much help. Solomon addressed all Israel—the commanders and captains, the judges, every leader, and all the heads of families. Then Solomon and the entire company went to the worship center at Gibeon—that's where the Tent of Meeting of God was, the one that Moses the servant of GOD had made in the wilderness. The Chest of God, though, was in Jerusalem—David had brought it up from Kiriath Jearim, prepared a special place for it, and pitched a tent for it. But the Bronze Altar that Bezalel son of Uri, the son of Hur, had made was in Gibeon, in its place before the Tabernacle of GOD; and that is where Solomon and the congregation gathered to pray. Solomon worshiped GOD at the Bronze Altar in front of the Tent of Meeting; he sacrificed a thousand Whole-Burnt-Offerings on it.

That night God appeared to Solomon. 'God said, "What do you want from me? Ask."

Solomon answered, "You were extravagantly generous with David my father, and now you have made me king in his place. Establish, GOD, the words you spoke to my father, for you've given me a staggering task, ruling this mob of people. Yes, give me wisdom and knowledge as I come and go among this people—for who on his own is capable of leading these, your glorious people?"

God answered Solomon, "This is what has come out of your heart: You didn't grasp for money, wealth, fame, and the doom of your enemies; you didn't even ask for a long life. You asked for wisdom and knowledge so you could govern well my people over whom I've made you king. Because of this, you get what you asked for—wisdom and knowledge. And I'm presenting you the rest as a bonus—money, wealth, and fame beyond anything the kings before or after you had or will have."

Then Solomon left the worship center at Gibeon and the Tent of Meeting and went to Jerusalem. He set to work as king of Israel.

Solomon collected chariots and horses: 1,400 chariots and 12,000 horses! He stabled them in the special chariot-cities as well as in Jerusalem. The king made silver and gold as common as rocks, and cedar as common as the fig trees in the lowland hills. His horses were brought in from Egypt and Cilicia, specially acquired by the king's agents. Chariots from Egypt went for fifteen pounds of silver and a horse for about three and three-quarters of a pound of silver. Solomon carried on a brisk horse-trading business with the Hittite and Aramean royal houses.

THE TEMPLE CONSTRUCTION BEGINS

2 Solomon gave orders to begin construction on the house of worship in honor of GOD and a palace for himself.

Solomon assigned 70,000 common laborers, 80,000 to work the quarries in the mountains, and 3,600 foremen to manage the workforce.

Then Solomon sent this message to King Hiram of Tyre: "Send me cedar logs, the same kind you sent David my father for building his palace. I'm about to build a house of worship in honor of GOD, a holy place for burning perfumed incense, for setting out holy bread, for making Whole-Burnt-Offerings at morning and evening worship, and for Sabbath, New Moon, and Holy Day services of worship—the acts of worship required of Israel.

"The house I am building has to be the best, for our God is the best, far better than competing gods. But who is capable of building such a structure? Why, the skies—the entire cosmos!—can't begin to contain him. And me, who am I to think I can build a house adequate for God—burning incense to him is about all I'm good for! I need your help: Send me a master artisan in gold, silver, bronze, iron, textiles of purple, crimson, and violet, and who knows the craft of engraving; he will supervise the trained craftsmen in Judah and Jerusalem that my father provided. Also send cedar, cypress, and algum logs from Lebanon; I know you have lumberjacks experienced in the Lebanon forests. I'll send workers to join your crews to cut plenty of timber—I'm going to need a lot, for this house I'm building is going to be absolutely stunning—a showcase temple! I'll provide all the food necessary for your crew of lumberjacks and loggers: 130,000 bushels of wheat, 120,000 gallons of wine, and 120,000 gallons of olive oil."

Hiram king of Tyre wrote Solomon in reply: "It's plain that GOD loves his people—he made you king over them!"

He wrote on, "Blessed be the GOD of Israel, who made heaven and earth, and who gave King David a son so wise, so knowledgeable and shrewd, to build a temple for GOD and a palace for himself. I've sent you Huram-Abi—he's already on his way—he knows the construction business inside and out. His mother is from Dan and his father from Tyre. He knows how to work in gold, silver, bronze, iron, stone, and wood, in purple, violet, linen, and crimson textiles; he is also an expert engraver and competent to work out designs with your artists and architects, and those of my master David, your father.

"Go ahead and send the wheat, barley, olive oil, and wine you promised for my work crews. We'll log the trees you need from the Lebanon forests and raft them down to Joppa. You'll have to get the timber up to Jerusalem yourself."

Solomon then took a census of all the foreigners living in Israel, using the same census-taking method employed by his father. They numbered 153,600. He assigned 70,000 of them as common laborers, 80,000 to work the quarries in the mountains, and 3,600 as foremen to manage the work crews.

3 So Solomon broke ground, launched construction of the house of GOD in Jerusalem on Mount Moriah, the place where GOD had appeared to his father David. The precise site, the threshing floor of Araunah the Jebusite, had been designated by David. He broke ground on the second day in the second month of the fourth year of his rule. These are the dimensions that Solomon set for the construction of the house of God: ninety feet long and thirty feet wide. The porch in front stretched the width of the building, that is, thirty feet; and it was thirty feet high.

The interior was gold-plated. He paneled the main hall with cypress and veneered it with fine gold engraved with palm tree and chain designs. He decorated the building with precious stones and gold from Parvaim. Everything was coated with gold veneer: rafters, doorframes, walls, and doors. Cherubim were engraved on the walls.

He made the Holy of Holies a cube, thirty feet wide, long, and high. It was veneered with 600 talents (something over twenty-two tons) of gold. The gold nails weighed fifty shekels (a little over a pound). The upper rooms were also veneered in gold.

He made two sculptures of cherubim, gigantic angel-like figures, for the Holy of Holies, both veneered with gold. The combined wingspread of the side-by-side cherubim (each wing measuring seven and a half feet) stretched from wall to wall, thirty feet. They stood erect facing the main hall.

He fashioned the curtain of violet, purple, and crimson fabric and worked a cherub design into it.

He made two huge free-standing pillars, each fifty-two feet tall, their capitals extending another seven and a half feet. The top of each pillar was set off with an elaborate filigree of chains, like necklaces, from which hung a hundred pomegranates. He placed the pillars in front of The Temple, one on the right, and the other on the left. The right pillar he named Jakin (Security) and the left pillar he named Boaz (Stability).

TEMPLE FURNISHINGS

4 He made the Bronze Altar thirty feet long, thirty feet wide, and ten feet high.

He made a Sea—an immense round basin of cast metal fifteen feet in diameter, seven and a half feet high, and forty-five feet in circumference. Just under the rim, there were two parallel bands of something like bulls, ten to each foot and a half. The figures were cast in one piece with the Sea. The Sea was set on twelve bulls, three facing north, three facing west, three facing south, and three facing east. All the bulls faced outward and supported the Sea on their hindquarters. The Sea was three inches thick and flared at the rim like a cup, or a lily. It held about 18,000 gallons.

He made ten Washbasins, five set on the right and five on the left, for rinsing the things used for the Whole-Burnt-Offerings. The priests washed themselves in the Sea.

He made ten gold Lampstands, following the specified pattern, and placed five on the right and five on the left.

He made ten tables and set five on the right and five on the left. He also made a hundred gold bowls.

He built a Courtyard especially for the priests and then the great court and doors for the court. The doors were covered with bronze.

He placed the Sea on the right side of The Temple at the southeast corner.

He also made ash buckets, shovels, and bowls.

And that about wrapped it up: Huram completed the work he had contracted to do for King Solomon:

two pillars;
two bowl-shaped capitals for the tops of the pillars;
two decorative filigrees for the capitals;
four hundred pomegranates for the filigrees (a double row of
    pomegranates for each filigree);

ten washstands with their basins;
one Sea and the twelve bulls under it;
miscellaneous buckets, forks, shovels, and bowls.

All these artifacts that Huram-Abi made for King Solomon for The Temple of GOD were made of burnished bronze. The king had them cast in clay in a foundry on the Jordan plain between Succoth and Zarethan. These artifacts were never weighed—there were far too many! Nobody has any idea how much bronze was used.

Solomon was also responsible for the furniture and accessories in The Temple of God:

the gold Altar;
the tables that held the Bread of the Presence;
the Lampstands of pure gold with their lamps, to be lighted
    before the Inner Sanctuary, the Holy of Holies;
the gold flowers, lamps, and tongs (all solid gold);
the gold wick trimmers, bowls, ladles, and censers;
the gold doors of The Temple, doors to the Holy of Holies, and
    the doors to the main sanctuary.

5 That completed the work King Solomon did on The Temple of GOD. He then brought in the holy offerings of his father David, the silver and the gold and the artifacts. He placed them all in the treasury of God's Temple.

INSTALLING THE CHEST

Bringing all this to a climax, Solomon got all the leaders together in Jerusalem—all the chiefs of tribes and the family patriarchs—to move the Chest of the Covenant of GOD from Zion and install it in The Temple. All the men of Israel assembled before the king on the feast day of the seventh month, the Feast of Booths.

When all the leaders of Israel were ready, the Levites took up the Chest. They carried the Chest, the Tent of Meeting, and all the sacred things in the Tent used in worship. The priests, all Levites, carried them. King Solomon and the entire congregation of Israel were there before the Chest, worshiping and sacrificing huge numbers of sheep and cattle—so many that no one could keep track.

The priests brought the Chest of the Covenant of GOD to its place in the Inner Sanctuary, the Holy of Holies, under the wings of the cherubim. The outspread wings of the cherubim formed a canopy over the Chest and its poles. The ends of the poles were so long that they stuck out from the entrance of the Inner Sanctuary, but were not noticeable further out— they're still there today. There was nothing in the Chest itself but the two stone tablets that Moses had placed in it at Horeb where GOD made a covenant with Israel after bringing them up from Egypt.

The priests then left the Holy Place. All the priests there were consecrated, regardless of rank or assignment; and all the Levites who were musicians were there—Asaph, Heman, Jeduthun, and their families, dressed in their worship robes; the choir and orchestra assembled on the east side of the Altar and were joined by 120 priests blowing trumpets. The choir and trumpets made one voice of praise and thanks to GOD—orchestra and choir in perfect harmony singing and playing praise to GOD:

Yes! God is good!
His loyal love goes on forever!

Then a billowing cloud filled The Temple of GOD. The priests couldn't even carry out their duties because of the cloud—the glory of GOD!—that filled The Temple of God.

SOLOMON'S DEDICATION AND PRAYER

6 Then Solomon said,

GOD said he would dwell in a cloud,
But I've built a temple most splendid,
A place for you to live in forever.

The king then turned to face the congregation that had come together and blessed them:

"Blessed be GOD, the God of Israel, who spoke personally to my father David. Now he has done what he promised when he said, 'From the day I brought my people Israel up from Egypt, I haven't set apart one city among the tribes of Israel in which to build a temple to honor my Name, or chosen one person to be the leader. But now I have chosen both a city and a person: Jerusalem for honoring my Name and David to lead my people Israel.'

"My father David very much wanted to build a temple honoring the Name of GOD, the God of Israel, but GOD told him, 'It was good that you wanted to build a temple in my honor—most commendable! But you are not the one to do it. Your son, who will carry on your dynasty, will build it for my Name.'

"And now you see the promise completed. GOD has done what he said he would do; I have succeeded David my father and now rule Israel; and I have built a temple to honor GOD, the God of Israel, and have secured a place for the Chest that holds the Covenant of GOD, the covenant he made with the people of Israel."

Before the entire congregation of Israel, Solomon took his position at the Altar of GOD and stretched out his hands. Solomon had made a bronze dais seven and a half feet square and four and a half feet high and placed it inside the court; that's where he now stood. Then he knelt in full view of the whole congregation, stretched his hands to heaven, and prayed:

GOD, O God of Israel, there is no God like you in the skies above or on the earth below, who unswervingly keeps covenant with his servants and unfailingly loves them while they sincerely live in obedience to your way. You kept your word to David my father, your promise. You did exactly what you promised—every detail. The proof is before us today!

Keep it up, GOD, O God of Israel! Continue to keep the promises you made to David my father when you said, "You'll always have a descendant to represent my rule on Israel's throne, on the one condition that your sons are as careful to live obediently in my presence as you have."

O GOD, God of Israel, let this all happen—
confirm and establish it!

Can it be that God will actually move into our neighborhood? Why, the cosmos itself isn't large enough to give you breathing room, let alone this Temple I've built. Even so, I'm bold to ask: Pay attention to these my prayers, both intercessory and personal, O GOD, my God. Listen to my prayers, energetic and devout, that I'm setting before you right now. Keep your eyes open to this

Temple day and night, this place you promised to dignify with your Name. And listen to the prayers that I pray in this place. And listen to your people Israel when they pray at this place.

Listen from your home in heaven
    and when you hear, forgive.

When someone hurts a neighbor and promises to make things right, and then comes and repeats the promise before your Altar in this Temple,

Listen from heaven and act;
    judge your servants, making the offender pay for the offense
And set the offended free,
    dismissing all charges.

When your people Israel are beaten by an enemy because they've sinned against you, but then turn to you and acknowledge your rule in prayers desperate and devout in this Temple,

Listen from your home in heaven;
    forgive the sin of your people Israel,
    return them to the land you gave to them and their ancestors.

When the skies shrivel up and there is no rain because your people have sinned against you, but then they pray at this place, acknowledging your rule and quit their sins because you have scourged them,

Listen from your home in heaven,
    forgive the sins of your servants, your people Israel.
Then start over with them;
    train them to live right and well;
Send rain on the land
    you gave as inheritance to your people.

When disasters strike, famine or catastrophe, crop failure or disease, locust or beetle, or when an enemy attacks their defenses—calamity of any sort—any prayer that's prayed from

anyone at all among your people Israel, their hearts penetrated
by disaster, hands and arms thrown out for help to this Temple,

Listen from your home in heaven, forgive and reward us:
    reward each life and circumstance,
For you know each life from the inside,
    (you're the only one with such inside knowledge!),
So they'll live before you in lifelong reverence and believing
    obedience on this land you gave our ancestors.

And don't forget the foreigner who is not a member of
your people Israel but has come from a far country because
of your reputation—people *are* going to be attracted here by
your great reputation, your wonderworking power—and who
come to pray to this Temple.

Listen from your home in heaven
    and honor the prayers of the foreigner,
So that people all over the world
    will know who you are and what you're like,
And live in reverent obedience before you,
    just as your own people Israel do,
So they'll know that you personally
    make this Temple that I've built what it is.

When your people go to war against their enemies at the
time and place you send them and they pray to GOD toward the
city you chose and The Temple I've built to honor your Name,

Listen from heaven to what they pray and ask for
    and do what is right for them.

When they sin against you—and they certainly will; there's
no one without sin!—and in anger you turn them over to the
enemy and they are taken off captive to the enemy's land,
whether far or near, but then repent in the country of their
captivity and pray with changed hearts in their exile, "We've
sinned; we've done wrong; we've been most wicked," and they
turn back to you heart and soul in the land of the enemy who

conquered them, and pray to you toward their homeland, the land you gave their ancestors, toward the city you chose, and this Temple I have built to the honor of your Name,

Listen from your home in heaven
    to their prayers desperate and devout;
Do what is best for them.
    Forgive your people who have sinned against you.

And now, dear God, be alert and attentive to prayer, all prayer, offered in this place.

Up, GOD, enjoy your new place of quiet repose,
    you and your mighty covenant Chest;
Dress your priests up in salvation clothes,
    let your holy people celebrate goodness.
And don't, GOD, back out on your anointed ones,
    keep in mind the love promised to David your servant.

THE TEMPLE DEDICATION

7 When Solomon finished praying, a bolt of lightning out of heaven struck the Whole-Burnt-Offering and sacrifices and the Glory of GOD filled The Temple. The Glory was so dense that the priests couldn't get in—GOD so filled The Temple that there was no room for the priests! When all Israel saw the fire fall from heaven and the Glory of GOD fill The Temple, they fell on their knees, bowed their heads, and worshiped, thanking GOD:

Yes! God is good!
His love never quits!

Then the king and all Israel worshiped, offering sacrifices to GOD. King Solomon worshiped by sacrificing 22,000 cattle and 120,000 sheep at the dedication of The Temple. The priests were all on duty; the choir and orchestra of Levites that David had provided for singing and playing anthems to the praise and love of GOD were all there; across the courtyard the priests blew trumpets. All Israelites were on their feet.

Solomon set apart the central area of the courtyard in front of GOD's Temple for sacred use and there sacrificed the Whole-Burnt-Offerings,

Grain-Offerings, and fat from the Peace-Offerings—the Bronze Altar was too small to handle all these offerings. This is how Solomon kept the great autumn Feast of Booths. For seven days there were people there all the way from the far northeast (the Entrance to Hamath) to the far southwest (the Brook of Egypt)—a huge congregation. They started out celebrating for seven days, and then did it for another seven days, a week for dedicating the Altar and another for the Feast itself—two solid weeks of celebration! On the twenty-third day of the seventh month Solomon dismissed his congregation. They left rejoicing, exuberant over all the good GOD had done for David and Solomon and his people Israel.

GOD'S CONFIRMATION

Solomon completed building The Temple of GOD and the royal palace—the projects he had set his heart on doing. Everything was done—success! Satisfaction!

GOD appeared to Solomon that very night and said, "I accept your prayer; yes, I have chosen this place as a temple for sacrifice, a house of worship. If I ever shut off the supply of rain from the skies or order the locusts to eat the crops or send a plague on my people, and my people, my God-defined people, respond by humbling themselves, praying, seeking my presence, and turning their backs on their wicked lives, I'll be there ready for you: I'll listen from heaven, forgive their sins, and restore their land to health. From now on I'm alert day and night to the prayers offered at this place. Believe me, I've chosen and sanctified this Temple that you have built: My Name is stamped on it forever; my eyes are on it and my heart in it always. As for you, if you live in my presence as your father David lived, pure in heart and action, living the life I've set out for you, attentively obedient to my guidance and judgments, then I'll back your kingly rule over Israel—make it a sure thing on a sure foundation. The same covenant guarantee I gave to David your father I'm giving to you, namely, 'You can count on always having a descendant on Israel's throne.'

"But if you or your sons betray me, ignoring my guidance and judgments, taking up with alien gods by serving and worshiping them, then the guarantee is off: I'll wipe Israel right off the map and repudiate this Temple I've just sanctified to honor my Name. And Israel will be nothing but a bad joke among the peoples of the world. And this Temple, splendid as it now is, will become an object of contempt; tourists will shake their heads, saying, 'What happened here? What's the story behind these ruins?' Then they'll be told, 'The people who used to live here betrayed their GOD, the very God who rescued their ancestors from Egypt; they took up with alien gods, worshiping and serving them. That's what's behind this God-visited devastation.'"

MORE ON SOLOMON

8 At the end of twenty years, Solomon had quite a list of accomplishments. He had:

> built The Temple of GOD and his own palace;
> rebuilt the cities that Hiram had given him and colonized them with Israelites;
> marched on Hamath Zobah and took it;
> fortified Tadmor in the desert and all the store-cities he had founded in Hamath;
> built the fortress cities Upper Beth Horon and Lower Beth Horon, complete with walls, gates, and bars;
> built Baalath and store-cities;
> built chariot-cities for his horses.

Solomon built impulsively and extravagantly—whenever a whim took him. And in Jerusalem, in Lebanon—wherever he fancied.

The remnants from the original inhabitants of the land (Hittites, Amorites, Perizzites, Hivites, Jebusites—all non-Israelites), survivors of the holy wars, were rounded up by Solomon for his gangs of slave labor. The policy is in effect today. But true Israelites were not treated this way; they were used in his army and administration—government leaders and commanders of his chariots and charioteers. They were also the project managers responsible for Solomon's building operations—250 in all in charge of the workforce.

Solomon brought Pharaoh's daughter from the City of David to a house built especially for her, "Because," he said, "my wife cannot live in the house of David king of Israel, for the areas in which the Chest of GOD has entered are sacred."

Then Solomon offered Whole-Burnt-Offerings to GOD on the Altar of GOD that he had built in front of The Temple porch. He kept to the regular schedule of worship set down by Moses: Sabbaths, New Moons, and the three annual feasts of Unraised Bread (Passover), Weeks (Pentecost), and Booths.

He followed the practice of his father David in setting up groups of priests carrying out the work of worship, with the Levites assigned to lead the sacred music for praising God and to assist the priests in the daily worship; he assigned security guards to be on duty at each gate— that's what David the man of God had ordered. The king's directions to the priests and Levites and financial stewards were kept right down to the fine print—no innovations—including the treasuries.

All that Solomon set out to do, from the groundbreaking of The Temple of God to its finish, was now complete.

Then Solomon went to Ezion Geber and Elath on the coast of Edom. Hiram sent him ships and with them veteran sailors. Joined by Solomon's men they sailed to Ophir (in east Africa), loaded on fifteen tons of gold, and brought it back to King Solomon.

✛

9 The queen of Sheba heard of Solomon's reputation and came to Jerusalem to put his reputation to the test, asking all the tough questions. She made a showy entrance—an impressive retinue of attendants and camels loaded with perfume and much gold and precious stones. She emptied her heart to Solomon, talking over everything she cared about. And Solomon answered everything she put to him—nothing stumped him. When the queen of Sheba experienced for herself Solomon's wisdom and saw with her own eyes the palace he had built, the meals that were served, the impressive array of court officials, the sharply dressed waiters, the cupbearers, and then the elaborate worship extravagant with Whole-Burnt-Offerings at The Temple of God, it all took her breath away.

She said to the king, "It's all true! Your reputation for accomplishment and wisdom that reached all the way to my country is confirmed. I wouldn't have believed it if I hadn't seen it for myself; they didn't exaggerate! Such wisdom and elegance—far more than I could ever have imagined. Lucky the men and women who work for you, getting to be around you every day and hear your wise words firsthand! And blessed be your God who has taken such a liking to you, making you king. Clearly, God's love for Israel is behind this, making you king to keep a just order and nurture a God-pleasing people."

She then gave the king four and a half tons of gold and sack after sack of spices and precious stones. There hasn't been a cargo of spices like the shipload the queen of Sheba brought to King Solomon. The ships of Hiram also imported gold from Ophir along with fragrant sandalwood and expensive gems. The king used the sandalwood for fine cabinetry in The Temple of GOD and the royal palace, and for making harps and dulcimers for the musicians. Nothing like that shipment of sandalwood has been seen since.

King Solomon, for his part, gave the queen of Sheba all her heart's desire—everything she asked for. She took away more than she brought. Satisfied, she returned home with her train of servants.

✝

Solomon received twenty-five tons of gold annually. This was above and beyond the taxes and profit on trade with merchants and traders. All kings of Arabia and various and assorted governors also brought silver and gold to Solomon.

King Solomon crafted 200 body-length shields of hammered gold—about fifteen pounds of gold to each shield—and about 300 small shields about half that size. He stored the shields in the House of the Forest of Lebanon.

The king made a massive throne of ivory with a veneer of gold. The throne had six steps leading up to it with an attached footstool of gold. The armrests on each side were flanked by lions. Lions, twelve of them, were placed at either end of the six steps. There was no throne like it in any other kingdom.

King Solomon's chalices and tankards were made of gold, and all the dinnerware and serving utensils in the House of the Forest of Lebanon were pure gold. Nothing was made of silver; silver was considered common and cheap in the time of Solomon.

The king's ships, manned by Hiram's sailors, made a round trip to Tarshish every three years, returning with a cargo of gold, silver, and ivory, apes and peacocks.

King Solomon was richer and wiser than all the kings of the earth—he surpassed them all. Kings came from all over the world to be with Solomon and get in on the wisdom God had given him. Everyone who came brought gifts—artifacts of gold and silver, fashionable robes and gowns, the latest in weapons, exotic spices, horses, and mules—parades of visitors, year after year.

Solomon collected horses and chariots. He had 4,000 stalls for horses and chariots, and 12,000 horsemen in barracks in the chariot-cities and in Jerusalem. He ruled over all the kings from the River

Euphrates in the east, throughout the Philistine country, and as far west as the border of Egypt. The king made silver as common as rocks and cedar as common as the fig trees in the lowland hills. He carried on a brisk horse-trading business with Egypt and other places.

⊹

The rest of Solomon's life and rule, from start to finish, one can read in the records of Nathan the prophet, the prophecy of Ahijah of Shiloh, and in the visions of Iddo the seer concerning Jeroboam son of Nebat. Solomon ruled in Jerusalem over all Israel for forty years. Solomon died and was buried in the City of David his father. His son Rehoboam was the next king.

KING REHOBOAM

10Rehoboam traveled to Shechem where all Israel had gathered to inaugurate him as king. Jeroboam was then in Egypt, where he had taken asylum from King Solomon; when he got the report of Solomon's death, he came back.

Summoned by Israel, Jeroboam and all Israel went to Rehoboam and said, "Your father made life hard for us—worked our fingers to the bone. Give us a break; lighten up on us and we'll willingly serve you."

"Give me," said Rehoboam, "three days to think it over; then come back." So the people left.

King Rehoboam talked it over with the elders who had advised his father when he was alive: "What's your counsel? How do you suggest that I answer the people?"

They said, "If you will be a servant to this people, be considerate of their needs and respond with compassion, work things out with them, they'll end up doing anything for you."

But he rejected the counsel of the elders and asked the young men he'd grown up with who were now currying his favor, "What do you think? What should I say to these people who are saying, 'Give us a break from your father's harsh ways—lighten up on us'?"

The young turks he'd grown up with said, "These people who complain, 'Your father was too hard on us; lighten up'—well, tell them this: 'My little finger is thicker than my father's waist. If you think life under my father was hard, you haven't seen the half of it. My father thrashed you with whips; I'll beat you bloody with chains!'"

Three days later Jeroboam and the people showed up, just as Rehoboam had directed when he said, "Give me three days to think it over; then come back." The king's answer was harsh and rude. He spurned the counsel of the elders and went with the advice of the younger set: "If you think life under my father was hard, you haven't seen the half of it: my father thrashed you with whips; I'll beat you bloody with chains!"

Rehoboam turned a deaf ear to the people. God was behind all this, confirming the message that he had given to Jeroboam son of Nebat through Ahijah of Shiloh.

When all Israel realized that the king hadn't listened to a word they'd said, they stood up to him and said,

Get lost, David!
We've had it with you, son of Jesse!
Let's get out of here, Israel, and fast!
From now on, David, mind your own business.

And with that they left. Rehoboam continued to rule only those who lived in the towns of Judah.

When King Rehoboam next sent out Adoniram, head of the work-force, the Israelites ganged up on him, pelted him with stones, and killed him. King Rehoboam jumped in his chariot and escaped to Jerusalem as fast as he could. Israel has been in rebellion against the Davidic dynasty ever since.

11 When Rehoboam got back to Jerusalem he called up the men of the tribes of Judah and Benjamin, 180,000 of their best soldiers, to go to war against Israel and recover the kingdom.

At the same time the word of GOD came to Shemaiah, a holy man, "Tell this to Rehoboam son of Solomon, king of Judah, along with all the Israelites in Judah and Benjamin, This is GOD's word: Don't march out; don't fight against your brothers the Israelites. Go back home, every last one of you; I'm in charge here." And they did it; they did what GOD said and went home.

Rehoboam continued to live in Jerusalem but built up a defense system for Judah all around: in Bethlehem, Etam, Tekoa, Beth Zur, Soco, Adullam, Gath, Mareshah, Ziph, Adoraim, Lachish, Azekah, Zorah, Aijalon, and Hebron—a line of defense protecting Judah and Benjamin. He beefed up the fortifications, appointed commanders, and put in supplies of food, olive oil, and wine. He installed arms—large shields and spears—in all the forts, making them very strong. So Judah and Benjamin were secure for the time.

The priests and Levites from all over Israel came and made themselves available to Rehoboam. The Levites left their pastures and properties and moved to Judah and Jerusalem because Jeroboam and his sons had dismissed them from the priesthood of GOD and replaced them with his own priests to preside over the worship centers at which he had installed goat and calf demon-idols. Everyone from all the tribes of Israel who determined to seek the GOD of Israel migrated with the priests and Levites to Jerusalem to worship there, sacrificing to the GOD of their ancestors. That gave a tremendous boost to the kingdom of Judah. They stuck with Rehoboam son of Solomon for three years, loyal to the ways of David and Solomon for this period.

Rehoboam married Mahalath daughter of Jerimoth, David's son, and Abihail daughter of Eliab, Jesse's son. Mahalath bore him Jeush, Shemariah, and Zaham. Then he married Maacah, Absalom's daughter, and she bore him Abijah, Attai, Ziza, and Shelomith. Maacah was Rehoboam's favorite wife; he loved her more than all his other wives and concubines put together (and he had a lot—eighteen wives and sixty concubines who produced twenty-eight sons and sixty daughters!).

Rehoboam designated Abijah son of Maacah as the "first son" and leader of the brothers—he intended to make him the next king. He was shrewd in deploying his sons in all the fortress cities that made up his defense system in Judah and Benjamin; he kept them happy with much food and many wives.

12 By the time Rehoboam had secured his kingdom and was strong again, he, and all Israel with him, had virtually abandoned GOD and his ways.

✛

In Rehoboam's fifth year, because he and the people were unfaithful to GOD, Shishak king of Egypt invaded as far as Jerusalem. He came with 1,200 chariots and 60,000 cavalry, and soldiers from all over—the Egyptian army included Libyans, Sukkites, and Ethiopians. They took the fortress cities of Judah and advanced as far as Jerusalem itself.

Then the prophet Shemaiah, accompanied by the leaders of Judah who had retreated to Jerusalem before Shishak, came to Rehoboam and said, "GOD's word: You abandoned me; now I abandon you to Shishak."

The leaders of Israel and the king were repentant and said, "GOD is right."

When GOD saw that they were humbly repentant, the word of GOD came to Shemaiah: "Because they are humble, I'll not destroy them—I'll give them a break; I won't use Shishak to express my wrath against Jerusalem. What I will do, though, is make them Shishak's subjects—they'll learn the difference between serving me and serving human kings."

Then Shishak king of Egypt attacked Jerusalem. He plundered the treasury of The Temple of GOD and the treasury of the royal palace—he took everything he could lay his hands on. He even took the gold shields that Solomon had made.

King Rehoboam replaced the gold shields with bronze shields and gave them to the guards who were posted at the entrance to the royal palace. Whenever the king went to GOD's Temple, the guards went with him carrying the shields, but they always returned them to the guardroom.

Because Rehoboam was repentant, GOD's anger was blunted, so he wasn't totally destroyed. The picture wasn't entirely bleak—there were some good things going on in Judah.

King Rehoboam regrouped and reestablished his rule in Jerusalem. He was forty-one years old when he became king and continued as king for seventeen years in Jerusalem, the city GOD chose out of all the tribes of Israel as the special presence of his Name. His mother was Naamah from Ammon. But the final verdict on Rehoboam was that he was a bad king—GOD was not important to him; his heart neither cared for nor sought after GOD.

The history of Rehoboam, from start to finish, is written in the memoirs of Shemaiah the prophet and Iddo the seer that contain the family trees. There was war between Rehoboam and Jeroboam the whole time. Rehoboam died and was buried with his ancestors in the City of David. His son Abijah ruled after him.

KING ABIJAH

13 In the eighteenth year of the rule of King Jeroboam, Abijah took over the throne of Judah. He ruled in Jerusalem three years. His mother was Maacah daughter of Uriel of Gibeah.

War broke out between Abijah and Jeroboam. Abijah started out with 400,000 of his best soldiers; Jeroboam countered with 800,000 of his best.

Abijah took a prominent position on Mount Zemaraim in the hill country of Ephraim and gave this speech: "Listen, Jeroboam and all Israel! Don't you realize that GOD, the one and only God of Israel, established David and his sons as the permanent rulers of Israel, ratified by a 'covenant of salt'—GOD's kingdom ruled by GOD's king? And what happened? Jeroboam, the son of Solomon's slave Nebat, rebelled against his master. All the riff-raff joined his cause and were too much for Rehoboam, Solomon's true heir. Rehoboam didn't know his way around—besides he was a real wimp; he couldn't stand up against them.

"Taking advantage of that weakness, you are asserting yourself against the very rule of GOD that is delegated to David's descendants—you think you are so big with your huge army backed up by the golden-calf idols that Jeroboam made for you as gods! But just look at what you've done—you threw out the priests of GOD, the sons of Aaron, and the Levites, and made priests to suit yourselves, priests just like the pagans have. Anyone who shows up with enough money to pay for it can be a priest! A priest of No-God!

"But for the rest of us in Judah, we're sticking with GOD. We have not traded him in for the latest model—we're keeping the tried and true priests of Aaron to lead us to GOD and the Levites to lead us in worship by sacrificing Whole-Burnt-Offerings and aromatic incense to GOD at the daily morning and evening prayers, setting out fresh holy bread on a clean table, and lighting the lamps on the golden Lampstand every night. We continue doing what GOD told us to in the way he told us to do it; but you have rid yourselves of him.

"Can't you see the obvious? God is on our side; he's our leader. And his priests with trumpets are all ready to blow the signal to battle. O Israel—don't fight against GOD, the God of your ancestors. You will not win this battle."

While Abijah was speaking, Jeroboam had sent men around to take them by surprise from the rear: Jeroboam in front of Judah and the ambush behind. When Judah looked back, they saw they were attacked front and back. They prayed desperately to GOD, the priests blew their trumpets, and the soldiers of Judah shouted their battle cry. At the battle cry, God routed Jeroboam and all Israel before Abijah and Judah. The army of Israel scattered before Judah; God gave them the victory. Abijah and his troops slaughtered them—500,000 of Israel's best fighters were killed that day. The army of Israel fell flat on its face—a humiliating defeat. The army of Judah won hands down because they trusted GOD, the God of their ancestors.

Abijah followed up his victory by pursuing Jeroboam, taking the towns of Bethel, Jeshanah, and Ephron with their surrounding villages. Jeroboam never did recover from his defeat while Abijah lived. Later on GOD struck him down and he died. Meanwhile Abijah flourished; he married fourteen wives and ended up with a family of twenty-two sons and sixteen daughters.

The rest of the history of Abijah, what he did and said, is written in the study written by Iddo the prophet.

KING ASA

14 Abijah died and was buried with his ancestors in the City of David. His son Asa became the next king.

For ten years into Asa's reign the country was at peace.

Asa was a good king. He did things right in GOD's eyes. He cleaned house: got rid of the pagan altars and shrines, smashed the sacred stone pillars, and chopped down the sex-and-religion groves (Asherim). He told Judah to center their lives in GOD, the God of their fathers, to do what the law said, and to follow the commandments. Because he got rid of all the pagan shrines and altars in the cities of Judah, his kingdom was at peace. Because the land was quiet and there was no war, he was able to build up a good defense system in Judah. GOD kept the peace.

Asa said to his people, "While we have the chance and the land is quiet, let's build a solid defense system, fortifying our cities with walls, towers, gates, and bars. We have this peaceful land because we sought GOD; he has given us rest from all troubles." So they built and enjoyed prosperity.

Asa had an army of 300,000 Judeans, equipped with shields and spears, and another 280,000 Benjaminites who were shield bearers and archers. They were all courageous warriors.

Zerah the Ethiopian went to war against Asa with an army of a million plus 300 chariots and got as far as Mareshah. Asa met him there and prepared to fight from the Valley of Zephathah near Mareshah. Then Asa prayed to GOD, "O GOD, you aren't impressed by numbers or intimidated by a show of force once you decide to help: Help us, O GOD; we have come out to meet this huge army because we trust in you and who you are. Don't let mere mortals stand against you!"

GOD defeated the Ethiopians before Asa and Judah; the Ethiopians ran for their lives. Asa and his men chased them as far as Gerar; so many of the Ethiopians were killed that there was no fight left in them—a massacre before GOD and his troops; Judah carted off loads of plunder. They devastated all the towns around Gerar whose people were helpless, paralyzed by the fear of GOD, and looted the country. They also attacked herdsmen and brought back a lot of sheep and camels to Jerusalem.

15 Then Azariah son of Obed, moved by the Spirit of God, went out to meet Asa. He said, "Listen carefully, Asa, and listen Judah and Benjamin: GOD will stick with you as long as you stick with him. If you look for him he will let himself be found; but if you leave him he'll leave you. For a long time Israel didn't have the real God, nor did they have the help of priest or teacher or book. But when they were in trouble and got serious, and decided to seek GOD, the God of Israel, GOD let himself be found. At that time it was a dog-eat-dog world; life was constantly up for grabs—no one, regardless of country, knew what the next day might bring. Nation battered nation, city pummeled city. God let loose every kind of trouble among them.

"But it's different with you: Be strong. Take heart. Payday is coming!"

Asa heard the prophecy of Azariah son of Obed, took a deep breath, then rolled up his sleeves, and went to work: He cleaned out the obscene and polluting sacred shrines from the whole country of Judah and Benjamin and from the towns he had taken in the hill country of Ephraim. He spruced up the Altar of GOD that was in front of The Temple porch. Then he called an assembly for all Judah and Benjamin, including those from Ephraim, Manasseh, and Simeon who were living there at the time (for many from Israel had left their homes and joined forces with Asa when they saw that GOD was on his side).

They all arrived in Jerusalem in the third month of the fifteenth year of Asa's reign for a great assembly of worship. From their earlier plunder they offered sacrifices of 700 oxen and 7,000 sheep for the worship. Then they bound themselves in a covenant to seek GOD, the God of their fathers, wholeheartedly, holding nothing back. And they agreed that anyone who refused to seek GOD, the God of Israel, should be killed, no matter who it was, young or old, man or woman. They shouted out their promise to GOD, a joyful sound accompanied with blasts from trumpets and rams' horns. The whole country felt good about the covenant promise—they had given their promise joyfully from the heart. Anticipating the best, they had sought God—and he showed up, ready to be found. GOD gave them peace within and without—a most peaceable kingdom!

In his clean-up of the country, Asa went so far as to remove his mother, Queen Maacah, from her throne because she had built a shockingly obscene image of the sex goddess Asherah. Asa tore it down, smashed it, and burned it up in the Kidron Valley. Unfortunately he didn't get rid of the local sex-and-religion shrines. But he was well-intentioned—his heart was in the right place, loyal to GOD. All the gold and silver vessels and artifacts that he and his father had consecrated for holy use he installed in The Temple of God. There wasn't a trace of war up to the thirty-fifth year of Asa's reign.

16 But in the thirty-sixth year of Asa's reign, Baasha king of Israel attacked. He started it by building a fort at Ramah and closing the border between Israel and Judah to keep Asa king of Judah from leaving or entering.

Asa took silver and gold from the treasuries of The Temple of GOD and the royal palace and sent it to Ben-Hadad, king of Aram who lived in Damascus, with this message: "Let's make a treaty like the one between our fathers. I'm showing my good faith with this gift of silver and gold. Break your deal with Baasha king of Israel so he'll quit fighting against me."

Ben-Hadad went along with King Asa and sent his troops against the towns of Israel. They sacked Ijon, Dan, Abel Maim, and all the store-cities of Naphtali. When Baasha got the report, he quit fortifying Ramah.

Then King Asa issued orders to his people in Judah to haul away the logs and stones Baasha had used in the fortification of Ramah and used them himself to fortify Geba and Mizpah.

Just after that, Hanani the seer came to Asa king of Judah and said, "Because you went for help to the king of Aram and didn't ask GOD for help, you've lost a victory over the army of the king of Aram. Didn't the Ethiopians and Libyans come against you with superior forces, completely outclassing you with their chariots and cavalry? But you asked GOD for help and he gave you the victory. GOD is always on the alert, constantly on the lookout for people who are totally committed to him. You were foolish to go for human help when you could have had God's help. Now you're in trouble—one round of war after another."

At that, Asa lost his temper. Angry, he put Hanani in the stocks. At the same time Asa started abusing some of the people.

A full account of Asa is written in *The Chronicles of the Kings of Judah*. In the thirty-ninth year of his reign Asa came down with a severe case of foot infection. He didn't ask GOD for help, but went instead to the doctors. Then Asa died; he died in the forty-first year of his reign. They buried him in a mausoleum that he had built for himself in the City of David. They laid him in a crypt full of aromatic oils and spices. Then they had a huge bonfire in his memory.

JEHOSHAPHAT OF JUDAH

17 Asa's son Jehoshaphat was the next king; he started out by working on his defense system against Israel. He put troops in all the fortress cities of Judah and deployed garrisons throughout Judah and in the towns of Ephraim that his father Asa had captured. GOD was on Jehoshaphat's side because he stuck to the ways of his father Asa's early years. He didn't fool around with the popular Baal religion—he was a seeker and follower of the God of his father and was obedient to him; he wasn't like Israel. And GOD secured the kingdom under his rule, gave him a firm grip on it. And everyone in Judah showed their appreciation by bringing gifts. Jehoshaphat ended up very rich and much honored. He was single-minded in following GOD; and he got rid of the local sex-and-religion shrines.

In the third year of his reign he sent his officials—excellent men, every one of them—Ben-Hail, Obadiah, Zechariah, Nethanel, and Micaiah on a teaching mission to the cities of Judah. They were accompanied by Levites—Shemaiah, Nethaniah, Zebadiah, Asahel, Shemiramoth, Jehonathan, Adonijah, Tobijah, and Tob-Adonijah; the priests Elishama and Jehoram were also in the company. They made a circuit of the towns of Judah, teaching the people and using the Book of The Revelation of GOD as their text.

There was a strong sense of the fear of GOD in all the kingdoms around Judah—they didn't dare go to war against Jehoshaphat. Some Philistines even brought gifts and a load of silver to Jehoshaphat, and the desert bedouin brought flocks—7,700 rams and 7,700 goats. So Jehoshaphat became stronger by the day, and constructed more and more forts and store-cities—an age of prosperity for Judah!

He also had excellent fighting men stationed in Jerusalem. The captains of the military units of Judah, classified according to families, were: Captain Adnah with 300,000 soldiers; his associate Captain Jehohanan with 280,000; his associate Amasiah son of Zicri, a volunteer for GOD, with 200,000. Officer Eliada represented Benjamin with 200,000 fully equipped with bow and shield; and his associate was

Jehozabad with 180,000 armed and ready for battle. These were under the direct command of the king; in addition there were the troops assigned to the fortress cities spread all over Judah.

18 But even though Jehoshaphat was very rich and much honored, he made a marriage alliance with Ahab of Israel. Some time later he paid a visit to Ahab at Samaria. Ahab celebrated his visit with a feast—a huge barbecue with all the lamb and beef you could eat. But Ahab had a hidden agenda; he wanted Jehoshaphat's support in attacking Ramoth Gilead. Then Ahab brought it into the open: "Will you join me in attacking Ramoth Gilead?" Jehoshaphat said, "You bet. I'm with you all the way; you can count on me and my troops."

Then Jehoshaphat said, "But before you do anything, ask GOD for guidance."

The king of Israel got the prophets together—all 400 of them—and put the question to them: "Should I attack Ramoth Gilead or should I hold back?"

"Go for it," they said. "God will hand it over to the king."

But Jehoshaphat dragged his feet, "Is there another prophet of GOD around here we can consult? Let's get a second opinion."

The king of Israel told Jehoshaphat, "As a matter of fact, there is another. But I hate him. He never preaches anything good to me, only doom, doom, doom—Micaiah son of Imlah."

"The king shouldn't talk about a prophet like that!" said Jehoshaphat.

So the king of Israel ordered one of his men, "Quickly, get Micaiah son of Imlah."

Meanwhile, the king of Israel and Jehoshaphat were seated on their thrones, dressed in their royal robes, resplendent in front of the Samaria city gates. All the prophets were staging a prophecy-performance for their benefit. Zedekiah son of Kenaanah had even made a set of iron horns, and brandishing them, called out, "GOD's word! With these horns you'll gore Aram until there's nothing left of them!" All the prophets chimed in, "Yes! Go for Ramoth Gilead! An easy victory! GOD's gift to the king!"

The messenger who went to get Micaiah told him, "The prophets have all said Yes to the king. Make it unanimous—vote Yes!"

But Micaiah said, "As sure as GOD lives, what God says, I'll say."

With Micaiah before him, the king asked him, "So, Micaiah—do we attack Ramoth Gilead? Or do we hold back?"

"Go ahead," he said, "an easy victory! God's gift to the king."

"Not so fast," said the king. "How many times have I made you promise under oath to tell me the truth and nothing but the truth?"

"All right," said Micaiah, "since you insist . . .

I saw all of Israel scattered over the hills,
    sheep with no shepherd.
Then GOD spoke, 'These poor people
    have no one to tell them what to do.
Let them go home and do
    the best they can for themselves.'"

The king of Israel turned to Jehoshaphat, "See! What did I tell you? He never has a good word for me from GOD, only doom."

Micaiah kept on, "I'm not done yet; listen to GOD's word:

I saw GOD enthroned,
    and all the Angel Armies of heaven
standing at attention,
    ranged on his right and his left.
And GOD said, "How can we seduce Ahab
    into attacking Ramoth Gilead?"
Some said this,
    and some said that.
Then a bold angel stepped out,
    stood before GOD, and said,
"I'll seduce him."
    "And how will you do it?" said GOD.
"Easy," said the angel,
    "I'll get all the prophets to lie."
"That should do it," said GOD;
    "On your way—seduce him!"

"And that's what has happened. GOD filled the mouths of your puppet prophets with seductive lies. GOD has pronounced your doom."

Just then Zedekiah son of Kenaanah came up and slapped Micaiah in the face, saying, "Since when did the Spirit of GOD leave me and take up with you?"

Micaiah said, "You'll know soon enough; you'll know it when you're frantically and futilely looking for a place to hide."

The king of Israel had heard enough: "Get Micaiah out of here! Turn him over to Amon the city magistrate and to Joash the king's son with this message: 'King's orders! Lock him up in jail; keep him on bread and water until I'm back in one piece.'"

Micaiah said,

If you ever get back in one piece,
    I'm no prophet of GOD.

He added,

When it happens, O people,
    remember where you heard it!

So the king of Israel and Jehoshaphat king of Judah went ahead and attacked Ramoth Gilead. The king of Israel said to Jehoshaphat, "Wear my kingly robe; I'm going into battle disguised." So the king of Israel entered the battle in disguise.

Meanwhile, the king of Aram had ordered his chariot commanders (there were thirty-two of them), "Don't bother with anyone whether small or great; go after the king of Israel and him only."

When the chariot commanders saw Jehoshaphat, they said, "There he is! The king of Israel!" and took after him. Jehoshaphat yelled out, and the chariot commanders realized they had the wrong man—it wasn't the king of Israel after all. God intervened and they let him go.

Just then someone, without aiming, shot an arrow into the crowd and hit the king of Israel in the chink of his armor. The king told his charioteer, "Turn back! Get me out of here—I'm wounded."

All day the fighting continued, hot and heavy. Propped up in his chariot, the king watched from the sidelines. He died that evening.

19 But Jehoshaphat king of Judah got home safe and sound. Jehu, son of Hanani the seer, confronted King Jehoshaphat: "You have no business helping evil, cozying up to GOD-haters. Because you did this, GOD is good and angry with you. But you're not all bad—you made a clean sweep of the polluting sex-and-religion shrines; and you were single-minded in seeking God."

Jehoshaphat kept his residence in Jerusalem but made a regular round of visits among the people, from Beersheba in the south to Mount Ephraim in the north, urging them to return to GOD, the God of their ancestors.

And he was diligent in appointing judges in the land—each of the fortress cities had its judge. He charged the judges: "This is serious work; do it carefully. You are not merely judging between men and women; these are GOD's judgments that you are passing on. Live in the fear of GOD—be most careful, for GOD hates dishonesty, partiality, and bribery."

In Jerusalem Jehoshaphat also appointed Levites, priests, and family heads to decide on matters that had to do with worship and mediating local differences. He charged them: "Do your work in the fear of GOD; be dependable and honest in your duties. When a case comes before you involving any of your fellow citizens, whether it seems large (like murder) or small (like matters of interpretation of the law), you are responsible for warning them that they are dealing with GOD. Make that explicit, otherwise both you and they are going to be dealing with GOD's wrath. Do your work well or you'll end up being as guilty as they are.

"Amariah the chief priest is in charge of all cases regarding the worship of GOD; Zebadiah son of Ishmael, the leader of the tribe of Judah, is in charge of all civil cases; the Levites will keep order in the courts. Be bold and diligent. And GOD be with you as you do your best."

☩

20 Some time later the Moabites and Ammonites, accompanied by Meunites, joined forces to make war on Jehoshaphat. Jehoshaphat received this intelligence report: "A huge force is on its way from beyond the Dead Sea to fight you. There's no time to waste—they're already at Hazazon Tamar, the oasis of En Gedi."

Shaken, Jehoshaphat prayed. He went to GOD for help and ordered a nationwide fast. The country of Judah united in seeking GOD's help—they came from all the cities of Judah to pray to GOD.

Then Jehoshaphat took a position before the assembled people of Judah and Jerusalem at The Temple of GOD in front of the new courtyard and said, "O GOD, God of our ancestors, are you not God in heaven above and ruler of all kingdoms below? You hold all power and might in your fist—no one stands a chance against you! And didn't you make the natives of this land leave as you brought your people Israel in, turning it over permanently to your people Israel, the descendants of Abraham your friend? They have lived here and built a holy house of worship to honor you, saying, 'When the worst happens—whether war or flood or disease or famine—and we take our place before this Temple (we know you are personally present in this place!) and pray out our pain and trouble, we know that you will listen and give victory.'

"And now it's happened: men from Ammon, Moab, and Mount Seir have shown up. You didn't let Israel touch them when we got here at first—we detoured around them and didn't lay a hand on them. And now they've come to kick us out of the country you gave us. O dear God, won't you take care of them? We're helpless before this vandal horde ready to attack us. We don't know what to do; we're looking to you."

Everyone in Judah was there—little children, wives, sons—all present and attentive to GOD.

Then Jahaziel was moved by the Spirit of GOD to speak from the midst of the congregation. (Jahaziel was the son of Zechariah, the son of Benaiah, the son of Jeiel, the son of Mattaniah the Levite of the Asaph clan.) He said, "Attention everyone—all of you from out of town, all you from Jerusalem, and you King Jehoshaphat—GOD's word: Don't be afraid; don't pay any mind to this vandal horde. This is God's war, not yours. Tomorrow you'll go after them; see, they're already on their way up the slopes of Ziz; you'll meet them at the end of the ravine near the wilderness of Jeruel. You won't have to lift a hand in this battle; just stand firm, Judah and Jerusalem, and watch GOD's saving work for you take shape. Don't be afraid, don't waver. March out boldly tomorrow—GOD is with you."

Then Jehoshaphat knelt down, bowing with his face to the ground. All Judah and Jerusalem did the same, worshiping GOD. The Levites (both Kohathites and Korahites) stood to their feet to praise GOD, the God of Israel; they praised at the top of their lungs!

They were up early in the morning, ready to march into the wilderness of Tekoa. As they were leaving, Jehoshaphat stood up and said, "Listen Judah and Jerusalem! Listen to what I have to say! Believe firmly in GOD, your God, and your lives will be firm! Believe in your prophets and you'll come out on top!"

After talking it over with the people, Jehoshaphat appointed a choir for GOD; dressed in holy robes, they were to march ahead of the troops, singing,

Give thanks to GOD,
His love never quits.

As soon as they started shouting and praising, GOD set ambushes against the men of Ammon, Moab, and Mount Seir as they were attacking Judah, and they all ended up dead. The Ammonites and Moabites mistakenly attacked those from Mount Seir and massacred them. Then, further confused, they went at each other, and all ended up killed.

As Judah came up over the rise, looking into the wilderness for the horde of barbarians, they looked on a killing field of dead bodies— not a living soul among them.

When Jehoshaphat and his people came to carry off the plunder they found more loot than they could carry off—equipment, clothing, valuables. It took three days to cart it away! On the fourth day they came together at the Valley of Blessing (Beracah) and blessed GOD (that's how it got the name, Valley of Blessing).

Jehoshaphat then led all the men of Judah and Jerusalem back to Jerusalem—an exuberant parade. GOD had given them joyful relief from their enemies! They entered Jerusalem and came to The Temple of GOD with all the instruments of the band playing.

When the surrounding kingdoms got word that GOD had fought Israel's enemies, the fear of God descended on them. Jehoshaphat heard no more from them; as long as Jehoshaphat reigned, peace reigned.

That about sums up Jehoshaphat's reign over Judah. He was thirty-five years old when he became king and ruled as king in Jerusalem for twenty-five years. His mother was Azubah daughter of Shilhi. He continued the kind of life characteristic of his father Asa—no detours, no dead-ends—pleasing GOD with his life. But he failed to get rid of the neighborhood sex-and-religion shrines—people continued to pray and worship at these idolatrous god shops.

The rest of Jehoshaphat's life, from start to finish, is written in the memoirs of Jehu son of Hanani, which are included in the *Royal Annals of Israel's Kings*.

Late in life Jehoshaphat formed a trading syndicate with Ahaziah king of Israel—which was very wrong of him to do. He went in as partner with him to build ocean-going ships at Ezion Geber to trade with Tarshish. Eliezer son of Dodavahu of Mareshah preached against Jehoshaphat's venture: "Because you joined forces with Ahaziah, GOD has shipwrecked your work." The ships were smashed and nothing ever came of the trade partnership.

21 Jehoshaphat died and was buried in the family cemetery in the City of David. Jehoram his son was the next king.

KING JEHORAM

Jehoram's brothers were Azariah, Jehiel, Zechariah, Azariahu, Michael, and Shephatiah—the sons of Jehoshaphat king of Judah. Their father had lavished them with gifts—silver, gold, and other valuables, plus the fortress cities in Judah. But Jehoram was his firstborn son and he gave him the kingdom of Judah. But when Jehoram had taken over his father's kingdom and had secured his position, he killed all his brothers along with some of the government officials.

Jehoram was thirty-two years old when he became king and ruled in Jerusalem for eight years. He imitated Israel's kings and married into the Ahab dynasty. GOD considered him an evil man. But despite that, because of his covenant with David, GOD was not yet ready to destroy the descendants of David; he had, after all, promised to keep a light burning for David and his sons.

During Jehoram's reign, Edom revolted from Judah's rule and set up their own king. Jehoram responded by setting out with his officers and chariots. Edom surrounded him, but in the middle of the night he and his charioteers broke through the lines and hit Edom hard.

Edom continues in revolt against Judah right up to the present. Even little Libnah revolted at that time. The evidence accumulated: Since Jehoram had abandoned GOD, the God of his ancestors, God was abandoning him. He even went so far as to build pagan sacred shrines in the mountains of Judah. He brazenly led Jerusalem away from God, seducing the whole country.

One day he got a letter from Elijah the prophet. It read, "From GOD, the God of your ancestor David—a message: Because you have not kept to the ways of Jehoshaphat your father and Asa your grandfather, kings of Judah, but have taken up with the ways of the kings of Israel in the north, leading Judah and Jerusalem away from God, going step by step down the apostate path of Ahab and his crew—why, you even killed your own brothers, all of them better men than you!— GOD is going to afflict your people, your wives, your sons, and everything you have with a terrible plague. And you are going to come down

393

with a terrible disease of the colon, painful and humiliating."

The trouble started with an invasion. GOD incited the Philistines and the Arabs who lived near the Ethiopians to attack Jehoram. They came to the borders of Judah, forced their way in, and plundered the place—robbing the royal palace of everything in it including his wives and sons. One son, his youngest, Ahaziah, was left behind. The terrible and fatal disease in his colon followed. After about two years he was totally incontinent and died writhing in pain. His people didn't honor him by lighting a great bonfire, as was customary with his ancestors. He was thirty-two years old when he became king and reigned for eight years in Jerusalem. There were no tears shed when he died—it was good riddance!—and they buried him in the City of David, but not in the royal cemetery.

KING AHAZIAH

22 The people of Jerusalem made Ahaziah, Jehoram's youngest son, king. Raiders from the desert, who had come with the Arabs against the settlement, had killed all the older sons. That's how Ahaziah son of Jehoram king of Judah became king. Ahaziah was twenty-two years old when he became king, but reigned only one year in Jerusalem. His mother was Athaliah, granddaughter of Omri. He lived and ruled just like the Ahab family had done, his mother training him in evil ways. GOD also considered him evil, related by both marriage and sin to the Ahab clan. After the death of his father, he attended the sin school of Ahab, and graduated with a degree in doom. He did what they taught him, went with Joram son of Ahab king of Israel in the war against Hazael king of Aram at Ramoth Gilead. Joram, wounded by the Arameans, retreated to Jezreel to recover from the wounds he received in Ramah in his war with Hazael king of Aram. Ahaziah son of Jehoram king of Judah paid a visit to Joram son of Ahab on his sickbed at Jezreel.

The fate of Ahaziah when he went to visit was God's judgment on him. When Ahaziah arrived at Jezreel, he and Joram met with Jehu son of Nimshi, whom GOD had already authorized to destroy the dynasty of Ahab. Jehu, already at work, executing doom on the dynasty of Ahab, came upon the captains of Judah and Ahaziah's nephews, part of the Ahaziah delegation, and killed them outright. Then he sent out a search party looking for Ahaziah himself. They found him hiding out in Samaria and hauled him back to Jehu. And Jehu killed him.

They didn't, though, just leave his body there. Out of respect for his grandfather Jehoshaphat, famous as a sincere seeker after GOD, they gave him a decent burial. But there was no one left in Ahaziah's family capable of ruling the kingdom.

QUEEN ATHALIAH

When Ahaziah's mother Athaliah saw that her son was dead, she took over. She began by massacring the entire royal family. Jehosheba, daughter of King Jehoram, took Ahaziah's son Joash, and kidnapped him from among the king's sons slated for slaughter. She hid him and his nurse in a private room away from Athaliah. So Jehosheba, daughter of King Jehoram and Ahaziah's sister—she was also the wife of Jehoiada the priest—saved Joash from the murderous Queen Athaliah. He was there with her, hidden away for six years in The Temple of God. Athaliah, oblivious to his existence, ruled the country.

23 In the seventh year the priest Jehoiada decided to make his move and worked out a strategy with certain influential officers in the army. He picked Azariah son of Jeroham, Ishmael son of Jehohanan, Azariah son of Obed, Maaseiah son of Adaiah, and Elishaphat son of Zicri as his associates. They dispersed throughout Judah and called in the Levites from all the towns in Judah along with the heads of families. They met in Jerusalem. The gathering met in The Temple of God. They made a covenant there in The Temple.

The priest Jehoiada showed them the young prince and addressed them: "Here he is—the son of the king. He is going to rule just as GOD promised regarding the sons of David. Now this is what you must do: A third of you priests and Levites who come on duty on the Sabbath are to be posted as security guards at the gates; another third will guard the palace; and the other third will guard the foundation gate. All the people will gather in the courtyards of The Temple of GOD. No one may enter The Temple of GOD except the priests and designated Levites—they are permitted in because they've been consecrated, but all the people must do the work assigned them. The Levites are to form a ring around the young king, weapons at the ready. Kill anyone who tries to break through your ranks. Your job is to stay with the king at all times and places, coming and going."

All the Levites and officers obeyed the orders of Jehoiada the priest. Each took charge of his men, both those who came on duty on the

Sabbath and those who went off duty on the Sabbath, for Jehoiada the priest hadn't exempted any of them from duty. Then the priest armed the officers with spears and the large and small shields originally belonging to King David that were stored in The Temple of God. Well-armed, the guards took up their assigned positions for protecting the king, from one end of The Temple to the other, surrounding both Altar and Temple.

Then the priest brought the prince into view, crowned him, handed him the scroll of God's covenant, and made him king. As Jehoiada and his sons anointed him they shouted, "Long live the king!"

Athaliah, hearing all the commotion, the people running around and praising the king, came to The Temple to see what was going on. Astonished, she saw the young king standing at the entrance flanked by the captains and heralds, with everybody beside themselves with joy, trumpets blaring, the choir and orchestra leading the praise. Athaliah ripped her robes in dismay and shouted, "Treason! Treason!"

Jehoiada the priest ordered the military officers, "Drag her outside—and kill anyone who tries to follow her!" (The priest had said, "Don't kill her inside The Temple of GOD.") So they dragged her out to the palace's horse corral and there they killed her.

Jehoiada now made a covenant between himself and the king and the people: they were to be GOD's special people.

The people poured into the temple of Baal and tore it down, smashing altar and images to smithereens. They killed Mattan the priest of Baal in front of the altar.

Jehoiada turned the care of GOD's Temple over to the priests and Levites, the way David had directed originally. They were to offer the Whole-Burnt-Offerings of GOD as set out in The Revelation of Moses, and with praise and song as directed by David. He also assigned security guards at the gates of GOD's Temple so that no one who was unprepared could enter. Then he got everyone together—officers, nobles, governors, and the people themselves—and escorted the king down from The Temple of GOD, through the Upper Gate, and placed him on the royal throne. Everybody celebrated the event. And the city was safe and undisturbed—Athaliah had been killed; no more Athaliah terror.

KING JOASH

24 Joash was seven years old when he became king; he was king for forty years in Jerusalem. His mother's name was Gazelle (Zibiah). She was from Beersheba.

396

Taught and trained by Jehoiada the priest, Joash did what pleased GOD throughout Jehoiada's lifetime. Jehoiada picked out two wives for him; he had a family of both sons and daughters.

The time came when Joash determined to renovate The Temple of GOD. He got the priests and Levites together and said, "Circulate through the towns of Judah every year and collect money from the people to repair The Temple of your God. You are in charge of carrying this out." But the Levites dragged their feet and didn't do anything.

Then the king called in Jehoiada the chief priest and said, "Why haven't you made the Levites bring in from Judah and Jerusalem the tax Moses, servant of GOD and the congregation, set for the upkeep of the place of worship? You can see how bad things are—wicked Queen Athaliah and her sons let The Temple of God go to ruin and took all its sacred artifacts for use in Baal worship."

Following the king's orders, they made a chest and placed it at the entrance to The Temple of GOD. Then they sent out a tax notice throughout Judah and Jerusalem: "Pay the tax that Moses the servant of GOD set when Israel was in the wilderness."

The people and their leaders were glad to do it and cheerfully brought their money until the chest was full.

Whenever the Levites brought the chest in for a royal audit and found it to be full, the king's secretary and the official of the chief priest would empty the chest and put it back in its place. Day after day they did this and collected a lot of money. The king and Jehoiada gave the money to the managers of The Temple project; they in turn paid the masons and carpenters for the repair work on The Temple of GOD. The construction workers kept at their jobs steadily until the restoration was complete—the house of GOD as good as new! When they had finished the work, they returned the surplus money to the king and Jehoiada, who used the money for making sacred vessels for Temple worship, vessels for the daily worship, for the Whole-Burnt-Offerings, bowls, and other gold and silver liturgical artifacts.

Whole-Burnt-Offerings were made regularly in The Temple of GOD throughout Jehoiada's lifetime. He died at a ripe old age—130 years old! They buried him in the royal cemetery because he had such a distinguished life of service to Israel and God and God's Temple.

But after the death of Jehoiada things fell apart. The leaders of Judah made a formal presentation to the king and he went along with them.

Things went from bad to worse; they deserted The Temple of GOD and took up with the cult of sex goddesses. An angry cloud hovered over Judah and Jerusalem because of this sin. GOD sent prophets to straighten them out, warning of judgment. But nobody paid attention.

Then the Spirit of God moved Zechariah son of Jehoiada the priest to speak up: "God's word: Why have you deliberately walked away from GOD's commandments? You can't live this way! If you walk out on GOD, he'll walk out on you."

But they worked out a plot against Zechariah, and with the complicity of the king—he actually gave the order!—they murdered him, pelting him with rocks, right in the court of The Temple of GOD. That's the thanks King Joash showed the loyal Jehoiada, the priest who had made him king. He murdered Jehoiada's son. Zechariah's last words were, "Look, GOD! Make them pay for this!"

A year or so later Aramean troops attacked Joash. They invaded Judah and Jerusalem, massacred the leaders, and shipped all their plunder back to the king in Damascus. The Aramean army was quite small, but GOD used them to wipe out Joash's large army—their punishment for deserting GOD, the God of their ancestors. Arameans implemented God's judgment against Joash.

They left Joash badly wounded and his own servants finished him off—it was a palace conspiracy, avenging the murder of the son of Jehoiada the priest. They killed him in his bed. Afterward they buried him in the City of David, but he was not honored with a grave in the royal cemetery. The temple conspirators were Zabad, whose mother was Shimeath from Ammon, and Jehozabad, whose mother was Shimrith from Moab. The story of his sons, the many sermons preached to Joash, and the account of his repairs on The Temple of God can be found contained in the commentary on the royal history.

Amaziah, Joash's son, was the next king.

KING AMAZIAH

25 Amaziah was twenty-five years old when he became king and reigned twenty-nine years in Jerusalem. His mother was Jehoaddin from Jerusalem. He lived well before GOD, doing the right thing for the most part. But he wasn't wholeheartedly devoted to God. When he had the affairs of the kingdom well in hand, he executed the palace guard who had assassinated his father the king. But he didn't kill the sons of the assassins—he was mindful of what GOD commanded in The Revelation of

Moses, that parents shouldn't be executed for their childrens' sins, nor children for their parents'. We each pay personally for our sins.

Amaziah organized Judah and sorted out Judah and Benjamin by families and by military units. Men twenty years and older had to register—they ended up with 300,000 judged capable of military service. In addition he hired 100,000 soldiers from Israel in the north at a cost of about four and a half tons of silver.

A holy man showed up and said, "No, O king—don't let those northern Israelite soldiers into your army; GOD is not on their side, nor with any of the Ephraimites. Instead, you go by yourself and be strong. God and God only has the power to help or hurt your cause."

But Amaziah said to the holy man, "But what about all this money—these tons of silver I have already paid out to hire these men?"

"GOD's help is worth far more to you than that," said the holy man.

So Amaziah fired the soldiers he had hired from the north and sent them home. They were very angry at losing their jobs and went home seething.

But Amaziah was optimistic. He led his troops into the Valley of Salt and killed 10,000 men of Seir. They took another 10,000 as prisoners, led them to the top of the Rock, and pushed them off a cliff. They all died in the fall, smashed on the rocks.

But the troops Amaziah had dismissed from his army, angry over their lost opportunity for plunder, rampaged through the towns of Judah all the way from Samaria to Beth Horon, killing 3,000 people and taking much plunder.

On his return from the destruction of the Edomites, Amaziah brought back the gods of the men of Seir and installed them as his own gods, worshiping them and burning incense to them. *That* ignited GOD's anger; a fiery blast of GOD's wrath put into words by a God-sent prophet: "What is this? Why on earth would you pray to inferior gods who couldn't so much as help their own people from you—gods weaker than Amaziah?"

Amaziah interrupted him, "Did I ask for your opinion? Shut up or get thrown out!"

The prophet quit speaking, but not before he got in one last word: "I have it on good authority: God has made up his mind to throw *you* out because of what you've done, and because you wouldn't listen to me."

✠

One day Amaziah sent envoys to Jehoash son of Jehoahaz, the son of Jehu, king of Israel, challenging him to a fight: "Come and meet with me, I dare you. Let's have it out face to face!"

Jehoash king of Israel replied to Amaziah king of Judah, "One day a thistle in Lebanon sent word to a cedar in Lebanon, 'Give your daughter to my son in marriage.' But then a wild animal of Lebanon passed by and stepped on the thistle, crushing it. Just because you've defeated Edom in battle, you now think you're a big shot. Go ahead and be proud, but stay home. Why press your luck? Why bring defeat on yourself and Judah?"

Amaziah wouldn't take no for an answer—God had already decided to let Jehoash defeat him because he had defected to the gods of Edom. So Jehoash king of Israel came on ahead and confronted Amaziah king of Judah. They met at Beth Shemesh, a town of Judah. Judah was thoroughly beaten by Israel—all the soldiers straggled home in defeat.

Jehoash king of Israel captured Amaziah king of Judah, the son of Joash, the son of Ahaziah, at Beth Shemesh. But Jehoash didn't stop at that; he went on to attack Jerusalem. He demolished the Wall of Jerusalem all the way from the Ephraim Gate to the Corner Gate—a stretch of about six hundred feet. He looted the gold, silver, and furnishings—anything he found that was worth taking—from both the palace and The Temple of God—and, for good measure, he took hostages. Then he returned to Samaria.

Amaziah son of Joash king of Judah continued as king fifteen years after the death of Jehoash son of Jehoahaz king of Israel. The rest of the life and times of Amaziah from start to finish is written in the *Royal Annals of the Kings of Judah and Israel.*

During those last days, after Amaziah had defected from GOD, they cooked up a plot against Amaziah in Jerusalem, and he had to flee to Lachish. But they tracked him down in Lachish and killed him there. They brought him back on horseback and buried him in Jerusalem with his ancestors in the City of David.

KING UZZIAH

26 The people of Judah then took Uzziah, who was only sixteen years old, and made him king in place of his father Amaziah. The first thing he did after his father was dead and buried was to recover Elath for Judah and rebuild it.

Uzziah was sixteen years old when he became king and reigned for fifty-two years in Jerusalem. His mother was Jecoliah from Jerusalem. He behaved well in the eyes of GOD, following in the footsteps of his father Amaziah. He was a loyal seeker of God. He was well trained by his pastor and teacher Zechariah to live in reverent obedience before God, and for as long as Zechariah lived, Uzziah lived a godly life. And God prospered him.

He ventured out and fought the Philistines, breaking into the fortress cities of Gath, Jabneh, and Ashdod. He also built settlements around Ashdod and other Philistine areas. God helped him in his wars with the Philistines, the Arabs in Gur Baal, and the Meunites. The Ammonites also paid tribute. Uzziah became famous, his reputation extending all the way to Egypt. He became quite powerful.

Uzziah constructed defense towers in Jerusalem at the Corner Gate, the Valley Gate, and at the corner of the wall. He also built towers and dug cisterns out in the country. He had herds of cattle down in the foothills and out on the plains, had farmers and vinedressers at work in the hills and fields—he loved growing things.

On the military side, Uzziah had a well-prepared army ready to fight. They were organized by companies under the direction of Jeiel the secretary, Maaseiah the field captain, and Hananiah of the general staff. The roster of family leaders over the fighting men accounted for 2,600. Under them were reinforcement troops numbering 307,000, with 500 of them on constant alert—a strong royal defense against any attack. Uzziah had them well-armed with shields, spears, helmets, armor, bows, and slingshots. He also installed the latest in military technology on the towers and corners of Jerusalem for shooting arrows and hurling stones. He became well known for all this—a famous king. Everything seemed to go his way.

But then the strength and success went to his head. Arrogant and proud, he fell. One day, contemptuous of GOD, he walked into The Temple of GOD like he owned it and took over, burning incense on the Incense Altar. The priest Azariah, backed up by eighty brave priests of GOD, tried to prevent him. They confronted Uzziah: "You must not, you *cannot* do this, Uzziah—only the Aaronite priests, especially consecrated for the work, are permitted to burn incense. Get out of God's Temple; you are unfaithful and a disgrace!"

But Uzziah, censer in hand, was already in the middle of doing it and angrily rebuffed the priests. He lost his temper; angry words were exchanged—and then, even as they quarreled, a skin disease appeared on his forehead. As soon as they saw it, the chief priest Azariah and the other priests got him out of there as fast as they could. He hurried out—he knew that GOD then and there had given him the disease. Uzziah had his skin disease for the rest of his life and had to live in quarantine; he was not permitted to set foot in The Temple of GOD. His son Jotham, who managed the royal palace, took over the government of the country.

The rest of the history of Uzziah, from start to finish, was written by the prophet Isaiah son of Amoz. When Uzziah died, they buried him with his ancestors in a field next to the royal cemetery. His skin disease disqualified him from burial in the royal cemetery. His son Jotham became the next king.

KING JOTHAM

27Jotham was twenty-five years old when he became king; he reigned sixteen years at Jerusalem. His mother was Jerusha the daughter of Zadok. In GOD's eyes he lived a good life, following the path marked out by his father Uzziah. Unlike his father, though, he didn't desecrate The Temple of GOD. But the people pushed right on in their lives of corruption.

Jotham constructed the Upper Gate of The Temple of GOD, considerably extended the Wall of the Ophel, and built cities in the high country of Judah and forts and towers down in the forests. He fought and beat the king of the Ammonites—that year the Ammonites turned over three and a quarter tons of silver and about sixty-five bushels of wheat, and another sixty-five bushels of barley. They repeated this for the next two years. Jotham's strength was rooted in his steady and determined life of obedience to GOD.

The rest of the history of Jotham, including his wars and achievements, are all written in the *Royal Annals of the Kings of Israel and Judah*. He was twenty-five years old when he became king; he reigned for sixteen years at Jerusalem. Jotham died and was buried in the City of David. His son Ahaz became the next king.

KING AHAZ

28Ahaz was twenty years old when he became king and reigned sixteen years in Jerusalem. He didn't live right in the eyes of GOD; he wasn't at all like his ancestor David. Instead he followed in the track of Israel in the north, even casting metal figurines for worshiping the pagan Baal gods. He participated in the outlawed burning of incense in the Valley of Ben Hinnom and—incredibly!—indulged in the outrageous practice of "passing his sons through the fire," a truly abominable thing he picked up from the pagans GOD had earlier thrown out of the country. He also joined in the activities of the neighborhood sex-and-religion shrines that flourished all over the place.

GOD, fed up, handed him over to the king of Aram, who beat him badly and took many prisoners to Damascus. God also let the king of Israel loose on him and that resulted in a terrible slaughter: Pekah son of Remaliah killed 120,000 in one day, all of them first-class soldiers, and all because they had deserted GOD, the God of their ancestors. Furthermore, Zicri, an Ephraimite hero, killed the king's son Maaseiah, Azrikam the palace steward, and Elkanah, second in command to the king. And that wasn't the end of it—the Israelites captured 200,000 men, women, and children, besides huge cartloads of plunder that they took to Samaria.

GOD's prophet Oded was in the neighborhood. He met the army when it entered Samaria and said, "Stop right where you are and listen! GOD, the God of your ancestors, was angry with Judah and used you to punish them; but you took things into your own hands and used *your* anger, uncalled for and irrational, to turn your brothers and sisters from Judah and Jerusalem into slaves. Don't you see that this is a terrible sin against your GOD? Careful now; do exactly what I say—return these captives, every last one of them. If you don't, you'll find out how real anger, GOD's anger, works."

Some of their Ephraimite leaders—Azariah son of Jehohanan, Berekiah son of Meshillemoth, Jehizkiah son of Shallum, and Amasa son of Hadlai—stood up against the returning army and said, "Don't bring the captives here! We've already sinned against GOD; and now you are about to compound our sin and guilt. We're guilty enough as it is, enough to set off an explosion of divine anger."

So the soldiers turned over both the captives and the plunder to the leaders and the people. Personally designated men gathered the captives together, dressed the ones who were naked using clothing from the stores of plunder, put shoes on their feet, gave them all a square meal, provided first aid to the injured, put the weak ones on donkeys, and then escorted them to Jericho, the City of Palms, restoring them to their families. Then they went back to Samaria.

At about that time King Ahaz sent to the king of Assyria asking for personal help. The Edomites had come back and given Judah a bad beating, taking off a bunch of captives. Adding insult to injury the Philistines raided the cities in the foothills to the west and the southern desert and captured Beth Shemesh, Aijalon, and Gederoth, along with Soco, Timnah, and Gimzo, with their surrounding villages, and moved in, making themselves at home. Arrogant King Ahaz, acting as if he could do without God's help, had unleashed an epidemic of depravity. Judah, brought to its knees by GOD, was now reduced to begging for a handout. But the king of Assyria, Tiglath-Pileser, wouldn't help—he came instead and humiliated Ahaz even more by attacking and bullying him. Desperate, Ahaz ransacked The Temple of GOD, the royal palace, and every other place he could think of, scraping together everything he could, and gave it to the king of Assyria—and got nothing in return, not a bit of help.

But King Ahaz didn't learn his lesson—at the very time that everyone was turning against him, he continued to be against GOD! He offered sacrifices to the gods of Damascus. He had just been defeated by Damascus; he thought, "If I worship the gods who helped Damascus, those gods just might help me too." But things only went from bad to worse: first Ahaz in ruins and then the country. He cleaned out The Temple of God of everything useful and valuable, boarded up the doors of The Temple, and then went out and set up pagan shrines for his own use all over Jerusalem. And not only in Jerusalem, but all over Judah— neighborhood shrines for worshiping any and every god on sale. And was GOD ever angry!

The rest of Ahaz's infamous life, all that he did from start to finish, is written in the *Royal Annals of the Kings of Judah and Israel.* When Ahaz died, they buried him in Jerusalem, but he was not honored with a burial in the cemetery of the kings. His son Hezekiah was the next king.

KING HEZEKIAH

29 Hezekiah became king when he was twenty-five years old and was king in Jerusalem for twenty-nine years. His mother was Abijah daughter of Zechariah. In GOD's opinion he was a good king; he kept to the standards of his ancestor David.

In the first month of the first year of his reign, Hezekiah, having first repaired the doors of The Temple of GOD, threw them open to the public. He assembled the priests and Levites in the court on the east side and said, "Levites, listen! Consecrate yourselves and consecrate The

Temple of GOD—give this much-defiled place a good housecleaning. Our ancestors went wrong and lived badly before GOD—they discarded him, turned away from this house where we meet with GOD, and walked off. They boarded up the doors, turned out the lights, and canceled all the acts of worship of the GOD of Israel in the holy Temple. And because of that, GOD's anger flared up and he turned those people into a public exhibit of disaster, a moral history lesson—look and read! This is why our ancestors were killed, and this is why our wives and sons and daughters were taken prisoner and made slaves.

"I have decided to make a covenant with the GOD of Israel and turn history around so that GOD will no longer be angry with us. Children, don't drag your feet in this! GOD has chosen you to take your place before him to serve in conducting and leading worship—*this* is your life work; make sure you do it and do it well."

The Levites stood at attention: Mahath son of Amasai and Joel son of Azariah from the Kohathites; Kish son of Abdi and Azariah son of Jehallelel from the Merarites; Joah son of Zimmah and Eden son of Joah from the Gershonites; Shimri and Jeiel sons of Elizaphan; Zechariah and Mattaniah sons of Asaph; Jehiel and Shimei of the family of Heman; Shemaiah and Uzziel of the family of Jeduthun. They presented themselves and their brothers, consecrated themselves, and set to work cleaning up The Temple of GOD as the king had directed—as GOD directed! The priests started from the inside and worked out; they emptied the place of the accumulation of defiling junk—pagan rubbish that had no business in that holy place—and the Levites hauled it off to the Kidron Valley. They began the Temple cleaning on the first day of the first month and by the eighth day they had worked their way out to the porch—eight days it took them to clean and consecrate The Temple itself, and in eight more days they had finished with the entire Temple complex.

Then they reported to Hezekiah the king, "We have cleaned up the entire Temple of GOD, including the Altar of Whole-Burnt-Offering and the Table of the Bread of the Presence with their furnishings. We have also cleaned up and consecrated all the vessels which King Ahaz had gotten rid of during his misrule. Take a look; we have repaired them. They're all there in front of the Altar of GOD."

Then Hezekiah the king went to work: He got all the leaders of the city together and marched to The Temple of GOD. They brought with them seven bulls, seven rams, seven lambs, and seven he-goats to sacrifice as an Absolution-Offering for the royal family, for the Sanctuary, and for Judah as a whole; he directed the Aaronite priests to sacrifice them on the Altar of GOD. The priests butchered the bulls and then took the blood and sprinkled it on the Altar, and then the same with the rams and lambs. Finally they brought the goats up; the king and congregation laid their hands upon them. The priests butchered them and made an Absolution-Offering with their blood at the Altar to atone for the sin of all Israel—the king had ordered that the Whole-Burnt-Offering and the Absolution-Offering be for all Israel.

The king ordered the Levites to take their places in The Temple of GOD with their musical instruments—cymbals, harps, zithers—following the original instructions of David, Gad the king's seer, and Nathan the prophet; this was GOD's command conveyed by his prophets. The Levites formed the orchestra of David, while the priests took up the trumpets.

Then Hezekiah gave the signal to begin: The Whole-Burnt-Offering was offered on the Altar; at the same time the sacred choir began singing, backed up by the trumpets and the David orchestra while the entire congregation worshiped. The singers sang and the trumpeters played all during the sacrifice of the Whole-Burnt-Offering. When the offering of the sacrifice was completed, the king and everyone there knelt to the ground and worshiped. Then Hezekiah the king and the leaders told the Levites to finish things off with anthems of praise to GOD using lyrics by David and Asaph the seer. They sang their praises with joy and reverence, kneeling in worship.

Hezekiah then made this response: "The dedication is complete—you're consecrated to GOD. Now you're ready: Come forward and bring your sacrifices and Thank-Offerings to The Temple of GOD."

And come they did. Everyone in the congregation brought sacrifices and Thank-Offerings and some, overflowing with generosity, even brought Whole-Burnt-Offerings, a generosity expressed in seventy bulls, a hundred rams, and two hundred lambs—all for Whole-Burnt-Offerings for GOD! The total number of animals consecrated for sacrifice that day amounted to 600 bulls and 3,000 sheep. They ran out of priests qualified to slaughter all the Whole-Burnt-Offerings so their brother Levites stepped in and helped out while other priests consecrated themselves for the work. It turned out that the Levites had been more responsible in making sure they were properly consecrated than the priests had been. Besides the overflow of Whole-Burnt-Offerings there were also choice pieces for the Peace-Offerings and lavish libations that went with the Whole-Burnt-Offerings. The worship in The Temple of GOD was on a firm footing again!

Hezekiah and the congregation celebrated: God had established a firm foundation for the lives of the people—and so quickly!

✛

30 Then Hezekiah invited all of Israel and Judah, with personal letters to Ephraim and Manasseh, to come to The Temple of GOD in Jerusalem to celebrate the Passover to Israel's God. The king and his officials and the congregation in Jerusalem had decided to celebrate Passover in the second month. They hadn't been able to celebrate it at the regular time because not enough of the priests were yet personally prepared and the people hadn't had time to gather in Jerusalem. Under these circumstances, the revised date was approved by both king and people and they sent out the invitation from one end of the country to the other, from Beersheba in the south to Dan in the north: "Come and celebrate the Passover to Israel's God in Jerusalem." No one living had ever celebrated it properly.

The king gave the orders, and the couriers delivered the invitations from the king and his leaders throughout Israel and Judah. The invitation read: "O Israelites! Come back to GOD, the God of Abraham, Isaac, and Israel, so that he can return to you who have survived the predations of the kings of Assyria. Don't repeat the sins of your ancestors who turned their backs on GOD, the God of their ancestors who then brought them to ruin—you can see the ruins all around you. Don't be pigheaded as your ancestors were. Clasp GOD's outstretched hand. Come to his Temple of holy worship, consecrated for all time. Serve GOD, *your* God. You'll no longer be in danger of his hot anger. If you come back to GOD, your captive relatives and children will be treated compassionately and allowed to come home. Your GOD is gracious and kind and won't snub you—come back and he'll welcome you with open arms."

So the couriers set out, going from city to city through the country of Ephraim and Manasseh, as far north as Zebulun. But the people poked fun at them, treated them as a joke. But not all; some from Asher, Manasseh, and Zebulun weren't too proud to accept the invitation and come to Jerusalem. It was better in Judah—God worked powerfully among them to make it unanimous, responding to the orders sent out by the king and his officials, orders backed up by the word of GOD.

It turned out that there was a tremendous crowd of people when the time came in the second month to celebrate the Passover (sometimes called the Feast of Unraised Bread). First they went to work and got rid of all the pagan altars that were in Jerusalem—hauled them off and dumped them in the Kidron Valley. Then, on the fourteenth day of the second month, they slaughtered the Passover lambs. The priests and Levites weren't ready; but now, embarrassed in their laziness, they consecrated themselves and brought Whole-Burnt-Offerings to The Temple of GOD. Ready now, they stood at their posts as designated by The Revelation of Moses the holy man; the priests sprinkled the blood the Levites handed to them. Because so many in the congregation had not properly prepared themselves by consecration and so were not qualified, the Levites took charge of the slaughter of the Passover lambs so that they would be properly consecrated to GOD.

There were a lot of people, especially those from Ephraim, Manasseh, Issachar, and Zebulun, who did not eat the Passover meal because they had not prepared themselves adequately. Hezekiah prayed for these as follows: "May GOD who is all good, pardon and forgive everyone who sincerely desires GOD, the God of our ancestors. Even— especially!—these who do not meet the literal conditions stated for access to The Temple."

GOD responded to Hezekiah's prayer and healed the people.

All the Israelites present in Jerusalem celebrated the Passover (Feast of Unraised Bread) for seven days, celebrated exuberantly. The Levites and priests praised GOD day after day, filling the air with praise sounds of percussion and brass. Hezekiah commended the Levites for the superb way in which they had led the people in the worship of GOD.

When the feast and festival—that glorious seven days of worship, the making of offerings, and the praising of GOD, the God of their ancestors—were over, the tables cleared and the floors swept, they all decided to keep going for another seven days! So they just kept on celebrating, and as joyfully as they began.

Hezekiah king of Judah gave 1,000 bulls and 7,000 sheep for the congregation's worship; the officials gave an additional 1,000 bulls and 10,000 sheep. And there turned out to be plenty of consecrated priests—qualified and well-prepared. The whole congregation of Judah, the priests and Levites, the congregation that came in from Israel, and the resident aliens from both Israel and Judah, were all in on the joyous celebration. Jerusalem was bursting with joy—nothing like this had taken place in Jerusalem since Solomon son of David king of Israel had built and dedicated The Temple.

The priests and Levites had the last word: they stood and blessed the people. And God listened, listened as the ascending sound of their prayers entered his holy heaven.

✝

31 After the Passover celebration, they all took off for the cities of Judah and smashed the phallic stone monuments, chopped down the sacred Asherah groves, and demolished the neighborhood sex-and-religion shrines and local god shops. They didn't stop until they had been all through Judah, Benjamin, Ephraim, and Manasseh. Then they all went back home and resumed their everyday lives.

Hezekiah organized the groups of priests and Levites for their respective tasks, handing out job descriptions for conducting the services of worship: making the various offerings, and making sure that thanks and praise took place wherever and whenever GOD was worshiped.

He also designated his personal contribution for the Whole-Burnt-Offerings for the morning and evening worship, for Sabbaths, for New Moon festivals, and for the special worship days set down in The Revelation of GOD.

In addition, he asked the people who lived in Jerusalem to be responsible for providing for the priests and Levites so they, without distraction or concern, could give themselves totally to The Revelation of GOD.

As soon as Hezekiah's orders had gone out, the Israelites responded generously: firstfruits of the grain harvest, new wine, oil, honey—everything they grew. They didn't hold back, turning over a tithe of everything. They also brought in a tithe of their cattle, sheep, and anything else they owned that had been dedicated to GOD. Everything was sorted and piled in mounds. They started doing this in the third month and didn't finish until the seventh month.

When Hezekiah and his leaders came and saw the extent of the mounds of gifts, they praised GOD and commended God's people Israel. Hezekiah then consulted the priests and Levites on how to handle the abundance of offerings.

Azariah, chief priest of the family of Zadok, answered, "From the moment of this huge outpouring of gifts to The Temple of GOD, there has been plenty to eat for everyone with food left over. GOD has blessed his people—just look at the evidence!"

Hezekiah then ordered storerooms to be prepared in The Temple of GOD. When they were ready, they brought in all the offerings of tithes and sacred gifts. They put Conaniah the Levite in charge with his brother Shimei as assistant. Jehiel, Azaziah, Nahath, Asahel, Jerimoth, Jozabad, Eliel, Ismakiah, Mahath, and Benaiah were project managers under the direction of Conaniah and Shimei, carrying out the orders of King Hezekiah and Azariah the chief priest of The Temple of God. Kore son of Imnah the Levite, security guard of the East Gate, was in charge of the Freewill-Offerings of God and responsible for distributing the offerings and sacred gifts. Faithful support out in the priestly cities was provided by Eden, Miniamin, Jeshua, Shemaiah, Amariah, and Shecaniah. They were even-handed in their distributions to their coworkers (all males thirty years and older) in each of their respective divisions as they entered The Temple of GOD each day to do their assigned work (their work was all organized by divisions). The divisions comprised officially registered priests by family and Levites twenty years and older by job description. The official family tree included everyone in the entire congregation—their small children, wives, sons, and daughters. The ardent dedication they showed in bringing themselves and their gifts to worship was total—no one was left out.

The Aaronites, the priests who lived out on the pastures that belonged to the priest-cities, had reputable men on hand to distribute regular rations to every priest—everyone listed in the official family tree of the Levites.

Hezekiah carried out this work and kept it up everywhere in Judah. He was the very best—good, right, and true before his GOD. Everything he took up, whether it had to do with worship in God's Temple or the carrying out of God's Law and Commandments, he did well in a spirit of prayerful worship. He was a great success.

✢

32 And then, after this exemplary track record, this: Sennacherib king of Assyria came and attacked Judah. He put the fortified cities under siege, determined to take them.

When Hezekiah realized that Sennacherib's strategy was to take Jerusalem, he talked to his advisors and military leaders about eliminating all the water supplies outside the city; they thought it was a good idea. There was a great turnout of people to plug the springs and tear down the aqueduct. They said, "Why should the kings of Assyria march in and be furnished with running water?"

Hezekiah also went to work repairing every part of the city wall that was damaged, built defensive towers on it, built another wall of defense further out, and reinforced the defensive rampart (the Millo) of the old City of David. He also built up a large store of armaments—spears and shields. He then appointed military officers to be responsible for the people and got them all together at the public square in front of the city gate.

Hezekiah rallied the people, saying, "Be strong! Take courage! Don't be intimidated by the king of Assyria and his troops—there are more on our side than on their side. He only has a bunch of mere men; we have our GOD to help us and fight for us!"

Morale surged. Hezekiah's words put steel in their spines.

Later on, Sennacherib, who had set up camp a few miles away at Lachish, sent messengers to Jerusalem, addressing Judah through Hezekiah: "A proclamation of Sennacherib king of Assyria: You poor people—do you think you're safe in that so-called fortress of Jerusalem? You're sitting ducks. Do you think Hezekiah will save you? Don't be stupid—Hezekiah has fed you a pack of lies. When he says, 'GOD will save us from the power of the king of Assyria,' he's lying—you're all going to end up dead. Wasn't it Hezekiah who cleared out all the neighborhood worship shrines and told you, 'There is only one legitimate place to worship'? Do you have any idea what I and my ancestors have done to all the countries around here? Has there been a single god anywhere strong enough to stand up against me? Can you name one god among all the nations that either I or my ancestors have ravaged that so much as lifted a finger against me? So what makes you think you'll make out any better with your god? Don't let Hezekiah fool you; don't let him get by with his barefaced lies; don't trust him. No god of any country or kingdom ever has been one bit of help against me or my ancestors—what kind of odds does that give your god?"

The messengers felt free to throw in their personal comments, putting down both GOD and God's servant Hezekiah.

Sennacherib continued to send letters insulting the GOD of Israel: "The gods of the nations were powerless to help their people; the god of Hezekiah is no better, probably worse."

The messengers would come up to the wall of Jerusalem and shout up to the people standing on the wall, shouting their propaganda in Hebrew, trying to scare them into demoralized submission. They contemptuously lumped the God of Jerusalem in with the handmade gods of other peoples.

King Hezekiah, joined by the prophet Isaiah son of Amoz, responded by praying, calling up to heaven. GOD answered by sending an angel who wiped out everyone in the Assyrian camp, both warriors and officers. Sennacherib was forced to return home in disgrace, tail between his legs. When he went into the temple of his god, his own sons killed him.

GOD saved Hezekiah and the citizens of Jerusalem from Sennacherib king of Assyria and everyone else. And he continued to take good care of them. People streamed into Jerusalem bringing offerings for the worship of GOD and expensive presents to Hezekiah king of Judah. All the surrounding nations were impressed—Hezekiah's stock soared.

✝

Some time later Hezekiah became deathly sick. He prayed to GOD and was given a reassuring sign.

But the sign, instead of making Hezekiah grateful, made him arrogant. This made GOD angry, and his anger spilled over on Judah and Jerusalem. But then Hezekiah, and Jerusalem with him, repented of his arrogance, and GOD withdrew his anger while Hezekiah lived.

Hezekiah ended up very wealthy and much honored. He built treasuries for all his silver, gold, precious stones, spices, shields, and valuables, barns for the grain, new wine, and olive oil, stalls for his various breeds of cattle, and pens for his flocks. He founded royal cities for himself and built up huge stocks of sheep and cattle. God saw to it that he was extravagantly rich. Hezekiah was also responsible for diverting the upper outlet of the Gihon spring and rerouting the water to the west side of the City of David. Hezekiah succeeded in everything he did. But when the rulers of Babylon sent emissaries to find out about the sign from God that had taken place earlier, God left him on his own to see what he would do; he wanted to test his heart.

✝

The rest of the history of Hezekiah and his life of loyal service, you can read for yourself—it's written in the vision of the prophet Isaiah son of Amoz in the *Royal Annals of the Kings of Judah and Israel*. When Hezekiah died, they buried him in the upper part of the King David cemetery. Everyone in Judah and Jerusalem came to the funeral. He was buried in great honor.

Manasseh his son was the next king.

KING MANASSEH

33 Manasseh was twelve years old when he became king. He ruled for fifty-five years in Jerusalem. In GOD's opinion he was a bad king—an evil king. He reintroduced all the moral rot and spiritual corruption that had been scoured from the country when GOD dispossessed the pagan nations in favor of the children of Israel. He rebuilt the sex-and-religion shrines that his father Hezekiah had torn down, he built altars and phallic images for the sex god Baal and the sex goddess Asherah and worshiped the cosmic powers, taking orders from the constellations. He built shrines to the cosmic powers and placed them in both courtyards of The Temple of GOD, the very Jerusalem Temple dedicated exclusively by GOD's decree to GOD's Name ("in Jerusalem I place my Name"). He burned his own sons in a sacrificial rite in the Valley of Ben Hinnom. He practiced witchcraft and fortune-telling. He held séances and consulted spirits from the underworld. Much evil—in GOD's view a career in evil. And GOD was angry.

As a last straw he placed a carved image of the sex goddess Asherah that he had commissioned in The Temple of God, a flagrant and provocative violation of God's well-known command to both David and Solomon, "In this Temple and in this city Jerusalem, my choice out of all the tribes of Israel, I place my Name—exclusively and forever." He had promised, "Never again will I let my people Israel wander off from this land I've given to their ancestors. But on this condition, that they keep everything I've commanded in the instructions my servant Moses passed on to them."

But Manasseh led Judah and the citizens of Jerusalem off the beaten path into practices of evil exceeding even the evil of the pagan nations that GOD had earlier destroyed. When GOD spoke to Manasseh and his people about this, they ignored him.

Then GOD directed the leaders of the troops of the king of Assyria to come after Manasseh. They put a hook in his nose, shackles on his feet, and took him off to Babylon. Now that he was in trouble, he went to his knees in prayer asking for help—total repentance before the God of his ancestors. As he prayed, GOD was touched; GOD listened and brought him back to Jerusalem as king. That convinced Manasseh that GOD was in control.

After that Manasseh rebuilt the outside defensive wall of the City of David to the west of the Gihon spring in the valley. It went from the Fish Gate and around the hill of Ophel. He also increased its height. He tightened up the defense system by posting army captains in all the fortress cities of Judah. He also did a good spring cleaning on The Temple, carting out the pagan idols and the goddess statue. He took all the altars he had set up on The Temple hill and throughout Jerusalem and dumped them outside the city. He put the Altar of GOD back in working order and restored worship, sacrificing Peace-Offerings and Thank-Offerings. He issued orders to the people: "You shall serve and worship GOD, the God of Israel." But the people didn't take him seriously—they used the name "GOD" but kept on going to the old pagan neighborhood shrines and doing the same old things.

The rest of the history of Manasseh—his prayer to his God, and the sermons the prophets personally delivered by authority of GOD, the God of Israel—this is all written in *The Chronicles of the Kings of Israel.* His prayer and how God was touched by his prayer, a list of all his sins and the things he did wrong, the actual places where he built the pagan shrines, the installation of the sex-goddess Asherah sites, and the idolatrous images that he worshiped previous to his conversion—this is all described in the records of the prophets.

When Manasseh died, they buried him in the palace garden. His son Amon was the next king.

KING AMON

Amon was twenty-two years old when he became king. He was king for two years in Jerusalem. In GOD's opinion he lived an evil life, just like his father Manasseh, but he never did repent to GOD as Manasseh repented. He just kept at it, going from one thing to another.

In the end Amon's servants revolted and assassinated him—killed the king right in his own palace. The citizens in their turn then killed the king's assassins. The citizens then crowned Josiah, Amon's son, as king.

KING JOSIAH

34 Josiah was eight years old when he became king. He ruled for thirty-one years in Jerusalem. He behaved well before GOD. He kept straight on the path blazed by his ancestor David, not one step to the left or right.

When he had been king for eight years—he was still only a teenager—he began to seek the God of David his ancestor. Four years later, the twelfth year of his reign, he set out to cleanse the neighborhood of sex-and-religion shrines, and get rid of the sacred Asherah groves and the god and goddess figurines, whether carved or cast, from Judah. He wrecked the Baal shrines, tore down the altars connected with them, and scattered the debris and ashes over the graves of those who had worshiped at them. He burned the bones of the priests on the same altars they had used when alive. He scrubbed the place clean, Judah and Jerusalem, clean inside and out. The clean-up campaign ranged outward to the cities of Manasseh, Ephraim, Simeon, and the surrounding neighborhoods—as far north as Naphtali. Throughout Israel he demolished the altars and Asherah groves, pulverized the god and goddess figures, chopped up the neighborhood shrines into firewood. With Israel once more intact, he returned to Jerusalem.

One day in the eighteenth year of his kingship, with the cleanup of country and Temple complete, King Josiah sent Shaphan son of Azaliah, Maaseiah the mayor of the city, and Joah son of Joahaz the historian to renovate The Temple of God. First they turned over to Hilkiah the high priest all the money collected by the Levitical security guards from Manasseh and Ephraim and the rest of Israel, and from Judah and Benjamin and the citizens of Jerusalem. It was then put into the hands of the foremen managing the work on The Temple of God who then passed it on to the workers repairing God's Temple—the carpenters, construction workers, and masons—so they could buy the lumber and dressed stone for rebuilding the foundations the kings of Judah had allowed to fall to pieces. The workmen were honest and diligent. Their foremen were Jahath and Obadiah, the Merarite Levites, and Zechariah and Meshullam from the Kohathites—these managed the project. The Levites—they were all skilled musicians—were in charge of the common laborers and supervised the workers as they went from job to job. The Levites also served as accountants, managers, and security guards.

While the money that had been given for The Temple of God was being received and dispersed, Hilkiah the high priest found a copy of The Revelation of Moses. He reported to Shaphan the royal secretary, "I've just found the Book of God's Revelation, instructing us in God's way—found it in The Temple!" He gave it to Shaphan, who then gave it to the king. And along with the book, he gave this report: "The job is complete—everything you ordered done is done. They took all the money that was collected in The Temple of God and handed it over to the managers and workers."

And then Shaphan told the king, "Hilkiah the priest gave me a book." Shaphan proceeded to read it out to the king.

When the king heard what was written in the book, GOD's Revelation, he ripped his robes in dismay. And then he called for Hilkiah, Ahikam son of Shaphan, Abdon son of Micah, Shaphan the royal secretary, and Asaiah the king's personal aide. He ordered them all: "Go and pray to GOD for me and what's left of Israel and Judah. Find out what we must do in response to what is written in this book that has just been found! GOD's anger must be burning furiously against us—our ancestors haven't obeyed a thing written in this book of GOD, followed none of the instructions directed to us."

Hilkiah and those picked by the king went straight to Huldah the prophetess. She was the wife of Shallum son of Tokhath, the son of Hasrah, who was in charge of the palace wardrobe. She lived in Jerusalem in the Second Quarter. The men consulted with her. In response to them she said, "GOD's word, the God of Israel: Tell the man who sent you here, 'GOD has spoken, I'm on my way to bring the doom of judgment on this place and this people. Every word written in the book read by the king of Judah will happen. And why? Because they've deserted me and taken up with other gods; they've made me thoroughly angry by setting up their god-making businesses. My anger is raging white-hot against this place and nobody is going to put it out.'

"And also tell the king of Judah, since he sent you to ask GOD for direction, GOD's comment on what he read in the book: 'Because you took seriously the doom of judgment I spoke against this place and people, and because you responded in humble repentance, tearing your robe in dismay and weeping before me, I'm taking you seriously. GOD's word. I'll take care of you; you'll have a quiet death and be buried in peace. You won't be around to see the doom that I'm going to bring upon this place and people.'"

The men took her message back to the king.

The king acted immediately, assembling all the elders of Judah and Jerusalem, and then proceeding to The Temple of GOD bringing everyone in his train—priests and prophets and people ranging from the least to the greatest. Then he read out publicly everything written in the Book of the Covenant that was found in The Temple of GOD. The king stood by his pillar and before GOD solemnly committed himself to the covenant: to follow GOD believingly and obediently; to follow his instructions, heart and soul, on what to believe and do; to confirm with his life the entire covenant, all that was written in the book.

Then he made everyone in Jerusalem and Benjamin commit themselves. And they did it. They committed themselves to the covenant of God, the God of their ancestors.

Josiah did a thorough job of cleaning up the pollution that had spread throughout Israelite territory and got everyone started fresh again, serving and worshiping their GOD. All through Josiah's life the people kept to the straight and narrow, obediently following GOD, the God of their ancestors.

✠

35 Josiah celebrated the Passover to GOD in Jerusalem. They killed the Passover lambs on the fourteenth day of the first month. He gave the priests detailed instructions and encouraged them in the work of leading worship in The Temple of GOD. He also told the Levites who were in charge of teaching and guiding Israel in all matters of worship (they were especially consecrated for this), "Place the sacred Chest in The Temple that Solomon son of David, the king of Israel, built. You don't have to carry it around on your shoulders any longer! Serve GOD and God's people Israel. Organize yourselves by families for your respective responsibilities, following the instructions left by David king of Israel and Solomon his son.

"Take your place in the sanctuary—a team of Levites for every grouping of your fellow citizens, the laity. Your job is to kill the Passover lambs, then consecrate yourselves and prepare the lambs so that everyone will be able to keep the Passover exactly as GOD commanded through Moses."

Josiah personally donated 30,000 sheep, lambs, and goats and 3,000 bulls—everything needed for the Passover celebration was there. His officials also pitched in on behalf of the people, including the priests and the Levites. Hilkiah, Zechariah, and Jehiel, leaders in The Temple of God, gave 2,600 lambs and 300 bulls to the priests for the Passover offerings. Conaniah, his brothers Shemaiah and Nethanel, along with the Levitical chiefs Hashabiah, Jeiel, and Jozabad, donated 5,000 lambs and 500 bulls to the Levites for the Passover offerings.

Preparations were complete for the service of worship; the priests took up their positions and the Levites were at their posts as instructed by the king. They killed the Passover lambs, and while the priests sprinkled the blood from the lambs, the Levites skinned them out.

Then they set aside the Whole-Burnt-Offering for presentation to the family groupings of the people so that each group could offer it to GOD following the instructions in the Book of Moses. They did the same with the cattle. They roasted the Passover lamb according to the instructions and boiled the consecrated offerings in pots and kettles and pans and promptly served the people.

After the people had eaten the holy meal, the Levites served themselves and the Aaronite priests—the priests were busy late into the night making the offerings at the Altar.

The Asaph singers were all in their places following the instructions of David, Asaph, Heman, and Jeduthun the king's seer. The security guards were on duty at each gate—the Levites also served them because they couldn't leave their posts.

Everything went without a hitch in the worship of GOD that day as they celebrated the Passover and the offering of the Whole-Burnt-Offering on the Altar of GOD. It went just as Josiah had ordered. The Israelites celebrated the Passover, also known as the Feast of Unraised Bread, for seven days. The Passover hadn't been celebrated like this since the days of Samuel the prophet. None of the kings had done it. But Josiah, the priests, the Levites, all Judah and Israel who were there that week, plus the citizens of Jerusalem—*they* did it. In the eighteenth year of the rule of King Josiah, this Passover was celebrated.

✠

Some time later, after Josiah's reformation of The Temple, Neco king of Egypt marched out toward Carchemish on the Euphrates River on his way to war. Josiah went out to fight him.

Neco sent messengers to Josiah saying, "What do we have against each other, O king of Judah? I haven't come to fight against you but against the country with whom I'm at war. God commanded me to hurry, so don't get in my way; you'll only interfere with God, who is on my side in this, and he'll destroy you."

But Josiah was spoiling for a fight and wouldn't listen to a thing Neco said (in actuality it was God who said it). Though King Josiah disguised himself when they met on the plain of Megiddo, archers shot him anyway.

The king said to his servants, "Get me out of here—I'm badly wounded."

So his servants took him out of his chariot and laid him down in an ambulance chariot and drove him back to Jerusalem. He died there and was buried in the family cemetery. Everybody in Judah and Jerusalem attended the funeral. Jeremiah composed an anthem of lament for Josiah. The anthem is still sung by the choirs of Israel to this day. The anthem is written in the Laments.

The rest of the history of Josiah, his exemplary and devout life, conformed to The Revelation of GOD. The whole story, from start to finish, is written in the *Royal Annals of the Kings of Israel and Judah*. By popular choice, Jehoahaz son of Josiah was made king at Jerusalem, succeeding his father.

KING JEHOAHAZ

36 Jehoahaz was twenty-three years old when he began to rule. He was king in Jerusalem for a mere three months. The king of Egypt dethroned him and forced the country to pay him nearly four tons of silver and seventy-five pounds of gold.

KING JEHOIAKIM

Neco king of Egypt then made Eliakim, Jehoahaz's brother, king of Judah and Jerusalem, but changed his name to Jehoiakim; then he took Jehoahaz back with him to Egypt.

Jehoiakim was twenty-five years old when he began to rule; he was king for eleven years in Jerusalem. In GOD's opinion he was an evil king.

Nebuchadnezzar king of Babylon made war against him, and bound him in bronze chains, intending to take him prisoner to Babylon. Nebuchadnezzar also took things from The Temple of GOD to Babylon and put them in his royal palace.

The rest of the history of Jehoiakim, the outrageous sacrilege he committed and what happened to him as a consequence, is all written in the *Royal Annals of the Kings of Israel and Judah*.

Jehoiachin his son became the next king.

KING JEHOIACHIN

Jehoiachin was eighteen years old when he became king. But he ruled for only three months and ten days in Jerusalem. In GOD's opinion he was an evil king. In the spring King Nebuchadnezzar ordered him brought to Babylon along with the valuables remaining in The Temple of GOD. Then he made his uncle Zedekiah a puppet king over Judah and Jerusalem.

KING ZEDEKIAH

Zedekiah was twenty-one years old when he started out as king. He was king in Jerusalem for eleven years. As far as GOD was concerned, he was just one more evil king; there wasn't a trace of contrition in him when the prophet Jeremiah preached GOD's word to him. Then he compounded his troubles by rebelling against King Nebuchadnezzar, who earlier had made him swear in God's name that he would be loyal. He became set in his own stubborn ways—he never gave GOD a thought; repentance never entered his mind.

The evil mindset spread to the leaders and priests and filtered down to the people—it kicked off an epidemic of evil, repeating the abominations of the pagans and polluting The Temple of GOD so recently consecrated in Jerusalem.

GOD, the God of their ancestors, repeatedly sent warning messages to them. Out of compassion for both his people and his Temple he wanted to give them every chance possible. But they wouldn't listen; they poked fun at God's messengers, despised the message itself, and in general treated the prophets like idiots. GOD became more and more angry until there was no turning back—GOD called in Nebuchadnezzar king of Babylon, who came and killed indiscriminately—and right in The Temple itself; it was a ruthless massacre: young men and virgins, the elderly and weak—they were all the same to him.

And then he plundered The Temple of everything valuable, cleaned it out completely; he emptied the treasuries of The Temple of God, the treasuries of the king and his officials, and hauled it all, people and possessions, off to Babylon. He burned The Temple of God to the ground, knocked down the wall of Jerusalem, and set fire to all the buildings—everything valuable was burned up. Any survivor was taken prisoner into exile in Babylon and made a slave to Nebuchadnezzar and his family. The exile and slavery lasted until the kingdom of Persia took over.

This is exactly the message of GOD that Jeremiah had preached: the desolate land put to an extended sabbath rest, a seventy-year Sabbath rest making up for all the unkept Sabbaths.

KING CYRUS

In the first year of Cyrus king of Persia—this fulfilled the message of GOD preached by Jeremiah—GOD moved Cyrus king of Persia to make an official announcement throughout his kingdom; he wrote it out as follows: "From Cyrus king of Persia a proclamation: GOD, the God of the heavens, has given me all the kingdoms of the earth. He has also assigned me to build him a Temple of worship at Jerusalem in Judah. All who belong to GOD's people are urged to return—and may your GOD be with you! Move forward!"

EZRA

History had not treated the People of Israel well and they were in decline. A superpower military machine, Babylon, had battered them and then, leaving their city and temple a mound of rubble, hauled them off into exile. Now, 128 years later, a few Jews back in Jerusalem had been trying to put the pieces back together decade after weary decade. But it was not going well at all. They were hanging on by their fingernails. And then Ezra arrived.

This is an extreme case of a familiar story, repeated with variations in most centuries and in most places in the world. Men and women who find their basic identity in God, as God reveals himself in Israel and Messiah, don't find an easy time of it. They never have. They never will. Their identity is under constant challenge and threat—sometimes by hostile assault, at other times by subtle and smiling seductions. Whether by assault or seduction, the People of God have come perilously close to obliteration several times. We are never out of danger.

Because of Ezra, Israel made it through. God didn't leave Ezra to do this single-handedly; he gave him substantial and critical help in the rescue operation in the person of Nehemiah, whose work providentially converged with his. (Important details of the Ezra story are in the memoirs of Nehemiah, the book that follows this one.) The People-of-God identity was recovered and preserved. Ezra used Worship and Text to do it. Ezra engaged them in the worship of God, the most all-absorbing, comprehensive act in which men and women can engage. This is how our God-formed identities become most deeply embedded in us. And Ezra led them into an obedient listening to the text of Scripture. Listening and following God's revelation are the primary ways in which we keep attentively obedient to the living presence of God among us.

Ezra made his mark: Worship and Text continue to be foundational for recovering and maintaining identity as the People of God.

EZRA

1 In the first year of Cyrus king of Persia—this fulfilled the Message of GOD preached by Jeremiah—GOD prodded Cyrus king of Persia to make an official announcement throughout his kingdom. He wrote it out as follows:

From Cyrus king of Persia, a Proclamation: GOD, the God of the heavens, has given me all the kingdoms of the earth. He has also assigned me to build him a Temple of worship in Jerusalem, Judah. Who among you belongs to his people? God be with you! Go to Jerusalem which is in Judah and build The Temple of GOD, the God of Israel, Jerusalem's God. Those who stay behind, wherever they happen to live, will support them with silver, gold, tools, and pack animals, along with Freewill-Offerings for The Temple of God in Jerusalem.

The heads of the families of Judah and Benjamin, along with the priests and Levites—everyone, in fact, God prodded—set out to build The Temple of GOD in Jerusalem. Their neighbors rallied behind them enthusiastically with silver, gold, tools, pack animals, expensive gifts, and, over and above these, Freewill-Offerings.

Also, King Cyrus turned over to them all the vessels and utensils from The Temple of GOD that Nebuchadnezzar had hauled from Jerusalem and put in the temple of his gods. Cyrus king of Persia put Mithredath the treasurer in charge of the transfer; he provided a full inventory for Sheshbazzar the prince of Judah, including the following:

30 gold dishes
1,000 silver dishes
29 silver pans
30 gold bowls
410 duplicate silver bowls
1,000 miscellaneous items.

All told, there were 5,400 gold and silver articles that Sheshbazzar took with him when he brought the exiles back from Babylon to Jerusalem.

2 These are the people from the province who now returned from the captivity, exiles whom Nebuchadnezzar king of Babylon had carried off captive. They returned to Jerusalem and Judah, each to his home town. They came in company with Zerubbabel, Jeshua, Nehemiah, Seraiah, Reelaiah, Mordecai, Bilshan, Mispar, Bigvai, Rehum, and Baanah.

The numbers of the returning Israelites by families of origin were as follows:

> Parosh, 2,172
> Shephatiah, 372
> Arah, 775
> Pahath-Moab (sons of Jeshua and Joab), 2,812
> Elam, 1,254
> Zattu, 945
> Zaccai, 760
> Bani, 642
> Bebai, 623
> Azgad, 1,222
> Adonikam, 666
> Bigvai, 2,056
> Adin, 454
> Ater (sons of Hezekiah), 98
> Bezai, 323
> Jorah, 112
> Hashum, 223
> Gibbar, 95.

Israelites identified by place of origin were as follows:
> Bethlehem, 123
> Netophah, 56
> Anathoth, 128
> Azmaveth, 42
> Kiriath Jearim, Kephirah, and Beeroth, 743
> Ramah and Geba, 621
> Micmash, 122
> Bethel and Ai, 223
> Nebo, 52

Magbish, 156
Elam (the other one), 1,254
Harim, 320
Lod, Hadid, and Ono, 725
Jericho, 345
Senaah, 3,630.
Priestly families:
Jedaiah (sons of Jeshua), 973
Immer, 1,052
Pashhur, 1,247
Harim, 1,017.
Levitical families:
Jeshua and Kadmiel (sons of Hodaviah), 74.
Singers:
Asaph's family line, 128.
Security guard families:
Shallum, Ater, Talmon, Akkub, Hatita, and Shobai, 139.
Families of temple support staff:
Ziha, Hasupha, Tabbaoth,
Keros, Siaha, Padon,
Lebanah, Hagabah, Akkub,
Hagab, Shalmai, Hanan,
Giddel, Gahar, Reaiah,
Rezin, Nekoda, Gazzam,
Uzza, Paseah, Besai,
Asnah, Meunim, Nephussim,
Bakbuk, Hakupha, Harhur,
Bazluth, Mehida, Harsha,
Barkos, Sisera, Temah,
Neziah, and Hatipha.
Families of Solomon's servants:
Sotai, Hassophereth, Peruda,
Jaala, Darkon, Giddel,
Shephatiah, Hattil, Pokereth-Hazzebaim, and Ami.
Temple support staff and Solomon's servants added up to 392.

These are those who came from Tel Melah, Tel Harsha, Kerub, Addon, and Immer. They weren't able to prove their ancestry, whether they were true Israelites or not:

Delaiah, Tobiah, and Nekoda, 652 in all.
Likewise with these priestly families:
Hobaiah, Hakkoz, and Barzillai, who had married a daughter of Barzillai the Gileadite and took that name.

They had thoroughly searched for their family records but couldn't find them. And so they were barred from priestly work as ritually unclean. The governor ruled that they could not eat from the holy food until a priest could determine their status with the Urim and Thummim.

The total count for the congregation was 42,360. That did not include the male and female slaves, which numbered 7,337. There were also 200 male and female singers, and they had 736 horses, 245 mules, 435 camels, and 6,720 donkeys.

✛

Some of the heads of families, on arriving at The Temple of GOD in Jerusalem, made Freewill-Offerings toward the rebuilding of The Temple of God on its site. They gave to the building fund as they were able, about 1,100 pounds of gold, about three tons of silver, and 100 priestly robes.

The priests, Levites, and some of the people lived in Jerusalem. The singers, security guards, and temple support staff found places in their home towns. All the Israelites found a place to live.

THE BUILDING BEGUN: "THE FOUNDATION OF THE TEMPLE WAS LAID"

3 When the seventh month came and the Israelites had settled into their towns, the people assembled together in Jerusalem. Jeshua son of Jozadak and his brother priests, along with Zerubbabel, the son of Shealtiel, and his relatives, went to work and built the Altar of the God of Israel to offer Whole-Burnt-Offerings on it as written in The Revelation of Moses the man of God.

Even though they were afraid of what their non-Israelite neighbors might do, they went ahead anyway and set up the Altar on its foundations and offered Whole-Burnt-Offerings on it morning and evening. They also celebrated the Festival of Booths as prescribed and the daily Whole-Burnt-Offerings set for each day. And they presented the regular Whole-Burnt-Offerings for Sabbaths, New Moons, and GOD's Holy Festivals, as well as Freewill-Offerings for GOD.

They began offering Whole-Burnt-Offerings to GOD from the very first day of the seventh month, even though The Temple of GOD's foundation had not yet been laid.

They gave money to hire masons and carpenters. They gave food, drink, and oil to the Sidonians and Tyrians in exchange for the cedar lumber they had brought by sea from Lebanon to Joppa, a shipment authorized by Cyrus the king of Persia.

In the second month of the second year after their arrival at The Temple of God in Jerusalem, Zerubbabel son of Shealtiel, and Jeshua son of Jozadak, in company with their brother priests and Levites and everyone else who had come back to Jerusalem from captivity, got started. They appointed the Levites twenty years of age and older to direct the rebuilding of The Temple of GOD. Jeshua and his family joined Kadmiel, Binnui, and Hodaviah, along with the extended family of Henadad—all Levites—to direct the work crew on The Temple of God.

When the workers laid the foundation of The Temple of GOD, the priests in their robes stood up with trumpets, and the Levites, sons of Asaph, with cymbals, to praise GOD in the tradition of David king of Israel. They sang antiphonally praise and thanksgiving to GOD:

Yes! GOD is good!
Oh yes—he'll never quit loving Israel!

All the people boomed out hurrahs, praising GOD as the foundation of The Temple of GOD was laid. As many were noisily shouting with joy, many of the older priests, Levites, and family heads who had seen the first Temple, when they saw the foundations of this Temple laid, wept loudly for joy. People couldn't distinguish the shouting from the weeping. The sound of their voices reverberated for miles around.

THE BUILDING STOPPED: CEASE REBUILDING IN THAT CITY

4 Old enemies of Judah and Benjamin heard that the exiles were building The Temple of the GOD of Israel. They came to Zerubbabel and the family heads and said, "We'll help you build. We worship your God the same as you. We've been offering sacrifices to him since Esarhaddon king of Assyria brought us here."

Zerubbabel, Jeshua, and the rest of the family heads of Israel said to them, "Nothing doing. Building The Temple of our God is not the same thing to you as to us. We alone will build for the GOD of Israel. We're the ones King Cyrus of Persia commanded to do it."

So these people started beating down the morale of the people of Judah, harassing them as they built. They even hired propagandists to sap their resolve. They kept this up for about fifteen years, throughout the lifetime of Cyrus king of Persia and on into the reign of Darius king of Persia.

In fact, in the reign of Xerxes, at the beginning of his reign, they wrote an accusation against those living in Judah and Jerusalem.

Again later, in the time of Artaxerxes, Bishlam, Mithredath, Tabeel, and their associates wrote regarding the Jerusalem business to Artaxerxes king of Persia. The letter was written in Aramaic and translated. (What follows is written in Aramaic.)

Rehum the commanding officer and Shimshai the secretary wrote a letter against Jerusalem to Artaxerxes the king as follows:

From: Rehum the commanding officer and Shimshai the secretary, backed by the rest of their associates, the judges and officials over the people from Tripolis, Persia, Erech, and Babylon, Elamites of Susa, and all the others whom the great and honorable Ashurbanipal deported and settled in the city of Samaria and other places in the land across the Euphrates.

(This is the copy of the letter they sent to him.)

To: King Artaxerxes from your servants from the land across the Euphrates.

We are here to inform the king that the Jews who came from you to us have arrived in Jerusalem and have set about rebuilding that rebellious and evil city. They are busy at work finishing the walls and rebuilding the foundations. The king needs to know that once that city is rebuilt and the wall completed they will no longer pay a penny of tribute, tax, or duty. The royal treasury will feel the loss. We're loyal to the king and cannot sit idly by while our king is being insulted—that's why we are passing this information on. We suggest that you look into the court records of your ancestors; you'll learn from those books that that city is a rebellious city, a thorn in the side to kings and provinces, an historic center of unrest and revolt. That's why the city was wiped out. We are letting the king know that if that city gets rebuilt and its walls restored, you'll end up with nothing in your province beyond the Euphrates.

The king sent his reply to Rehum the commanding officer, Shimshai the secretary, and the rest of their associates who lived in Samaria and other places beyond the Euphrates.

Peace be with you. The letter that you sent has been translated and read to me. I gave orders to search the records, and sure enough it turns out that this city has revolted against kings time and again—rebellion is an old story there. I find that they've had their share of strong kings who have taken over beyond the Euphrates and exacted taxes, tribute, and duty. So do this: Order these men to stop work immediately—not a lick of rebuilding in that city unless I order it. Act quickly and firmly; they've done enough damage to kings!

The letter of King Artaxerxes was read to Rehum and Shimshai the secretary and their associates. They lost no time. They went to the Jews in Jerusalem and made them quit work.

That put a stop to the work on The Temple of God in Jerusalem. Nothing more was done until the second year of the reign of Darius king of Persia.

THE BUILDING RESUMED: "HELP THE LEADERS IN THE REBUILDING"

5 Meanwhile the prophets Haggai and Zechariah son of Iddo were preaching to the Jews in Judah and Jerusalem in the authority of the God of Israel who ruled them. And so Zerubbabel son of Shealtiel and Jeshua son of Jozadak started again, rebuilding The Temple of God in Jerusalem. The prophets of God were right there helping them.

Tattenai was governor of the land beyond the Euphrates at this time. Tattenai, Shethar-Bozenai, and their associates came to the Israelites and asked, "Who issued you a permit to rebuild this Temple and restore it to use?" Then we told them the names of the men responsible for this construction work.

But God had his eye on the leaders of the Jews, and the work wasn't stopped until a report could reach Darius and an official reply be returned.

Tattenai, governor of the land beyond the Euphrates, and Shethar-Bozenai and his associates—the officials of that land—sent a letter to Darius the king. This is what they wrote to him:

To Darius the king. Peace and blessing!

We want to report to the king that we went to the province of Judah, to The Temple of the great God that is being rebuilt with large stones. Timbers are being fitted into the walls; the work is going on with great energy and in good time.

We asked the leaders, "Who issued you the permit to rebuild this Temple and restore it to use?" We also asked for their names so we could pass them on to you and have a record of the men at the head of the construction work.

This is what they told us: "We are servants of the God of the heavens and the earth. We are rebuilding The Temple that was built a long time ago. A great king of Israel built it, the entire structure. But our ancestors made the God of the heavens really angry and he turned them over to Nebuchadnezzar, king of Babylon, the Chaldean, who knocked this Temple down and took the people to Babylon in exile.

"But when Cyrus became king of Babylon, in his first year he issued a building permit to rebuild this Temple of God. He also gave back the gold and silver vessels of The Temple of God that Nebuchadnezzar had carted off and put in the Babylon temple. Cyrus the king removed them from the temple of Babylon and turned them over to Sheshbazzar, the man he had appointed governor. He told him, 'Take these vessels and place them in The Temple of Jerusalem and rebuild The Temple of God on its original site.' And Sheshbazzar did it. He laid the foundation of The Temple of God in Jerusalem. It has been under construction ever since but it is not yet finished."

So now, if it please the king, look up the records in the royal archives in Babylon and see if it is indeed a fact that Cyrus the king issued an official building permit authorizing the rebuilding of The Temple of God in Jerusalem. And then send the king's ruling on this matter to us.

6 So King Darius ordered a search through the records in the archives in Babylon. Eventually a scroll was turned up in the fortress of Ecbatana over in the province of Media, with this writing on it:

Memorandum

In his first year as king, Cyrus issued an official decree regarding The Temple of God in Jerusalem, as follows:

The Temple where sacrifices are offered is to be rebuilt on new foundations. It is to be ninety feet high and ninety feet wide with three courses of large stones topped with one course of timber. The cost is to be paid from the royal bank. The gold and silver vessels from The Temple of God that Nebuchadnezzar carried to Babylon are to be returned to The Temple at Jerusalem, each to its proper place; place them in The Temple of God.

Now listen, Tattenai governor of the land beyond the Euphrates, Shethar-Bozenai, associates, and all officials of that land: Stay out of their way. Leave the governor and leaders of the Jews alone so they can work on that Temple of God as they rebuild it.

I hereby give official orders on how you are to help the leaders of the Jews in the rebuilding of that Temple of God:

1. All construction costs are to be paid to these men from the royal bank out of the taxes coming in from the land beyond the Euphrates. And pay them on time, without delays.

2. Whatever is required for their worship—young bulls, rams, and lambs for Whole-Burnt-Offerings to the God-of-Heaven; and whatever wheat, salt, wine, and anointing oil the priests of Jerusalem request—is to be given to them daily without delay so that they may make sacrifices to the God-of-Heaven and pray for the life of the king and his sons.

I've issued an official decree that anyone who violates this order is to be impaled on a timber torn out of his own house, and the house itself made a manure pit. And may the God who put his Name on that place wipe out any king or people who dares to defy this decree and destroy The Temple of God at Jerusalem.

I, Darius, have issued an official decree. Carry it out precisely and promptly.

Tattenai governor of the land across the Euphrates, Shethar-Bozenai, and their associates did it: They carried out the decree of Darius precisely and promptly.

THE BUILDING COMPLETED:
"EXUBERANTLY CELEBRATED THE DEDICATION"

So the leaders of the Jews continued to build; the work went well under the preaching of the prophets Haggai and Zechariah son of Iddo. They completed the rebuilding under orders of the God of Israel and authorization by Cyrus, Darius, and Artaxerxes, kings of Persia. The Temple was completed on the third day of the month Adar in the sixth year of the reign of King Darius.

And then the Israelites celebrated—priests, Levites, every last exile, exuberantly celebrated the dedication of The Temple of God. At the dedication of this Temple of God they sacrificed a hundred bulls, two hundred rams, and four hundred lambs—and, as an Absolution-Offering for all Israel, twelve he-goats, one for each of the twelve tribes of Israel. They placed the priests in their divisions and the Levites in their places for the service of God at Jerusalem—all as written out in the Book of Moses.

✝

On the fourteenth day of the first month, the exiles celebrated the Passover.

All the priests and Levites had purified themselves—all, no exceptions. They were all ritually clean. The Levites slaughtered the Passover lamb for the exiles, their brother priests, and themselves.

Then the Israelites who had returned from exile, along with everyone who had removed themselves from the defilements of the nations to join them and seek GOD, the God of Israel, ate the Passover. With great joy they celebrated the Feast of Unraised Bread for seven days. GOD had plunged them into a sea of joy; he had changed the mind of the king of Assyria to back them in rebuilding The Temple of God, the God of Israel.

EZRA ARRIVES

7 After all this, Ezra. It was during the reign of Artaxerxes king of Persia. Ezra was the son of Seraiah, son of Azariah, son of Hilkiah, son of Shallum, son of Zadok, son of Ahitub, son of Amariah, son of Azariah, son of Meraioth, son of Zerahiah, son of Uzzi, son of Bukki, son of Abishua, son of Phinehas, son of Eleazar, son of Aaron the high priest.

That's Ezra. He arrived from Babylon, a scholar well-practiced in the Revelation of Moses that the GOD of Israel had given. Because GOD's hand was on Ezra, the king gave him everything he asked for. Some of the Israelites—priests, Levites, singers, temple security guards, and temple slaves—went with him to Jerusalem. It was in the seventh year of Artaxerxes the king.

They arrived at Jerusalem in the fifth month of the seventh year of the king's reign. Ezra had scheduled their departure from Babylon on the first day of the first month; they arrived in Jerusalem on the first day of the fifth month under the generous guidance of his God. Ezra had committed himself to studying the Revelation of GOD, to living it, and to teaching Israel to live its truths and ways.

✝

What follows is the letter that King Artaxerxes gave Ezra, priest and scholar, expert in matters involving the truths and ways of GOD concerning Israel:

> Artaxerxes, King of Kings, to Ezra the priest, a scholar of the Teaching of the God-of-Heaven.
>
> Peace. I hereby decree that any of the people of Israel living in my kingdom who want to go to Jerusalem, including their priests and Levites, may go with you. You are being sent by the king and his seven advisors to carry out an investigation of Judah and Jerusalem in relation to the Teaching of your God that you are carrying with you. You are also authorized to take the silver and gold that the king and his advisors are giving for the God of Israel, whose residence is in Jerusalem, along with all the silver and gold that has been collected from the generously donated offerings all over Babylon, including that from the people and the priests, for The Temple of their God in Jerusalem. Use this money carefully to buy bulls, rams, lambs, and the ingredients for Grain-Offerings and Drink-Offerings

. and then offer them on the Altar of The Temple of your God in Jerusalem. You are free to use whatever is left over from the silver and gold for what you and your brothers decide is in keeping with the will of your God. Deliver to the God of Jerusalem the vessels given to you for the services of worship in The Temple of your God. Whatever else you need for The Temple of your God you may pay for out of the royal bank.

I, Artaxerxes the king, have formally authorized and ordered all the treasurers of the land across the Euphrates to give Ezra the priest, scholar of the Teaching of the God-of-Heaven, the full amount of whatever he asks for up to a hundred talents of silver, six hundred and fifty bushels of wheat, and six hundred and seven gallons each of wine and olive oil. There is no limit on the salt. Everything the God-of-Heaven requires for The Temple of God must be given without hesitation. Why would the king and his sons risk stirring up his wrath?

Also, let it be clear that no one is permitted to impose tribute, tax, or duty on any priest, Levite, singer, temple security guard, temple servant, or any other worker connected with The Temple of God.

I authorize you, Ezra, exercising the wisdom of God that you have in your hands, to appoint magistrates and judges so they can administer justice among all the people of the land across the Euphrates who live by the Teaching of your God. Anyone who does not know the Teaching, you teach them.

Anyone who does not obey the Teaching of your God and the king must be tried and sentenced at once — death, banishment, a fine, prison, whatever.

EZRA: "I WAS READY TO GO"

Blessed be GOD, the God-of-Our-Fathers, who put it in the mind of the king to beautify The Temple of GOD in Jerusalem! Not only that, he caused the king and all his advisors and influential officials actually to like me and back me. My God was on my side and I was ready to go. And I organized all the leaders of Israel to go with me.

8 These are the family heads and those who signed up to go up with me from Babylon in the reign of Artaxerxes the king:

From the family of Phinehas: Gershom
Family of Ithamar: Daniel
Family of David: Hattush
Family of Shecaniah
Family of Parosh: Zechariah, and with him 150 men signed up
Family of Pahath-Moab: Eliehoenai son of Zerahiah, and 200 men
Family of Zattu: Shecaniah son of Jahaziel, and 300 men
Family of Adin: Ebed son of Jonathan, and 50 men
Family of Elam: Jeshaiah son of Athaliah, and 70 men
Family of Shephatiah: Zebadiah son of Michael, and 80 men
Family of Joab: Obadiah son of Jehiel, and 218 men
Family of Bani: Shelomith son of Josiphiah, and 160 men
Family of Bebai: Zechariah son of Bebai, and 28 men
Family of Azgad: Johanan son of Hakkatan, and 110 men
Family of Adonikam (bringing up the rear): their names were
    Eliphelet, Jeuel, Shemaiah, and 60 men
Family of Bigvai: Uthai and Zaccur, and 70 men.

I gathered them together at the canal that runs to Ahava. We camped there three days. I looked them over and found that they were all laymen and priests but no Levites. So I sent for the leaders Eliezer, Ariel, Shemaiah, Elnathan, Jarib, Elnathan, Nathan, Zechariah, and Meshullam, and for the teachers Joiarib and Elnathan. I then sent them to Iddo, who is head of the town of Casiphia, and told them what to say to Iddo and his relatives who lived there in Casiphia: "Send us ministers for The Temple of God."

Well, the generous hand of our God was on us, and they brought back to us a wise man from the family of Mahli son of Levi, the son of Israel. His name was Sherebiah. With sons and brothers they numbered eighteen. They also brought Hashabiah and Jeshaiah of the family of Merari, with brothers and their sons, another twenty. And then there were 220 temple servants, descendants of the temple servants that David and the princes had assigned to help the Levites in their work. They were all signed up by name.

I proclaimed a fast there beside the Ahava Canal, a fast to humble ourselves before our God and pray for wise guidance for our journey— all our people and possessions. I was embarrassed to ask the king for a cavalry bodyguard to protect us from bandits on the road. We had just told the king, "Our God lovingly looks after all those who seek

him, but turns away in disgust from those who leave him."
So we fasted and prayed about these concerns. And he listened.

Then I picked twelve of the leading priests—Sherebiah and
Hashabiah with ten of their brothers. I weighed out for them the silver,
the gold, the vessels, and the offerings for The Temple of our God that
the king, his advisors, and all the Israelites had given:

> 25 tons of silver
> 100 vessels of silver valued at three and three-quarter tons
> three and three-quarter tons of gold
> 20 gold bowls weighing eighteen and a half pounds
> 2 vessels of bright red copper, as valuable as gold.

I said to them, "You are holy to GOD and these vessels are holy. The
silver and gold are Freewill-Offerings to the GOD of your ancestors.
Guard them with your lives until you're able to weigh them out in a
secure place in The Temple of our God for the priests and Levites and
family heads who are in charge in Jerusalem."
The priests and Levites took charge of all that had been weighed out
to them, and prepared to deliver it to Jerusalem to The Temple of our God.

We left the Ahava Canal on the twelfth day of the first month to
travel to Jerusalem. God was with us all the way and kept us safe from
bandits and highwaymen.
We arrived in Jerusalem and waited there three days. On the fourth
day the silver and gold and vessels were weighed out in The Temple of
our God into the hands of Meremoth son of Uriah, the priest. Eleazar
son of Phinehas was there with him, also the Levites Jozabad son of
Jeshua and Noadiah son of Binnui. Everything was counted and
weighed and the totals recorded.

When they arrived, the exiles, now returned from captivity, offered
Whole-Burnt-Offerings to the God of Israel:

> 12 bulls, representing all Israel
> 96 rams
> 77 lambs
> 12 he-goats as an Absolution-Offering.

All of this was sacrificed as a Whole-Burnt-Offering to God.

They also delivered the king's orders to the king's provincial administration assigned to the land beyond the Euphrates. They, in turn, gave their support to the people and The Temple of God.

Ezra Prays: "Look at Us . . . Guilty Before You"

9 After all this was done, the leaders came to me and said, "The People of Israel, priests and Levites included, have not kept themselves separate from the neighboring people around here with all their vulgar obscenities—Canaanites, Hittites, Perizzites, Jebusites, Ammonites, Moabites, Egyptians, Amorites. They have given some of their daughters in marriage to them and have taken some of their daughters for marriage to their sons. The holy seed is now all mixed in with these other peoples. And our leaders have led the way in this betrayal."

When I heard all this, I ripped my clothes and my cape; I pulled hair from my head and out of my beard; I slumped to the ground, appalled.

Many were in fear and trembling because of what God was saying about the betrayal by the exiles. They gathered around me as I sat there in despair, waiting for the evening sacrifice. At the evening sacrifice I picked myself up from my utter devastation, and in my ripped clothes and cape fell to my knees and stretched out my hands to God, my God. And I prayed:

"My dear God, I'm so totally ashamed, I can't bear to face you. O my God—our iniquities are piled up so high that we can't see out; our guilt touches the skies. We've been stuck in a muck of guilt since the time of our ancestors until right now; we and our kings and priests, because of our sins, have been turned over to foreign kings, to killing, to captivity, to looting, and to public shame—just as you see us now.

"Now for a brief time God, our God, has allowed us, this battered band, to get a firm foothold in his holy place so that our God may brighten our eyes and lighten our burdens as we serve out this hard sentence. We were slaves; yet even as slaves, our God didn't abandon us. He has put us in the good graces of the kings of Persia and given us the heart to build The Temple of our God, restore its ruins, and construct a defensive wall in Judah and Jerusalem.

"And now, our God, after all this what can we say for ourselves? For we have thrown your commands to the wind, the commands you gave us through your servants the prophets. They told us, 'The land you're taking over is a polluted land, polluted with the obscene vulgarities of the people who live there; they've filled it with their moral rot from one end to the other. Whatever you do, don't give your daughters in marriage to their sons nor marry your sons to their daughters. Don't cultivate their good opinion; don't make over them and get them to like you so you can make a lot of money and build up a tidy estate to hand down to your children.'

"And now this, on top of all we've already suffered because of our evil ways and accumulated guilt, even though you, dear God, punished us far less than we deserved and even went ahead and gave us this present escape. Yet here we are, at it again, breaking your commandments by intermarrying with the people who practice all these obscenities! Are you angry to the point of wiping us out completely, without even a few stragglers, with no way out at all? You are the righteous GOD of Israel. We are, right now, a small band of escapees. Look at us, openly standing here, guilty before you. No one can last long like this."

EZRA TAKES CHARGE

10 Ezra wept, prostrate in front of The Temple of God. As he prayed and confessed, a huge number of the men, women, and children of Israel gathered around him. All the people were now weeping as if their hearts would break.

Shecaniah son of Jehiel of the family of Elam, acting as spokesman, said to Ezra: "We betrayed our God by marrying foreign wives from the people around here. But all is not lost; there is still hope for Israel. Let's make a covenant right now with our God, agreeing to get rid of all these wives and their children, just as my master and those who honor God's commandment are saying. It's what The Revelation says, so let's do it.

"Now get up, Ezra. Take charge—we're behind you. Don't back down."

So Ezra stood up and had the leaders of the priests, the Levites, and all Israel solemnly swear to do what Shecaniah proposed. And they did it.

Then Ezra left the plaza in front of The Temple of God and went to the home of Jehohanan son of Eliashib where he stayed, still fasting from food and drink, continuing his mourning over the betrayal by the exiles.

✛

A notice was then sent throughout Judah and Jerusalem ordering all the exiles to meet in Jerusalem. Anyone who failed to show up in three days, in compliance with the ruling of the leaders and elders, would have all his possessions confiscated and be thrown out of the congregation of the returned exiles.

All the men of Judah and Benjamin met in Jerusalem within the three days. It was the twentieth day of the ninth month. They all sat down in the plaza in front of The Temple of God. Because of the business before them, and aggravated by the buckets of rain coming down on them, they were restless, uneasy, and anxious.

Ezra the priest stood up and spoke: "You've broken trust. You've married foreign wives. You've piled guilt on Israel. Now make your confession to GOD, the God of your ancestors, and do what he wants you to do: Separate yourselves from the people of the land and from your foreign wives."

The whole congregation responded with a shout, "Yes, we'll do it—just the way you said it!"

They also said, "But look, do you see how many people there are out here? And it's the rainy season; you can't expect us to stand out here soaking wet until this is done—why, it will take days! A lot of us are deeply involved in this transgression. Let our leaders act on behalf of the whole congregation. Have everybody who lives in cities and who has married a foreign wife come at an appointed time, accompanied by the elders and judges of each city. We'll keep at this until the hot anger of our God over this thing is turned away."

Only Jonathan son of Asahel and Jahzeiah son of Tikvah, supported by Meshullam and Shabbethai the Levite, opposed this. So the exiles went ahead with the plan. Ezra the priest picked men who were family heads, each one by name. They sat down together on the first day of the tenth month to pursue the matter. By the first day of the first month they had finished dealing with every man who had married a foreign wife.

✝

Among the families of priests, the following were found to have married foreign wives:

The family of Jeshua son of Jozadak and his brothers: Maaseiah, Eliezer, Jarib, and Gedaliah. They all promised to divorce their wives and sealed it with a handshake. For their guilt they brought a ram from the flock as a Compensation-Offering.

The family of Immer: Hanani and Zebadiah.

The family of Harim: Maaseiah, Elijah, Shemaiah, Jehiel, and Uzziah.

The family of Pashhur: Elioenai, Maaseiah, Ishmael, Nethanel, Jozabad, and Elasah.

From the Levites: Jozabad, Shimei, Kelaiah—that is, Kelita—Pethahiah, Judah, and Eliezer.

From the singers: Eliashib.

From the temple security guards: Shallum, Telem, and Uri.

And from the other Israelites:

The family of Parosh: Ramiah, Izziah, Malkijah, Mijamin, Eleazar, Malkijah, and Benaiah.

The family of Elam: Mattaniah, Zechariah, Jehiel, Abdi, Jeremoth, and Elijah.

The family of Zattu: Elioenai, Eliashib, Mattaniah, Jeremoth, Zabad, and Aziza.

The family of Bebai: Jehohanan, Hananiah, Zabbai, and Athlai.

The family of Bani: Meshullam, Malluch, Adaiah, Jashub, Sheal, and Jeremoth.

The family of Pahath-Moab: Adna, Kelal, Benaiah, Maaseiah, Mattaniah, Bezalel, Binnui, and Manasseh.

The family of Harim: Eliezer, Ishijah, Malkijah, Shemaiah, Shimeon, Benjamin, Malluch, and Shemariah.

The family of Hashum: Mattenai, Mattattah, Zabad, Eliphelet, Jeremai, Manasseh, and Shimei.

The family of Bani: Maadai, Amram, Uel, Benaiah, Bedeiah, Keluhi, Vaniah, Meremoth, Eliashib, Mattaniah, Mattenai, and Jaasu.

The family of Binnui: Shimei, Shelemiah, Nathan, Adaiah, Macnadebai, Shashai, Sharai, Azarel, Shelemiah, Shemariah, Shallum, Amariah, and Joseph.

The family of Nebo: Jeiel, Mattithiah, Zabad, Zebina, Jaddai, Joel, and Benaiah.

All these had married foreign wives and some had also had children by them.

NEHEMIAH

Separating life into distinct categories of "sacred" and "secular" damages, sometimes irreparably, any attempt to live a whole and satisfying life, a coherent life with meaning and purpose, a life lived to the glory of God. Nevertheless, the practice is widespread. But where did all these people come up with the habit of separating themselves and the world around them into these two camps? It surely wasn't from the Bible. The Holy Scriptures, from beginning to end, strenuously resist such a separation.

The damage to life is most obvious when the separation is applied to daily work. It is common for us to refer to the work of pastors, priests, and missionaries as "sacred," and that of lawyers, farmers, and engineers as "secular." It is also wrong. Work, by its very nature, is holy. The biblical story is dominated by people who have jobs in gardening, shepherding, the military, politics, carpentry, tent making, homemaking, fishing, and more.

Nehemiah is one of these. He started out as a government worker in the employ of a foreign king. Then he became — and this is the work he tells us of in these memoirs — a building contractor, called in to rebuild the walls of Jerusalem. His coworker Ezra was a scholar and teacher, working with the Scriptures. Nehemiah worked with stones and mortar. The stories of the two men are interwoven in a seamless fabric of vocational holiness. Neither job was more or less important or holy than the other. Nehemiah needed Ezra; Ezra needed Nehemiah. God's people needed the work of both of them. We still do.

NEHEMIAH

1 The memoirs of Nehemiah son of Hacaliah.

It was the month of Kislev in the twentieth year. At the time I was in the palace complex at Susa. Hanani, one of my brothers, had just arrived from Judah with some fellow Jews. I asked them about the conditions among the Jews there who had survived the exile, and about Jerusalem.

They told me, "The exile survivors who are left there in the province are in bad shape. Conditions are appalling. The wall of Jerusalem is still rubble; the city gates are still cinders."

When I heard this, I sat down and wept. I mourned for days, fasting and praying before the God-of-Heaven.

I said, "GOD, God-of-Heaven, the great and awesome God, loyal to his covenant and faithful to those who love him and obey his commands: Look at me, listen to me. Pay attention to this prayer of your servant that I'm praying day and night in intercession for your servants, the People of Israel, confessing the sins of the People of Israel. And I'm including myself, I and my ancestors, among those who have sinned against you.

"We've treated you like dirt: We haven't done what you told us, haven't followed your commands, and haven't respected the decisions you gave to Moses your servant. All the same, remember the warning you posted to your servant Moses: 'If you betray me, I'll scatter you to the four winds, but if you come back to me and do what I tell you, I'll gather up all these scattered peoples from wherever they ended up and put them back in the place I chose to mark with my Name.'

"Well, there they are—your servants, your people whom you so powerfully and impressively redeemed. O Master, listen to me, listen to your servant's prayer—and yes, to all your servants who delight in honoring you—and make me successful today so that I get what I want from the king."

I was cupbearer to the king.

2 It was the month of Nisan in the twentieth year of Artaxerxes the king. At the hour for serving wine I brought it in and gave it to the king. I had never been hangdog in his presence before, so he asked me, "Why the long face? You're not sick are you? Or are you depressed?"

That made me all the more agitated. I said, "Long live the king! And why shouldn't I be depressed when the city, the city where all my family is buried, is in ruins and the city gates have been reduced to cinders?"

The king then asked me, "So what do you want?"

Praying under my breath to the God-of-Heaven, I said, "If it please the king, and if the king thinks well of me, send me to Judah, to the city where my family is buried, so that I can rebuild it."

The king, with the queen sitting alongside him, said, "How long will your work take and when would you expect to return?"

I gave him a time, and the king gave his approval to send me.

Then I said, "If it please the king, provide me with letters to the governors across the Euphrates that authorize my travel through to Judah; and also an order to Asaph, keeper of the king's forest, to supply me with timber for the beams of The Temple fortress, the wall of the city, and the house where I'll be living."

The generous hand of my God was with me in this and the king gave them to me. When I met the governors across The River (the Euphrates) I showed them the king's letters. The king even sent along a cavalry escort.

When Sanballat the Horonite and Tobiah the Ammonite official heard about this, they were very upset, angry that anyone would come to look after the interests of the People of Israel.

"COME—LET'S BUILD THE WALL OF JERUSALEM"

And so I arrived in Jerusalem. After I had been there three days, I got up in the middle of the night, I and a few men who were with me. I hadn't told anyone what my God had put in my heart to do for Jerusalem. The only animal with us was the one I was riding.

Under cover of night I went past the Valley Gate toward the Dragon's Fountain to the Dung Gate looking over the walls of Jerusalem, which had been broken through and whose gates had been burned up. I then crossed to the Fountain Gate and headed for the King's Pool but there wasn't enough room for the donkey I was riding to get through. So I went up the valley in the dark continuing my inspection of the wall. I came back in through the Valley Gate. The local officials had no idea where I'd gone or what I was doing—I hadn't breathed a word to the Jews, priests, nobles, local officials, or anyone else who would be working on the job.

Then I gave them my report: "Face it: we're in a bad way here. Jerusalem is a wreck; its gates are burned up. Come—let's build the wall of Jerusalem and not live with this disgrace any longer." I told them how God was supporting me and how the king was backing me up.

They said, "We're with you. Let's get started." They rolled up their sleeves, ready for the good work.

When Sanballat the Horonite, Tobiah the Ammonite official, and Geshem the Arab heard about it, they laughed at us, mocking, "Ha! What do you think you're doing? Do you think you can cross the king?"

I shot back, "The God-of-Heaven will make sure we succeed. We're his servants and we're going to work, rebuilding. You can keep your nose out of it. You get no say in this—Jerusalem's none of your business!"

✛

3 The high priest Eliashib and his fellow priests were up and at it: They went to work on the Sheep Gate; they repaired it and hung its doors, continuing on as far as the Tower of the Hundred and the Tower of Hananel. The men of Jericho worked alongside them; and next to them, Zaccur son of Imri.

The Fish Gate was built by the Hassenaah brothers; they repaired it, hung its doors, and installed its bolts and bars. Meremoth son of Uriah, the son of Hakkoz, worked; next to him Meshullam son of Berekiah, the son of Meshezabel; next to him Zadok son of Baana; and next to him the Tekoites (except for their nobles, who wouldn't work with their master and refused to get their hands dirty with such work).

The Jeshanah Gate was rebuilt by Joiada son of Paseah and Meshullam son of Besodeiah; they repaired it, hung its doors, and installed its bolts and bars. Melatiah the Gibeonite, Jadon the Meronothite, and the men of Gibeon and Mizpah, which was under the rule of the governor from across the Euphrates, worked alongside them. Uzziel son of Harhaiah of the goldsmiths' guild worked next to him, and next to him Hananiah, one of the perfumers. They rebuilt the wall of Jerusalem as far as the Broad Wall.

The next section was worked on by Rephaiah son of Hur, mayor of a half-district of Jerusalem. Next to him Jedaiah son of Harumaph rebuilt the front of his house; Hattush son of Hashabneiah worked next to him.

Malkijah son of Harim and Hasshub son of Pahath-Moab rebuilt another section that included the Tower of Furnaces. Working next to him was Shallum son of Hallohesh, mayor of the other half-district of Jerusalem, along with his daughters.

The Valley Gate was rebuilt by Hanun and villagers of Zanoah; they repaired it, hung its doors, and installed its bolts and bars. They went on to repair 1,500 feet of the wall, as far as the Dung Gate.

The Dung Gate itself was rebuilt by Malkijah son of Recab, the mayor of the district of Beth Hakkerem; he repaired it, hung its doors, and installed its bolts and bars.

The Fountain Gate was rebuilt by Shallun son of Col-Hozeh, mayor of the Mizpah district; he repaired it, roofed it, hung its doors, and installed its bolts and bars. He also rebuilt the wall of the Pool of Siloam at the King's Garden as far as the steps that go down from the City of David.

After him came Nehemiah son of Azbuk, mayor of half the district of Beth Zur. He worked from just in front of the Tomb of David as far as the Pool and the House of Heroes.

Levites under Rehum son of Bani were next in line. Alongside them, Hashabiah, mayor of half the district of Keilah, represented his district in the rebuilding. Next to him their brothers continued the rebuilding under Binnui son of Henadad, mayor of the other half-district of Keilah.

The section from in front of the Ascent to the Armory as far as the Angle was rebuilt by Ezer son of Jeshua, the mayor of Mizpah. From the Angle to the door of the house of Eliashib the high priest was done by Baruch son of Zabbai. Meremoth son of Uriah, the son of Hakkoz, took it from the door of Eliashib's house to the end of Eliashib's house. Priests from the neighborhood went on from there. Benjamin and Hasshub worked on the wall in front of their house, and Azariah son of Maaseiah, the son of Ananiah, did the work alongside his house.

The section from the house of Azariah to the Angle at the Corner was rebuilt by Binnui son of Henadad. Palal son of Uzai worked opposite the Angle and the tower that projects from the Upper Palace of the king near the Court of the Guard. Next to him Pedaiah son of Parosh and The Temple support staff who lived on the hill of Ophel worked up to the point opposite the Water Gate eastward and the projecting tower. The men of Tekoa did the section from the great projecting tower as far as the wall of Ophel.

Above the Horse Gate the priests worked, each priest repairing the wall in front of his own house. After them Zadok son of Immer rebuilt in front of his house and after him Shemaiah son of Shecaniah, the keeper of the East Gate; then Hananiah son of Shelemiah and Hanun, the sixth son of Zalaph; then Meshullam son of Berekiah rebuilt the wall in front of his storage shed.

Malkijah the goldsmith repaired the wall as far as the house of The Temple support staff and merchants, up to the Inspection Gate, and the Upper Room at the Corner. The goldsmiths and the merchants made the repairs between the Upper Room at the Corner and the Sheep Gate.

"I STATIONED ARMED GUARDS"

4 When Sanballat heard that we were rebuilding the wall he exploded in anger, vilifying the Jews. In the company of his Samaritan cronies and military he let loose: "What are these miserable Jews doing? Do they think they can get everything back to normal overnight? Make building stones out of make-believe?"

At his side, Tobiah the Ammonite jumped in and said, "That's right! What do they think they're building? Why, if a fox climbed that wall, it would fall to pieces under his weight."

Nehemiah prayed, "Oh listen to us, dear God. We're so despised: Boomerang their ridicule on their heads; have their enemies cart them off as war trophies to a land of no return; don't forgive their iniquity, don't wipe away their sin—they've insulted the builders!"

We kept at it, repairing and rebuilding the wall. The whole wall was soon joined together and halfway to its intended height because the people had a heart for the work.

When Sanballat, Tobiah, the Arabs, the Ammonites, and the Ashdodites heard that the repairs of the walls of Jerusalem were going so well—that the breaks in the wall were being fixed—they were absolutely furious. They put their heads together and decided to fight against Jerusalem and create as much trouble as they could. We countered with prayer to our God and set a round-the-clock guard against them.

But soon word was going around in Judah,

The builders are pooped,
 the rubbish piles up;
We're in over our heads,
 we can't build this wall.

And all this time our enemies were saying, "They won't know what hit them. Before they know it we'll be at their throats, killing them right and left. *That* will put a stop to the work!" The Jews who were their neighbors kept reporting, "They have us surrounded; they're going to attack!" If we heard it once, we heard it ten times.

So I stationed armed guards at the most vulnerable places of the wall and assigned people by families with their swords, lances, and bows. After looking things over I stood up and spoke to the nobles, officials, and everyone else: "Don't be afraid of them. Put your minds on the Master, great and awesome, and then fight for your brothers, your sons, your daughters, your wives, and your homes."

Our enemies learned that we knew all about their plan and that God had frustrated it. And we went back to the wall and went to work. From then on half of my young men worked while the other half stood guard with lances, shields, bows, and mail armor. Military officers served as backup for everyone in Judah who was at work rebuilding the wall. The common laborers held a tool in one hand and a spear in the other. Each of the builders had a sword strapped to his side as he worked. I kept the trumpeter at my side to sound the alert.

Then I spoke to the nobles and officials and everyone else: "There's a lot of work going on and we are spread out all along the wall, separated from each other. When you hear the trumpet call, join us there; our God will fight for us."

And so we kept working, from first light until the stars came out, half of us holding lances.

I also instructed the people, "Each person and his helper is to stay inside Jerusalem—guards by night and workmen by day."

We all slept in our clothes—I, my brothers, my workmen, and the guards backing me up. And each one kept his spear in his hand, even when getting water.

The "Great Protest"

5 A great protest was mounted by the people, including the wives, against their fellow Jews. Some said, "We have big families, and we need food just to survive."

Others said, "We're having to mortgage our fields and vineyards and homes to get enough grain to keep from starving."

And others said, "We're having to borrow money to pay the royal tax on our fields and vineyards. Look: We're the same flesh and blood as our brothers here; our children are just as good as theirs. Yet here we are having to sell our children off as slaves—some of our daughters have already been sold—and we can't do anything about it because our fields and vineyards are owned by somebody else."

I got really angry when I heard their protest and complaints. After thinking it over, I called the nobles and officials on the carpet. I said, "Each one of you is gouging his brother."

Then I called a big meeting to deal with them. I told them, "We did everything we could to buy back our Jewish brothers who had to sell themselves as slaves to foreigners. And now you're selling these same brothers back into debt slavery! Does that mean that we have to buy them back again?"

They said nothing. What could they say?

"What you're doing is wrong. Is there no fear of God left in you? Don't you care what the nations around here, our enemies, think of you?

"I and my brothers and the people working for me have also loaned them money. But this gouging them with interest has to stop. Give them back their foreclosed fields, vineyards, olive groves, and homes right now. And forgive your claims on their money, grain, new wine, and olive oil."

They said, "We'll give it all back. We won't make any more demands on them. We'll do everything you say."

Then I called the priests together and made them promise to keep their word. Then I emptied my pockets, turning them inside out, and said, "So may God empty the pockets and house of everyone who doesn't keep this promise—turned inside out and emptied."

Everyone gave a wholehearted "Yes, we'll do it!" and praised GOD. And the people did what they promised.

"REMEMBER IN MY FAVOR, O MY GOD"

From the time King Artaxerxes appointed me as their governor in the land of Judah—from the twentieth to the thirty-second year of his reign, twelve years—neither I nor my brothers used the governor's food allowance. Governors who had preceded me had oppressed the people by taxing them forty shekels of silver (about a pound) a day for food and wine while their underlings bullied the people unmercifully. But out of fear of God I did none of that. I had work to do; I worked on this wall. All my men were on the job to do the work. We didn't have time to line our own pockets.

I fed one hundred and fifty Jews and officials at my table in addition to those who showed up from the surrounding nations. One ox, six choice sheep, and some chickens were prepared for me daily, and every ten days a large supply of wine was delivered. Even so, I didn't use the food allowance provided for the governor—the people had it hard enough as it was.

Remember in my favor, O my God,
Everything I've done for these people.

"I'M DOING A GREAT WORK; I CAN'T COME DOWN"

6 When Sanballat, Tobiah, Geshem the Arab, and the rest of our ene-mies heard that I had rebuilt the wall and that there were no more breaks in it—even though I hadn't yet installed the gates—Sanballat and Geshem sent this message: "Come and meet with us at Kephirim in the valley of Ono."

I knew they were scheming to hurt me so I sent messengers back with this: "I'm doing a great work; I can't come down. Why should the work come to a standstill just so I can come down to see you?"

Four times they sent this message and four times I gave them my answer.

The fifth time—same messenger, same message—Sanballat sent an unsealed letter with this message:

"The word is out among the nations—and Geshem says it's true—that you and the Jews are planning to rebel. That's why you are rebuilding the wall. The word is that you want to be king and that you have appointed prophets to announce in Jerusalem, 'There's a king in Judah!' The king is going to be told all this—don't you think we should sit down and have a talk?"

I sent him back this: "There's nothing to what you're saying. You've made it all up."

They were trying to intimidate us into quitting. They thought, "They'll give up; they'll never finish it."

I prayed, "Give me strength."

✛

Then I met secretly with Shemaiah son of Delaiah, the son of Mehetabel, at his house. He said:

Let's meet at the house of God,
        inside The Temple;

Let's find safety behind locked doors
>   because they're coming to kill you,
Yes, coming by night to kill you.

I said, "Why would a man like me run for cover? And why would a man like me use The Temple as a hideout? I won't do it."

I sensed that God hadn't sent this man. The so-called prophecy he spoke to me was the work of Tobiah and Sanballat; they had hired him. He had been hired to scare me off—trick me—a layman, into desecrating The Temple and ruining my good reputation so they could accuse me.

"O my God, don't let Tobiah and Sanballat get by with all the mischief they've done. And the same goes for the prophetess Noadiah and the other prophets who have been trying to undermine my confidence."

✛

The wall was finished on the twenty-fifth day of Elul. It had taken fifty-two days. When all our enemies heard the news and all the surrounding nations saw it, our enemies totally lost their nerve. They knew that God was behind this work.

All during this time letters were going back and forth constantly between the nobles of Judah and Tobiah. Many of the nobles had ties to him because he was son-in-law to Shecaniah son of Arah and his son Jehohanan had married the daughter of Meshullam son of Berekiah. They kept telling me all the good things he did and then would report back to him anything I would say. And then Tobiah would send letters to intimidate me.

THE WALL REBUILT: NAMES AND NUMBERS

7 After the wall was rebuilt and I had installed the doors, and the security guards, the singers, and the Levites were appointed, I put my brother Hanani, along with Hananiah the captain of the citadel, in charge of Jerusalem because he was an honest man and feared God more than most men.

I gave them this order: "Don't open the gates of Jerusalem until the sun is up. And shut and bar the gates while the guards are still on duty. Appoint the guards from the citizens of Jerusalem and assign them to posts in front of their own homes."

The city was large and spacious with only a few people in it and the houses not yet rebuilt.

God put it in my heart to gather the nobles, the officials, and the people in general to be registered. I found the genealogical record of those who were in the first return from exile. This is the record I found:

These are the people of the province who returned from the captivity of the Exile, the ones Nebuchadnezzar king of Babylon had carried off captive; they came back to Jerusalem and Judah, each going to his own town. They came back in the company of Zerubbabel, Jeshua, Nehemiah, Azariah, Raamiah, Nahamani, Mordecai, Bilshan, Mispereth, Bigvai, Nehum, and Baanah.

The numbers of the men of the People of Israel by families of origin:

Parosh, 2,172
Shephatiah, 372
Arah, 652
Pahath-Moab (sons of Jeshua and Joab), 2,818
Elam, 1,254
Zattu, 845
Zaccai, 760
Binnui, 648
Bebai, 628
Azgad, 2,322
Adonikam, 667
Bigvai, 2,067
Adin, 655
Ater (sons of Hezekiah), 98
Hashum, 328
Bezai, 324
Hariph, 112
Gibeon, 95.

Israelites identified by place of origin:

Bethlehem and Netophah, 188
Anathoth, 128
Beth Azmaveth, 42
Kiriath Jearim, Kephirah, and Beeroth, 743
Ramah and Geba, 621
Micmash, 122

Bethel and Ai, 123
Nebo (the other one), 52
Elam (the other one), 1,254
Harim, 320
Jericho, 345
Lod, Hadid, and Ono, 721
Senaah, 3,930.
Priestly families:
Jedaiah (sons of Jeshua), 973
Immer, 1,052
Pashhur, 1,247
Harim, 1,017.
Levitical families:
Jeshua (sons of Kadmiel and of Hodaviah), 74.
Singers:
Asaph's family line, 148.
Security guard families:
Shallum, Ater, Talmon, Akkub, Hatita, and Shobai, 138.
Families of support staff:
Ziha, Hasupha, Tabbaoth,
Keros, Sia, Padon,
Lebana, Hagaba, Shalmai,
Hanan, Giddel, Gahar,
Reaiah, Rezin, Nekoda,
Gazzam, Uzza, Paseah,
Besai, Meunim, Nephussim,
Bakbuk, Hakupha, Harhur,
Bazluth, Mehida, Harsha,
Barkos, Sisera, Temah,
Neziah, and Hatipha.
Families of Solomon's servants:
Sotai, Sophereth, Perida,
Jaala, Darkon, Giddel,
Shephatiah, Hattil, Pokereth-Hazzebaim, and Amon.
The Temple support staff and Solomon's servants added up to 392.

These are those who came from Tel Melah, Tel Harsha, Kerub, Addon, and Immer. They weren't able to prove their ancestry, whether they were true Israelites or not:

The sons of Delaiah, Tobiah, and Nekoda, 642.

Likewise with these priestly families:

The sons of Hobaiah, Hakkoz, and Barzillai, who had married a daughter of Barzillai the Gileadite and took that name.

They looked high and low for their family records but couldn't find them. And so they were barred from priestly work as ritually unclean. The governor ruled that they could not eat from the holy food until a priest could determine their status by using the Urim and Thummim.

The total count for the congregation was 42,360. That did not include the male and female slaves who numbered 7,337. There were also 245 male and female singers. And there were 736 horses, 245 mules, 435 camels, and 6,720 donkeys.

Some of the heads of families made voluntary offerings for the work. The governor made a gift to the treasury of 1,000 drachmas of gold (about nineteen pounds), 50 bowls, and 530 garments for the priests. Some of the heads of the families made gifts to the treasury for the work; it came to 20,000 drachmas of gold and 2,200 minas of silver (about one and a third tons). Gifts from the rest of the people totaled 20,000 drachmas of gold (about 375 pounds), 2,000 minas of silver, and 67 garments for the priests.

The priests, Levites, security guards, singers, and Temple support staff, along with some others, and the rest of the People of Israel, all found a place to live in their own towns.

EZRA AND THE REVELATION

8 By the time the seventh month arrived, the People of Israel were settled in their towns. Then all the people gathered as one person in the town square in front of the Water Gate and asked the scholar Ezra to bring the Book of The Revelation of Moses that GOD had commanded for Israel.

So Ezra the priest brought The Revelation to the congregation, which was made up of both men and women—everyone capable of understanding. It was the first day of the seventh month. He read it facing the town square at the Water Gate from early dawn until noon in the hearing of the men and women, all who could understand it. And all the people listened—they were all ears—to the Book of The Revelation.

The scholar Ezra stood on a wooden platform constructed for the occasion. He was flanked on the right by Mattithiah, Shema, Anaiah, Uriah, Hilkiah, and Maaseiah, and on the left by Pedaiah, Mishael,

Malkijah, Hashum, Hashbaddanah, Zechariah, and Meshullam.

Ezra opened the book. Every eye was on him (he was standing on the raised platform) and as he opened the book everyone stood. Then Ezra praised GOD, the great God, and all the people responded, "Oh Yes! Yes!" with hands raised high. And then they fell to their knees in worship of GOD, their faces to the ground.

Jeshua, Bani, Sherebiah, Jamin, Akkub, Shabbethai, Hodiah, Maaseiah, Kelita, Azariah, Jozabad, Hanan, and Pelaiah, all Levites, explained The Revelation while people stood, listening respectfully. They translated the Book of The Revelation of God so the people could understand it and then explained the reading.

Nehemiah the governor, along with Ezra the priest and scholar and the Levites who were teaching the people, said to all the people, "This day is holy to GOD, your God. Don't weep and carry on." They said this because all the people were weeping as they heard the words of The Revelation.

He continued, "Go home and prepare a feast, holiday food and drink; and share it with those who don't have anything: This day is holy to God. Don't feel bad. The joy of GOD is your strength!"

The Levites calmed the people, "Quiet now. This is a holy day. Don't be upset."

So the people went off to feast, eating and drinking and including the poor in a great celebration. Now they got it; they understood the reading that had been given to them.

⊹

On the second day of the month the family heads of all the people, the priests, and the Levites gathered around Ezra the scholar to get a deeper understanding of the words of The Revelation. They found written in The Revelation that GOD commanded through Moses that the People of Israel are to live in booths during the festival of the seventh month. So they published this decree and had it posted in all their cities and in Jerusalem: "Go into the hills and collect olive branches, pine branches, myrtle branches, palm branches, and any other leafy branches to make booths, as it is written."

⊹

So the people went out, brought in branches, and made themselves booths on their roofs, courtyards, the courtyards of The Temple of God, the Water Gate plaza, and the Ephraim Gate plaza. The entire congregation that had come back from exile made booths and lived in them. The People of Israel hadn't done this from the time of Joshua son of Nun until that very day—a terrific day! Great joy!

Ezra read from the Book of The Revelation of God each day, from the first to the last day—they celebrated the feast for seven days. On the eighth day they held a solemn assembly in accordance with the decree.

9 Then on the twenty-fourth day of this month, the People of Israel gathered for a fast, wearing burlap and faces smudged with dirt as signs of repentance. The Israelites broke off all relations with foreigners, stood up, and confessed their sins and the iniquities of their parents. While they stood there in their places, they read from the Book of The Revelation of GOD, their God, for a quarter of the day. For another quarter of the day they confessed and worshiped their GOD.

A group of Levites—Jeshua, Bani, Kadmiel, Shebaniah, Bunni, Sherebiah, Bani, and Kenani—stood on the platform and cried out to GOD, their God, in a loud voice. The Levites Jeshua, Kadmiel, Bani, Hashabneiah, Sherebiah, Hodiah, Shebaniah, and Pethahiah said, "On your feet! Bless GOD, your God, for ever and ever!"

Blessed be your glorious name,
    exalted above all blessing and praise!
You're the one,
    GOD, you alone;
You made the heavens,
    the heavens of heavens, and all angels;
The earth and everything on it,
    the seas and everything in them;
You keep them all alive;
    heaven's angels worship you!

You're the one, GOD, *the* God
    who chose Abram
And brought him from Ur of the Chaldees
    and changed his name to Abraham.
You found his heart to be steady and true to you
    and signed a covenant with him,

455

A covenant to give him the land of the Canaanites,
    the Hittites, and the Amorites,
The Perizzites, Jebusites, and Girgashites,
    —to give it to his descendants.
And you kept your word
    because you are righteous.

You saw the anguish of our parents in Egypt.
    You heard their cries at the Red Sea;
You amazed Pharaoh, his servants, and the people of his land
    with wonders and miracle-signs.
You knew their bullying arrogance against your people;
    you made a name for yourself that lasts to this day.
You split the sea before them;
    they crossed through and never got their feet wet;
You pitched their pursuers into the deep;
    they sank like a rock in the storm-tossed sea.
By day you led them with a Pillar of Cloud,
    and by night with a Pillar of Fire
To show them the way
    they were to travel.
You came down onto Mount Sinai,
    you spoke to them out of heaven;
You gave them instructions on how to live well,
    true teaching, sound rules and commands;
You introduced them
    to your Holy Sabbath;
Through your servant Moses you decreed
    commands, rules, and instruction.
You gave bread from heaven for their hunger,
    you sent water from the rock for their thirst.
You told them to enter and take the land,
    which you promised to give them.

But they, our ancestors, were arrogant;
    bullheaded, they wouldn't obey your commands.
They turned a deaf ear, they refused
    to remember the miracles you had done for them;

They turned stubborn, got it into their heads
    to return to their Egyptian slavery.
And you, a forgiving God,
    gracious and compassionate,
Incredibly patient, with tons of love—
    you didn't dump them.
Yes, even when they cast a sculpted calf
    and said, "This is your god
Who brought you out of Egypt,"
    and continued from bad to worse,
You in your amazing compassion
    didn't walk off and leave them in the desert.
The Pillar of Cloud didn't leave them;
    daily it continued to show them their route;
The Pillar of Fire did the same by night,
    showed them the right way to go.

You gave them your good Spirit
    to teach them to live wisely.
You never stinted with your manna,
    gave them plenty of water to drink.
You supported them forty years in that desert;
    they had everything they needed;
Their clothes didn't wear out
    and their feet never blistered.
You gave them kingdoms and peoples,
    establishing generous boundaries.
They took over the country of Sihon king of Heshbon
    and the country of Og king of Bashan.
You multiplied children for them,
    rivaling the stars in the night skies,
And you brought them into the land
    that you promised their ancestors
    they would get and own.

Well, they entered all right,
    they took it and settled in.
The Canaanites who lived there
    you brought to their knees before them.

You turned over their land, kings, and peoples
    to do with as they pleased.
They took strong cities and fertile fields,
    they took over well-furnished houses,
Cisterns, vineyards, olive groves,
    and lush, extensive orchards.
And they ate, grew fat on the fat of the land;
    they reveled in your bountiful goodness.

But then they mutinied, rebelled against you,
    threw out your laws and killed your prophets,
The very prophets who tried to get them back on your side—
    and then things went from bad to worse.
You turned them over to their enemies,
    who made life rough for them.
But when they called out for help in their troubles
    you listened from heaven;
And in keeping with your bottomless compassion
    you gave them saviors:
Saviors who saved them
    from the cruel abuse of their enemies.
But as soon as they had it easy again
    they were right back at it—more evil.
So you turned away and left them again to their fate,
    to the enemies who came right back.
They cried out to you again; in your great compassion
    you heard and helped them again.
    This went on over and over and over.
You warned them to return to your Revelation,
    they responded with haughty arrogance:
They flouted your commands, spurned your rules
    —the very words by which men and women live!
They set their jaws in defiance,
    they turned their backs on you and didn't listen.
You put up with them year after year
    and warned them by your spirit through your prophets;
But when they refused to listen
    you abandoned them to foreigners.

Still, because of your great compassion,
> you didn't make a total end to them.
You didn't walk out and leave them for good;
> yes, you *are* a God of grace and compassion.

And now, our God, the great God,
> God majestic and terrible, loyal in covenant and love,
Don't treat lightly the trouble that has come to us,
> to our kings and princes, our priests and prophets,
Our ancestors, and all your people from the time
> of the Assyrian kings right down to today.
You are not to blame
> for all that has come down on us;
You did everything right,
> we did everything wrong.
None of our kings, princes, priests, or ancestors
> followed your Revelation;
They ignored your commands,
> dismissed the warnings you gave them.
Even when they had their own kingdom
> and were enjoying your generous goodness,
Living in that spacious and fertile land
> that you spread out before them,
They didn't serve you
> or turn their backs on the practice of evil.
And here we are, slaves again today;
> and here's the land you gave our ancestors
So they could eat well and enjoy a good life,
> and now look at us—no better than slaves on this land.
Its wonderful crops go to the kings
> you put over us because of our sins;
They act like they own our bodies
> and do whatever they like with our cattle.
> We're in deep trouble.

"Because of all this we are drawing up a binding pledge, a sealed document signed by our princes, our Levites, and our priests."

✞

10 The sealed document bore these signatures:
Nehemiah the governor, son of Hacaliah,
Zedekiah, Seraiah, Azariah, Jeremiah,
Pashhur, Amariah, Malkijah,
Hattush, Shebaniah, Malluch,
Harim, Meremoth, Obadiah,
Daniel, Ginnethon, Baruch,
Meshullam, Abijah, Mijamin,
Maaziah, Bilgai, and Shemaiah.
These were the priests.

The Levites:
Jeshua son of Azaniah, Binnui of the sons of Henadad, Kadmiel,
and their kinsmen: Shebaniah, Hodiah, Kelita, Pelaiah, Hanan,
Mica, Rehob, Hashabiah,
Zaccur, Sherebiah, Shebaniah,
Hodiah, Bani, and Beninu.

The heads of the people:
Parosh, Pahath-Moab, Elam, Zattu, Bani,
Bunni, Azgad, Bebai,
Adonijah, Bigvai, Adin,
Ater, Hezekiah, Azzur,
Hodiah, Hashum, Bezai,
Hariph, Anathoth, Nebai,
Magpiash, Meshullam, Hezir,
Meshezabel, Zadok, Jaddua,
Pelatiah, Hanan, Anaiah,
Hoshea, Hananiah, Hasshub,
Hallohesh, Pilha, Shobek,
Rehum, Hashabnah, Maaseiah,
Ahiah, Hanan, Anan,
Malluch, Harim, and Baanah.

The rest of the people, priests, Levites, security guards, singers, Temple staff, and all who separated themselves from the foreign neighbors to keep The Revelation of God, together with their wives, sons, daughters—everyone old enough to understand—all joined their noble kinsmen in a binding oath to follow The Revelation of God given through Moses the servant of God, to keep and carry out all the commandments of GOD our Master, all his decisions and standards. Thus:

We will not marry our daughters to our foreign neighbors nor let our sons marry their daughters.

When the foreign neighbors bring goods or grain to sell on the Sabbath we won't trade with them—not on the Sabbath or any other holy day.

Every seventh year we will leave the land fallow and cancel all debts.

We accept the responsibility for paying an annual tax of one-third of a shekel (about an eighth ounce) for providing The Temple of our God with

bread for the Table

regular Grain-Offerings

regular Whole-Burnt-Offerings

offerings for the Sabbaths, New Moons, and appointed
feasts

Dedication-Offerings

Absolution-Offerings to atone for Israel

maintenance of The Temple of our God.

We—priests, Levites, and the people—have cast lots to see when each of our families will bring wood for burning on the Altar of our GOD, following the yearly schedule set down in The Revelation.

We take responsibility for delivering annually to The Temple of GOD the firstfruits of our crops and our orchards, our firstborn sons and cattle, and the firstborn from our herds and flocks for the priests who serve in The Temple of our God—just as it is set down in The Revelation.

We will bring the best of our grain, of our contributions, of the fruit of every tree, of wine, and of oil to the priests in the storerooms of The Temple of our God.

We will bring the tithes from our fields to the Levites, since the Levites are appointed to collect the tithes in the towns where we work. We'll see to it that a priest descended from Aaron will supervise the Levites as they collect the tithes and make sure that they take a tenth of the tithes to the treasury in The Temple of our God. We'll see to it that the People of Israel and Levites bring the grain, wine, and oil to the storage rooms where the vessels of the Sanctuary are kept and where the priests who serve, the security guards, and the choir meet.

We will not neglect The Temple of our God.

11 The leaders of the people were already living in Jerusalem, so the rest of the people drew lots to get one out of ten to move to Jerusalem, the holy city, while the other nine remained in their towns. The people applauded those who voluntarily offered to live in Jerusalem.

These are the leaders in the province who resided in Jerusalem (some Israelites, priests, Levites, Temple staff, and descendants of Solomon's slaves lived in the towns of Judah on their own property in various towns; others from both Judah and Benjamin lived in Jerusalem):

From the family of Judah:

Athaiah son of Uzziah, the son of Zechariah, the son of Amariah, the son of Shephatiah, the son of Mahalalel, from the family line of Perez; Maaseiah son of Baruch, the son of Col-Hozeh, the son of Hazaiah, the son of Adaiah, the son of Joiarib, the son of Zechariah, the son of the Shilonite. The descendants of Perez who lived in Jerusalem numbered 468 valiant men.

From the family of Benjamin:

Sallu son of Meshullam, the son of Joed, the son of Pedaiah, the son of Kolaiah, the son of Maaseiah, the son of Ithiel, the son of Jeshaiah, and his brothers Gabbai and Sallai: 928 men. Joel son of Zicri was their chief and Judah son of Hassenuah was second in command over the city.

From the priests:

Jedaiah son of Joiarib; Jakin; Seraiah son of Hilkiah, the son of Meshullam, the son of Zadok, the son of Meraioth, the son of Ahitub, supervisor of The Temple of God, along with their associates responsible for work in The Temple: 822 men. Also Adaiah son of Jeroham, the son of Pelaliah, the son of Amzi, the son of Zechariah, the son of Pashhur, the son of Malkijah, and his associates who were heads of families: 242 men; Amashsai son of Azarel, the son of Ahzai, the son of Meshillemoth, the son of Immer, and his associates, all valiant men: 128 men. Their commander was Zabdiel son of Haggedolim.

From the Levites:

Shemaiah son of Hasshub, the son of Azrikam, the son of Hashabiah, the son of Bunni; Shabbethai and Jozabad, two of the leaders of the Levites who were in charge of the outside work of The Temple

462

of God; Mattaniah son of Mica, the son of Zabdi, the son of Asaph, the director who led in thanksgiving and prayer; Bakbukiah, second among his associates; and Abda son of Shammua, the son of Galal, the son of Jeduthun. The Levites in the holy city totaled 284.

From the security guards:

Akkub, Talmon, and their associates who kept watch over the gates: 172 men.

The rest of the Israelites, priests, and Levites were in all the towns of Judah, each on his own family property.

The Temple staff lived on the hill Ophel. Ziha and Gishpa were responsible for them.

The chief officer over the Levites in Jerusalem was Uzzi son of Bani, the son of Hashabiah, the son of Mattaniah, the son of Mica. Uzzi was one of Asaph's descendants, singers who led worship in The Temple of God. The singers got their orders from the king, who drew up their daily schedule.

Pethahiah son of Meshezabel, a descendant of Zerah son of Judah, represented the people's concerns at the royal court.

Some of the Judeans lived in the villages near their farms:
Kiriath Arba (Hebron) and suburbs
Dibon and suburbs
Jekabzeel and suburbs
Jeshua
Moladah
Beth Pelet
Hazar Shual
Beersheba and suburbs
Ziklag
Meconah and suburbs
En Rimmon
Zorah
Jarmuth
Zanoah
Adullam and their towns
Lachish and its fields
Azekah and suburbs.
They were living all the way from Beersheba to the Valley of Hinnom.

The Benjaminites from Geba lived in:
Micmash
Aijah
Bethel and its suburbs
Anathoth
Nob and Ananiah
Hazor
Ramah and Gittaim
Hadid, Zeboim, and Neballat
Lod and Ono and the Valley of the Craftsmen.
Also some of the Levitical groups of Judah were assigned to Benjamin.

12 These are the priests and Levites who came up with Zerubbabel son of Shealtiel and with Jeshua:
Seraiah, Jeremiah, Ezra,
Amariah, Malluch, Hattush,
Shecaniah, Rehum, Meremoth,
Iddo, Ginnethon, Abijah,
Mijamin, Moadiah, Bilgah,
Shemaiah, Joiarib, Jedaiah,
Sallu, Amok, Hilkiah, and Jedaiah.
These were the leaders of the priests during the time of Jeshua.
And the Levites:
Jeshua, Binnui, Kadmiel, Sherebiah, Judah;
Mattaniah, with his brothers, was in charge of songs of
praise, and their brothers Bakbukiah and Unni stood oppo-
site them in the services of worship.

Jeshua fathered Joiakim,
Joiakim fathered Eliashib,
Eliashib fathered Joiada,
Joiada fathered Jonathan,
and Jonathan fathered Jaddua.

During the time of Joiakim, these were the heads of the priestly
families:
of the family of Seraiah, Meraiah;
of Jeremiah, Hananiah;
of Ezra, Meshullam;

of Amariah, Jehohanan;
of Malluch, Jonathan;
of Shecaniah, Joseph;
of Harim, Adna;
of Meremoth, Helkai;
of Iddo, Zechariah;
of Ginnethon, Meshullam;
of Abijah, Zicri;
of Miniamin and Moadiah, Piltai;
of Bilgah, Shammua;
of Shemaiah, Jehonathan;
of Joiarib, Mattenai;
of Jedaiah, Uzzi;
of Sallu, Kallai;
of Amok, Eber;
of Hilkiah, Hashabiah;
and of Jedaiah, Nethanel.

During the time of Eliashib, Joiada, Johanan, and Jaddua, the Levites were registered as heads of families. During the reign of Darius the Persian, the priests were registered.

The Levites who were heads of families were registered in the Book of the Chronicles until the time of Johanan son of Eliashib. These were:

Hashabiah,
Sherebiah,
and Jeshua son of Kadmiel.

Their brothers stood opposite them to give praise and thanksgiving, one side responding to the other, as had been directed by David the man of God.

The security guards included:

Mattaniah,
Bakbukiah,
Obadiah,
Meshullam,
Talmon,
and Akkub.

They guarded the storerooms at the gates. They lived during the time of Joiakim son of Jeshua, the son of Jozadak, the time of Nehemiah the governor and of Ezra the priest and scholar.

DEDICATION OF THE WALL

When it came time for the dedication of the wall, they tracked down and brought in the Levites from all their homes in Jerusalem to carry out the dedication exuberantly: thanksgiving hymns, songs, cymbals, harps, and lutes. The singers assembled from all around Jerusalem, from the villages of the Netophathites, from Beth Gilgal, from the farms at Geba and Azmaveth—the singers had built villages for themselves all around Jerusalem.

The priests and Levites ceremonially purified themselves; then they did the same for the people, the gates, and the wall.

I had the leaders of Judah come up on the wall, and I appointed two large choirs. One proceeded on the wall to the right toward the Dung Gate. Hashaiah and half the leaders of Judah followed them, including Azariah, Ezra, Meshullam, Judah, Benjamin, Shemaiah, and Jeremiah. Some of the young priests had trumpets. Next, playing the musical instruments of David the man of God, came Zechariah son of Jonathan, the son of Shemaiah, the son of Mattaniah, the son of Micaiah, the son of Zaccur, the son of Asaph, and his brothers Shemaiah, Azarel, Milalai, Gilalai, Maai, Nethanel, Judah, and Hanani. Ezra the scholar led them.

At the Fountain Gate they went straight ahead, up the steps of the City of David using the wall stairway above the house of David to the Water Gate on the east.

The other choir proceeded to the left. I and half of the people followed them on the wall from the Tower of Furnaces to the Broad Wall, over the Ephraim Gate, the Jeshanah Gate, the Fish Gate, the Tower of Hananel, and the Tower of the Hundred as far as the Sheep Gate, stopping at the Prison Gate.

The two choirs then took their places in The Temple of God. I was there with half of the officials, along with the priests Eliakim, Maaseiah, Miniamin, Micaiah, Elioenai, Zechariah, and Hananiah with their trumpets. Also Maaseiah, Shemaiah, Eleazar, Uzzi, Jehohanan, Malkijah, Elam, and Ezer. The singers, directed by Jezrahiah, made the rafters ring.

That day they offered great sacrifices, an exuberant celebration because God had filled them with great joy. The women and children raised their happy voices with all the rest. Jerusalem's jubilation was heard far and wide.

✠

That same day men were appointed to be responsible for the store-rooms for the offerings, the firstfruits, and the tithes. They saw to it that the portion directed by The Revelation for the priests and Levites was brought in from the farms connected to the towns. Judah was so appreciative of the priests and Levites and their service; they, along with the singers and security guards, had done everything so well, conducted the worship of their God and the ritual of ceremonial cleansing in a way that would have made David and his son Solomon proud. That's the way it was done in the olden days, the days of David and Asaph, when they had choir directors for singing songs of praise and thanksgiving to God.

During the time of Zerubbabel and Nehemiah, all Israel contributed the daily allowances for the singers and security guards. They also set aside what was dedicated to the Levites, and the Levites did the same for the Aaronites.

✠

13 Also on that same day there was a reading from the Book of Moses in the hearing of the people. It was found written there that no Ammonite or Moabite was permitted to enter the congregation of God, because they hadn't welcomed the People of Israel with food and drink; they even hired Balaam to work against them by cursing them, but our God turned the curse into a blessing. When they heard the reading of The Revelation, they excluded all foreigners from Israel.

✠

Some time before this, Eliashib the priest had been put in charge of the storerooms of The Temple of God. He was close to Tobiah and had made available to him a large storeroom that had been used to store Grain-Offerings, incense, worship vessels, and the tithes of grain, wine, and oil for the Levites, singers, and security guards, and the offerings for the priests.

When this was going on I wasn't there in Jerusalem; in the thirty-second year of Artaxerxes king of Babylon, I had traveled back to the king. But later I asked for his permission to leave again. I arrived in Jerusalem and learned of the wrong that Eliashib had done in turning over to him a room in the courts of The Temple of God. I was angry, really angry, and threw everything in the room out into the street, all of Tobiah's stuff. Then I ordered that they ceremonially cleanse the room. Only then did I put back the worship vessels of The Temple of God, along with the Grain-Offerings and the incense.

And then I learned that the Levites hadn't been given their regular food allotments. So the Levites and singers who led the services of worship had all left and gone back to their farms. I called the officials on the carpet, "Why has The Temple of God been abandoned?" I got everyone back again and put them back on their jobs so that all Judah was again bringing in the tithe of grain, wine, and oil to the storerooms. I put Shelemiah the priest, Zadok the scribe, and a Levite named Pedaiah in charge of the storerooms. I made Hanan son of Zaccur, the son of Mattaniah, their right-hand man. These men had a reputation for honesty and hard work. They were responsible for distributing the rations to their brothers.

Remember me, O my God, for this. Don't ever forget the devoted work I have done for The Temple of God and its worship.

During those days, while back in Judah, I also noticed that people treaded wine presses, brought in sacks of grain, and loaded up their donkeys on the Sabbath. They brought wine, grapes, figs, and all kinds of stuff to sell on the Sabbath. So I spoke up and warned them about selling food on that day. Tyrians living there brought in fish and whatever else, selling it to Judeans—*in Jerusalem*, mind you!—on the Sabbath.

I confronted the leaders of Judah: "What's going on here? This evil! Profaning the Sabbath! Isn't this exactly what your ancestors did? And because of it didn't God bring down on us and this city all this misery? And here you are adding to it—accumulating more wrath on Jerusalem by profaning the Sabbath."

As the gates of Jerusalem were darkened by the shadows of the approaching Sabbath, I ordered the doors shut and not to be opened until the Sabbath was over. I placed some of my servants at the gates to make sure that nothing to be sold would get in on the Sabbath day.

Traders and dealers in various goods camped outside the gates once or twice. But I took them to task. I said, "You have no business camping out here by the wall. If I find you here again, I'll use force to drive you off."

And that did it; they didn't come back on the Sabbath.

Then I directed the Levites to ceremonially cleanse themselves and take over as guards at the gates to keep the sanctity of the Sabbath day.

Remember me also for this, my God. Treat me with mercy according to your great and steadfast love.

✠

Also in those days I saw Jews who had married women from Ashdod, Ammon, and Moab. Half the children couldn't even speak the language of Judah; all they knew was the language of Ashdod or some other tongue. So I took those men to task, gave them a piece of my mind, even slapped some of them and jerked them by the hair. I made them swear to God: "Don't marry your daughters to their sons; and don't let their daughters marry your sons—and don't you yourselves marry them! Didn't Solomon the king of Israel sin because of women just like these? Even though there was no king quite like him, and God loved him and made him king over all Israel, foreign women were his downfall. Do you call this obedience—engaging in this extensive evil, showing yourselves faithless to God by marrying foreign wives?"

One of the sons of Joiada, the son of Eliashib the high priest, was a son-in-law of Sanballat the Horonite; I drove him out of my presence.

Remember them, O my God, how they defiled the priesthood and the covenant of the priests and Levites.

✠

All in all I cleansed them from everything foreign. I organized the orders of service for the priests and Levites so that each man knew his job. I arranged for a regular supply of altar wood at the appointed times and for the firstfruits.

Remember me, O my God, for good.

ESTHER

I t seems odd that the awareness of God, or even of the people of God, brings out the worst in some people. God, the source of all goodness and blessing and joy, at times becomes the occasion for nearly unimaginable acts of cruelty, atrocity, and evil.

There is a long history of killing men and women simply because they are perceived as reminders or representatives of the living God, as if killing people who worship God gets rid of God himself. We've recently completed a century marked by an extraordinary frenzy of such "god" killings. To no one's surprise, God is still alive and present.

The Book of Esther opens a window on this world of violence directed, whether openly or covertly, against God and God's people. The perspective it provides transcends the occasion that provoked it, a nasty scheme to massacre all the exiled Jews who lived in the vast expanse of fifth-century B.C. Persia. Three characters shape the plot. Mordecai, identified simply as "the Jew," anchors the story. He is solid, faithful, sane, godly. His goodness is more than matched by the evil and arrogant vanity of Haman, who masterminds the planned massacre. Mordecai's young, orphaned, and ravishing cousin, Esther, whom he has raised, emerges from the shadows of the royal harem to take on the title role.

It turns out that no God-representing men and women get killed in this story—in a dramatic turnaround, the plot fails. But millions before and after Esther have been and, no doubt, will continue to be killed. There is hardly a culture or century that doesn't eventually find a Haman determined to rid the world of evidence and reminders of God. Meanwhile, Esther continues to speak the final and definitive word: You can't eliminate God's people. No matter how many of them you kill, you can't get rid of the communities of God-honoring, God-serving, God-worshiping people scattered all over the earth. This is still the final and definitive word.

ESTHER

1 This is the story of something that happened in the time of Xerxes, the Xerxes who ruled from India to Ethiopia—127 provinces in all. King Xerxes ruled from his royal throne in the palace complex of Susa. In the third year of his reign he gave a banquet for all his officials and ministers. The military brass of Persia and Media were also there, along with the princes and governors of the provinces.

For six months he put on exhibit the huge wealth of his empire and its stunningly beautiful royal splendors. At the conclusion of the exhibit, the king threw a weeklong party for everyone living in Susa, the capital—important and unimportant alike. The party was in the garden courtyard of the king's summer house. The courtyard was elaborately decorated with white and blue cotton curtains tied with linen and purple cords to silver rings on marble columns. Silver and gold couches were arranged on a mosaic pavement of porphyry, marble, mother-of-pearl, and colored stones. Drinks were served in gold chalices, each chalice one-of-a-kind. The royal wine flowed freely—a generous king!

The guests could drink as much as they liked—king's orders!—with waiters at their elbows to refill the drinks. Meanwhile, Queen Vashti was throwing a separate party for women inside King Xerxes' royal palace.

On the seventh day of the party, the king, high on the wine, ordered the seven eunuchs who were his personal servants (Mehuman, Biztha, Harbona, Bigtha, Abagtha, Zethar, and Carcas) to bring him Queen Vashti resplendent in her royal crown. He wanted to show off her beauty to the guests and officials. She was extremely good-looking.

But Queen Vashti refused to come, refused the summons delivered by the eunuchs. The king lost his temper. Seething with anger over her insolence, the king called in his counselors, all experts in legal matters. It was the king's practice to consult his expert advisors. Those closest to him were Carshena, Shethar, Admatha, Tarshish, Meres, Marsena, and Memucan, the seven highest-ranking princes of Persia and Media, the inner circle with access to the king's ear. He asked them what legal recourse they had against Queen Vashti for not obeying King Xerxes' summons delivered by the eunuchs.

Memucan spoke up in the council of the king and princes: "It's not only the king Queen Vashti has insulted, it's all of us, leaders and people alike in every last one of King Xerxes' provinces. The word's going to get out: 'Did you hear the latest about Queen Vashti? King Xerxes ordered her to be brought before him and she wouldn't do it!' When the women hear it, they'll start treating their husbands with contempt. The day the wives of the Persian and Mede officials get wind of the queen's insolence, they'll be out of control. Is that what we want, a country of angry women who don't know their place?

"So, if the king agrees, let him pronounce a royal ruling and have it recorded in the laws of the Persians and Medes so that it cannot be revoked, that Vashti is permanently banned from King Xerxes' presence. And then let the king give her royal position to a woman who knows her place. When the king's ruling becomes public knowledge through-out the kingdom, extensive as it is, every woman, regardless of her social position, will show proper respect to her husband."

The king and the princes liked this. The king did what Memucan proposed. He sent bulletins to every part of the kingdom, to each province in its own script, to each people in their own language: "Every man is master of his own house; whatever he says, goes."

2 Later, when King Xerxes' anger had cooled and he was having second thoughts about what Vashti had done and what he had ordered against her, the king's young attendants stepped in and got the ball rolling: "Let's begin a search for beautiful young virgins for the king. Let the king appoint officials in every province of his kingdom to bring every beautiful young virgin to the palace complex of Susa and to the harem run by Hegai, the king's eunuch who oversees the women; he will put them through their beauty treatments. Then let the girl who best pleases the king be made queen in place of Vashti."

The king liked this advice and took it.

✢

Now there was a Jew who lived in the palace complex in Susa. His name was Mordecai the son of Jair, the son of Shimei, the son of Kish—a Benjaminite. His ancestors had been taken from Jerusalem with the exiles and carried off with King Jehoiachin of Judah by King Nebuchadnezzar of Babylon into exile. Mordecai had reared his cousin Hadassah, otherwise known as Esther, since she had no father or mother. The girl had a good figure and a beautiful face. After her parents died, Mordecai had adopted her.

When the king's order had been publicly posted, many young girls were brought to the palace complex of Susa and given over to Hegai who was overseer of the women. Esther was among them.

Hegai liked Esther and took a special interest in her. Right off he started her beauty treatments, ordered special food, assigned her seven personal maids from the palace, and put her and her maids in the best rooms in the harem. Esther didn't say anything about her family and racial background because Mordecai had told her not to.

Every day Mordecai strolled beside the court of the harem to find out how Esther was and get news of what she was doing.

Each girl's turn came to go in to King Xerxes after she had completed the twelve months of prescribed beauty treatments—six months' treatment with oil of myrrh followed by six months with perfumes and various cosmetics. When it was time for the girl to go to the king, she was given whatever she wanted to take with her when she left the harem for the king's quarters. She would go there in the evening; in the morning she would return to a second harem overseen by Shaashgaz, the king's eunuch in charge of the concubines. She never again went back to the king unless the king took a special liking to her and asked for her by name.

When it was Esther's turn to go to the king (Esther the daughter of Abihail the uncle of Mordecai, who had adopted her as his daughter), she asked for nothing other than what Hegai, the king's eunuch in charge of the harem, had recommended. Esther, just as she was, won the admiration of everyone who saw her.

She was taken to King Xerxes in the royal palace in the tenth month, the month of Tebeth, in the seventh year of the king's reign.

The king fell in love with Esther far more than with any of his other women or any of the other virgins—he was totally smitten by her. He placed a royal crown on her head and made her queen in place of Vashti. Then the king gave a great banquet for all his nobles and officials— "Esther's Banquet." He proclaimed a holiday for all the provinces and handed out gifts with royal generosity.

✜

On one of the occasions when the virgins were being gathered together, Mordecai was sitting at the King's Gate. All this time, Esther had kept her family background and race a secret as Mordecai had ordered;

Esther still did what Mordecai told her, just as when she was being raised by him.

On this day, with Mordecai sitting at the King's Gate, Bigthana and Teresh, two of the king's eunuchs who guarded the entrance, had it in for the king and were making plans to kill King Xerxes. But Mordecai learned of the plot and told Queen Esther, who then told King Xerxes, giving credit to Mordecai. When the thing was investigated and confirmed as true, the two men were hanged on a gallows. This was all written down in a logbook kept for the king's use.

⊹

3 Some time later, King Xerxes promoted Haman son of Hammedatha the Agagite, making him the highest-ranking official in the government. All the king's servants at the King's Gate used to honor him by bowing down and kneeling before Haman—that's what the king had commanded.

Except Mordecai. Mordecai wouldn't do it, wouldn't bow down and kneel. The king's servants at the King's Gate asked Mordecai about it: "Why do you cross the king's command?" Day after day they spoke to him about this but he wouldn't listen, so they went to Haman to see whether something shouldn't be done about it. Mordecai had told them that he was a Jew.

When Haman saw for himself that Mordecai didn't bow down and kneel before him, he was outraged. Meanwhile, having learned that Mordecai was a Jew, Haman hated to waste his fury on just one Jew; he looked for a way to eliminate not just Mordecai but all Jews throughout the whole kingdom of Xerxes.

In the first month, the month of Nisan, of the twelfth year of Xerxes, the *pur*—that is, the lot—was cast under Haman's charge to determine the propitious day and month. The lot turned up the thirteenth day of the twelfth month, which is the month of Adar.

Haman then spoke with King Xerxes: "There is an odd set of people scattered through the provinces of your kingdom who don't fit in. Their customs and ways are different from those of everybody else. Worse, they disregard the king's laws. They're an affront; the king shouldn't put up with them. If it please the king, let orders be given that they be destroyed. I'll pay for it myself. I'll deposit 375 tons of silver in the royal bank to finance the operation."

The king slipped his signet ring from his hand and gave it to Haman son of Hammedatha the Agagite, archenemy of the Jews.

"Go ahead," the king said to Haman. "It's your money—do whatever you want with those people."

The king's secretaries were brought in on the thirteenth day of the first month. The orders were written out word for word as Haman had addressed them to the king's satraps, the governors of every province, and the officials of every people. They were written in the script of each province and the language of each people in the name of King Xerxes and sealed with the royal signet ring.

Bulletins were sent out by couriers to all the king's provinces with orders to massacre, kill, and eliminate all the Jews—youngsters and old men, women and babies—on a single day, the thirteenth day of the twelfth month, the month Adar, and to plunder their goods. Copies of the bulletin were to be posted in each province, publicly available to all peoples, to get them ready for that day.

At the king's command, the couriers took off; the order was also posted in the palace complex of Susa. The king and Haman sat back and had a drink while the city of Susa reeled from the news.

4 When Mordecai learned what had been done, he ripped his clothes to shreds and put on sackcloth and ashes. Then he went out in the streets of the city crying out in loud and bitter cries. He came only as far as the King's Gate, for no one dressed in sackcloth was allowed to enter the King's Gate. As the king's order was posted in every province, there was loud lament among the Jews—fasting, weeping, wailing. And most of them stretched out on sackcloth and ashes.

Esther's maids and eunuchs came and told her. The queen was stunned. She sent fresh clothes to Mordecai so he could take off his sackcloth but he wouldn't accept them. Esther called for Hathach, one of the royal eunuchs whom the king had assigned to wait on her, and told him to go to Mordecai and get the full story of what was happening. So Hathach went to Mordecai in the town square in front of the King's Gate. Mordecai told him everything that had happened to him. He also told him the exact amount of money that Haman had promised to deposit in the royal bank to finance the massacre of the Jews. Mordecai also gave him a copy of the bulletin that had been posted in Susa ordering the massacre so he could show it to Esther when he reported back with instructions to go to the king and intercede and plead with him for her people.

Hathach came back and told Esther everything Mordecai had said. Esther talked it over with Hathach and then sent him back to Mordecai with this message: "Everyone who works for the king here, and even the people out in the provinces, knows that there is a single fate for every man or woman who approaches the king without being invited: death. The one exception is if the king extends his gold scepter; then he or she may live. And it's been thirty days now since I've been invited to come to the king."

When Hathach told Mordecai what Esther had said, Mordecai sent her this message: "Don't think that just because you live in the king's house you're the one Jew who will get out of this alive. If you persist in staying silent at a time like this, help and deliverance will arrive for the Jews from someplace else; but you and your family will be wiped out. Who knows? Maybe you were made queen for just such a time as this."

Esther sent back her answer to Mordecai: "Go and get all the Jews living in Susa together. Fast for me. Don't eat or drink for three days, either day or night. I and my maids will fast with you. If you will do this, I'll go to the king, even though it's forbidden. If I die, I die."

Mordecai left and carried out Esther's instructions.

⊹

5 Three days later Esther dressed in her royal robes and took up a position in the inner court of the palace in front of the king's throne room. The king was on his throne facing the entrance. When he noticed Queen Esther standing in the court, he was pleased to see her; the king extended the gold scepter in his hand. Esther approached and touched the tip of the scepter. The king asked, "And what's your desire, Queen Esther? What do you want? Ask and it's yours—even if it's half my kingdom!"

"If it please the king," said Esther, "let the king come with Haman to a dinner I've prepared for him."

"Get Haman at once," said the king, "so we can go to dinner with Esther."

So the king and Haman joined Esther at the dinner she had arranged. As they were drinking the wine, the king said, "Now, what is it you want? Half of my kingdom isn't too much to ask! Just ask."

Esther answered, "Here's what I want. If the king favors me and is pleased to do what I desire and ask, let the king and Haman come again tomorrow to the dinner that I will fix for them. Then I'll give a straight answer to the king's question."

✝

Haman left the palace that day happy, beaming. And then he saw Mordecai sitting at the King's Gate ignoring him, oblivious to him. Haman was furious with Mordecai. But he held himself in and went on home. He got his friends together with his wife Zeresh and started bragging about how much money he had, his many sons, all the times the king had honored him, and his promotion to the highest position in the government. "On top of all that," Haman continued, "Queen Esther invited me to a private dinner she gave for the king, just the three of us. And she's invited me to another one tomorrow. But I can't enjoy any of it when I see Mordecai the Jew sitting at the King's Gate."

His wife Zeresh and all his friends said, "Build a gallows seventy-five feet high. First thing in the morning speak with the king; get him to order Mordecai hanged on it. Then happily go with the king to dinner."

Haman liked that. He had the gallows built.

✝

6 That night the king couldn't sleep. He ordered the record book, the day-by-day journal of events, to be brought and read to him. They came across the story there about the time that Mordecai had exposed the plot of Bigthana and Teresh—the two royal eunuchs who guarded the entrance and who had conspired to assassinate King Xerxes.

The king asked, "What great honor was given to Mordecai for this?"

"Nothing," replied the king's servants who were in attendance. "Nothing has been done for him."

The king said, "Is there anybody out in the court?"

Now Haman had just come into the outer court of the king's palace to talk to the king about hanging Mordecai on the gallows he had built for him.

The king's servants said, "Haman is out there, waiting in the court."

"Bring him in," said the king.

When Haman entered, the king said, "What would be appropriate for the man the king especially wants to honor?"

Haman thought to himself, "He must be talking about honoring me—who else?" So he answered the king, "For the man the king delights to honor, do this: Bring a royal robe that the king has worn and a horse the king has ridden, one with a royal crown on its head. Then give the robe and the horse to one of the king's most noble princes. Have him robe the man whom the king especially wants to honor; have the prince lead him on horseback through the city square, proclaiming before him, 'This is what is done for the man whom the king especially wants to honor!'"

"Go and do it," the king said to Haman. "Don't waste another minute. Take the robe and horse and do what you have proposed to Mordecai the Jew who sits at the King's Gate. Don't leave out a single detail of your plan."

So Haman took the robe and horse; he robed Mordecai and led him through the city square, proclaiming before him, "This is what is done for the man whom the king especially wants to honor!"

Then Mordecai returned to the King's Gate, but Haman fled to his house, thoroughly mortified, hiding his face. When Haman had finished telling his wife Zeresh and all his friends everything that had happened to him, his knowledgeable friends who were there and his wife Zeresh said, "If this Mordecai is in fact a Jew, your bad luck has only begun. You don't stand a chance against him—you're as good as ruined."

While they were still talking, the king's eunuchs arrived and hurried Haman off to the dinner that Esther had prepared.

⊹

7 So the king and Haman went to dinner with Queen Esther. At this second dinner, while they were drinking wine the king again asked, "Queen Esther, what would you like? Half of my kingdom! Just ask and it's yours."

Queen Esther answered, "If I have found favor in your eyes, O King, and if it please the king, give me my life, and give my people their lives.

"We've been sold, I and my people, to be destroyed—sold to be massacred, eliminated. If we had just been sold off into slavery, I wouldn't even have brought it up; our troubles wouldn't have been worth bothering the king over."

King Xerxes exploded, "Who? Where is he? This is monstrous!"

"An enemy. An adversary. This evil Haman," said Esther.

Haman was terror-stricken before the king and queen.

The king, raging, left his wine and stalked out into the palace garden.

Haman stood there pleading with Queen Esther for his life—he could see that the king was finished with him and that he was doomed.

As the king came back from the palace garden into the banquet hall, Haman was groveling at the couch on which Esther reclined. The king roared out, "Will he even molest the queen while I'm just around the corner?"

When that word left the king's mouth, all the blood drained from Haman's face.

Harbona, one of the eunuchs attending the king, spoke up: "Look over there! There's the gallows that Haman had built for Mordecai, who saved the king's life. It's right next to Haman's house — seventy-five feet high!"

The king said, "Hang him on it!"

So Haman was hanged on the very gallows that he had built for Mordecai. And the king's hot anger cooled.

✠

8 That same day King Xerxes gave Queen Esther the estate of Haman, archenemy of the Jews. And Mordecai came before the king because Esther had explained their relationship. The king took off his signet ring, which he had taken back from Haman, and gave it to Mordecai. Esther appointed Mordecai over Haman's estate.

Then Esther again spoke to the king, falling at his feet, begging with tears to counter the evil of Haman the Agagite and revoke the plan that he had plotted against the Jews. The king extended his gold scepter to Esther. She got to her feet and stood before the king. She said, "If it please the king and he regards me with favor and thinks this is right, and if he has any affection for me at all, let an order be written that cancels the bulletins authorizing the plan of Haman son of Hammedatha the Agagite to annihilate the Jews in all the king's provinces. How can I stand to see this catastrophe wipe out my people? How can I bear to stand by and watch the massacre of my own relatives?"

King Xerxes said to Queen Esther and Mordecai the Jew: "I've given Haman's estate to Esther and he's been hanged on the gallows because he attacked the Jews. So go ahead now and write whatever you decide on behalf of the Jews; then seal it with the signet ring." (An order written in the king's name and sealed with his signet ring is irrevocable.)

So the king's secretaries were brought in on the twenty-third day of the third month, the month of Sivan, and the order regarding the Jews was written word for word as Mordecai dictated and was addressed to the satraps, governors, and officials of the provinces from India to

Ethiopia, 127 provinces in all, to each province in its own script and each people in their own language, including the Jews in their script and language.

He wrote under the name of King Xerxes and sealed the order with the royal signet ring; he sent out the bulletins by couriers on horseback, riding the fastest royal steeds bred from the royal stud.

The king's order authorized the Jews in every city to arm and defend themselves to the death, killing anyone who threatened them or their women and children, and confiscating for themselves anything owned by their enemies. The day set for this in all King Xerxes' provinces was the thirteenth day of the twelfth month, the month of Adar. The order was posted in public places in each province so everyone could read it, authorizing the Jews to be prepared on that day to avenge themselves on their enemies.

The couriers, fired up by the king's order, raced off on their royal horses. At the same time, the order was posted in the palace complex of Susa.

Mordecai walked out of the king's presence wearing a royal robe of violet and white, a huge gold crown, and a purple cape of fine linen. The city of Susa exploded with joy. For Jews it was all sunshine and laughter: they celebrated, they were honored. It was that way all over the country, in every province, every city when the king's bulletin was posted: the Jews took to the streets in celebration, cheering, and feasting. Not only that, but many non-Jews became Jews—now it was dangerous *not* to be a Jew!

⊹

9 On the thirteenth day of the twelfth month, the month of Adar, the king's order came into effect. This was the very day that the enemies of the Jews had planned to overpower them, but the tables were now turned: the Jews overpowered those who hated them! The Jews had gathered in the cities throughout King Xerxes' provinces to lay hands on those who were seeking their ruin. Not one man was able to stand up against them—fear made cowards of them all. What's more, all the government officials, satraps, governors—everyone who worked for the king—actually helped the Jews because of Mordecai; they were afraid of him. Mordecai by now was a power in the palace. As Mordecai became more and more powerful, his reputation had grown in all the provinces.

So the Jews finished off all their enemies with the sword, slaughtering them right and left, and did as they pleased to those who hated them. In the palace complex of Susa the Jews massacred five hundred men. They also killed the ten sons of Haman son of Hammedatha, the archenemy of the Jews:

Parshandatha	Dalphon
Aspatha	Poratha
Adalia	Aridatha
Parmashta	Arisai
Aridai	Vaizatha

But they took no plunder. That day, when it was all over, the number of those killed in the palace complex was given to the king. The king told Queen Esther, "In the palace complex alone here in Susa the Jews have killed five hundred men, plus Haman's ten sons. Think of the killing that must have been done in the rest of the provinces! What else do you want? Name it and it's yours. Your wish is my command."

"If it please the king," Queen Esther responded, "give the Jews of Susa permission to extend the terms of the order another day. And have the bodies of Haman's ten sons hanged in public display on the gallows."

The king commanded it: The order was extended; the bodies of Haman's ten sons were publicly hanged.

The Jews in Susa went at it again. On the fourteenth day of Adar they killed another three hundred men in Susa. But again they took no plunder.

Meanwhile in the rest of the king's provinces, the Jews had organized and defended themselves, freeing themselves from oppression. On the thirteenth day of the month of Adar, they killed 75,000 of those who hated them but did not take any plunder. The next day, the fourteenth, they took it easy and celebrated with much food and laughter. But in Susa, since the Jews had banded together on both the thirteenth and fourteenth days, they made the fifteenth their holiday for laughing and feasting. (This accounts for why Jews living out in the country in the rural villages remember the fourteenth day of Adar for celebration, their day for parties and the exchange of gifts.)

✠

Mordecai wrote all this down and sent copies to all the Jews in all King Xerxes' provinces, regardless of distance, calling for an annual celebration on the fourteenth and fifteenth days of Adar as the occasion when Jews got relief from their enemies, the month in which their sorrow turned to joy, mourning somersaulted into a holiday for parties and fun and laughter, the sending and receiving of presents and of giving gifts to the poor.

And they did it. What started then became a tradition, continuing the practice of what Mordecai had written to them.

✠

Haman son of Hammedatha, the Agagite, the archenemy of all Jews, had schemed to destroy all Jews. He had cast the *pur* (the lot) to throw them into a panic and destroy them. But when Queen Esther intervened with the king, he gave written orders that the evil scheme that Haman had worked out should boomerang back on his own head. He and his sons were hanged on the gallows. That's why these days are called "Purim," from the word *pur* or "lot."

Therefore, because of everything written in this letter and because of all that they had been through, the Jews agreed to continue. It became a tradition for them, their children, and all future converts to remember these two days every year on the specified dates set down in the letter. These days are to be remembered and kept by every single generation, every last family, every province and city. These days of Purim must never be neglected among the Jews; the memory of them must never die out among their descendants.

Queen Esther, the daughter of Abihail, backed Mordecai the Jew, using her full queenly authority in this second Purim letter to endorse and ratify what he wrote. Calming and reassuring letters went out to all the Jews throughout the 127 provinces of Xerxes' kingdom to fix these days of Purim their assigned place on the calendar, dates set by Mordecai the Jew—what they had agreed to for themselves and their descendants regarding their fasting and mourning. Esther's word confirmed the tradition of Purim and was written in the book.

✠

10 King Xerxes imposed taxes from one end of his empire to the other. For the rest of it, King Xerxes' extensive accomplishments, along with a detailed account of the brilliance of Mordecai, whom the king had promoted, that's all written in *The Chronicles of the Kings of Media and Persia.*

Mordecai the Jew ranked second in command to King Xerxes. He was popular among the Jews and greatly respected by them. He worked hard for the good of his people; he cared for the peace and prosperity of his race.